*Social Science and the Politics*
*of Modern Jewish Identity*

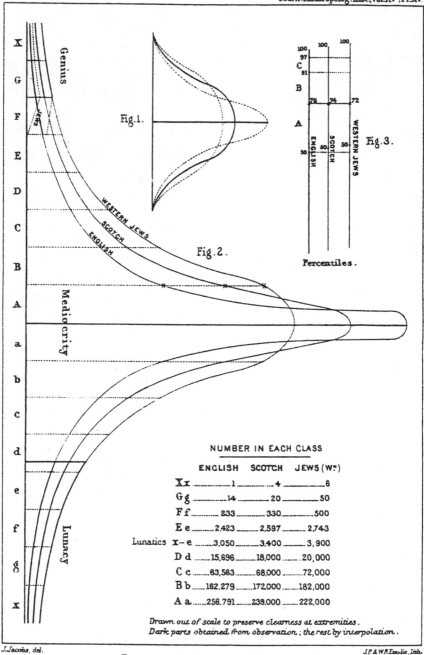

Fig. 1.

Fig. 2.

Fig. 3.

Percentiles.

WESTERN JEWS

SCOTCH

ENGLISH

Genius

Mediocrity

Lunacy

NUMBER IN EACH CLASS

| | ENGLISH | SCOTCH | JEWS (W.) |
|---|---|---|---|
| Xx | 1 | 4 | 6 |
| Gg | 14 | 20 | 50 |
| Ff | 233 | 330 | 500 |
| Ee | 2,423 | 2,597 | 2,743 |
| Lunatics x–e | 3,050 | 3,400 | 3,900 |
| Dd | 15,696 | 18,000 | 20,000 |
| Cc | 63,583 | 68,000 | 72,000 |
| Bb | 162,279 | 172,000 | 182,000 |
| Aa | 256,791 | 239,000 | 222,000 |

*Drawn out of scale to preserve clearness at extremities.*
*Dark parts obtained from observation; the rest by interpolation.*

J. Jacobs, del.

J.P. & W.R. Emslie, lith.

## DISTRIBUTION OF ABILITY
### AMONG
### ENGLISHMEN, SCOTCHMEN & JEWS

# Social Science and the Politics of Modern Jewish Identity

Mitchell B. Hart

*Stanford Series in Jewish History and Culture*
*Edited by Aron Rodrigue and Steven J. Zipperstein*

Stanford University Press
*Stanford, California* 2000

Stanford University Press
Stanford, California
© 2000 by the Board of Trustees of the
Leland Stanford Junior University
Printed in the United States of America

Library of Congress Cataloging-in-Publication Data

Hart, Mitchell Bryan
    Social science and the politics of modern Jewish identity / Mitchell B. Hart.
        p.   cm. — (Stanford studies in Jewish history and culture)
    Includes bibliographical references and index.
    ISBN 0-8047-3824-6 (cloth : alk. paper)
        1. Jews—Social conditions—20th century.  2. Jews—Identity.  3. Jews—
    Statistics.  4. Jews—Cultural assimilation.  5. Jews—History—1789–1945—
    Historiography.  I. Title.  II. Series.

DS140 .H37 2000
305.8924—dc21                                                    99-059745

⊗ This book is printed on acid-free, archival quality paper.

Original printing 2000
Last figure below indicates year of this printing:
09  08  07  06  05  04  03  02  01  00
Typeset by Robert C. Ehle in 10/12 ITC Galliard.

*To the Memory of My Mother*
(ז״ל)

# *Acknowledgments*

This book began as a dissertation under the supervision of Steven J. Zipperstein, who shaped the work from start to finish. He read carefully and critically, and his comments were always tempered with encouragement. I have benefited and continue to benefit greatly from his intelligence, patience, sense of humor, and friendship. Amos Funkenstein (ז״ל) shaped my thinking about history and historiography in profound ways. I am grateful for having had the opportunity to study with him. Steven Aschheim, Arnold Band, David Biale, David Ellenson, David Myers, and Aron Rodrigue read and commented on early versions of parts of this work. Their comments are much appreciated. Derek Penslar offered particularly perceptive criticism on revised versions of the manuscript. His suggestions helped me reshape the book in fundamental ways. The idea for this project came from suggestions made long ago by Todd Endelman and David Sorkin. This may not be the book they had in mind, but I thank them for encouraging it.

Over the years I've also had the privilege of learning from a number of friends and colleagues. I'd like to thank Gil Anidjar, Bonnie Effros, Peter Gordon, Noah Isenberg, Wulf Kansteiner, Tony Michels, Erika Rappaport, Steve Rappaport, Aaron Rubenstein, Alan Steinweis, David Rechter, Kevin Tyner Thomas, Lori Weintrob, and Michael Wintroub. In Miami I have had the good fortune to be part of a lively and engaged history department that makes it not only possible but also pleasurable to do one's work. In particular, I'd like to thank Mark Szuchman, whose collegiality, friendship, and knowledge of Nota Bene enabled me to survive in the first few years.

I am grateful to the following libraries for the use of their facilities: UCLA; Berkeley; Stanford; the Hebrew University, Jerusalem; The Jewish Theological Seminary in New York City; and the Jewish Division of the New York Public Library. And I wish to thank the staffs of the Central Zionist Archives, the Archive for the History of the Jewish People, YIVO, and the Leo Baeck Institute for their assistance. Grants from the National Foundation for Jewish Culture and the Memorial Foundation for Jewish Culture made the initial research and writing possible. Generous support from the Florida International University Foundation and from the Florida International University College of Arts and Sciences allowed me to do subsequent research and turn the dissertation into a book. It's a pleasure to thank Norris Pope and Anna Eberhard Friedlander at Stanford University Press for shepherding the manuscript through, and Ruth Barzel for editing it. I feel fortunate to have had their assistance and support.

I'm also happy to thank the following presses for their permission to reprint portions of published articles. Parts of this book have appeared in *Studies in Contemporary Jewry*, vol. 11, 1995 (Oxford University Press); *Isis*, vol. 90, no. 2, 1999 (University of Chicago Press); and *Jewish Social Studies: History, Culture, Society*, vol. 2, no. 1, 1995 (Indiana University Press).

A number of other friends also helped me along the way, and I am grateful to all of them. In particular I'd like to thank Kyle Todd, with whom I've been friends now for over twenty-five years. Since we first started discussing books and ideas on the baseball diamond in junior high school, he has profoundly shaped and influenced my thinking about so many important things. Finally, I owe the deepest debt of gratitude to my wife, Nina. She is my closest friend and intellectual companion. Nothing I write here could possibly suffice.

This book is dedicated to the memory of my mother, Janet Rose Hart (ז״ל), who taught me to love Judaism, books, music, and baseball—although not always in that order.

M.B.H.

# Contents

*Social Science and the Politics*
*of Modern Jewish Identity*

# Introduction

In 1991 the Council of Jewish Federations published its National Jewish Population Survey. The survey, spanning the years 1985–90, provided statistics on various aspects of American Jewish life, including birthrates, education, involvement in Jewish communal organizations, intermarriage, and conversion. The survey quickly became the source of intense public debate among Jewish academics and community leaders. One finding in particular generated heated controversy and a great deal of concern: 52 percent of Jews in the United States were married to Gentiles. It was this statistic that made the population survey a source of newspaper headlines, editorials, and public debate.[1]

Intermarriage was "another Holocaust"; Jews were "an endangered species." Images of decline and disappearance captured—at least for a while—the imagination of many American Jews. And the fact that the notion of decline was undergirded with demographic statistics, and thus delivered in the name and with the authority of social science, probably made the purported threat to American Jewry's future that much more urgent.

Critics of the survey's methodology and conclusions argued that, rather than a 52 percent intermarriage rate, the number was closer to 40 percent, and that this had been the figure, more or less, for decades. Thus, there is no genuine American Jewish demographic crisis. One of the fiercest critics of the study, the Hebrew University sociologist Steven M. Cohen, faulted it on methodological and conceptual grounds. Cohen suggested that American Jewry was not intermarrying at the rate claimed, and that even if one were to grant such a high rate of intermarriage, the conclusion reached by the study—that American Jewry might ultimately disappear—is unwarranted. In response, the twelve social scientists involved in the population study attacked Cohen, calling into question his "standing in the community of scholars." They accused him of cloaking an "ideological peroration and professional diatribe in the garb of social science."[2]

Dire warnings about the eventual disappearance of American Jewry are nothing new. Over two decades ago, for instance, Elihu Bergman, writing in the Jewish magazine *Moment*, argued that because of intermarriage there would be "no more than 944,000 [Jews], and conceivably as few as 10,240" in the United States in 2076. "If present trends are not arrested or reversed the American Jewish community faces extinction as a significant entity, and by its own hand, during the first half of the 21st century."[3] Nor are these warnings of Jewish decline and disappearance limited to the American scene. In 1967 the French sociologist Georges Friedmann published *The End of the Jewish People?*, in which he examined demographic and sociological trends and predicted the imminent disappearance of Jewry.[4] More recently the British historian Bernard Wasserstein has examined what he calls "the vanishing Diaspora" of European Jewry. While the "Jewish Question" may remain a vital source of concern for some Europeans, the reality is that the Jews are literally disappearing from the continent. Wasserstein begins his book on a rather dire note: "The Jews are vanishing from Europe—and not only because of Hitler. . . . Demographic projections for the next two or three decades vary greatly, depending on such factors as the rate of emigration from the Soviet Union; but the range of possibilities extends only downward—at best the Jews in Europe face slow diminution, at worst virtual extinction."[5]

The late twentieth century, then, is not without its prophets of decline and disappearance (and those who, in turn, warn against such overly pessimistic, Cassandra-like predictions). Predicting the demise of the Jewish People, and drawing moral lessons from this, are of course well-established Jewish traditions. As the philosopher of Jewish history Simon Rawidowicz noted a half century ago, the Jews are an "ever-dying people," intently focused on their imminent disappearance.[6] However, while the fear of collective decline may be millennia-old, the shape of the current debates is the product of quite particular, modern forces. For, regardless of which side of the debate over Jewish decline one stands on,[7] those involved in the debate appear united in their faith in the power of numbers and of social science to grasp the reality of the situation, to provide the tools with which to understand the questions of contemporary Jewish collective life, identify problems and challenges, and even help solve them. Moreover, those engaged in the debate share a willingness to draw moral and political lessons from the social scientific data. Individual decisions about marriage and divorce, childbearing and child raising, and where to live and work and worship as Jews are meaningful mainly in the aggregate, insofar as they both influence and indicate collective Jewish identity and vitality. And, ultimately, such judgments bear on the issues of assimilation, and the viability of the Diaspora; on the encounter of Jews and Judaism with a benign, hospitable society; and on the ability of "the Jewish People" to survive not the age-old hostility of anti-Semitism, but the "kindness" of a relatively open, capitalist state and culture. As one prominent Jewish historian has written, low birth rates and high intermarriage rates are not problems facing any one Diaspora Jewish community, but are "part of a general pattern in open societies. It is the downside of the affluence, the range of opportunities, the social mobility, and the cultural integration which postwar modernity has offered to the Jews."[8]

Whether the participants are aware of it or not, the current debate—undertaken with the tools of social science—over assimilation and its impact on Jewish identity and demography is the latter-day incarnation of a sustained debate engaged in by Jews (and non-Jews), in Europe and the United States, close to a century ago. This book explores that debate, and the relationship between social science, Jewish scholarship, and Jewish politics. It analyzes the crucial ideas and issues that preoccupied Jewish social scientists, the multiple contexts out of which these ideas emerged, and the political or ideological purposes to which they were put. And it traces the origins and development of Jewish social science at the institutional level, and connects this with particular political developments at the time.[9]

Between the years 1880 and 1930 Jewish demographers, anthropologists, physicians, and political economists produced a large body of literature on the Jews as a religious, national, and racial group. The scope of this research, termed at the time "Jewish statistics," covered a broad array of disciplinary fields and research categories. These included demography, anthropology, medicine and biology, political or national economy, migration, intermarriage and conversion, education, criminality, and suicide. Methodologically this research relied heavily upon descriptive statistics, but it also utilized history, ethnography, and iconography. Between 1902 and 1925 the institutional center of this new Jewish social science was Berlin, where the Verein für jüdische Statistik (Organization for Jewish Statistics) set up its main bureau, and where the official journal of the statistical movement, the *Zeitschrift für Demographie und Statistik der Juden*, was published. Important research was also undertaken in ancillary bureaus, and by unaffiliated Jewish individuals and organizations in continental Europe,

England, and the United States. Jewish social scientists—Jewish scholars who used the methods and concepts of social science to analyze Jews and Judaism—published their work in monographs and academic journals (both "Jewish" and "non-Jewish"). This scientific or scholarly research also found its way into more popular venues—newspapers, popular journals, encyclopedias—and hence, potentially at least, to a broader audience.

Jewish social science constituted an important development within modern Jewish scholarship, yet it has received little attention.[10] In terms of methods, objects of research, and goals, the emergence of Jewish social science signaled a shift, or at least a broadening, in the very definition of "science" within Jewish scholarship. In contrast to history and philology, Jewish social science focused on the contemporary or present-day condition of Jewry, and shifted interest from religion and philosophy to demography, economy, health, and social organization. Methodologically, it made use of statistics, and drew upon disciplines such as anthropology, biology, and medicine. This shift was impelled by a number of forces and developments—material, intellectual, and political. Numerically the Jewish population, to an even greater extent than the general European population, increased dramatically during the nineteenth century. This was due to a variety of factors, including improvements in medical care and public-health conditions and the resultant drop in mortality rates. Demography and vital statistics, including birth, death, and marriage rates, measured these changes. Jewish social science was impelled in part by notable demographic growth over the course of the nineteenth century, even though, as we shall see, the debate among Jewish social scientists in the first decades of the twentieth century revolved around the fear of Jewish demographic decline.

The migrations of East European Jews westward, beginning in the late 1860s, called forth research into the socioeconomic and cultural conditions of Russian, Rumanian, and Galician Jewries, as well as into the immigrant communities that had formed in major Western cities. Moreover, the twin processes of industrialization and urbanization that occurred at such a rapid pace in Central Europe in the last quarter of the nineteenth century produced fundamental changes in Jewish life, and compelled Jewish social scientists to describe and analyze conditions among the Jewish working and middle classes. Increasing numbers moved from rural and border regions to major cities, a demographic shift that brought with it dramatic changes in social, economic, educational, and cultural patterns.[11]

## The Power of Numbers

Jewish social scientists and their proponents argued that such recent developments in Jewish life necessitated new methods of analysis, methods capable of grasping conditions and changes at the mass level. Statistics, together with the interpretive models of the social and biomedical sciences, could be used to make sense, it was argued, of the enormous changes experienced by modern Jewry. Statistics, broadly defined, offered, in the words of one Jewish social scientist, "the ability to measure and produce knowledge about mass phenomena"; it provided "rhythm, measure, and order" to the confusing multiplicities of social life.[12]

Throughout this work I use the terms Jewish statistics and Jewish social science interchangeably.[13] Numbers did indeed possess a newfound power and prestige, and this helps to explain the emergence of Jewish social science. Statistics, however, was only one component of a broader social scientific interpretive framework composed of ideas and theories drawn from a host of related disciplines. Measurements of crania, noses and chests, and distributions of eye, hair, and skin color were elements of the anthropological analysis of racial identity and difference, purity and impurity, superiority and inferiority. Statistics on birth and death, marriage, intermarriage and conversion, physical and mental health, and disease, criminality, and suicide were often, though not always, interpreted in light of contemporary theories such as degeneration and eugenics, social Darwinism and Lamarckism. Lastly, the quantification of Jewish economic behavior and conditions was part of a larger debate over the relationship between Jews, capitalism, and modern culture.

Nonetheless, the assertion about the ability of numbers to capture the complexities of modern, mass phenomena, and to order them into something manageable, was of increasing importance in public debates about Jewry in the last half of the nineteenth century. Jewish social scientists who voiced their enthusiasm for the power of numbers were echoing a widely held, though by no means uncontested, article of faith.[14] As one historian of social science has written, this faith in numbers was "the leitmotif of nineteenth century statistical thinking."[15]

Beginning already in the late eighteenth century, governmental agencies and bureaucracies, as well as private groups and individuals, generated numerical data on everything "from geography and climate to government, economics, agriculture, trade, population and culture," as well as sanitation, education, labor, poverty, and crime.[16] Demographers monitored rates of birth—legitimate and illegitimate—and death, marriage and divorce, immigration and emigration, crime and suicide. Anatomists and physical anthropologists measured and compared head shapes and cranial capacities, lengths of noses and widths of chests. Physicians and psychologists counted the numbers of physically and mentally ill, and speculated on the causes of immunity from and susceptibility to particular diseases on the part of individuals and groups.

This "avalanche of numbers" produced, inter alia, a growing "trust in numbers."[17] This was a trust, in the first place, in the ability of numbers to capture or reflect social realities, to reveal the patterns or laws of society, apart from individual idiosyncratic behavior. At an early stage statistics offered, it was believed, nomothetic, or lawlike, truths, and the science was characterized by a strong determinism. Over the course of the nineteenth century this faith in statistical laws was replaced by the idea of probability, and an element of chance or indeterminacy was factored in. Nonetheless, the belief in an unmediated, direct relationship between numbers and reality, between the measurement and the thing measured, remained.

Significantly, the gradual shift from determinism to probability, and the emergence of the idea of variation, focused attention on the idea and ideal of "normalcy." According to the philosopher of science Ian Hacking, the erosion of determinism was not of great immediate importance to most people. Rather,

something else was pervasive and everybody came to know about it: the enumeration of people and their habits. Society became statistical. A new type of law came into being, analogous to the laws of nature, but pertaining to people. These new laws were expressed in terms of probability. They carried with them the connotations of normalcy and of deviations from the norm. The cardinal concept of the psychology of the Enlightenment had been, simply, human nature. By the end of the nineteenth century, it was being replaced by something different: normal people.[18]

Just as significantly, the social sciences, in formulating and disseminating "laws" of behavior at the collective level, possessed the power to transform their object of study. While social scientists sought at times to equate their discoveries of "social laws" with discoveries made by natural scientists, the analogy could not hold. The definitions generated by social scientists of "normal" and "pathological," "healthy" and "diseased"—categories that would figure prominently, as we shall see, in Jewish social scientific analyses—directly affected the ways in which individuals and groups thought and acted, about themselves and others. As Hacking points out, the desire to be normal, and to be considered normal, is a powerful one. "Few of us fancy being pathological, so 'most of us' try to make ourselves normal, which in turn affects what is normal. Atoms have no such inclinations. The human sciences display a feedback effect not to be found in physics."[19]

Social science, in other words, was a compelling instrument of power and control. Indeed, the avalanche of numbers was intimately tied up from the start with technologies of government and state. Classifying and enumerating on the part of official bureaucracies were tools of authority. More than this, certain categories quickly became especially important for social scientists interested in questions of control and reform. "Most of the law-like regularities were first perceived in connection with deviancy: suicide, crime, vagrancy, madness, prostitution, disease."[20] The power of statistics to define normal and pathological was easily extended into the cultural and social realms.

What is of significance for this study is that the Jews quickly became objects of such classification and enumeration. Already in the middle of the eighteenth century, for example, with the founding of the official Prussian Statistical Bureau, the *Judenliste* appeared as a category of investigation.[21] The census forms of individual German states contained the category *Religionsbekenntnis* (religious affiliation), and "Israelite" was one of the options offered; the 1870 census of the newly established German Reich listed the same category.[22] The category "religious affiliation" was also a component of the survey cards filled out by judicial administrators; hence, official German criminal statistics had a confessional element to them.[23] This category disappeared in the judicial forms of the Weimar period. General population statistics—birth and death; marriage, divorce, and intermarriage; migration—continued, however, to include "religion" as a category during Weimar.[24] The category of religion was part of the official censuses of a number of countries, in addition to Germany, with Jewish populations, including Russia, Austria, Hungary, Rumania, Italy, Switzerland, Bulgaria, Greece, Denmark, and Sweden. These censuses would constitute a principal source of data on Jewry for working Jewish social scientists.

There were, on the other hand, countries that forbade enumeration along religious lines. These included France, Great Britain, Belgium, the United States, Canada, and the countries of Latin America. There were times, it is true, when governmental agencies in some of these countries did count Jews.[25] Still, religion did not become a regular component of the general decennial censuses of these countries. Thus, numbers generated about the Jewish populations within such countries were oftentimes the product of guesswork, arrived at by indirect, highly questionable methods (such as calculating from the number of schoolchildren missing from public schools on Yom Kippur). Jewish communal and voluntary organizations tended to figure more prominently in the collection of statistical data on Jews in these countries.[26]

As we shall see, just how to classify the Jews—as a religion, race, nation, *Volk*—remained open to debate well into the twentieth century. And their enumeration could and did change depending on how one classified or categorized them. Still, the Jews were a category of research for European and Anglo-American social scientists, and social scientists were responsible in large part for constructing and disseminating scientific images or notions of Jews and Judaism. Moreover, the Jews were more and more defined and described in the evaluative terms that had gained greater power over the course of the nineteenth century, such as normal and pathological, and healthy and diseased. The debate over Jewish collective decline, which was at the heart of the Jewish social scientific enterprise, was framed largely in such terms. Counting Jews was the preliminary step in a more complex evaluative process of the modern Jewish condition.

The Jews, however, were not solely an *object* of social scientific study. The universality of science demanded that Jews, as objects, be included with all the other races, ethnos, nations in scientific research, but it also allowed Jews to enter into these disciplines, to master the language, arguments, and ideas, and to appropriate these for their own purposes. One historian of statistics has recently written that "the aim of statistics is to reduce the abundance of situations and to provide a summarized description of them that can be remembered and used as a basis of action."[27] By the end of the nineteenth century Jews, too, were using statistics increasingly to order and make sense of their situations, and to prescribe action. In short, Jews became *subjects*, or participants, as well as objects within the social sciences, empowered to construct their own narratives around the statistics about the Jewish present and future.

## Genealogies of Jewish Social Science

While an organized, institutionalized Jewish statistical enterprise only emerged in the first decade of the twentieth century, there already existed by that time numerous individual efforts undertaken along such lines. By the turn of the twentieth century, an extensive corpus of social scientific material on Jewry had been produced.[28] This literature has a complex history of its own that deserves fuller treatment. Yet within the context of a discussion of Jewish statistics this earlier work represents the intellectual foundation upon which the project was built. It formed what can be termed the collective thought structure or intellectual grammar, the style of scientific thinking for Jewish social scientists. It provided a particular language and method, categories, themes, and issues of research (as well as much of the raw data) with which Jewish writers would construct their own narratives.[29]

A number of works written by Jews, and bearing upon the statistical study of Jewry, were produced over the course of the nineteenth century. These included the eminent Jewish historian Leopold Zunz's 1823 article "Prolegomenon to a Future Statistic of the Jews," proffered by many as the earliest systematic statement on the subject;[30] the 1871 study of the Jewish communities of Germany, Austria-Hungary, and Switzerland sponsored by the Israelite Synod of Augsburg;[31] and the works on the question of the immigration of East European Jews into Germany published by the German Jewish physician Salomon Neumann. In 1880 Neumann entered into a public dispute over Jewish immigration and assimilation when he published *The Fable of Mass Jewish Immigration: A Chapter in Prussian Statistics*. Employing official Prussian statistics, he responded to scientific and popular articles that argued that the enormous influx of East European Jews, combined with the demographic advantage German Jews enjoyed—their rates of birth, it was argued, were significantly higher than their rates of death—threatened the Christian, Anglo-Saxon nature of the German state.[32] During this same period the Anglo-Jewish social scientist, historian, and folklorist Joseph Jacobs wrote a series of articles, in both academic and popular forums, dealing with Jewish demography, health, and the issue of the Jews as a race.[33] In 1886–87 Alfred Nossig, who was instrumental in the creation of Jewish statistics, published his *Materials Related to a Statistic of the Jewish People*, a work that presented the latest numbers, together with Nossig's analysis, of Jewish communities around the world.[34] Jewish newspapers, from across the political spectrum, also took to publishing social scientific analysis, as well as to reproducing official government statistics generated by national and local bureaus.[35]

Jewish communal and extra-communal institutions were active during the last decades of the nineteenth century in statistical research projects of their own. These constituted an important primary source for later Jewish social scientists. The Jewish Colonization Association (ICA), for example, conducted a survey in 1898–99 on the living and working conditions of Russian-Jewish agriculturists, craftsmen, and productive laborers in the Russian Pale of Settlement. The B'nai Brith Lodge of Mannheim studied the influence of general economic factors on the occupational structure of rural Jewish populations in Baden. Beginning in 1879 the Deutsch-Israelitische Gemeindebund (DIGB) published an annual statistical yearbook on German Jewry, a task that would eventually become one of the projects taken over by the Bureau for Jewish Statistics.[36] Jewish communities in other countries also took up the task of gathering and publishing statistics. In France, beginning in the middle of the nineteenth century, the Alliance Israélite Universelle took an interest in statistics and in social scientific questions, publishing studies related to these themes. The subject also found its way into the pages of the *Revue des Études Juives*.[37] In England the Board of Deputies had been collecting and publishing vital statistics—birth, death, and marriage rates—since at least the 1870s.[38] In 1875 the Board of Delegates of American Israelites joined with the Union of American Hebrew Congregations in an effort to collect statistical material on the Jews of the United States. This was the first such systematic survey of American Jews.[39] Statistical and social scientific material would also soon appear, and figure prominently, in more ambitious American-Jewish scholarly projects such as the *American Jewish Yearbook* and the *Jewish Encyclopedia*.[40]

Genealogies of the Jewish statistical project, composed by various participants or observers between the years 1903–40, invested these early studies with an exaggerated significance, representing them, in toto, as a precursor to their own endeavors and hence as proof that Jewish statistics was firmly rooted in the Jewish scholarly past.[41] However, the vast majority of social scientific work about Jews produced during the nineteenth century emanated from non-Jewish authorities. And this work was of far greater importance for the development of Jewish social science. The European paradigm provided Jewish social scientists with the main thematic categories, and many, though not all, of the images and arguments of Jewish statistics.[42] This remained so during the lifetime of the enterprise.

These non-Jewish authorities were either statisticians and social scientists working under the auspices of the state, or independent researchers. Official governmental studies, such as the 1897 census in Russia, the 1882 and 1897 censuses in Poland,[43] or the censuses and surveys undertaken by the various German statistical bureaus, constituted one of the main sources of primary data for Jewish social scientists, who would continue to rely heavily on this official material throughout the decades under discussion. Moreover, the writings of individual non-Jewish social scientists—such as Rudolf Virchow, Felix von Luschan, Georg von Mayr, Wilhelm Roscher, Adolf Wagner, and Werner Sombart in Germany; Anatole Leroy Beaulieu in France; and Francis Galton in England—shaped in profound ways the thinking of Jewish social scientists.

The appropriation by Jewish scholars of non-Jewish social scientific work was a critical, dialectical process, a matter of reinterpretation and rejection as well as of incorporation. On the one hand, Jewish social scientists were members of the general social scientific community. Educated in European universities, they spoke the language of European science; this was, by definition, the only scientific language they could speak. On the other hand, they were Jews, engaged with their own community or people at both the intellectual and the practical levels. This tension helped define Jewish social science to a significant degree.[44] European science had made the Jews an object of study, and constructed a scientific discourse permeated with particular political and moral value judgments. To be sure, this discourse was by no means monolithic. It is important to note that, while attention has focused overwhelmingly, and for perfectly understandable reasons, on the anti-Semitic impulse to much of the European scientific literature dealing with Jews produced over the past two centuries, there was a "liberal" tradition within the sciences that developed parallel to it.[45] Jewish social scientists of various ideological persuasions would draw in important ways on the authority and research of these "liberal" non-Jewish scholars. The heterogenous, dynamic nature of social scientific analyses in general meant that the "nature" of the Jew(s) remained open to reevaluation and re-imagination.

The heterogeneity of the scientific discourse about Jews allowed Jewish scientists to fashion responses out of elements drawn from this same scientific discourse, to construct their own narratives of "Jewish race," health and disease, Jews and capitalism, and so forth. Especially important in this regard was the "environmentalist" explanation for physiological and psychological, as well as socioeconomic and cultural, traits. Such an explanation emphasized historical and social forces as determinative, and embraced the concept of acquired traits or characteristics. By the late nineteenth century the theory of acquired traits had come to be associated almost exclusively with the early-eighteenth-century French naturalist Jean-Baptiste Lamarck—though, as commentators on Lamarck point out, the notion of acquired traits was already universally accepted at the time Lamarck utilized it.[46] Lamarckism posited a tight connection between an organism and its surroundings, and explained evolutionary transformation in an organism as a direct response to environmental conditions or challenges. In order to maintain (or regain) an equilibrium or harmony with its particular environment, a species will adapt, by either using individual requisite organs or limbs more frequently—thereby strengthening and enlarging them—or by developing new parts that meet the new conditions. The anatomical and physiological changes that occurred as a result of this adaptation process were, according to this theory, heritable. Significant structural changes, necessitated by environmental challenges, produced in turn transformations at the genetic level. New or altered structures become part of what gets inherited by subsequent generations. Lamarckism, as it came to be formulated in the late nineteenth century, was associated almost exclusively with this notion of acquired characteristics, or "soft inheritance." It would be this theory that brought Lamarckians into conflict with Mendelians, and supporters of August Weismann's germ plasm theory.[47] While Mendelian genetics, of course, eventually proved the more satisfactory theory, the dispute was by no means settled by the first decades of the twentieth century. Neither the ascendancy of Darwin's theory of natural selection, nor the rediscovery of Mendel's laws of inheritance, meant the demise of the notion of acquired traits. As Ludmilla Jordanova has written, for decades after 1900, indeed, as late as the 1950s, "prominent biologists continued to defend Lamarck's biological philosophy of the inheritance of acquired characteristics."[48] Certainly, during the period in which Jewish social scientists were relying so heavily upon this sort of environmentalist argument, the theory was a legitimate, if contested, one within the scientific community.

Jewish social scientists, however, were by no means entirely consistent in their adoption of this sort of environmentalism. They could, at times, put forth ideas and images of Jewry that relied on essentialist notions, and that strike us as biological or "racialist." Nonetheless, Jewish social scientists did rely heavily on a Lamarckian environmentalism, so much so that adherence to Lamarckian theory itself came to be identified as "Jewish" in some circles.[49] And the theory of acquired traits did serve Jewish social scientists' purposes nicely.[50] It allowed them, in the first place, to explain the particular physical or mental traits oftentimes identified as racially Jewish as historically or socially determined. This was an attempt to undermine an explanatory framework that relied on an overly rigid biological determinism, and which undergirded a racialized anti-Semitism aimed at achieving a variety of political goals, including the restriction or reversal of the civil and social rights attained by Jews over the course of the nineteenth century.

The politics of anti-Semitism assumed different shapes in different countries, each with their own political tradition vis-à-vis Jews and other minority groups. Nonetheless, in fundamental respects the scientific discourse on race and disease was international, and one finds the same or similar images and ideas circulating in academic texts produced in every language in which scientists wrote.[51] Thus, by the end of the nineteenth century a "scientific anti-Semitism" had emerged in Europe and the United States that did not merely draw on the language and ideas of the social and biological sciences, but that counted prominent scientists among its vocal advocates. This meant, as Nancy Leys Stepan and Sander Gilman have argued, that Jewish social scientists found themselves, qua Jews, defined negatively by the very discourse they had come to accept as true. We shall see the extent to which notions such as normal and pathological, healthy and diseased were not only used generally to define Jewry, but were also internalized by Jewish writers and applied to contemporary Jewish life. The strategy of response developed by Jews was a complex one, revealing an uneasy relation with the non-Jewish scholarship produced about Jewry. For even as Jewish social scientists sought to dispel the dominant image of the Jews as racially pathological or diseased, they put forth many of these same images. Resistance and rejection were accompanied by acceptance and appropriation:

As Jews (and other groups stereotyped in the biological and social sciences of the day) were drawn more deeply into the sciences of racial difference, whether in measuring themselves as a race by craniometry and other methods, or by comparing one fraction of the Jewish "race" with another, or by commenting on or contesting the thesis of Jewish pathology and illness, they were tempted simultaneously to embrace and reject the field: to embrace science's methods, concepts, and the promise it held out for discovering knowledge, and to reject, in a variety of ways, the conclusions of science as they appeared to apply negatively to themselves.[52]

In fact, most Jewish social scientists accepted not only the methods and concepts of science but also a number of the conclusions, negative though these undoubtedly were. This acceptance of negative images promulgated by non-Jewish authorities helps explain the complex, ambivalent image of Jewry that emerges from a reading of most Jewish social scientific texts. Jews evince numerous pathological traits; they suffer from a host of physical, mental, and social diseases that threaten their vitality and viability as a group. At the same time, the Jews display markedly healthy traits, which at times leads Jewish scientists to speak of, at the least, a Jewish equality with "superior" nations and races; at times, the Jews are even defined as superior. In simultaneously embracing and rejecting the European scientific discourse on Jewry, Jewish social scientists were fulfilling the roles of apologist and reformer. They defended their own people from attacks by anti-Semites, while offering a self-critique and suggestions for self-improvement based on the knowledge and insights of science.

Thus, Jewish social scientists did not merely internalize negative images of Jews and reproduce them in their own work. They contextualized and explained them within the framework of the development of European or American society as a whole. Jewish social scientific analysis, it must be emphasized, was both self-congratulatory and self-critical. It was often apologetic, yet it simultaneously aimed at illuminating Jewish deficiencies, with an eye to collective reform and improvement. It also constituted, it is important to note, a broader, more far-reaching critique of European (and, at times, American) society, and of modernity in general.

Without doubt, the need to respond to negative images of the Jews, constructed out of the language of science, impelled Jewish statistics to a degree. In his introductory survey to the 1903 maiden volume of the Verein für jüdische Statistik (Organization for Jewish Statistics), the head of the *Verein*, Alfred Nossig, sought at one point to explain why eighty years had elapsed between Zunz's 1823 call for a statistic of the Jews and the publication of the *Verein*'s initial volume. He offered a number of reasons, among them what he called the "psychological motives" behind Jewish statistics. "Is what the anti-Semites say correct? Are we corrupt and corrupting as a whole? Are we really greedy and wealthy, hoarding riches?"[53] Nossig certainly would have answered in the negative; his own work was largely apologetic, representing the Jews in a highly favorable light. Yet he left the above questions unanswered, an indication of the ambivalence with which Jewish social scientists as a whole approached the question of the Jewish condition.

Other Jewish social scientists would indeed answer yes, albeit with significant qualifications. They would incorporate such negative imagery into their own work, yet would use it as an opportunity to analyze and explain the reasons for this condition. The debate over "Jewish decline" focused to a significant degree on the question of causality, on how to account for the various indicators of collective degeneration: lower birthrates, increasing levels of physical and mental disorders, crime, suicide, intermarriage, and so forth. The explanation lay not in the nature of the Jews per se, as those inspired by racial anti-Semitism would have had it, but in the environment—those forces and conditions, both historical and contemporary, external to the Jewish self.

However, while the emergence of a racialized and politicized "scientific anti-Semitism" was an important impetus to Jewish statistics, it would be a mistake to interpret Jewish social science as merely, or even chiefly, a reaction to modern anti-Semitism. A complex nexus of intellectual, political, and socioeconomic forces combined to make social science appear, at the end of the nineteenth century, a necessary undertaking.[54] Jewish social science emerged in part out of a desire to respond to the anti-Semitic images framed in scientific terms, but it also offered a framework for understanding and explaining fundamental changes in modern European Jewish life. From mass migrations and shifts in patterns of reproduction and marriage, education and occupation to the purported changes in their physical and mental makeup, "modernity" had dramatically transformed the Jews. These monumental changes in Jewish life, set in motion, according to Jewish scholars, by the processes of emancipation, integration, and assimilation, and the responses to these, constituted the bulk of the research matter for Jewish social scientists.

Jewish social science emerged not only as one means of understanding or intellectually organizing fundamental shifts in the material conditions of European Jewry. It was also a response to, and a shaper of, fundamental questions about Jewish collective identity. As one popular anthropological tract—written in fact by a non-Jew—framed it, "What are the Jews?" (*Was sind Juden?*).[55] Are they a religion, tribe, nation, people, race? What physical, psychological, social, and economic characteristics define and unite Jews, and serve at the same time to set them apart from other groups? And how has modernity affected this collective identity? Nossig's second chief "psychological motive" to Jewish statistics was this deeply felt need to redefine Jewry. This impulse—and here Nossig articulated a view held in common by many, though by no means all, of the early Jewish social scientists—arose out of the purported failure of emancipation and assimilation, and, more important, out of the rise of Jewish nationalism. A "new Jewish consciousness" had developed, but it remained vague and uncertain. "Who is a Jew?" Nossig asked. "How many are there? Where and under what conditions [do they live]?"[56]

To be sure, not all Jewish social scientists believed in the failure of emancipation, or for that matter that Jewish nationalism was the answer. Yet it was the repudiation of what the historian of German Jewry David Sorkin has called the "ideology of emancipation,"[57] and to an extent a repudiation of an "ideology of modernity" itself, which added impetus to the initial efforts at an organized Jewish social science. Moreover, Nossig's willingness to link Jewish statistics with Zionism, and to the purported "failure of emancipation," illustrates the generalization that there was indeed an identifiable political and ideological impulse to institutionalized Jewish social science.

## The Politics of Jewish Scholarship

This ideological thrust to Jewish scholarship was not of course limited to, nor did it begin with, Jewish nationalists. Since its inception, the evolving definition of a science or scholarship of Judaism and Jewry (*Wissenschaft des Judentums*) had been closely intertwined with reformulations of modern Jewish identity.[58] For much of the nineteenth century the focus of Jewish scholarship had been on Judaism—on religious belief and practice, on Jewish literature, and on the leading religious and intellectual figures involved in its creation and interpretation. The reasons for this were in part conceptual. German Jewish historians, for instance, conceived their own work along the lines of *Ideengeschichte*, following their non-Jewish German counterparts. Yet these conceptual and methodological innovations were impelled by ideological as well as intellectual forces. As historians of modern Jewish scholarship argue, *Wissenschaft* assumed a particular shape in the first half of the nineteenth century as an integral part of the effort to reconfigure Jewish identity according to modern demands, and hence facilitate the emancipatory process. The emergence of the modern bourgeois nation-state necessitated a reformation of both individual and collective Jewish identity. Jewish scholarship was part of that process. In the case of Central European Jewry in particular, *Wissenschaft des Judentums* was one component of an ideology of emancipation and integration. On the one hand, defining the Jews as a "faith community," united solely by ties of religious belief and practice, allowed proponents of Jewish emancipation and integration to argue that Jews, as individuals, were capable of identifying with and participating in the modern nation-state. On the other hand, the historicization of Judaism—the explication of Judaism's contingent and developmental nature—permitted Jewish elites to carry out the reform of the religion, and by extension the reform and "regeneration" of Jewry.

By the end of the century this ideology of emancipation had come under increasing challenge. Jewish social science emerged within the context of the fin-de-siècle debate over emancipation and assimilation carried out among Jewish and non-Jewish cultural and political elites. Its representatives understood their work as a contribution to the solution of what had come to be termed "the Jewish Question." The civil and legal emancipation of Jewry had been formally granted in most Central and Western European states by the 1880s. The process of social and cultural integration or assimilation had been under way since at least the late eighteenth century. This integrative process occurred in different ways, with varying degrees of success, in different countries.[59] Yet by the end of the nineteenth century the emancipation of the Jews in Central and Western Europe appeared secured, and successful socioeconomic integration into the general non-Jewish environment realized.

However, just what to make of this modernization process, how to evaluate its impact on Jewry, was the open question. Thus, the debate over emancipation turned not so much on political-legal principles as on the consequences of emancipation and assimilation. The focus of research, therefore, would shift from Judaism to Jewry, from religion to the Jewish people or *Volk*. What transformations had been effected upon the Jews by these new conditions? How had increasing freedom and tolerance, economic, social, and cultural advancement, worked changes on the Jews? Judaism, as a set of ritual beliefs and practices, was important now more and more in a sociological sense, insofar as it functioned to bring about or retard particular Jewish characteristics. So, for instance, orthodox dietary or sexual practices, and their impact on the physical health of Jews, were reexamined in the light of social hygiene. Or, to take another example, to be explored in depth in a later chapter: the importance of the ban on intermarriage now purportedly lay in its effect on the anthropological and biological character of Jewry.

Social scientific inquiry into the effects of assimilation was ultimately an inquiry into collective Jewish identity, historical and contemporary, and into the question of Jewish survival. For many, social science, as part of a reconceived Jewish scholarship, became an instrument with which to challenge the ideology of emancipation, which in turn involved a reformulation of Jewish identity, a refutation of the idea that Jewry (*Judentum*) could be "reduced" or limited to a religious identity and community. Jewish nationalists in particular embraced such a redefinition of Jewish identity, and made it part of their political agenda. The Jews were a *Volk* and a nation, sharing far more than a commitment to a set of religious beliefs and practices. This *völkish* identity of Jewry was assumed to be an essential attribute; at the same time it required empirical, scientific demonstration. Just as significant, emancipation and assimilation, it was argued, were disintegrative forces, acting as agents for the dissolution of this identity, and hence as a threat to the Jewish future. Social science charted this dissolution and decline; nationalism offered the means to reverse the process.

On the other hand, there were those who, even as they admitted that a "loss" to Jewry was discernible as a result of the emancipatory process, conceived of integration or assimilation as a positive thing, as a necessary and progressive step in the modernization of Jewry. There were still others who refused to embrace assimilation as a goal, yet nonetheless continued to embrace the possibility of Jewish collective life in the Diaspora, and used social science to argue this position. As we shall see, social scientists who retained a faith in the viability of Jewish integration, or at least in life in the Diaspora, were engaged in an ideological battle on at least two fronts: against, on the one hand, the anti-Semitic forces that came to rely increasingly on scientific evidence—including statistics—to support their claims about the essential incompatibility of the Jews and the modern European nation-state, and, on the other hand, those Zionists whose grave concerns were not so much with the failure of emancipation (i.e., with anti-Semitism), as with the unparalleled success of Jewish integration into European society, and hence the impossibility of a Jewish future in *galut*.

Still, this study argues that the social scientific approach to contemporary Jewry appealed, at least at the outset, disproportionately to Zionists. Zionism sought proof for a Jewish national identity and unity, and sought to reinvest contemporary Jews with a vital national consciousness, through a number of different avenues. These included historical memory, language, folklore, art, and literature. Social science was a fundamental and fertile source for this nationalist endeavor. This new type of knowledge was a means by which the liberal, emancipationist identification of the Jews as solely a religious community could be proven false, and the Jews redefined as a *Volk* and nation.

Intent on demonstrating the difference between the Jew and the non-Jew, and the identity of Jewry despite geographic dispersion and temporal distance, Zionists were attracted by social scientific disciplines that took seriously the idea of reconceptualizing and reorganizing collectives along organic national and racial lines. Moreover, social science—strongly influenced as it was during this period by the biological and medical sciences—provided Zionists with the language with which to prove the degeneration of the Jews in the Diaspora, and the possibility of regeneration through a return to the "healthy" conditions of Jewish Palestine. More generally, the creation of statistical bureaus and the production of social scientific knowledge about "the nation" or "the people" represented for Zionists an appropriation of tasks traditionally associated in Europe with state and municipal administrations. The social scientific enterprise, therefore, aided Zionists in fashioning themselves as a Jewish "government" *in potentia*, in possession of the social knowledge required to make social policy.

Surely there was a great irony in the Zionist insistence on the negative, disintegrative effects of assimilation on Jewish identity. For the majority of these social scientists were products of the very process they now set out to delegitimize and reverse. The highly assimilated, or acculturated, nature of many Central and Western European Zionists is widely acknowledged and noted by historians of the movement.[60] It is axiomatic that Zionism drew for inspiration not only on Jewish history and thought, but also on European intellectual and political currents. This is, of course, nowhere clearer than in the very notion of modern nationalism.[61] There was, then, as David Vital has written, something a bit absurd (or at least it could easily be construed as such) about a highly assimilated Jew—one who had "adopted the language, culture, and social habits of the non-Jew"—calling for Jewish separateness and isolation. Yet, as Vital notes, "an assimilated Western Jew who had concluded, for whatever reason, that the Emancipation had failed, or was to be rejected, or both, had little choice." A "return to the ghetto," to pre-emancipation life, was not a serious option.[62] A "third way," as one Zionist social scientist put it, was necessary: A regeneration at every level—physical, political, social, economic.[63] The tools with which to accomplish this, however, would be derived from the very same culture that Jewish nationalists came to define as inimical to Jewish existence. Even as they worked out, through social scientific analysis, the mechanisms by which emancipation and assimilation threatened to destroy modern Jewry, Jewish social scientists derived their expertise and authority from the fruits of this process. They spoke in the name of European (as well as, of course, of Jewish) scholarship, and as they set about transforming Jewry—at least at the levels of discourse and imagination—into a normal and healthy nation and people, they did so along lines already delineated by European science.[64]

In representing Jewry through the language of the social sciences, Jewish social scientists were in effect reconstituting Jewish identity. Moreover, in analyzing the enormous effects worked on European Jewry by the transformations of nineteenth-century society and culture, Jewish social scientists redefined the notion of modern Jewish history, or "Jewish modernity," itself. By shifting the emphasis of analysis and explanation to the social and economic, and by attempting to grasp the impact on Jewish life and thought of industrialization, urbanization, and a culture defined more and more by capitalist relations, these scientists reconfigured the boundaries of premodern and modern vis-à-vis the Jewish past and present. The historians of the earlier *Wissenschaft* school had by and large located modernity in the political (i.e., the French Revolution) or intellectual (i.e., the Enlightenment) transformations that had occurred in Europe during the latter half of the eighteenth century. Social scientists, in contrast, saw the changes brought about by industrialization and urbanization as the primary causes of transformation within Jewish life. These produced the revolutionary shifts in social and economic relations, intellectual and cultural practices, and attitudes and beliefs that marked off the era as "modern."

In contrast to the extraordinary individuals whose ideas and actions propel Jewish history along in the narratives of the *Wissenschaft* writers, the characteristics and conditions of Jewry as a whole constitute the object of social scientific analysis. Physiological and physiognomic traits, rates of birth and death, health and disease, marriage, divorce, intermarriage and conversion, emigration and immigration, occupational and educational levels, criminality and suicide are the materials with which the texts of social science are constructed. The conversion of Heinrich Heine or of Moses Mendelssohn's children did not interest the social scientist (although such historical facts do appear in social scientific narratives as illustrative of larger trends). Rather, the movement of the Jewish masses—geographically, socially, economically, culturally—possessed meaning, and demanded explication and interpretation.

## *The Organization of the Study*

Jewish social science, then, was a product of a dynamic socioeconomic reality and of an ideologically charged interpretation of that reality. Jewish scholars sought to describe and analyze these transformations, and to provide them with a larger meaning and significance, with political as well as social and economic implications. This study explores the production by Jews of social scientific knowledge about Jews, and the multiple forces impelling this intellectual activity.

It focuses on, but does not limit its analysis to, the interest in and use of social science among Central European Zionists. I argue that Jewish statistics was conceived at the intellectual and institutional levels principally as a Zionist project, although a strong non-Zionist involvement can be adduced. Chapter 1 examines the interconnection between the creation and the development of an institutional framework for Jewish social scientific research and the politics of Jewish nationalism. It focuses first on the crucial years 1902–03, and the formation of the Verein für jüdische Statistik. The *Verein*, and Jewish statistics in general, were promoted as nonpartisan undertakings, intended to bring together all interested parties and organizations within Jewry. From the outset, however, the *Verein* was conceived by its founders as a Zionist project. More particularly, it was created by members of the Democratic Faction, who were aligned with the cultural wing of the movement, and it was intended to serve specific ideological purposes. At the institutional level, Jewish statistics represented a cultural achievement, visible proof of the sort of cultural regeneration advocated by the Faction. Moreover, it was also, at least potentially, a sign of strength and independence vis-à-vis the political, Herzlian faction of the Zionist movement. Intellectually, statistics would provide the knowledge necessary to carry out "present-day work" (*Gegenwartsarbeit*), a central goal of cultural, and then practical, Zionists.

The analysis then turns in chapter 2 to the creation and evolution of the Bureau für jüdische Statistik (1904), and to the ideas and influence of Arthur Ruppin, the first director of the bureau, and arguably the most important Jewish social scientist of the era. It examines the implications of two themes, nationalism and science, which were central to Ruppin's writings, and then places Ruppin within a broader circle of Jewish social scientists committed to Zionism. After evaluating the significance of Ruppin's brief tenure as head of the bureau, the chapter surveys the history of the bureau until its demise in 1931; it also briefly relates the emergence of other centers of Jewish statistical work between the years 1904 and 1925.

Central to the Jewish scientific discourse were debates over heredity and environment, progress and degeneration, normalcy and abnormality—debates that preoccupied nineteenth- and early-twentieth-century European and North American social scientists. I have tried throughout to demonstrate the degree to which Jewish statistics emerged within a multiplicity of contexts—Jewish and non-Jewish, intellectual and political. Chapters 3 through 7 explore the literature generated on demography, health and hygiene, physical anthropology, and national economy. They analyze the interconnections between ideas and ideology in Jewish social science, exploring the production and dissemination of statistics, ideas, and images about Jewry by Jewish scholars for specific political purposes.

At the heart of the debate over the effects of emancipation and integration on the Jews was the demographic question. Demography, or the study of population numbers and movements, constituted one of the central categories of Jewish social science. Although they admitted the extreme difficulty, if not impossibility, of procuring precise figures, Jewish statisticians set as one of their chief tasks the enumeration of the total number of Jews in the world, and of Jewish populations within particular countries or nations and within individual cities and communities. The mass movement of Jews, their emigration, immigration, and internal migrations, were also designated at the outset as important subjects for analysis.

More than anything else, though, Jewish social scientists were interested in the question of fertility. Jewish birthrates, it was commonly believed, had before the era of emancipation consistently exceeded death rates. Jewish demographic patterns, that is, could be described as healthy and vital before the Jews became "modern." In the centuries before the nineteenth, Jews reproduced at greater rates than Christians; more Jewish infants and children survived into adulthood; and the life span of Jews was longer than that of their neighbors. Statistics, however, appeared to show that Jewish fertility rates had indeed declined over the course of the nineteenth century, at least in Western industrialized countries. How to explain this demographic decline, and just what, if anything, it signified, were the issues of contention. Chapter 3 examines the discourse generated on Jewish fertility, and the question of decline. Central to this demographic question was the reconception of intermarriage and conversion in terms of medicine, biology, and racial science. This sort of reconception, which entailed the reinterpretation of phenomena pivotal to traditional Jewish religious history and thought, was fundamental to Jewish social science. Rather than being matters of theology, intermarriage and conversion now became significant primarily in terms of the threat they purportedly posed to Jewry at the demographic and biological levels. As such, intermarriage and conversion became fundamental elements in the larger debates over Jewish identity and difference, normalcy and abnormality, progress and decline.

As is evident from an analysis of specific phenomena such as intermarriage and conversion, the ideas and images drawn from the realms of medicine and biology were extremely important for Jewish social scientists. Chapter 4 explores in greater detail the impact of medicine, biology, and psychiatry on Jewish social science, and the uses made of the concepts of disease and degeneration. The majority of Jewish scientists accepted the tradition within general European science that identified the Jews as physically and morally degenerate, and they reproduced within their own works the statistics and images that proved this condition. At the same time, they rejected the racial determinism that often undergirded non-Jewish analyses. They insisted instead on an environmental causality. Casting European Jewry as either actually or potentially diseased, and identifying the causes of this with the very condition of modernity, Zionists (on whom I focus) were able to demonstrate scientifically that Jews literally had no future in the Diaspora. Social laws and forces seemingly beyond Jewry's control were working to eliminate its resistance to infectious and contagious illnesses, increase the rates of mental and nervous disorders, and lower fertility rates. At both the quantitative and qualitative levels, Zionist social scientists argued, modern Jewry was under attack.

This book is concerned in large part with the conjunction of social science and Zionism. Yet even as I underscore the fundamental nexus between this enterprise and Jewish nationalism, it is also necessary to call attention to the intellectual and ideological heterogeneity of Jewish social science. There was a significant countercurrent, a non-Zionist, at times even anti-

Zionist, presence within Jewish social science from the outset. I use the label "Diasporist" to refer to those non-Zionists who continued to believe in the feasibility and desirability of Jewish life in the Diaspora. Diasporists, like Zionists, understood their own work largely in instrumental terms. They wove social scientific facts and figures into narratives demonstrating the viability and normalcy—either actual or potential—of Jewish life in Europe and North America. For some, Diasporism translated into the ongoing effort for a successful integration or assimilation of the Jews into the wider Gentile society. For others, however, it meant territorial nationalism. Still others believed that the Jewish future could best be insured through a return to orthodox religious rituals. Chapter 5 deals exclusively with the Diasporist discourse as it came to be articulated through debates over Jewish demography, and health and disease. Succeeding chapters integrate discussions of non-Zionist and Zionist social scientists in the realms of racial science and national economy.

I turn in chapter 6 then to the representation of Jewish identity and difference through racial anthropology and iconography. An examination of texts dealing with physical anthropology and racial iconography reveals that Jewish social scientists looked to statistics and images of Jewish bodily traits and forms to prove that at the fundamental physical level Jews constituted a recognizable "type," one that set them apart from the people in whose midst they lived, and connected them, despite geographic divisions, with other Jews. Iconography from ancient Near Eastern monuments, juxtaposed with photographs of contemporary European Jews, served as proof for these scientists that Jews constituted a unified—if not necessarily pure—race despite the elapse of thousands of years. Moreover, for Zionists it established an empirical link between Jewry and Palestine based on scientific evidence established through anthropology, archaeology, and the technology of mechanical reproduction. Whether or not this purported physical, anthropological difference between Jews and non-Jews was a positive or negative condition; whether it was a set of attributes to be preserved—through the mechanism of isolation in their own homeland—or gradually eliminated—through the continuation of the integration process—was central to the debate. Like fertility, intermarriage, and matters of health and disease, the numbers and images generated about the size and shape of the Jewish anatomy were part of the more general debate over assimilation, decline and degeneration, and the means of regeneration.

Jewish social scientists, like Jewish historians, identified emancipation as a revolutionary turning point in Jewish history. However, unlike historians, who focused mainly on intellectual and political developments as causes of emancipation and assimilation, social scientists located the significant shift at the economic and social levels. Capitalism, and the social and cultural relations accompanying it, were the mechanisms of far-reaching transformations in modern Jewish life. Chapter 7 examines the descriptive representations of Jewish economic conditions and the theoretical analyses of the historical and contemporary links between Jews and capitalism. It looks at the comparative discussions of Jewish economic existence in Eastern and Western Europe, and at the debate over the interpretive categories of degeneration and decline applied to the economic realm. Through an analysis of the impact of the theories of two leading German national economists, Wilhelm Roscher and Werner Sombart, this chapter demonstrates how the appropriation by Zionists of two different theses regarding Jews and European economic development served as a response to anti-Semitic charges of Jewish inferiority by articulating a nexus between economic talent and intellectual acumen. Simultaneously, the purported relationship between Jews and capitalism offered further proof of the diseased and abnormal existence of the Jews, and of the impossibility of a future in the Diaspora. Moreover, analyses of Jewish economic history from a racial perspective allowed Zionists to connect Jews with other non-European trading peoples such as the Phoenicians and the Armenians, and hence to establish yet another connection between Jews and Palestine.

Finally, in a concluding chapter, I trace the impact of Jewish social science, and address some methodological questions raised by the use of this knowledge. Research produced by Jewish social scientists found its way immediately into contemporary Jewish and non-Jewish scholarship, was taken up and utilized by Jewish social workers and communal activists, and constituted an important source of material for later social historians of Jewry. What a cursory exploration of this sort of afterlife of Jewish social research demonstrates is not merely that this work exerted an influence, both at the time it was produced and after. It also makes clear that the faith in numbers, the implicit and unquestioned assumption about the objectivity of statistical data, extends far beyond the social scientific circles studied here. Faced with the various ways in which Jewish social scientific knowledge was used by others, by non-social scientists—in many cases by those quite distant ideologically or temporally—we need to inquire into why such utilization occurred so unproblematically. Why, for instance, did anti-Semitic researchers accept the knowledge produced by Jewish social scientists, given what they believed about the Jews' nature? Or, to take a more benign example: Why do Jewish social historians working today, or who have been working over the past few decades, uncritically utilize numbers produced close to a century ago, even when they are aware of the politically or ideologically charged nature of the narratives?

## Historical and Historicist Considerations

Of particular interest in this work is the question of why the social sciences became at a certain time and place so significant, why they emerged at a particular historical juncture as that body of knowledge believed to be best suited to, or capable of, describing reality. And, more particularly, how were statistics about Jewish life woven into narratives of progress or decline, health or degeneration, normalcy or abnormality? To explore these issues I adopt a constructivist approach to the history of statistics and the social sciences.[65] I approach social scientific texts as narratives, as interpretations and reconstructions of an historical reality—rather than as direct reflections of that reality—bound up with particular ideological commitments and goals. This study is not concerned chiefly with the degree to which the statistics used, or the explanations and conclusions generated around them by these scientists, corresponded to the reality or truth of Jewish life during the decades under discussion. For the cultural and intellectual historian, what is of primary interest is the meaning and significance assigned to the statistics; the way in which numbers and images were used to articulate evaluations of collective health or disease, of normalcy or abnormality; and the way in which these judgments then came to be part of broader debates over the Jewish present and future. Within these texts it is possible to identify a fundamental shift in the evaluation of Eastern and Western European Jewry, and in the notion of "modernity" itself. Such a reevaluation emerged out of an extended analysis of emancipation and assimilation, which itself emerged out of an analysis of the statistical and social scientific data.

Insisting that science, and social science especially, is distinct from the reality it purports to reflect and describe does not mean that the two are unrelated, that we do not or cannot learn about the realities of the past or present from these sources.[66] The point is rather that these texts, no matter how successful they may be in offering a sense of direct or transparent access to reality, are built of more than just the facts of social and economic life. It was, of course, the insistence on the part of social scientists that their work did objectively and dispassionately represent reality that, in part, lent the sciences such prestige and power. The ability to give order to mass society, to reveal the patterns and structures and trends, rendered social science increasingly indispensable. I contend that any attempt at making these texts speak about reality in such a way—as the creators of the texts themselves intended—is, at the least, problematic.

Nonetheless, this was usable knowledge. Moreover, as historians of science argue, scientific knowledge is also social knowledge. It emerges out of a particular, contingent context, a product of a complex set of political, social, economic, and intellectual factors. And, as texts or interpretations of reality, scientific narratives enter into particular contexts and help to shape and influence them. The import of an examination and analysis of these early social scientific texts lies, first of all, in what they reveal about the intellectual and cultural life of European and Anglo-American Jewry between 1880 and 1930. Jewish social science represented a startlingly different approach to the Jewish past and present than previous Jewish scholarship had. This was so in the first place, of course, because the categories of analysis were different: demography, economy, anthropology, pathology rather than the beliefs, practices, and intellectual creations of the Jewish religious imagination, or the great political transformations which affected Jewish communal life. The Jewish social science that emerged in the late nineteenth century shared important affinities with the Jewish scholarly tradition that preceded it. Just as significant, however, were the discontinuities that marked off Jewish social science as a distinct intellectual enterprise.

Probably nothing demonstrates the contingent nature of Jewish social science more dramatically than the prominent place racial theory and concepts occupied in it. In the post-Holocaust period, a phenomenon such as Jewish interest in, and contribution to, a racialized social science may strike us as strange, perhaps uncomfortably so. The widespread acceptance and utilization of racial ideas, by Jews and non-Jews alike throughout Europe in the half century before the rise of Nazism, has been well documented by recent scholarship.[67] This literature demonstrates that the belief in the viability of the notion of race was not limited to conservative, right-wing ideologues. Rather, thinkers from across the political and ideological spectrum took the idea of race seriously and incorporated it into their scientific and political writings. Racial science in all its aspects has, however, been so thoroughly identified with Nazism and the Holocaust that the important historical differences between racial thought, as it developed over the course of the nineteenth and early twentieth centuries, and the racial eugenics and genocidal policy implemented by the Nazi regime are oftentimes collapsed. Undoubtedly, Nazism built its racial ideology on the intellectual foundation of earlier racial science; yet a critical historicist approach forces us to recognize the distinction between the two. There were those within the scientific communities of Central and Western Europe who did indeed attack the use of racialist theories.[68] Yet, well into the 1920s racial thinking was a prominent and legitimate feature of the European intellectual landscape. Hence, Jewish social scientists, educated and trained in Central and Western European universities during a time when the language and concepts of biology and race exercised tremendous influence within the human sciences, could be expected to participate in this discourse.

Undoubtedly, racial images and ideas were critical to the emergence and development of what I choose to call Jewish social science. Debates over racial identity were instrumental in the shaping of Jewish social science, and they figure prominently in this study. But to categorize most of those involved in this scholarship as race scientists is to limit or reduce the purview of their intellectual interests and influences. They were social scientists because they were influenced by and partook of the numerous intellectual "disciplines" that were developing into the professional social sciences. And, just as important, the ultimate analytical interest of Jewish social scientists was the "social." Rather than focusing on the historical or biological—although they certainly engaged these categories, and oftentimes employed them as causal explanations—they were concerned with the condition of contemporary Jewish society (and individual communities). At the empirical or positive level this entailed research into the demographic makeup of Jewry, its levels of health and disease, education, migration, occupations, and so forth. At the theoretical level it meant asking questions about the impact of emancipation and assimilation on Jewish identity, and on the physical, social, economic, and cultural conditions just listed. It meant offering explanations for the patterns discerned through the statistics.

And here is the second major reason why this body of scholarship deserves the appellation "social." As I mentioned above, and as we shall have occasion to see throughout, the explanations proffered by Jewish writers for the condition of modern Jewry were overwhelmingly rooted in social conditions, broadly defined. This is not to say that factors drawn from the historical or biological realms played no part in the causal frameworks constructed by Jewish scholars. These were indeed very important elements. But, ultimately, social forces were deemed paramount. Chief among these was "assimilation." To a certain extent Jewish social science can be described as an extended encounter and confrontation with assimilation, an attempt to comprehend it as a phenomenon itself and to illuminate its myriad consequences for modern Jewish life. Certainly, the effects of assimilation were sometimes understood in biological or racial terms. Thus, for instance, some Jewish social scientists debated the impact of intermarriage on the physical and moral character of Jewry. However, the causes of such manifestations of assimilation were social or environmental.

The debate over the environmental or racio-biological etiology of individual and group conditions or traits had been central to the development of the social sciences in Europe and the United States over the previous century and a half. In weighing in on the debate over causality, Jewish social scientists placed their own work firmly within the broader corpus of social scientific literature, and made a contribution to this ongoing argument.

Jews now became subjects as well as objects of statistical social scientific research. Thus, the emergence of a significant number of texts written by Jews about Jews signaled a development *within the European social sciences* (as well as within Jewish scholarship) that historians of the social sciences have all but completely ignored. The work of Jewish social scientists belongs, therefore, to the history of the modern social sciences, as well as to modern Jewish history.

## CHAPTER ONE

# "Wir müssen mehr wissen"

## Institutional and Ideological Foundations of a Jewish Statistics

From the outset Jewish statistics was cast in inclusive, universalist terms. The introduction to *Jüdische Statistik*, the maiden publication of the Verein für jüdische Statistik, began by declaring that the interest among Jews in statistics "was linked to the general, human, cultural movement, the tendency of every civilized *Volk* to gain a conception of its condition. Statistics . . . is the only, indispensable foundation for the understanding of human groups." A Jewish statistics, in turn, "emerges out of the need of all of Jewry [*Gesamtjudentums*], out of the non-Jewish totality, out of the *Zeitgeist*. It is and will be defined by its allegiance to objectivity (*Objectivität*), science (*Wissenschaft*), and truth (*Wahrheit*)." Evidence for this homogeneity of purpose could be found, so it was claimed, in the ideologically heterogeneous makeup of the *Verein* and its supporters.[1]

Yet Jewish statistics was in fact conceived, though not wholly carried out, as a Zionist project. There were clear ideological, in addition to intellectual, impulses to the creation of statistical bureaus, to the collection, organization and publication of statistical materials; and to the scholarly analysis of modern Jewry along social scientific lines. Certainly, from the start non-Zionists contributed to the creation and development of Jewish statistics at every level. The community of Jewish social scientists extended beyond those committed to Zionism, to those who remained convinced of the viability and vitality of Jewish life in the Diaspora. Nonetheless, Jewish statistics was, conceptually, the child of Jewish nationalism. In the first years of the twentieth century Zionists succeeded in creating an institutional setting whose intellectual activities served their own ideological goals, while at the same time involving non-Zionist organizations in the enterprise. This chapter traces the creation of Jewish social science at the institutional level, and locates this within the context of early Zionist political and ideological developments. It places the emergence of the Verein für jüdische Statistik in a highly circumscribed moment in Zionist history: the crystallization of an oppositional force to Theodor Herzl's leadership of the movement around the concept of "culture." For Cultural Zionists the creation of a vital and viable "Jewish culture"—broadly defined to include not only art, music, and literature but also the revival of the Hebrew language and the establishment of a Jewish or Hebrew University—was an essential condition for, and component of, Jewish national life. Social science, I argue, was understood as a cultural undertaking, and as part of the concerted effort to establish Cultural Zionism as a force in Zionist politics. This chapter then addresses the question of non-Zionist participation, focusing on the move to define Jewish statistics as an objective and universal science, and the instrumental function of such a definition. My goal is to situate the statistical project within the context of Central European Jewish politics, elucidating how and why social scientific research on contemporary Jewry came to be conceived ideologically as part of the Zionist arsenal, while also being touted as objective, universal, and non-partisan.[2]

## *The Creation of the* Verein für jüdische Statistik

In December 1901, at the Fifth Zionist Congress in Basel, Max Nordau declared to his fellow delegates that "an exact statistical research of the Jewish people is an uppermost necessity for the Zionist movement."[3] Jewish statistics would provide a "solid foundation" for the Jewish nationalist movement, moving it from the "realm of feeling" to that of "practical preparation." "In the most important point, the positive knowledge of our people and their actual conditions, we are poorly or not at all prepared. We should be operating with incontestable, inflexible numbers, yet we have only general, vague sentiment."[4] Taking the opportunity to attack the liberal Jewish establishment, Nordau added that "the hypocrites and babblers who drivel on about a 'Mission of Judaism among the Jewish People' have no need to bother with Jewish statistics. They know enough about Judaism when they know their own incomes, and how many wealthy people there are in the community." Zionists, however,

must know more [*Wir müssen mehr wissen*]. We must know with greater precision about the national material [*das Volksmaterial*] with which we have to work. We need an exact anthropological, biological, economic and intellectual statistic of the

Jewish People. We must have quantitative answers to the following questions: How is the Jewish People physiologically constituted? What is the average size (of the Jew)? What are his anatomical characteristics? What are the numbers of diseased within it? What are the death rates? How many days, on the average, is the Jew ill during a year? What is the average life span? From which diseases do Jews die? What are the numbers related to marriage? Related to children? How many criminals, insane, deaf and dumb, cripples, blind, epileptics are there among the Jewish nation? Do the Jews have their own particular or characteristic criminality, and if so, what is it? How many Jews are city-dwellers, how many rural? What sorts of occupations do Jews pursue? What do they possess? What do they eat and drink? How do they live? How do they dress? How much income do they require for food, clothing, housing, intellectual and spiritual needs? All of this one must know, if one wants to really know a people. As long as this remains unknown, whatever one seeks to do for the nation will be a fumbling in the dark; and whatever one says about this nation will be, at best, poetry, and at worst empty chatter.[5]

Nordau unambiguously tied the statistical study of the Jews to the Zionist enterprise, while simultaneously delegitimizing the non-Zionist Jewish community. Equating ignorance of the Jewish present with the past from which Zionism marked a break, he identified non-Zionist Jewry with a sterile antiquarianism, tinged with the corruption that accompanied wealth.[6]

Zionism, in contrast, interested itself in the present and future of Jewish life. The "wealthy Jews" gave up nothing for the Jewish collective whole; they offered money, but nothing more. Zionists were prepared to sacrifice. "Despite the extraordinary difficulties involved in statistically examining the life of the nation in all its material and moral aspects, Zionists must not shirk away from this task." Nordau offered up the statistical enterprise as a pioneering effort, akin to the other pioneering tasks to be undertaken by the movement. The new scientific enterprise must be part of the larger national enterprise. The project of collecting and analyzing facts and figures about contemporary Jewish life, Nordau appeared to suggest, would in itself constitute part of the effort of national regeneration, while the knowledge produced was requisite for a renewed national consciousness and for nation building.

Nordau granted that Jewish statisticians would need to avail themselves of already existing methods and materials, produced mainly by various government offices and bureaus. Yet he was quick to point out that the quality of the extant research was uneven at best, and that for all intents and purposes Jewish researchers would have to begin de novo. One of the chief difficulties facing Jewish statistics, according to Nordau—and one that later Jewish social scientists complained about regularly—was the absence in many countries where Jews lived of officially generated statistics along confessional or religious lines. This was true, for example, of the governments of France, Italy, Belgium, Great Britain, and the United States. It made generating reliable numbers about such Jewish national communities terribly difficult.[7] Yet even in those countries where "confession" was a legitimate and legal category—Germany, Austria-Hungary, Rumania, and Russia—"we possess only a few scattered works, and these are not the most reliable or comprehensive."[8] Nordau seriously underestimated the number of already existing statistical works about Jewry. Whether this was due to genuine ignorance or to a desire to convince his audience of the need for immediate action is unclear. At any rate, his call for an organized Jewish statistics did indeed generate a vigorous response among Zionists. The speech was reprinted or paraphrased in a number of Zionist-oriented newspapers and journals, and his claim that statistical research was fundamental to the success of the Zionist project was echoed by lesser-known figures in the Zionist press.[9] Such pleas for a Jewish statistics were explicit calls for a body of knowledge that the Zionist movement could use. They spoke to a more general belief or conviction that Jewish nationalism must become "scientific" in order to achieve its goals. A mass movement, if it was systematically to reconstitute a *Volk*, required the tools by which mass phenomena could be known and understood. The "*Volksmaterial*" demanded, as Nordau said, a quantitative approach.

In early 1902 a "Committee for the Establishment of a Bureau for Jewish Statistics" formed in Berlin.[10] It sought, as its call for public support announced, to solve "the problem of the production of an exact scientific statistic of the complete development of the cultural life of Jewry" through the creation of a "central gathering place" [*Centralsammelstelle*], or bureau, for all statistical material related to Jews.[11] Over the following months the committee reconstituted itself into the Verein für jüdische Statistik, an organization intended to serve as a model and institutional center for a European-wide Jewish statistical movement. Satellite or regional sections quickly formed in cities throughout Central and Eastern Europe: Hamburg, Vienna, Bern, Lvov (Lemberg), Odessa, Warsaw, Tomsk, and Philippopolis.[12]

Organizationally, the *Verein* was composed of executive officers—chairman, vice chairman, general secretary, and treasurer, a board of directors (*Vorstand*), individual working groups, and dues-paying members. Executive officers and the board of directors, responsible for all matters administrative and financial, were to be elected yearly at the annual planning sessions of the *Verein*. Regional sections were made up of a section leader, who was directly answerable to the central Berlin *Verein*, and a working group.[13]

The primary goal of the *Verein*, according to its statutes, was to acquire "the knowledge of the conditions of all groups within the Jewish *Volk*" through the efforts of "a systematic statistics and demography." This was intended as a scientific (*wissenschaftlich*) enterprise, yet it was also conceived in practical terms (*praktisch*) along the lines of social policy or praxis. "Through its realization," the *Verein* stated, "the informational basis for all actions aimed at the improvement of the conditions of the Jewish masses will have been created."[14] This intersection of science and politics, captured in the concept of a *wissenschaftliche Sozialpolitik*, was present at the outset, and, as we shall see, it impelled Jewish social science throughout its career. The definition of such key terms as "reform," "improvement," or "regeneration" was certainly contested by different individuals and factions. But the assumption that Jewish statistics ought to serve the practical and political needs of the Jewish community, and that this political component in no way compromised the objective, scientific nature of the enterprise, went all but unchallenged by those involved. These are points to which we will return throughout this study.

The construction of a Jewish statistics was to be achieved through the collection, organization, and publication of all social scientific materials related to Jewry. The preliminary task set by the *Verein* was the production of a systematic bibliography of Jewish statistics, a task that fell to the working groups (*Arbeitsgruppen*). The central *Verein* in Berlin produced and disseminated a detailed set of instructions regarding this process.[15] Regional working groups were instructed to concern themselves solely with material related to their particular state or region. The Berlin working groups were to handle materials related to Prussia, Germany as a whole, and all those states or countries lacking a regional working group.

In June 1902 four Berlin working groups were organized. They were responsible for excerpting previously published material from the following sources: 1) bibliographical works, encyclopedias, books, and brochures; 2) scientific journals; 3) Jewish journals and newspapers; and 4) statistical publications. A fifth group was constituted shortly thereafter to translate the abundant Russian material. A redaction committee was responsible for ordering this material to be prepared for publication.

In creating a working bibliography of Jewish social science, emphasis was placed on already published sources, both Jewish and non-Jewish. Yet new research was also encouraged, and the instructional sheet included a guide on how to go about producing new work. Researchers were invited to investigate statistical archives of states, communities, and public organizations; Jewish *Gemeinde* records, tax records, matriculation books; and to devise questionnaires in order to survey the social conditions of Jewry.

Material was to be divided into two main groups: 1) general Jewish statistics, "encompassing all publications in which the conditions of Jews in diverse lands [*in mehreren Ländern*] are addressed," and 2) Jewish regional statistics [*Jüdische Landesstatistik*], "encompassing all publications concerned with the conditions of Jews in a particular country or region [*Land*]." Within both these groups material was to be further divided and organized into the following thematic categories: 1) population statistics (birth, marriage, death; population increase and decrease; immigration and emigration; conversions, both out of and into Judaism); 2) anthropological and ethnographic statistics; 3) health statistics; 4) economic statistics (occupational statistics, including the percentage of Jews in military service, and the description of the overall economic condition of Jewry; 5) statistics of social life (family life, communal organizations (*Vereine*), charity and mutual-aid establishments); 6) statistics of religious life (organization of the *Kultusgemeinden*, synagogue, etc., both orthodox and reform; 7) moral statistics (crime, suicide, etc.); 8) statistics of intellectual life (Jewish schools, attendance at non-Jewish schools, average education [*Bildung*], Jewish libraries, the Jewish press, the percentage of Jews involved in the intellectual life of a particular country); 9) political statistics (the civic-legal standing [*staatsrechtliche Stellung*] of the Jewish population, its rights in reality ("ihre Rechte in der Praxis"); relations of Jews with non-Jews; assimilation and national consciousness; 10) miscellaneous.

The product of this collective enterprise was a bibliography extending to over one hundred pages, which formed part of the *Verein*'s initial publication, *Jüdische Statistik* (1903). In addition to the bibliography, the volume included representative examples of original statistical research work undertaken by various Jewish organizations and individual Jewish social scientists.

In early 1904 the *Verein* established a board of curators (*Kuratorium*) for the purpose of raising funds, mainly in order to facilitate the creation of a bureau for Jewish statistics in Berlin.[16] Later that same year the *Verein* announced the establishment of the Bureau für jüdische Statistik in Berlin, and the appointment of the lawyer and social scientist Arthur Ruppin as director. The bureau was, as it was intended to be, the focal point of Jewish social scientific activity in Europe; it remained so until the mid-1920s. It was responsible for, inter alia, the production and publication of the official journal of the movement, the *Zeitschrift für Demographie und Statistik der Juden*, which appeared from 1905 until 1931, when the bureau closed.

In addition to the creation of the bureau, in 1904 the *Verein* also established the Union of Jewish Statistics (Verband der jüdische Statistik). The Verband served as an umbrella organization, linking Berlin with other Jewish statistical organizations being formed.[17] During the following two decades a number of other bureaus and Jewish social scientific institutions were founded throughout Central and Eastern Europe, each with ties to the Berlin *Verein* and bureau.

## Jewish Statistics and Jewish Politics

The Zionist impulse to this new Jewish statistical enterprise was evident at the outset.[18] Institutionally, the committee and the *Verein* were composed exclusively of Zionists; conceptually, the statistical enterprise was cast as a necessary ingredient for the Jewish nationalist undertaking. Alfred Nossig, chair of the committee and head of the *Verein*, had been active in Zionist politics since the late 1880s. Born in Lvov, in what was then Austrian Galicia, he had in his youth been an outspoken advocate of Polish-Jewish assimilation. As a poet, dramatist, and artist he had devoted his talents to celebrating Polish nationalism and demonstrating the love of the Jews for their adopted Polish homeland. Nossig, as Ezra Mendelsohn has written, was the product of a Jewish enlightenment tradition, romantic and idealist, intent on "uplifting" the Jewish people through cultural regeneration.[19] When in the late 1880s his enchantment with Polish nationalism faded, Nossig transferred his enormous creative energy to the nascent Jewish nationalist movement.

During the years 1886–87 he collected statistical materials related to the Jews, mainly from previously published monographs, journals, and government studies. He organized and published this material, in Polish and German, intending it as a first effort at a systematic Jewish statistics.[20] This work was, however, also a contribution to the political debate over the Jews, part of the post-liberal and post-emancipatory redefinition of Jews and Judaism utilizing the language of social science. According to Nossig, Jews must be defined anthropologically as a *Volk* or *Stamm*, rather than as a religious community.[21] They shared an historical homeland, particular physical characteristics that set them apart from other nations, and the common languages Hebrew and Yiddish.

Through a combination of comparative statistics and a priori assertions about the "character" and "habits" of Jews, Nossig sought to demonstrate the essential unity of the Jewish *Stamm*, a unity that inhered despite their geographic, political, and cultural differences. For Nossig, contemporary knowledge about the condition of Jewry constituted an essential part of the nationalist enterprise. His interest in statistics and in the social sciences was motivated in large part by the functional role he believed this type of knowledge could play in the reconstitution of a Jewish *Volk*. In his essay on the "Jewish Question" Nossig argued that, given the contemporary economic and religious tensions in Poland, the expulsion of Jewry was imminent. The only solution, he concluded, was mass migration to Palestine and the creation of a Jewish state. These pronouncements infuriated the assimilationists in Poland, with whom Nossig had once been aligned. They viewed him now "not only as a traitor, but as a man of science, who gave to Zionists the scientific tools required for an intellectually and scientifically based worldview."[22]

When in early 1902 Nossig organized the Committee for the Establishment of a Bureau for a Statistics of the Jewish People, he drew exclusively on the talents of his fellow Zionists. In addition to Nossig, the committee was made up of the following individuals, all of whom were actively involved in the Zionist movement: Natan Birnbaum, Martin Buber, David Farbstein, Berthold Feiwel, Alexander Hausmann, Abraham Kastelianski, Jacob Kohann-Bernstein, Abraham Korkis, Sigmund Kornfeld, Egon Lederer, Leo Motzkin, L. Felix Pinkus, Davis Trietsch, and Chaim Weizmann. In building the working groups or sections of the *Verein*—which were responsible for the initial collection and organization of statistical material—the executive committee successfully recruited, through lectures and advertisements, students associated with university-based Zionist associations such as *Kadimah*, *Emunah*, and *Ivria*.[23] In addition, the *Verein* gained the support of regional Zionist organizations. The working section in Tomsk, for example, was created as a direct result of the First Zionist *Landeskonferenz* in Siberia, which passed a resolution in January 1903 stating that "[a] comprehensive Jewish statistics is the primary basis of rational Zionist work." The resolution pledged to create a working group to collect data on the Jews of Siberia and a commission to establish a Central Bureau of Jewish statistics in Siberia. In reporting this the Zionist newspaper *Die Welt* took the opportunity to inform its readers of the significance of statistics to Zionism, and to urge their involvement. "[T]here rests upon all Zionist organizations, as well as all insightful members, the duty to support, through participation in scholarly work or the raising of funds, Jewish statistics, which from the national standpoint is an eminently significant undertaking."[24]

The nationalist impulse to Jewish statistics was written into the founding documents of the institution. The 1902 official declaration (*Aufruf*), issued by the committee, argued that the task of a Jewish statistics was made ever more urgent at present by the emergence of a Jewish nationalist movement, which "must and will succeed" (*Positives leisten soll und will*). Yet how can the Jewish nationalist movement possibly succeed, they asked,

when the material with which it must work remains unknown? How can social measures be taken when the economic and cultural structure of the population has not been determined, when the economic and intellectual constitution of the Jewish *Volk* remains unknown? In other words, we are at present in no position to attain to a sufficient solution to the Jewish Question. . . . If we wish to perform an operation on the body of the *Volk*, we must first possess an exact scientific diagnosis.[25]

## *Jewish Statistics and the Democratic Faction*

This first public formulation deliberately echoed Nordau's speech delivered at the Fifth Zionist Congress in 1901. It suggested a unity of purpose and intent within the Zionist movement as a whole. Jewish statistics emerged, however, out of a highly circumscribed political debate within the Zionist movement during the first few years of the twentieth century. Ironically, given Nordau's relationship with Herzl, Jewish statistics was one project of the Democratic Faction; as such, it represented part of the broader struggle between cultural Zionists—including the Faction—and Herzl, Nordau, and political Zionism.[26]

The initial committee, and the board of directors appointed to head the *Verein* in May 1902, were composed almost entirely of cultural Zionists active in the Faction.[27] Led by Chaim Weizmann, Leo Motzkin, Martin Buber, and Berthold Feiwel, the Faction emerged at the Fifth Zionist Congress in 1901 in opposition to what its members perceived as Herzl's authoritarian control over Zionist policy and procedure. It sought to exert greater influence over the shape and character of the movement through its calls for "democratization."[28] For the purposes of this study, what is of interest and significance is the emphasis placed by the Faction on the issue of culture, and the emergence of cultural, educational, and economic ideas and activities as central components of what practical Zionists identified as *Gegenwartsarbeit*—an action undertaken in the Diaspora in the present to further the Zionist cause.[29]

*Jüdische Kultur* and *Gegenwartsarbeit* were separate yet interrelated notions of how Zionism should be reconceptualized, and its activities redirected. Jewish statistics was conceived as one element in this reconceptualization. The scientific effort itself, on the one hand, constituted a type of cultural task or activity, and a form of *Gegenwartsarbeit*.[30] On the other hand, statistical knowledge came to be defined as essential to the identification and illumination of "areas" of Jewish life targeted for Zionist efforts. For example, the economic structures and activities, or the physical and mental health of Jews, were conceived of as realms of both scientific knowledge and practical action. Praxis, it was argued, demanded knowledge, and only statistics could offer the type of knowledge a mass movement like Zionism required. In other words, both the activity of producing knowledge about the contemporary conditions and relations (*Verhältnisse*) of

Jewry, and the knowledge produced, were integrated into the nationalist effort, and conceived as requisite to the transformation of Jewish life.

The act of creating a statistical bureau was one among many cultural tasks initiated by Faction members in the first few years of the new century. The Zionist publishing house Jüdischer Verlag (which counted the *Verein's Jüdische Statistik* as one of its first publications), the Jewish University project, the adult-education programs of the "Jewish" Toynbee Hall in Vienna (modeled after the famous English institution), the journal *Palästina*—devoted to economic research in Palestine, and edited by Nossig and Davis Trietsch—as well as the celebration of Jewish art, literature, and music all testify to the emphasis the Faction placed on culture and education. Each constituted an act of cultural production, conceived as an integral component of Jewish national regeneration.[31]

Like the endeavors enumerated above, the creation of a statistical institution, and social scientific research itself, were meant to serve as tangible evidence of cultural activity. For Weizmann, as for the others involved in the Faction, the value of the statistical bureau, as a site of scientific activity, lay in its ability to serve the cultural and propagandistic needs of the Faction and of the movement. In a letter to Ahad Ha'am, Weizmann described in clear terms the positive achievements of the Democratic Faction in bringing the question of culture to the fore: "But the most significant of all are the positive independ(ent) activities of the association which has been formed. These activities, to my mind, will show themselves in the first instance mainly in propaganda, campaigning and cultural work. The creation of an organ, the creation of a statistical bureau, these are, in my view, the two important tasks facing us."[32] The programmatic statement of the Faction, drafted in Heidelberg in 1902, provides further evidence of the ways in which social scientific knowledge came to be seen as a requisite element in cultural Zionist work.[33] The program asserted, in language echoing the social sciences, that the Jews were characterized by "a national, völkish-psychological individuality" ("*eine nationale, völkerpsychologische Individualität*"), which, despite historical forces, had maintained its "essential national characteristics" ("*wesentliche nationale Merkmale*"). This individuality and identity, this "essential difference," according to the Faction, was "manifested most clearly in *Kultur*."

On the one hand, then, the national identity of Jewry was assumed, and cultural activity constituted a manifestation of this identity. However, the Faction argued that assimilation had eroded the sense of an organic collective Jewish identity. Assimilation was unnatural and abnormal, for it both denied the individuality of nations, and placed "the interests of the individual over those of the whole." The goal of the Faction was the regeneration of Jewry, "the reconstruction of the Jewish *Volk* as an organic unity."

In order to accomplish this, Zionists would need to acquire the necessary knowledge (*Erkenntnis*) of the abnormal condition of the Jewish *Volk*.[34] "Among the most important and necessary preliminary tasks of Zionism," the program announced, "is the comprehensive research of the Jewish *Volk*," in particular with regard to colonization in Palestine.[35] Even as they asserted the organic, national identity of Jewry, the Faction insisted that this identity was in danger of disintegrating. Social scientific research was necessary for understanding and combating this phenomenon.

Moreover, the Faction's insistence on such dangers, and the proffering of a remedy—based in part on scientific research and knowledge—were means of asserting power and control vis-à-vis the entrenched Zionist leadership, and of maneuvering cultural or practical Zionists into a position of authority. As David Vital has written about the role of "culture" within the Democratic Faction's agenda, "the question of culture was thus, from the first, a subject for indirect dispute with Herzl and his 'political' school, and, by stages, a topic—in fact, a banner—around which opposition to him, overt and covert alike, tended to muster."[36] The appropriation by cultural Zionists of the prestige of science, the concerted effort on their part to "scientize" Jewish nationalism, was an assertion of power and authority vis-à-vis the mainstream Zionist power structure.

Within Europe in general over the course of the nineteenth century, social science was increasingly linked with social policy and with the workings of the modern state. State administrations and bureaucracies appropriated for themselves the tasks of collecting and disseminating statistical information on subjects or citizens, first for purposes of taxation and military conscription, and over time for more varied reasons related to questions of social policy and reform. By the last quarter of the nineteenth century, both the ability and the need to possess quantitative studies about one's own "people" were well-established indicators of state and administrative power.[37] The establishment of institutions of Jewish social scientific research by practical Zionists can be understood, therefore, as one expression of the impulse to assume the role of a "government of the Jews," undertaking those tasks—census taking, the shaping of economic and social policy, concern over public health and hygiene—usually associated with political and official administrative bodies. In assuming those tasks, again as part of a systematic ethic of *Gegenwartsarbeit*, cultural and practical Zionists were asserting their ability to function in a quasi-governmental fashion. Signaling the ability to organize at the institutional level, these cultural enterprises were intended as counterweights to Herzl's own institutional signs of authority. Together with the numerous other cultural institutions initiated by the Faction, the statistical bureau served a quite specific ideological and political function within the struggle for authority occurring in Zionist circles in the first years of the century.

## The Redefinition of a "jüdische Wissenschaft"

The talismanic power of the notion of "science" was crucial to this sort of political struggle carried out by the Faction with the Zionist mainstream; to the Faction's reconceptualization of Zionism along cultural lines; and to its identity as a whole.[38] The image of science/scholarship (*Wissenschaft*) as a quintessentially modern and constructive critical enterprise appealed to the Faction's image of itself as representative of a modern critical spirit within Zionist and Jewish life. In the first place, the turn toward contemporary Jewish life as an object of study, and the epistemological and methodological shifts accompanying this, signified a break with the well-established *Wissenschaft des Judentums* tradition of Jewish scholarship, and the liberal, assimilationist goals it purportedly came to represent. In his speech on "Jewish Science" at the Fifth Zionist Congress, Martin Buber contrasted the older, irrelevant *Wissenschaft des Judentums* (concerned solely with the philological exposition of ancient texts) with a *jüdische Wissenschaft* that addressed itself both to the "Jewish Question" and to Zionism. This revamped Jewish science—what Buber called a "*jüdische Wissenschaftscomplex*"—would broaden out the areas of scholarly investigation to include work "on the Jewish race, its development, its psycho-physiological particularities; work on ancient Jewish economy, on the social structure of our *Volk*, on the evolution of its specific customs and manners." Buber envisioned a full-blown Jewish social science, incorporating the disciplines of "anthropology, ethnology, economics, social and cultural studies."[39] Such a science would constitute one part of what Buber and others conceived of as the "renaissance" in Jewish cultural and intellectual life. This flowering of Jewish creativity would provide impetus to, and signal the success of, the Jewish nationalist rebirth.[40]

The call for a different Jewish *Wissenschaft*, a "national" *Wissenschaft*, was widespread at the turn of the century, and not limited to those with direct involvement in statistics.[41] In an article entitled "The Problem of Jewish Science," the Galician Zionist and Democratic Faction member Osias Thon employed the language of oppression and death to convey the need for a new Jewish science. He acknowledged the profound learning and talent of the luminaries of the *Wissenschaft* movement—S. J. L. Rappaport, Leopold Zunz, Isaac Marcus Jost, Abraham Geiger, and Heinrich Graetz. Nonetheless, he confessed, my soul remains estranged and distant from theirs. There is an abyss between their conception and sentiment regarding the Jewish people and mine, which cannot be bridged. I have read Graetz's eleven volume history with astonishment, and yet it leaves me in the end only with the sounds of lament of a funeral oration, and all around are tombstones and cemeteries. It is suffocation and frostbite. And this is Graetz, the most lively and warm-blooded of them all.[42]

In Thon's view, a revitalized Jewish science would shift its focus away from the past and onto the present. "Until now our *Wissenschaft* has known only a past, but no present. This accounts for its cadaverous odor." In reciting the deficiencies of the established *Wissenschaft* approach Thon set down the agenda of the emerging Jewish statistical movement:

Is there a science of Judaism that concerns itself with the economic conditions of the Jews? Is there a *Wissenschaft des Judentums* that illuminates in a sociological way the type of group-structure of the Jews? One could investigate the welfare system of Jews; the minyan as a group, with its hierarchy. Where is such a science that can provide us with reliable statistical numbers about the Jews? . . . Jews have colonized Palestine now for more than two decades. Where is the science that can tell us about the land and its condition, about the colonies and their management? Other *Völker* realize that *Wissenschaft* is only partly concerned with the past. Jews must realize that the problem of a Jewish science is one concerning the entire Jewish people as a living organism. A living organism has its immanent laws of life and development. It is the task of a Jewish science of Jewry to discern these, in all their aspects.[43]

It should be evident that one cannot take these descriptions of a degenerate and enfeebled *Wissenschaft des Judentums* as representative of the reality of Jewish scholarship at that time.[44] Rather, these were concerted attempts to delegitimize a complex and heterogeneous intellectual tradition by linking this scholarship to decay and death, and tarring the *Wissenschaft* tradition with the brush of assimilation. This was a clear and conscious political move on the part of Zionists. An assault upon the epistemological order was an assault upon the established political and social order. In formulating an alternative way of knowing Jewry, of understanding and explaining the Jewish past and present, Zionists asserted their ability to reconstitute the social, economic, and political conditions of Jewry in the present and future.

Nor was the Zionist interest in appropriating for itself the mantle of "science" limited to its struggle with liberal Central European Jewish authority. The demonstration of a serious engagement on the part of Zionists with contemporary Eastern European Jewish social and economic problems would also assist in defusing the criticisms of Jewish socialists. If Zionism wishes to compete with the Bund, Weizmann wrote to Herzl in 1903, it must address itself to social and economic issues; it must show the

Jewish youth of Russia that it is "a genuinely modern movement of cultural and scientific responsibility."[45] Indeed, in its initial phase the primary focus of Jewish statistics was on the socioeconomic condition of Eastern European Jewry, including those immigrant communities that had reconstituted themselves in Western Europe and the United States. "This volume," the editors of *Jüdische Statistik* informed their readers in 1903,

> is dedicated to researching the conditions of the oppressed part of the Jewish *Volk* who in their homelands are losing their means of existence and are turning more and more to emigration. Professional authors examine here in original work the condition of the mobile Jewish world proletariat, its movement out of the East toward the European West and America on the one hand and toward the Orient on the other. [Through this intellectual effort] the Verein für jüdische Statistik will create the foundations for the alleviation of Jewish mass misery.[46]

Again, the practical and political impulse to Jewish social scientific research is evident here. The ability to speak *about* Jews authoritatively meant the ability to speak *for* Jews. Control over Jewish knowledge was at least one fundamental aspect of control over Jewish life.

The significance of Jewish statistics for cultural Zionists lay, then, in its prestige as a science, and in the political and practical benefits promised by the knowledge social science produced. Revealingly, most of the individuals making up the founding committee of the Verein für jüdische Statistik evinced no serious or long-lasting intellectual interest in or organizational commitment to Jewish statistics. Only Nossig remained involved for an extended duration, mostly at the administrative level. Weizmann's interest in Jewish statistics, in contrast, peaked in late 1902 with the survey he initiated on Russian-Jewish university students throughout Europe (including Russia). The survey, prepared in the main by Berthold Feiwel, was envisioned by Weizmann as a prerequisite to the creation of a Jewish university. The empirical knowledge produced about the inadequate living and working conditions of Russian Jewish university students, and about the hostility and prejudice they encountered, would serve to convince those in the West, with the means to lend support, of the necessity of a *jüdische Hochschule*.[47] Weizmann pledged University Bureau money to Nossig (who in 1903 became a Berlin representative of the university project) and to the statistical *Verein* to aid in the costs of publishing the report. (In the end, only the results of the survey on students in Western European universities appeared.) Neither Weizmann nor Feiwel remained involved in Jewish statistics for long after the completion of the project. The limits of their interest and their participation provide a clear example of the way in which Jewish statistics was seen primarily in functional terms, as an instrument of Zionist goals.

For Natan Birnbaum and Leo Motzkin, both of whom were involved for a brief time in the initial stage of Jewish statistics, the worth of statistical investigations into the condition of Jewry resided in the use to which such knowledge could be put by Jewish nationalists. Birnbaum never engaged in actual statistical research, and his brief involvement with the *Verein* remained nominal. A few years later he renounced Zionism and committed himself to Diaspora nationalism, and then to religious orthodoxy.[48] Nonetheless, his pronouncements about statistics lend valuable insight into the role some Zionists insisted social science ought to play in the nationalist struggle. "One must research the biological, cultural, and economic conditions of the geographically dispersed Israel," Birnbaum declared as early as 1897. "This is the requisite scientific work for a judgment on the viability of the Jews as a nation."[49] Moreover, the social sciences were an invaluable tool because they possessed a predictive power. Taking up the theoretical debate regarding the differences between the natural and social sciences, Birnbaum argued that, "it is self-evident that the social sciences [like the natural sciences] lend insight into the future."[50] This assertion then led Birnbaum into a discussion of the importance of *Wissenschaft* for Zionism.

In a 1902 article, "The Value of Jewish statistics," Birnbaum stressed the particular significance of statistical research for the Zionist movement. He reproduced sections of the Committee for a Jewish Statistic's *Aufruf*, and argued that scientific knowledge must be the foundation for future national action.[51] In a veiled reference to Herzl's hold on the movement, he attacked those detractors of statistics "who would rely only upon party dogmas or the words of a leader to guide them politically or socially; who admit 'facts' but trust them only if they remain 'unordered and unarranged'; or those who distrust science, and rely only upon 'instinct' or intuition."[52] Jewish statistics offered, in Birnbaum's view, an "objective picture" of the Jewish condition, and this in turn made possible reliable judgments or predictions about the Jewish future.[53]

Motzkin, who eventually produced a statistically based work on the effects of the 1903 Russian pogroms,[54] sought to elevate the Zionist interest in statistics above that of other segments of the Jewish community by distancing it from the purely functional. "For Zionists, the study of the Jewish people is the goal in itself," he argued. Motzkin contrasted this approach favorably with those of other segments of the Jewish community, whose interests in statistics were impelled by the conceptually limited goals of "defense," "charity," or "class-struggle" (i.e., liberal integrationists such as the Centralverein deutscher Staatsbürger jüdischer Glaubens (CV) and the Verein zur Abwehr des Antisemitismus, the philanthropists, and the socialists).[55] For Motzkin, the Zionist engagement with statistics stemmed from an involvement with the whole of Jewish life, rather than with particular phenomena such as anti-Semitism, poverty, or socioeconomic tensions. As we shall see in a moment, this "universalist" claim for Jewish statistics was a central facet of Zionist self-representation.

Motzkin nevertheless went on to posit a number of functions or goals for Jewish statistics as a singularly Zionist project. In so doing he enunciated several of the fundamental themes of Zionist social scientific discourse. "Of course," he maintained, "we will use all of this material as testimony or evidence for our own purposes: the necessity of a radical historical solution to the Jewish Question." Zionists had to know the "material capabilities of the Jewish organism, and establish foundations for answering numerous questions about Jewish life." They must investigate ethnological differences between Jews and other peoples, and chart the effects of assimilation in the West; describe migration patterns, educational levels, and occupational status; explore the "abnormalities of Jewish economic life," and discover the "laws of Jewish social life."

In short, a Zionist Statistics would reveal "the abnormality of Jewish existence in all its nakedness."[56] Jewish statistics would demonstrate scientifically the "abnormal" nature of the contemporary Jewish condition, and would also help to reconstitute modern Jewish identity along national lines. This would be accomplished through an illumination of an essential Jewish particularity and difference, or "national essence."[57]

As we shall see throughout this study, Zionists drew heavily on medical language and metaphors, such as the conditions of "normal" and "abnormal," to describe what they understood as their task vis-à-vis the sick and degenerate body of Jewry. Yet this image of contemporary Jewry as pathological was only one side of a complex and ambiguous image. Throughout the writings of Zionists interested and involved in social science, one encounters two prominent themes, two preeminent tasks envisioned for this science: it will illuminate the fact of the existence of a Jewish national or ethnic identity, and the "worth" or "value" of Jewry as a distinct and different collective entity. Simultaneously, it will analyze and represent the causes for, and manifestations of, the dissolution of that identity—a process designated as "abnormal" and "diseased"—in the modern period.

## Non-Zionist Jewish Participation in the Statistical Project

Conceived at its outset as a Zionist project, Jewish statistics nonetheless quickly garnered the financial, administrative, and intellectual support and participation of many non-Zionist Jewish individuals and communal institutions. Over and again the inclusive nature of the enterprise was stressed.

Jewish statistics, according to the *Verein*'s official statement, "renounces this or that party of Judaism. Statistics is best able to capture the totality of Jewish experience. The greatest variety of organizations and institutions who are participating in the statistical enterprise testify to the nonpartisanship of the *Verein. For the first time successfully almost all great Jewish organizations have united as one in their dedication to the task*" (emphasis in the original).[58]

Indeed, the scientific community created around the idea of a Jewish statistics was an inclusive one. Communal and international organizations such as the ICA, the CV, the B'nai Brith of Germany, the DIGB, the Gesellschaft zur Förderung der Wissenschaft des Judentums, the Öster-reichische-Israelitische Union, and the Hilfsvereins für Galizien, together with dozens of individual Jewish Gemeinde, lent their financial support to the project. Between 1904 and 1905 and 1905 and 1906, subventions collected from organizations and communities doubled, from 4,032DM to 9,685DM.[59]

Nossig failed, however, to secure what he considered adequate financial backing from the executive committee of the central Zionist organization. The significance of statistics for the national movement was certainly acknowledged. Still, the Smaller Actions Committee (SAC) decided that the project demanded a commitment of far more money (an estimated 1 million marks) than the movement could afford. The SAC did, however, pledge a three-thousand-DM annual subvention, and it subsidized a study of the social conditions of Russian Jewry.[60]

A number of factors help to account for the unwillingness on the part of the Central Zionist Office to adequately fund Jewish statistics. The Zionist organization habitually suffered from a shortage of funds, and there were projects proposed or under way during this period deemed more significant for the ultimate success of the movement.[61] An unexpected event such as the 1903 Kishinev pogrom, for example, generated interest in the practical uses of statistics; yet the material assistance required to aid the victims made substantial claims on the Zionist Organization's limited financial resources. In addition, there surely was also resistance on the part of the SAC to fund a project spearheaded by an oppositional faction within the movement that clearly sought to challenge Herzl and political Zionism's authority and agenda. One finds evidence for this, in fact, in cultural Zionists' public rebukes of political Zionists who failed to follow Nordau's call of 1901.[62]

Despite the fact that the Zionist Organization provided less financial support than had been hoped for, by 1908 Nossig could announce at the annual meeting of the Verband that "the Verein für jüdische Statistik is now supported financially by all major Jewish organizations and fifty-five communities in Germany and abroad."[63] Further evidence of the extensive interest and involvement of non-Zionists can be seen in the composition of the *Verein*'s administration. After the initial formation period in which Zionists alone constituted the administrative personnel, non-Zionists assumed key positions. While Nossig served as the chair of the *Kuratorium* elected in 1904, Louis Maretzki, a Berlin *Sanitätsrat* and head of B'nai Brith, was appointed to the second position. A list of German Jewish elites attending the first plenary session of the Verband der jüdische Statistik that same year included the names of prominent representatives of the liberal German Jewish community, including Maretzki, Martin Philippson, Berthold Timendorfer, Paul Nathan, and Hirsch Hildesheimer. Two years later Philippson and Eugen Fuchs, one of the leaders of the CV, appeared on the list of board members.[64]

The interest of liberal Jewish organizations and communal elites in Jewish statistics is not in itself surprising. Non-Zionists as well as Zionists, in Europe and the United States, involved themselves in the production and dissemination of social scientific knowledge for intellectual, ideological, and practical purposes. The surveys undertaken at the end of the nineteenth century by groups such as the B'nai Brith in Germany and the Österreichische-Israelitische Union in Austria, for example, were utilitarian and philanthropic, part of the effort of social and economic reform aimed at the impoverished immigrants from Eastern Europe or the native Jewish underclasses.[65] As we shall see, there certainly were those Jewish social scientists in Europe and the United States who produced studies that sought to refute the critics of emancipation and assimilation. Through analyses of social scientific data on physical characteristics, rates of birth and death, health and disease, and immigration and economics, the notion of a successful Jewish integration into modern European or American society was represented as a reality, and/or affirmed as a still viable ideal.

Social science, then, was taken up and used by a variety of individuals and groups for different, even opposing ideological and political ends. Certainly, Jewish social science represented only one example of such a politicization of scholarship. Historians involved in the *Wissenschaft des Judentums* movement in the nineteenth century clearly understood their scholarly endeavors as part and parcel of the broader Jewish effort at modernization and integration into general European society. In this they followed trends within the German and European academic communities. In the twentieth century, historians committed to Zionism—the so-called "Jerusalem School" of Jewish historiography—reinterpreted and re-imagined the Jewish past (and repudiated the integrationist tendencies within the *Wissenschaft* school) with the idea of lending the power of historical scholarship to the Jewish nationalist effort. And if one looks at the programmatic statements of the numerous general statistical and social scientific societies that emerged throughout Europe and America over the course of the nineteenth and early twentieth centuries, one finds a similar conjunction of theory and praxis, intellectual and ideological commitment. In this sense Jewish statistics represented one example among many of the way in which a particular type of knowledge, of intellectual endeavor, emerges contingently, within a nexus of specific historical developments and demands, to become part of diverse, even opposing ideological and political programs.[66]

Yet, interestingly, the explicit declarations regarding the nexus of the ideological and intellectual did not obviate, in the minds of those involved, the objective and "universal" nature of their science. This, despite the fact that objectivity had come to be associated most intimately with a distance, or at least with the appearance of distance, from the political or ideological realm. Nor did the clear ideological commitments to Jewish nationalism of those who participated in the earliest planning of the *Verein* keep non-Zionist organizations from affiliating themselves with the project. Yet, with the exception of the CV (until 1913), all the major Central European organizations and communal representative bodies expressed an open hostility to Zionist ideas and activities. The denial by Zionism of the solely religious character of Jewry, and the attempt to redefine Jewry along national/racial lines, were anathema to the majority of Jews. This was so regardless of what German or Austrian Zionists believed or said about their own relationship to their countries, and their identities as (mainly) solid bourgeois citizens.[67] For most Jews, the liberal emancipationist dream of a complete Jewish integration into German society, and the acceptance of Jews as full and equal citizens, remained viable. The emphasis upon differences other than religious ones between Jews and Germans, and the (re-)elevation of Palestine as the "Home of the Jews"—even if only for Eastern European Jews—signified for liberal Jewry that Zionists had abandoned their faith in integration and their sense of belonging fully to the German *Vaterland*.

How, then, do we understand such a seemingly unproblematic juxtaposition of political and social engagement with the assertion of scientific objectivity? Would the explicit links between politics and scholarship—between Zionism or integrationism and social science—not obviate the objective status of the latter? Moreover, how might we explain the involvement of liberal Jewish institutions and their representatives in an enterprise that explicitly announced itself as inspired by, as Nossig wrote, the "end of the dream of Emancipation," and by the renewed ideal of Jewish nationalism?

These two points, in fact, are interrelated, and indeed serve in large measure to illuminate one another. On the one hand, to establish the objectivity of their work, the organizers of Jewish statistics relied on the assertion of the nonpartisan, nonpolitical nature of their enterprise. At the same time, a guarantee of the objectivity and of the universality of Jewish statistics created the conditions for non-Zionist participation. The creation of a community of Jewish social scientists that transcended the political, and hence constituted the scientific, depended on the universal nature of the enterprise. Yet the establishment of Jewish statistics as an objective, nonpartisan enterprise, encompassing the efforts of all the Jewish community, was itself a conscious political strategy on the part of Zionists.

## Universality, Objectivity, and the Creation of a Jewish Social Scientific Community

In order to understand the inclusive nature of Jewish statistics, and the politics of inclusivity, we need to examine the rhetoric of self-construction and representation. Far more than the particular nationalist impulse to Jewish statistics, what the programmatic statements of the movement repeatedly stressed was its objective and universal nature. The editors of *Jüdische Statistik* acknowledged the Zionist impulse, yet they insisted that this did not obviate the nonpartisan nature of the enterprise. The interest and work in Jewish statistics is "very widespread . . . and emerges out of the need of all of Jewry (*Gesamtjudentums*), out of the non-Jewish totality, out of the *Zeitgeist*."[68] Jews with a nationalist sensibility, they wrote, "have been most zealous in research, without demanding that the work serve their own purposes exclusively. Our *Verein* shall proceed from the same sensibility" ("In diesem Sinne geht auch unser Verein vor").[69] "If there exists a vantage point from which to deal with Jewry not in a polemical way, but with the most severe objectivity, as a complex whole, then it is statistics. Therefore, the Verein für jüdische Statistik does not place itself in the service of this or that party within Jewry, but in the service of all of Jewry and mankind, of science and of truth."[70]

Such assertions of objectivity, universality, and nonpartisanship were made repeatedly in the first few years of the statistical enterprise. They were impelled by a number of different concerns and goals. In the first place, objectivity was insisted upon because of two interrelated claims made by proponents of anti-Semitism: 1) scientific anti-Semitism was objective in its analysis of the Jews, and 2) the Jews (like women and blacks) were incapable of achieving such objectivity themselves.[71] An objective Jewish science would serve to counter, as one writer put it, the "deceitful objectivity" of "scientific anti-Semitism."[72]

Insistence on the nonpartisan nature of Jewish statistics was also intended to counter charges of partisanship from among members of the interested Jewish community. Such a charge had in fact already been made the year before from within the Zionist camp. Felix Lazar Pinkus had initially been a member of the Democratic Faction, and of the Committee for Jewish statistics. By 1903, however, he had become a vocal opponent of the Faction movement. In arguing against the Faction, Pinkus insisted that "those very organizations tied to the Faction—the Jüdischer Verlag, the statistical bureau, and the Hochschule—should remain the province of individuals within Zionism, not parties."[73]

The emphasis on nonpartisanship also points to an initial fear and concern on the part of non-Zionists that Jewish statistics might be made to serve as the handmaiden of Jewish nationalism. During the 1904 annual meeting of the *Verein*'s executive, for instance, Nossig felt it necessary to reassure the group that the *Verein* had no "separatist tendencies." "Within Jewry, the Verein does not identify itself with this or that group, but exists as a scientific organization for all parties."[74] An assurance of objectivity and universality permitted non-Zionists to view Jewish statistics as a unifying rather than a divisive enterprise, one whose function transcended the narrow ends of Jewish nationalism. Moreover, positing Jewish statistics as a prerequisite to the solution of the Jewish Question—while leaving the Jewish Question undefined—meant that Jewish groups other than Zionists could make use of such knowledge for their own purposes (i.e. internal reform, communal defense against anti-Semitism, welfare and charity work, etc.).[75]

The universal nature of Jewish statistics, it was argued, stemmed in part from the fact that Jewry's newly found urge to investigate its own conditions social scientifically was an urge shared by all civilized peoples and nations. The Jewish interest in statistics was linked to the "general human, cultural impulse felt by all civilized peoples for a progressively more precise representation of their actual conditions."[76] In addition, the knowledge produced by Jewish statistics would be of great value or use to the non-Jewish world. In his 1903 programmatic essay Nossig claimed that Jewish statistics was valuable and necessary not merely for Jewry, but for the states and peoples within whose midst Jews lived. The knowledge derived from the social sciences would provide the sure means by which the "full and just value of the Jews as a social element" could be judged. Such knowledge was essential for understanding and solving the *Judenfrage*, or Jewish Question, which at the same time was a *Weltfrage*, or universal question.[77] In addition, Jewish statistics would surely be of interest and importance to science. In positing this, Nossig placed Jewish statistics firmly within the tradition of *Wissenschaft des Judentums*, whose founders also felt it necessary to argue the case for their research in terms of universal scientific value. Moreover, in both cases the antiquity and centrality of Jews and Judaism to civilization were invoked to prove the importance of the inquiries.[78] Nossig wrote:

If anyone were inclined to admit that the Jews are the chosen people, it would be the demographers. The Jews are the ancient nation [*altes Volk*], the primordial tribe [*uralte Stamm*], which has survived not only legendary, but also numerous historical deluges. Yet they are no fossil, but remain a living being. Contemporaries of the Chaldeans and Egyptians, yet continuing on as a modern *Volk*, they are for science the most interesting and instructive objects of study. This is particularly so in that they evince actual biological peculiarities which, properly evaluated, offer valuable knowledge for all of mankind.[79]

The "peculiarity" of the Jews' nature, and the value of this to social scientists, were themes that Jewish and non-Jewish writers would stress over the coming decades. The Jews, it was claimed, were social "barometers," exemplars of a modern condition that would in the near future come to characterize all of Western society. Demographically and socioeconomically, the Jews had "modernized" to a far greater extent than Christians; but Christians could look upon the Jews in the present and see their collective future. For better or worse, Jewry and modernity were one, and Jewish statistics served to illuminate this fact. This was yet another way in which Jewish social science was universalized, and hence depoliticized.

## Defining Objectivity

For the most part, Jewish social scientists assumed and asserted, rather than debated, the objective nature of their investigations. Moments of such disciplinary self-reflection were few and far between. In the minutes from the *Verein*'s 1912 annual meeting, there is reference to a brief debate over the problem of *Werturteil*, or the place of value judgments in scientific discourse. The Munich-based demographer and physician Rudolf Wassermann, who in his own work demonstrated little aversion to tying social scientific research to Zionist politics, at a certain point voiced discomfort with the explicitly ideological nature of the enterprise. He pushed for the complete disengagement of Jewish statistics from political and practical concerns, arguing that such extra-scientific interests impaired the objective nature of the enterprise. His colleagues, it was reported, unanimously rejected this argument. Jewish social science as "propaganda," they agreed, was unacceptable, but "the striving of Jewish science to represent not only reality, but suggest shortcomings and corrections to this reality was also necessary, and appreciated by the entire Jewish community."[80] This brief debate was most probably prompted by the recent highly charged debates within German social scientific circles over the question of "value-free" science.[81] More than anything else, it demonstrates rather clearly the relative disinterest among Jewish social scientists in exploring the thorny issue of the relation between objectivity, and social activism or political commitment.

In what traits or elements did this more or less assumed objectivity of Jewish social science inhere? In order to answer this it is necessary to gain a sense of what the broader scientific community understood as objective during this time. For insofar as Jewish social scientists derived the definitional terms and concepts of social science from this scientific community, the idea of objectivity, even if contended by factions within the scientific community, would be shared by Jews and non-Jews alike. In other words, in appropriating the form and content of European social science, Jewish social scientists inherited the definition of scientific objectivity.

It is important to note that objectivity and truth are not identical in this context.[82] Jewish social scientists shared, necessarily, the belief in the objective status of social scientific knowledge, and the terms of defining this status. But they challenged in fundamental ways the truth of non-Jewish representations of Jewish life. Indeed, it was precisely in the violation of the terms of objectivity by anti-Semites that Jewish social scientists located the falsity of these claims.

The faith in the objectivity of social science stemmed first of all from the central role that statistics played in the definition of the enterprise. Insofar as science came to be defined as the numerical measure of mass phenomena, objective fact was intimately connected to the quantification process. "Science," the Anglo-Jewish social scientist Joseph Jacobs declared in 1885, "was to Condillac a hundred years ago only a well-constructed terminology [*une langage bien faite*]; nowadays science is measurement accurately calculated."[83] Quantification in this view was a mechanical process. It eliminated, by definition, the subjective vagaries that accompanied the study of individual human beings; that is, it permitted definitive generalizations in a way historicism could not. In a 1908 article entitled "Jewish Statistics," Bruno Blau, the recently appointed director of the Bureau for Jewish Statistics in Berlin, argued that statistics "by its very nature was an objective science." He pointed to its ability to represent mechanically the reality of mass phenomena as the sign of such objectivity. The essence of statistics is not merely numbers, Blau wrote, but the science of large numbers. It deals with mass phenomena; it cannot take the individual case as typical. "As such, statistics can unhesitatingly be designated the most objective science, since it deals only with facts that are directly obtained through mechanical means of computation, and whose accuracy can be determined every time."[84] A few years later Arthur Ruppin argued much the same thing:

"One cannot say anything with any certainty by observing individuals. Only observation of the mass offers the possibility of arriving at an objective judgment."[85]

Objectivity and scientificity, therefore, resided in part in the purported mimetic ability of social science, in its descriptive powers of mass movements and structures. It is often argued that an early model for the social scientific notion of objectivity was not history, but natural science, which discovered "laws" and laid claim to being both proscriptive and descriptive. The ideal of social science as a "social physics" or "social biology" offered the image of social scientists capable of reaching an understanding of the social body in a manner analogous to the natural scientist's understanding of the planets or the animal kingdom.[86] An image of the social scientist as natural scientist meant, among other things, that objective truth resulted from obtaining a requisite distance from the subject, from standing outside of the "thing" as an invisible observer; or, in Thomas Nagel's felicitous phrase, from securing "the view from nowhere."[87]

Yet the ideal of a "view from nowhere" was a particularly difficult one for social scientists to maintain. For, unlike natural scientists, the "somewhere" in which social scientists labored was the same as the object of their study. Well-established hierarchies of difference between the middle-class male scientist and the myriad groups within society that constituted the object of their study—workers, women, the poor, the sick, criminals and prostitutes, and so forth—provided some requisite "distance." (It is, of course, precisely this same distance, defined in terms of class, gender, religion, or race, that helps to explain the ease with which scientists established categorical hierarchies.) However, the clear-cut interventionist nature of social science; its association with governmental policies of control and reform; and the connection in the minds of many between social science and socialism, all led to an identification of politics with subjectivity. The semblance of a political or partisan agenda fueling scientific work obviated that work's "scientific" nature.

Objectivity, therefore, came in the nineteenth century to be linked more and more with the absence of political or moral engagement on the part of the social scientist. "Another concomitant of objectivity is the appearance, at least, of ideological neutrality, and hence identification with a community of researchers rather than with a movement of activists. This has provided an especially crucial incentive to objectivity in history and the social sciences."[88] A "pure" or objective social science could certainly take into account the historically important role played, for instance, by ethics or values in the development of particular forms of social or economic life. But the values of the scientist, his personal beliefs about particular political or social ideologies, were not to guide his research or conclusions. The social scientist must be concerned, as the German national economist Werner Sombart remarked, only with "what is," not with "what ought to be."[89] Indeed, one encounters the same formula in the introduction to Arthur Ruppin's seminal 1904 work *Die Juden der Gegenwart*: "The numerous writings on Jews and Jewry that appear year in and year out concern themselves more with prophecy and prediction than with representation, more with 'what ought to be' than with 'what is'." Ruppin saw as one of his chief tasks as a Jewish social scientist the correction of that deficiency.[90]

Objectivity, however, was not solely a matter of distancing one's work from the appearance of impropriety that came with an explicit political and ideological impetus. Rather, it was, minimally, a combination of the appearance of nonpartisanship and the engagement of a method or set of agreed-upon rules that indicated membership in an intellectual community. "Quantitative conclusions carry authority in part because they seem to be dictated by explicit procedures for gathering and processing numbers, and to be independent of the passions and interests that inform political debate. The key ingredient here is the faith that science works according to method, which raises it above the foibles of mere individuals."[91] Objectivity that emerges as knowledge comes to be seen as separate from the local contexts in which it is produced, and assumes a universality. In this way evidence, in the form of statistics and the narratives woven around them, can "travel." In the words of the historian of statistics Theodore Porter:

> The language of mathematics is highly structured and rule-bound. It exacts a severe discipline from its users, a discipline that is very nearly uniform over most of the globe. . . . Since the rules of collecting and manipulating numbers are widely shared, they can easily be transported across oceans and continents and used to coordinate activities or settle disputes. Perhaps most crucially, reliance on numbers and quantitative manipulation minimizes the need for intimate knowledge and personal trust. Quantification is well-suited for communication that goes beyond the boundaries of locality and community. A highly disciplined discourse helps to produce knowledge independent of the particular people who make it.[92]

Thus, the power of numbers resides in part in their ability to induce a trust in certain forms of knowledge that transcend ideological disparities. Numbers in particular are capable of constituting intellectual communities that not only transcend geographic boundaries but that, more to the point, go beyond ideological and personal differences. More generally, science could be termed universal, objective, and/or neutral insofar as it united or unified into a coherent community individuals who were otherwise divided. Science ideally, as the historian of science Robert Proctor has argued, "was a harmonizing force, a unifying force," permitting individuals and groups to transcend political, social, religious, and other differences. "Science united, where politics divided."[93]

## The Politics of Objectivity

Jewish social science, as I have argued above, was represented from the outset as just such a unifier of diverse and discordant Jewish groups. The objectivity and truth of Jewish statistics lay in the fact that it "renounces this or that party of Judaism." Statistics must be taken up and supported because it was best able to capture the totality of the Jewish experience. "We are dealing with a subject," the editors of *Jüdische Statistik* assured their readers, "which is of significance and interest for *all* of Jewry, and not merely for a fraction."[94]

In an article entitled "Jewish Statistics as Zionist Cultural Work," the cultural Zionist Bertold Feuchtwang made a clear case for the idea that by its nature statistics offered an unmediated reflection of reality, and that this objectivity could serve as a unifying factor within the Zionist movement and Jewry as a whole. "Statistics is one arm or branch of Jewish cultural work, which can unite all shades of Zionists. As an activity purely of verification it cannot interfere in the realm of belief or conviction. [In addition,] it provides the easiest way for Zionists to unite with all other groups in Jewry."[95] Feuchtwang found proof for Jewish statistics' power to bring various factions within the Zionist movement together in the fact that "Dr. Nordau, who as one of the most prominent representatives of political Zionism is taken by advocates of cultural Zionism as an opponent of their program, sounded a call for statistics. [This] demonstrates the correctness of our claim that this cultural task can bring together all Zionists."[96]

Nonetheless, the intimate institutional and ideological ties between Jewish statistics and Zionists—ties that Feuchtwang touted as fundamental to the Jewish nationalist enterprise—did not obviate, in his mind, the universality of Jewish social science. The *Verein*, Feuchtwang stressed, was not linked to "any one party within Jewry," but rather "desires to serve all of Jewry, humanity, science—and the truth." This was so because "the Jewish question is a universal question [*die Judenfrage ist eine Weltfrage*]."[97] After a long and detailed survey of the genealogy of Jewish statistics, and a summary of the work accomplished by the *Verein* up to 1905, Feuchtwang emphatically restated what he considered to be the real significance of this new endeavor:

Again, the main significance and importance of Jewish statistics, and the Verein für jüdische Statistik, is not that it offers individuals an opportunity to explore the field, but that it brings together all different types of Jewish organizations and committees. . . . *For the first time since the destruction of the Jewish state there exists an organi-zation devoted to the computation of and research into the conditions of the entire Jewish people. The ground for a scientific, officially administered statistic of Jewry has been laid.*[98] (emphasis in the original)

The status of Jewish statistics as an objective science, capable of producing not just knowledge but truth, depended in large part therefore on its ability to transcend party politics, on the definition of the enterprise as a universal, unifying effort.[99] The involvement of non-Zionist Jewish organizations, in turn, depended upon the assurance of the nonfactional nature of Jewish statistics.

The inclusive, universal nature and unifying function of Jewish statistics, however, was understood by Zionist proponents of the project as, ultimately, a means of furthering Zionist influence within the Jewish communities. If we explore in greater detail the ideal of objectivity within Jewish social science, we can more clearly illuminate the dialectical nature of the Zionist relation to Jewish statistics. The image of Jewish statistics as a representative voice for "the whole of Jewry" (*Gesamtjudentum*) served to reinforce the belief that *Zionism alone* represented the true interests of all of Jewry (even if this ideal remained unrealized in the present).[100]

Leo Motzkin, as we saw above, maintained that only the Zionists, among the various Jewish groups, were capable of producing a reliable and objective statistical portrait of Jewry. This was so because only Zionists "represent the most general goals; they cannot allow themselves to submit to any tendency to particularity or narrowing."[101] Drawing in non-Zionist Jewish organizations to the common effort of the statistical project would offer cultural Zionists a way of "gently" persuading their opponents of the validity of the cause. According to Bertold Feuchtwang,

The ground is hereby prepared for the opportunity to exhort the large non-Zionist organizations to their duty, and appeal to their desire for Jewish solidarity, not through vehement attacks, but in a more tactful manner. Official Zionism, which has taken the way of polemic and outright attack, has engendered only unwilling-ness and bitterness among Jewish organizations. The development of statistical associations [*Verbände*] assuredly constitutes a remedy to this phenomenon. If one were to make use of this experience, and consequently decide to adopt a concilia-tory tactic, it appears possible that the leading organizations and committees could be won over to the chief goals of the national-Jewish movement.[102]

This conflation of the Jewish nationalist movement with Jewry as a whole, for the purpose of serving the specific interests of Zionism, characterized the overall strategy of the Democratic Faction. It was evident, for example, in the way in which Chaim Weizmann framed his ideas about the Jewish university project to his colleague Martin Buber. Writing in September

1903, Weizmann made explicit his conception of the university and of knowledge as propaganda, and his belief that these were required to further the Zionist cause. But, he warned, any proposals regarding the university project must not mention Zionism. "I suggest that in this memorandum [setting out ideas for a university] you treat the entire question of the courses solely from the viewpoint of preparation for the university—include nothing about Zionism in it. Since we need the memorandum for large groups, bring in a lot about living Jewish scholarship, about current questions in Jewry (colonization, emigration, statistics)."[103]

If Zionism was to succeed as a national movement, giving voice to the needs and longings of the Jewish *Volk*, then it had to come to embody the Jewish *Volk* as a whole. Jewish culture took on such meaning in internal Zionist debates in part because it seemed best able to achieve this. E. M. Lilien's paintings, Martin Buber's Hasidic tales, Weizmann and Feiwel's university project, and the *Jüdischer Verlag* all sought to demonstrate through the medium of cultural expression the naturalness of the ties between an educated Jewish elite and the Jewish masses. Likewise, the statistical *Verein* was conceived as a cultural endeavor, whose scientific, objective nature allowed for universalism and inclusiveness.

The inclusive nature of the statistical institutions, and the spirit of objective, nonpartisan scholarship, both served particular political ends. The ability to unite a myriad of Jewish groups under the banner of Jewish statistics demonstrated, in the minds of its proponents, the ability of Zionism to unify the Jewish *Volk* under the banner of national regeneration. This "unification" occurred first of all (perhaps could only occur) at the conceptual or imaginary level.[104] Jewish social scientific narratives united Jewry at a representational level by positing a *Volk* and nation bound by genetic as well as historical ties, transcending the geographic and cultural disjunctions characteristic of the Diaspora. Secondly, unification was institutional and communal: the amalgamation of different and conflicting Jewish organizations within the Verein für jüdische Statistik gave concrete expression to the Zionist ideal of unity.

A functional analysis of the rhetoric of objectivity and universality returns us to Zionism, and more particularly to the Democratic Faction. At the institutional and scholarly levels Jewish social science was indeed inclusive, constructed and sustained by the financial, administrative, and intellectual contributions of a wide variety of Jewish individuals and groups. The tension between ideology and objectivity, between partisanship and universality, characterized Jewish social science from the start.

# The Bureau for Jewish Statistics and the Development of Jewish Social Science 1904–1931

In an entry dated April 26, 1904, Arthur Ruppin recorded the following in his diary:

I was quite surprised to receive in mid-March a letter from Dr. Alfred Nossig, of Halensee, in which he asked if I would be prepared to accept a place as scientific head of a Central Bureau for Jewish Statistics, which is now being established. I was in Berlin and negotiated in person with Nossig. It is likely that I will accept the position, with a 250DM a month stipend, beginning October 1, 1904, and settle in Berlin.[1]

Some months later Ruppin left the city of Magdeburg and took up residence in Berlin-Charlottenburg. On the first of October he assumed directorship of the Bureau für jüdische Statistik. He received a monthly salary of 200DM; he supplemented this with part-time work as a lawyer, having been hired on by Berthold Timendorfer.[2] Timendorfer had participated in some of the early plenary meetings of the Verein für jüdische Statistik, and during the Weimar years would become—together with a number of leading Jewish social scientists—an executive of the leading Jewish welfare organization in Germany.[3] Ruppin enlisted the assistance of Jakob Thon, also a lawyer by profession, and a leader in Galician Zionist circles.[4] Over the next few years Thon produced studies on Jewish demography, education, criminality, and economics, as well as a full-length study of Austrian Jewry.[5] He remained Ruppin's assistant at the bureau for four years, and then followed him to Palestine, where he served as his assistant in the Palestine Office of the World Zionist Organization.[6]

Born in 1876 in Rawitsch, Posen (then part of Prussia), Ruppin studied law and economics at the University of Halle and the University of Berlin, and served as a lawyer before taking up his position at the Bureau for Jewish Statistics.[7] He appeared to be the logical choice for the position of director. His reputation as a leading social scientist of Jewry had been established over the previous few years through the publication of numerous articles on Jewish demography and social conditions.[8] His full-length study *The Jews of Today*, which appeared in 1904, was immediately recognized as a seminal work in the nascent field.[9] In addition, he had gained attention in the general world of German scholarship through the publication, in 1903, of his prize-winning essay on Darwinism and social science.[10]

Indeed, Ruppin was one of the most important and influential Jewish social scientists at work during the three decades prior to World War II. He remained director of the bureau for only a short time, yet this period was significant both for his own development as a social scientist and for that of organized Jewish statistics. The following discussion of Ruppin's import extends the analysis, undertaken in the previous chapter, of the link between Jewish scholarship and Jewish nationalism. As we shall see, during the years under discussion Ruppin became a committed Zionist who placed his scientific interests and research at the service of his politics.[11] Yet an analysis of the institutional and intellectual development of Jewish social science also shows that by 1908, and the elevation of Jacob Segall to a position of authority within the bureau, the liberal, non-Zionist impulse had gained a secure footing at the editorial as well as the administrative levels. This approach to the history of the bureau, and the emergence, during the years 1905–25, of other organizations and centers of Jewish statistical research stresses the heterogeneity of Jewish statistics. It provides a sense of the degree to which Jewish social science was shaped by and gave shape to both Zionist and non-Zionist perspectives and agendas.

## *The Bureau for Jewish Statistics (1904–1908)*

As the bureau's financial and administrative duties were in the hands of the *Verein*'s executive, Ruppin's tasks as director were mainly scholarly. He and Thon prepared the bureau's official journal, the *Zeitschrift für Demographie und Statistik der Juden* (volume 1 appeared in 1905) for publication.[12] This entailed soliciting and editing articles from scholars internationally, and collecting and organizing already-published official statistical material related to Jewry. This material would be included in unattributed articles, written by Ruppin and Thon, and in a section entitled *Archiv*. The bureau also prepared and published, in conjunction with the DIGB, the annual statistical yearbook of the German Jewish community.[13] In addition to these projects, the bureau published monographs devoted to social scientific analyses of particular Jewish communities throughout Europe. In the first years of the bureau's existence most of the monographs and much of the *Zeitschrift* were products of Ruppin's and, to a lesser extent, Thon's efforts. According to Ruppin, more than half of the solicited articles for the first volume of the journal failed to arrive, and he ended up filling the journal with his own, mainly unattributed, pieces.[14]

At the outset Ruppin was enthusiastic about his new position. The move to Berlin afforded him the opportunity to attend lectures on anthropology and national economy at the university, which he did each weekday morning.[15] His position at the bureau, which required four hours in the afternoon, allowed him unparalleled access to the raw statistical data he needed to rework his book and prepare new studies of Jewry. "I have a great deal of work," Ruppin wrote in late 1904, "but it is work which I enjoy. My employment at the Bureau for Jewish Statistics is perhaps the first of my life of which I can say I feel it is a vocation [*Beruf*] . . . and for which I have an inclination."[16]

Ruppin's expressed enthusiasm for his position as director did not last long. He soon grew disenchanted with his life at the bureau and in Berlin. In part this dissatisfaction was due to his strained relationship with Nossig, with whom Ruppin clashed personally and professionally. Although he credited Nossig with enormous administrative skills, Ruppin found his presence at the bureau bothersome. He was, in Ruppin's view, a personally distasteful man. In addition, Nossig possessed no real training as a statistician, at least as far as Ruppin was concerned. And although Ruppin admitted that, for the most part, Nossig did not interfere in the scientific work of the bureau, he was nonetheless bothered by Nossig's stress on the propagandistic function of Jewish statistics. Although his own social scientific work was intimately bound up with Jewish politics, Ruppin nevertheless sought to distance himself, as the genuine scientist, from Nossig, the administrator and propagandist.

In addition to his difficulties with Nossig, Ruppin had grown tired, by the middle of 1905, of what he described as the "mechanical work" at the statistical bureau. He came to doubt the significance of social scientific research—which at one point he referred to as "scribbling" (*Schreiberei*)—for "the life of the Jewish people."[17] Moreover, he was discouraged by the "extraordinarily little amount of understanding" the journal had received, particularly among German Jews. According to Ruppin, German Jews as a whole suffered from an ignorance and confusion similar to Nossig's. "They do not understand the idea of an objective statistical journal," he wrote. "They are so preoccupied with the struggle against anti-Semitism that they only possess an understanding and interest for whatever can be of use in this struggle. If the *Zeitschrift* had as its task collecting statistics for this fight, certainly it would become the coddled darling of German Jewry."[18]

This lack of understanding on the part of the community was accompanied by a good amount of rage, largely precipitated by the publication in the first volume of the *Zeitschrift* of an article entitled "The Jewish Idea of Chosenness and its Biological Significance" by the non-Jewish anthropologist Curt Michaelis.[19] Arguing from the reference points of social biology and racial anthropology, Michaelis asserted that the idea of chosenness was the dominant Jewish racial trait, and that it explained the "characteristic" Jewish racial pride and sense of difference. "In the idea of chosenness there is only an absolute exclusivity, which expresses itself practically in strong endogamic laws, and in contempt and cruelty toward other nations." This, in turn, led to perpetual conflict between Jewry and the rest of the nations. "Racial pride produces racial hatred in its strongest forms, and the consequence was constant racial struggle. . . . The Jewish people stood principally in a struggle against the entire world; and therefore, naturally, the whole world is against the Jewish nation."[20]

The significance of racial and biological notions for Jewish social science will become evident in the chapters to follow, and cannot detain us here. Ruppin did not seem to think much of the intellectual quality of the piece; he recorded in his diary his disappointment that the article "was not scientifically worthy enough."[21] Yet the article is important here insofar as it illuminates Ruppin's desire to move Jewish statistics away from an overly apologetic or defensive role. Michaelis's assertion about the racial pride and difference of the Jews, and the conflicts this produces, certainly indicated that the *Zeitschrift*, and the *Verein*, were willing to countenance conflicting, even negative interpretations of Jewry. Moreover, the inclusion of an article by a non-Jewish authority signaled the sort of anti-parochialism that Ruppin, and others, desired. In the end, any doubts that had been raised about the *Verein* in the minds of communal Jewish leaders were not long sustained, and did not seem to have had much of an impact on the level of support for the statistical effort. The article nonetheless did precipitate objections, and it reinforced Ruppin's sense of alienation from the official German Jewish community.[22]

Ruppin also complained about the bureau's financial problems. These, he maintained, bore most heavily upon Thon and himself in their effort to publish the *Zeitschrift*. In contrast to the officially published reports of the *Verein*, which celebrated the strong financial support for Jewish statistics from Jewish organizations and communities, Ruppin repeatedly noted in his diaries the lack of sufficient funding.[23] In July 1905 he recorded that the bureau was already running a deficit. In September of the same year he noted that because of financial pressures, he was editing the journal without pay. And in December 1905 Ruppin wrote the following: "The financial situation of the bureau is miserable. It is running a deficit of 3,000DM. All of Nossig's promises have proven to be frivolous and vaporous. The Bureau wouldn't have been able to pay Thon if not for the Zionist Action Committee, which has requested a statistical work on Russian Jewry and offered a 1,000DM honorarium."[24] Over the next few years Nossig did manage to negotiate generous subventions from Jewish communal institutions. Nonetheless, the need to negotiate, and the brute fact of financial dependence undoubtedly had an impact on Ruppin.

In mid-1905 Ruppin decided to vacate his post as director of the Bureau for Jewish Statistics. "I have already edited the *Zeitschrift* for a year," he wrote sarcastically, "and have done enough to insure my own immortality." Yet he quickly regained an enthusiasm for work at the bureau. He agreed to edit the 1906 volume of the *Zeitschrift*, asserting that it still possessed "a definite worth for the Jewish *Volk*," as well as significance for his own social scientific research.[25] Nonetheless, he longed for more direct involvement in Zionist "practical activity."

During the little time that he had resided in Berlin, Ruppin's commitment to practical Zionism had intensified.[26] Although he evinced a deep antagonism to official Zionism, in 1907 he traveled to Palestine as an official representative of the Zionist Action Committee, and the following year accepted the job as director of the World Zionist Organization's Palestine Office. "I will go to Palestine," he wrote, "and hopefully finally find there the great field of work which I have sought so long."[27] Ruppin's active involvement with the Bureau for Jewish Statistics ceased at this point. Over the next few years his articles continued to appear in the *Zeitschrift*; after 1909, however, his contributions were few and far between.

Ruppin nonetheless remained a dominant force in Jewish social science, mainly through the publication of his synthetic studies of contemporary Jewry, *Die Juden der Gegenwart* and *Die Soziologie der Juden*.[28] In Palestine he continued his anthropological and sociological investigations, carrying out anthropometric and social and racial hygiene studies, and he lectured in sociology at the newly created Hebrew University. He kept abreast of developments in the social and natural sciences in Europe and America, and maintained contact with scientists, Jewish and non-Jewish, in Germany and elsewhere.[29]

## *Ruppin and the Idea of a Zionist Social Science*

More than any other single figure, Ruppin articulated a systematic, coherent social scientific analysis of modern Jewish life from a Zionist perspective. He incorporated history, statistics, and ideas drawn from sociology, anthropology, social biology, and political economy into his work. The numerous books he published between the years 1904 and 1940, while they display an active interest in contemporary scholarship, were variations and emendations of those themes and subjects that preoccupied him from the outset of his career. As a social scientist of the Jews he sought to identify the mechanisms by virtue of which traditional Jewish identity and community had been undermined in the modern period, and through which assimilation, as he saw it, had become the norm. He inquired into the effects of this assimilatory process on the Jews—the changes brought about to Jewry physically, socially, economically, and culturally. At the same time, he was intensely interested in continuities in Jewish life, particularly in physical or anthropological terms. This interest stemmed, as we shall see, not merely from Ruppin's identification of himself as an anthropologist of the Jews. It was also impelled by the desire, which he shared with other Zionist social scientists, to demonstrate scientifically the national, ethnic, and/or racial identity of Jewry, and thereby to offer empirical support to Jewish nationalist claims.

Ruppin's sense of the inextricability of Zionism and Jewry, of the success of Jewish national efforts in Palestine and of the viable future of Jewry, was intimately bound up with his self-understanding as a social scientist. His conviction that social science was a "vocation" stemmed in large part from the way in which the personal and the political came together in his intellectual pursuits.[30] A 1903 trip to Galicia, for instance, represented both a scientific excursion and a process of self-discovery. "I will travel to Galicia," he wrote in his diary, "in order to learn about the Jews there, who remain untouched by Western culture. . . . The consequences of this trip can be quite significant for me, as the trip will aid me in deciding whether to embrace Zionism or Assimilationism, a decision I have until now wavered on."[31] The journey was, first, an ethnographic or anthropological field trip, during which Ruppin played the observer of a "foreign" people and culture, and obtained images and facts he could later employ in his scientific writings. Yet these were also "his people," and their present condition, as it revealed itself to him, held some key to his own identity as a Jew.

Already before this encounter with Galician Jewry Ruppin had come to believe that the nation or *Volk* alone gave meaning to the life of an individual. In April 1903 he recorded in his diary: "For the first time in my life I believe I have developed a coherent worldview. This worldview culminates in the idea that human individuals as such are worthless, that only as part of a nation can they be said to be worth something, and that the nation is the means to the higher breeding or cultivation [*Züchtung*] of humanity."[32] Ruppin had already challenged the liberal notion of the supremacy of the individual a year before, in one of his first published arti-cles.[33] In it he argued that for fifteen hundred years Christianity had suc-ceeded in making the ideal of individual human life, the "unconditional worth of the individual," central to culture. But this, Ruppin asserted, is not a universal principle that must remain unchallenged. Perhaps there is justification for amending this idea, and making the worth of the individ-ual life contingent on something beyond it, like the good of the State. Rup-pin endorsed this view wholeheartedly. "Should not changes in the needs of the State entail revisions in morality?"[34] Invoking Nietzsche, Ruppin concluded that the quality of individuals was, and must be, of equal or greater importance as the quantity.

Yet, while he committed himself to the idea that the *Volk* and State demanded the individual's energies and loyalty, he remained undecided as to whether to commit himself to the German or the Jewish nation. He was traveling to Galicia in order "to see for myself how the condition of the Jews stands. There and then I will decide whether to make *Judentum* or *Deutschtum* my nation and my life's work. . . . It matters not to which nation a man belongs, as long as one belongs to a nation." Ruppin viewed his own confusion about his personal identity as a German and a Jew as symptomatic of all of German Jewry. German Jews today are "neither fish nor fowl," he concluded, "and they must decide what they are."[35]

The trip to Galicia exerted a profound impact on Ruppin, and directly influenced the shape and direction of his social scientific work. As the above quotation indicates, his ambivalence toward Germany and German Jewry was further heightened by his contact with "non-modern" Jews. In fact, Ruppin increasingly came to see Western Jewry as socially and cultur-ally compromised. Eastern European Jewry, in contrast, now represented authenticity and spiritual vitality. The abyss between Western and Eastern European Jewry in his mind was unbridgeable; it was among the Jewish masses in Russia, Rumania, and Galicia, who were still steeped in genuine Jewish culture and isolated from the disintegrative forces of social and eco-nomic modernization, that Ruppin located the Jewish future. As we shall see, the themes of Jewish national and cultural "worth" or "value," and modern Jewry's decline and degeneration—as the actual condition of Western Jewry, and the potential fate of Eastern Jewry—were central to the social scientific analyses of Ruppin and other Zionists.

This heightened interest in Western and Eastern European Jewry (including East European immigrant communities in the United States) was reflected in the contents of the *Zeitschrift*, and in the emphasis placed on European Jewry in the monographs produced by individual Jewish social scientists. Articles and analyses of non-European Jewish communi-ties periodically found their way into the body of literature, and ethnographic and anthropological treatments of North African and Near Eastern Jewries constituted an important part of the debates over the racial unity and purity of Jewry. Yet, for the most part, attention to these groups was minimal; it was limited to population counts rather than being the subject of extended discussions.[36] Thus, the overwhelming number of articles published over the two and one-half decades of the *Zeitschrift*'s existence dealt, not surprisingly, with Central and Eastern European Jewry.

This focus on European Jewry was due in part to financial considerations. The subventions for the monograph series published by the Bureau for Jewish Statistics, for instance, came largely from Jewish communities and organizations. They sponsored research on their own communities out of intellectual curiosity and practical need. The first statistical monograph published by the bureau, coauthored by Ruppin and Thon, was a study of Jews and education in Prussia, and was sponsored by the Berlin Jewish community.[37] It met an immediate practical need, "since a bill concerning the support of schools was just then being publicly discussed."[38] Jakob Thon's studies, *Die jüdische Gemeinden und Vereine in Deutschland* and *Die Juden in Österreich*, were published with subventions from the Gesellschaft zur Förderung der Wissenschaft des Judentums (Society for the Advancement of the Science of Judaism) and the Austrian B'nai Brith respectively.

In sum, in Bruno Blau's words, the works undertaken by the bureau on German and Austrian Jewry "were intended mainly for practical purposes; for the Jewish communities it was of the utmost importance to become acquainted with their population and its structure. This was not only indispensable for purposes of taxation and various administrative tasks but also for welfare activities of all sorts in so far as they were to be placed on a sound basis."[39]

Yet the political and personal engagement of the Jewish social scientist was also a factor in circumscribing the subject matter. Ruppin, like others we will encounter in this study, presented his social scientific research and writing on contemporary Jewry quite explicitly as a "rational justification" for Zionism. This included the elucidation of the "racial worth" of the Jews—the justification for their continued existence as a separate national entity—and the diagnosis of modern Jewry's ills. Social science would offer, in the first place, a response to Jewry's opponents, who claimed to prove the inferiority of the Jewish *Volk* through their own scientific research. As such, it would contribute to the generation of a new sense of Jewish national consciousness and pride among Jews. Yet it would also illuminate, for Jews themselves, the degree of physical, cultural, and economic degeneration from which Jewry suffered; it would locate its causes, and thereby point the way to a solution. Ruppin's inquiries into the quantitative and qualitative status or "nature" of Jewry were self-conscious investigations into the possibilities of practical Zionism; and they were, as Nordau and other early proponents of Jewish statistics had desired, productions of a usable knowledge.

Ruppin distinguished his own work from scholarly efforts that had come before, identifying his writings as marking the inauguration of a genuine scientific approach to modern Jewish life.[40] Earlier writers and proponents of Zionism, Ruppin argued, "had appealed to sentiments, to the historical and religious meaning of Palestine to Jews, to the instinctual strivings." In contrast, he would present the "more prosaic, factual basis for settlement on a national basis."[41] Nonetheless, his insistence that Jewish social science serve particular political ends linked him conceptually with his predecessors. Like those who initiated the statistical project, Ruppin understood his intellectual efforts largely—though by no means only—in instrumentalist terms. He acknowledged no tension or contradiction in the open declaration that his scholarship—objective and scientific—serve explicit ideological ends.

Ruppin's conviction regarding the fundamental interconnection between his social scientific research, his practical work as a Zionist, and the theoretical issues surrounding Jewish nationalism only grew stronger in the years after his departure from the bureau. Contemplating the reworking of *Die Juden der Gegenwart* in 1910, he wrote that social science "shall be the theoretical foundation for my practical work, and hopefully it will also contribute to a general clarification of the Jewish Question and Zionism." A few months later, upon the publication of the work, Ruppin claimed that "[t]he book still has many mistakes, yet it remains the first attempt at a social scientific analysis of the Jewish Question and the first scientific validation of Zionism. It must be translated now into English and Hebrew."[42]

## "An Arsenal of New Weapons"

The notion of social science as a tool of Zionist policy and propaganda was taken up by other Zionist writers, either social scientists themselves or those sympathetic to the project. An anonymous commentator on Ruppin's first major article on Jews and statistics, for instance, noted that his analysis gave the lie to assimilationist claims about "progress." "The self-congratulatory ideas of the assimilationists can now be addressed with dispassionate numbers, the misery of the Jews [*Judennot*] scientifically established, and Zionism represented as the only cure."[43] The Austrian physician, racial anthropologist and Zionist Ignaz Zollschan labeled his own social scientific work a "weapon" with which to battle against scientific anti-Semitism and for Jewish nationalism. "It is very desirable," Zollschan told an audience of American Zionists in 1914, "that we should employ the same weapons as our opponents: that is to say, the weapons of anthropology, sociology, and natural science, to investigate the social value of the Jews."[44] In a speech before the Tenth Zionist Congress in 1911 Zollschan attributed what he took to be the failure of Zionist propaganda to the movement's "lack of a sufficiently scientific mooring, the lack of a sufficiently stable theoretical foundation."[45] Zionism had continued to place too much emphasis in its definition of nationality on "subjective" aspects such as "thought and will"; it paid insufficient attention to "objective" factors such as blood, and the danger posed to Jewish identity by the assimilation of foreign blood through intermarriage. The identification of these "objective" factors, and the political and social issues that develop around them, would point clearly toward the practical work Zionists must do. "Only with an adequate sociological knowledge can the statesman create a worthwhile policy. A programmatic idea must be grounded in a viable theory, and this too produces effective propaganda."[46] Zollschan acknowledged the crucial role Ruppin's social scientific work played in identifying the "disintegration of modern Jewry" as the most profound problem facing Jewry, and Zionism as the only real solution. Zollschan viewed his own work as further evidence of these claims, as the scientific demonstration of the "racial and cultural worth" of Jewry, and hence of the possibility of national regeneration.

Adolf Böhm, the first major historian of the Jewish nationalist movement, in turn called Zollschan's work highly significant for Zionism. It served to clarify the evils of assimilation, degeneration, and lack of national and racial pride.[47] Zollschan had succeeded, Böhm argued, in refuting, by means of science, anti-Semitic notions of Jewish inferiority. He showed Jews that they had reason for asserting a "racial pride" (*Rassenstolz*), and proved that Jewry should be preserved as a unique and particular *Volk*:

He [Zollschan] searches out the enemy on his own battlefield, yet he does not negate the premises, since he, too, concludes that racial purity must be a demand in the sense of the highest political-anthropological goal. However, he proves in the strongest scientific manner the complete absurdity of the hypothesis of the superior Germanic and inferior Semitic races. Therewith, he has done an eternal service to Jewry and to humanity.[48]

Evident here in Böhm's review is the universalism and particularism that would characterize much of Jewish social science. Zollschan's research into racial purity, and the conclusions he drew about Aryan claims of superiority, provide "an eternal service to Jewry and to humanity." Yet Böhm understood the more immediate and important contribution of Zollschan's work to be the service it rendered to the Zionist movement. Zollschan's analysis, like Ruppin's, demonstrated that contemporary Jewry was in the process of decline and disintegration. It made a convincing case that "[t]he only possibility for its survival is Zionism." "A particular virtue of the book," Böhm concluded, "is that we finally possess a work that all scientific and educated circles, without differentiation, can acknowledge as a foundation of Zionism. Our propaganda has suffered until now above all from the fact that we have been unable to concern wider circles with our problems." Zollschan's work, he concluded, "has received approval from every corner. . . . [It is] an arsenal of new weapons."[49]

By the 1910s, therefore, the link between Zionism and social science was represented as a well-established and commonly recognized fact. "We know," the social scientist and physician Hugo Hoppe wrote in 1913, "that his [Zollschan's] work constitutes the theoretical, indeed the natural-scientific, anthropological formulation of Zionism, while Ruppin's work *Die Juden der Gegenwart*, on its side, offers the social scientific and biological formulation of Zionism."[50] Social scientific work itself was looked upon as a nationalist activity, as one of a number of cultural and practical undertakings constitutive of *jüdische Kultur* and *Gegenwartsarbeit*. Moreover, the knowledge produced by social science served to confirm, or establish, the identity and worth of the Jews as a nation, while simultaneously articulating a set of negative conditions requiring reform or negation.

Ruppin's studies, together with the social scientific writings of other Zionists such as Zollschan, Felix Theilhaber, Rudolf Wassermann, Elias Auerbach, and Hugo Hoppe, represented an extension and amplification of the goals of the founders of the Verein für jüdische Statistik. Through a descriptive statistical analysis of the physical, social, economic, and intellectual conditions of the Jews, their identity and unity as a nation and *Volk* would be made apparent, even as differences were acknowledged. The abnormal and pathological status of modern Jewish existence in the Diaspora—a product of historical and environmental rather than racial factors—would be empirically demonstrated, and a nationalist solution would be put forth as the only viable alternative.

## *The Bureau for Jewish Statistics and the Development of Jewish Social Science (1908–1931)*

In important respects, as the above analysis indicates, there were discernible continuities between the Jewish statistical enterprise envisioned by its founders, and the way it developed during the time of what might be termed its "professionalization" under Ruppin's tenure. At the same time, Ruppin's directorship of the *Verein* did mark a break or shift from the initial shape of Jewish statistics. Discontinuity was apparent, first of all, at the organizational level. The structural hierarchy of working groups, each with its own leader, answerable to a central administrative authority, did not appear to survive the start-up of the bureau. One finds little trace of the majority of individuals whose names appeared in the documents related to the Verein's activities during the years 1902–03. The working groups had been organized to compile the already existing bibliographic material (as well as to drum up financial support through subscriptions and memberships). With the publication of the 1903 volume, the groups—at least in Berlin—dissolved.

More important was the conceptual shift that occurred. At the outset, a Jewish statistics meant not only the study of Jewry by statistical means; just as important, it signaled the appropriation or control of the Jewish present through the active scholarly efforts of *Jewish* scientists. The ideals of objectivity and universality mandated the inclusion of all Jewish groups, without regard to partisan politics; it did not preclude a definition of Jewish statistics as an essentially Jewish enterprise, to be undertaken by Jews. Ruppin, on the other hand, sought to open up Jewish statistics to non-Jewish scholars, seeing in their contributions to the *Zeitschrift* and to the field an affirmation of the scientific objectivity and worth of the endeavor. Jewish social science, as it is defined in this study, was carried out by Jewish scholars. However, non-Jews continued to produce work on Jewry, and this work was vital to the Jewish social scientific enterprise.[51]

Upon Ruppin's departure to Palestine in 1908 the position of director fell to Bruno Blau (1881–1954).[52] Like Ruppin, Blau was a lawyer by training. He contributed articles to the *Zeitschrift für Demographie und Statistik der Juden* on a wide variety of subjects, including Jewish criminality, education, and marriage.[53] Blau was also a Zionist, and conceived of Jewish statistics in instrumental terms. In an article entitled "Jewish Statistics," published in *Die Welt* in the year he assumed control over the bureau, he argued that

the significance of statistics for the living conditions of a *Volk* is well known and acknowledged by every cultured state today. . . . There is no foundation for doubt regarding the necessity and worth of statistics today. [Statistics, however,] is of far greater significance for a *Volk* that finds itself living in abnormal conditions. And such a community [*Gemeinschaft*] is the Jewish one, which lacks a territory, is dispersed all over the earth, and which finds itself to a large extent in a condition of enormous need and the most extreme suffering.

The practical and political ends of statistical research were, in Blau's view, of greater significance than the "ideal or scientific." Linking the notion of abnormality with illness, Blau asserted that "[s]tatistics will provide the Jewish physicians of the *Volk* [*jüdische Volksheilskünstlern*] the means to

arrive at a correct diagnosis, and smooth the difficult path toward successful therapy."[54]

In 1909 Blau was joined by Jacob Segall, a statistician, political economist, and physician who had first become involved in Jewish statistics while
a student in Munich.[55] Segall quickly became the guiding editorial force at
the bureau, and remained so for the duration of the bureau's existence. As
a liberal—in 1911 he became an active member in the *CV*—his presence and
influence reflected and contributed to the non-Zionist character of Jewish
statistics at an even broader level. The inclusive, universal aspect of the
enterprise, which had been present from the outset at the rhetorical and
administrative levels, was now an integral component of the editorial
process.

Until World War I the *Verein* and the bureau carried out their respective
activities relatively uninterrupted, although by 1913 problems of funding
had begun to impose limitations on projects and personnel. Nossig
retained his position as chairman of the board of directors of the *Verein*
until that same year, when he was replaced by Blau. (Nossig remained on
the board of directors for another year, and then resigned completely). Blau
and Segall edited the *Zeitschrift*, which appeared regularly through 1916.

Aside from the *Zeitschrift*, the bureau's energies were focused mainly on
the production of what was called a "monumental work": A collection of
statistical tables, using material collected from sources from all over the
world, dealing with "the three faiths" (Protestantism, Catholicism, and
Judaism). "It will be not just the most comprehensive work on Jewry," an
official announcement declared, "but the standard work of religious statistics."[56] In addition, the bureau involved itself over the following years in
the preparation of studies sponsored by interested outside parties. The
Berlin Jewish Gemeinde offered a 3,000DM subvention for two studies of
the Berlin Jewish community, to be undertaken with the assistance of
Berlin's municipal statistical office. The B'nai Brith, in turn, sponsored an
extensive study of Jewish welfare and charity work in Germany.[57]

In the decade preceding World War I Jewish statistical bureaus and associations were also established in other cities in Germany and throughout
Europe, and they made important contributions to the body of Jewish
social scientific literature.[58] The most significant of these, at least in the first
decade of the century, was the Verein für jüdische Statistik in Munich,
founded in 1904.[59] This *Verein*, led by the statistician Arthur Cohen and the
sociologist Georg Halpern, was a member of the Verband der jüdische Statistik, and at least nominally fell under the administrative jurisdiction of
Berlin. Practically, though, it functioned independently. It established its
own board of directors and held its own annual meetings (while also sending delegates to the annual meetings of the *Verband*). The Munich *Verein*

sponsored courses and lectures on statistical method and themes at the university, from which it recruited most of its members. Programatically, the *Verein* devoted itself in the main to investigating Bavarian Jewry. Yet its most prominent representatives—Cohen, Segall, Felix Theilhaber, and Rudolf Wassermann—wrote monographs and contributed articles to the *Zeitschrift* on a broad range of themes.[60]

It is also worth noting that in 1914 the American Jewish Committee created a statistical bureau in order to gather data on American Jewry, and that the Berlin bureau was involved directly with this project. The first director of the American bureau was Joseph Jacobs, who had been one of the earliest advocates and practitioners of Jewish statistics. In 1900 Jacobs moved from England to the United States to become an editor of the new *Jewish Encyclopedia*. The editors of the encyclopedia made a point of calling attention to the place social scientific knowledge produced about Jewry would occupy in the encyclopedia. And Jacobs declared at one point that the encyclopedia would "give a complete Jewish history, a complete Jewish theology, a nearly complete account of Jewish literature, and the first sketch of a complete Jewish sociology."[61] There existed, then, an impetus to organized social scientific research within important circles of American Jewish scholarship at the turn of the century. At some point before 1914, Jacobs traveled to Berlin and met with Bruno Blau at the Bureau for Jewish Statistics. According to Blau, Jacobs learned about the organization and methods of the bureau, and modeled the Statistical Bureau of the American Jewish Committee on this.[62]

During the war years the overriding concern of the bureau in Berlin was, understandably, the collection and publication of statistics related to the Jewish involvement in and commitment to the German war effort. In October 1914 the Verband der deutschen Juden, a communal umbrella organization, created a special statistical commission made up of representatives of the Verein für jüdische Statistik, the CV, and the *Verband* itself. It was responsible for collecting and publishing statistics on Jewish participation in the war.[63] Some months later the German minister of the interior issued a call to all religious communities to compile and publish lists of their members who had fallen in battle, and the *Verband* enlisted the service of the Jewish statistical bureau as mediator between the government and the German Jewish communities. In early 1915 the bureau, appealing to German Jewry's "self-evident duty to the Fatherland," issued a call in the *Zeitschrift* for its readers to involve themselves in the collection of relevant information.[64]

Such an explicit declaration of loyalty and interest in the war effort by Jewish social scientists was not surprising. Like most other Jewish organizations and institutions in Germany at this time, the bureau's identity was, for the moment at least, as much German as Jewish.[65] The symbolic import of this declaration was heightened by the politics surrounding the issue of Jewish military service. The notion that Jews were both physically incapable and morally unwilling to serve militarily was a long-standing accusation of those who sought to challenge Jewish emancipation and integration into the modern nation-state. Social science played an integral role in this debate. The image of the "degenerate" Jewish body—individual and collective—unable to perform adequately the tasks of the nation was a staple of European social scientific discourse.[66] And, as we shall see, this image provided great impetus to the work of Jewish social scientists. Anthropologists and physicians debated what the peculiar shape of the "Jewish body" revealed about the Jew's martial talents. Statisticians, relying almost exclusively on surveys and censuses undertaken by Russian and Central European authorities, compared the percentages of Jews and non-Jews serving in the army, and from these drew conclusions about the "Jewish character."

Indeed, in 1916 German government and military circles published statistical reports attempting to show that Jews had shirked their military duty; hence, they were as unpatriotic as many German nationalists had long claimed. For its part, the Verband der deutschen Juden, together with the Bureau für jüdische Statistik, utilized the war statistics to demonstrate the statistical overrepresentation of Jews in the German war effort.[67] Leading Jewish social scientists, including Jacob Segall, published their own monographs, both during and after the war, with a similar goal in mind.[68]

Following the war the *Verein* and the bureau were plagued with financial burdens, and the preparation and publication of new statistical work became increasingly difficult. These problems only grew more severe over the next decade, as the profound economic crises of the Weimar Republic greatly limited the organization's ability to raise funds and pay personnel.[69] The *Zeitschrift* appeared intermittently, and often in a foreshortened form; nothing was published in the Bureau's monograph series.[70]

In no way does this mean that statistics and social science became less significant for Jewish communities in the interwar years. While, as we shall see, fear of population decline was a crucial motivating factor in Jewish social science in the decades before 1914, the enormous losses suffered during the war heightened these fears. Echoing concerns voiced throughout German society, Jewish elites embraced a "discourse of decline." Social science was fundamental to the expanding Jewish *Sozialpolitik*, or social welfare policy, developed during the Weimar Republic.[71] The new social-welfare institutions, particularly the Zentralwohlfahrtsstelle der deutschen Juden, carried out their own social scientific investigations, and disseminated them through their own conferences and publications.[72] The appearance of these new institutions may also help to explain the diminished interest in, and support for, the bureau's activities.

In addition, in the 1920s other Jewish social scientific research institutes emerged in Central and Eastern Europe that challenged the central role of the Berlin bureau. These testified to the increasing belief in the significance of such scholarship, yet also to the sense that the *Verein* and the bureau were faltering. In 1923 Jacob Segall, together with Jacob Lestschinsky and Boris Brutzkus, began publishing in Yiddish the *Blatter für Statistik, Demographie und Wirtschaftskunde der Juden*. One year later the *Gesellschaft für Statistik und Wirtschaftskunde der Juden* (Society for the Statistics and Economics of the Jews) was created, with the *Blatter* serving as its official organ. In addition to Segall, Lestschinsky, and Brutzkus, the society counted among its members the historians Simon Dubnow and Mark Wischnitzer, the national economist Abraham Coralnik, and the Berlin statistician Heinrich Silbergleit.[73] In 1927 a Jewish statistical bureau was also created in Lvov (Lemberg), funded by the Lvov Jewish community, and independent of the official Polish statistical bureau.[74]

Undoubtedly, the most important development was the creation in 1925 of the Yiddish Scientific Institute (YIVO). YIVO's center was Vilnius, but it also had institutes in Berlin, Warsaw, and New York. It designated "economics and statistics" as one of its four main sections of research (the other three were Yiddish linguistics, literature, and folklore; history; and psychology and education). Jacob Lestschinsky served as the director of the economic and statistical section.[75] There was a strong continuity, in terms of personnel and subject matter, between the YIVO statistical section and earlier Jewish social scientific endeavors. The YIVO *Shriften far Ekonomik un Statistik* was a direct continuation of the 1923/24 effort mentioned above.[76] A number of Jewish social scientists whose work had first appeared in the *Zeitschrift für Demographie und Statistik der Juden* were now invited to contribute to YIVO: Rudolf Wassermann, M. J. Guttmann, Raphael Becker, I. Koralnik, and Lestschinsky. In addition, scholars such as Simon Dubnow, Abraham Menes, Nahum Gelber, and Liebman Hersch contributed to the section's journal.[77] A few, like Wassermann and G. Gurewitsch, were members of the original working groups of the Verein für jüdische Statistik in 1902, and were responsible for putting together the 1903 volume *Jüdische Statistik*.

The emergence of these new institutions, which began publishing their own social scientifically based journals, and which also made explicit the link between social and economic research and the practical application of this knowledge,[78] helps explain the declining fortunes of the Bureau for Jewish Statistics in the Weimar period. In 1927, recognizing its financial and organizational difficulties, the bureau entered into what Segall called a "working relationship" (*Arbeitsgemeinschaft*) with the Akademie für die Wissenschaft des Judentums. Like the Verein für jüdische Statistik, the *Akademie* had been inspired by the ideal of "working groups" of Jewish scholars, in this case put forth by the German Jewish philosophers and ped-agogues Franz Rosenzweig and Hermann Cohen.[79]

It might appear ironic that an enterprise such as Jewish statistics, which started its career in explicit opposition to the *Wissenschaft des Judentums* tra-dition, should end up subsumed and supported by a *Wissenschaft* institu-tion. Yet, like the founders of the Verein für jüdische Statistik, both direc-tors of the *Akademie* during its brief existence (1919–34), Eugen Täubler and Julius Guttmann, envisioned a *Wissenschaft des Judentums* very different from the nineteenth-century movement. Both distanced themselves from the "narrow" *Literaturgeschichte* of the older tradition, and called for a Sci-ence of Judaism that incorporated new methods and disciplines in order to study both the Jewish past and present. Täubler, who had been a member of one of the Verein für jüdische Statistik working groups while a student at the University of Berlin in 1902–03, believed in the need for a "sociolog-ical" approach to Jewish history.[80] During his tenure as director, he had in fact pushed—albeit unsuccessfully—for a sociological section of the *Akademie*. Guttmann, under whose directorship the economic and statisti-cal section was put in place, "was especially intrigued by the application of sociological and economic modes of analysis to the Jewish past."[81] More-over, sociological and economic analysis had come to be recognized as a growing, if still not widely prevalent, element in Jewish historiography.[82] The bureau would combine its efforts with those of the *Akademie*'s section for economics and statistics, headed by Silbergleit. The *Zeitschrift*, still under Segall's editorship, would be published jointly by the bureau and the *Akademie*.[83] This relationship lasted until the demise of the bureau, and with it of the *Zeitschrift*, in 1931.

For the better part of its existence the Verein für jüdische Statistik, and the bureau it created, could justifiably lay claim to being at the center of Jewish social scientific research. True, the categories, themes, and methods of investigation were in large part inherited from the general European social sciences; and much, though by no means all, of the statistical data utilized by Jewish scientists was the product of official governmental cen-suses and surveys, and individual non-Jewish authorities. Nonetheless, the *Verein*'s accomplishments were many. It succeeded in defining the social sci-entific study of Jewry as a *Jewish* scholarly endeavor. Thus, Jews were both subjects and objects of research, and the knowledge produced was intended to serve, first and foremost, specifically Jewish needs and goals. The *Verein* established an institutional setting, funded and administered by Jews, within which social scientific work could be undertaken, and it produced an official journal for the dissemination of this work.

However, the Jewish social scientific community extended far beyond the Berlin *Verein* and bureau. We have already seen that numerous other *Vereine* and bureaus started up shortly after the organization came into being in Berlin, and that others were created in subsequent years. Beyond this, there were those who claimed no affiliation with an organization for Jewish statistics, yet whose writings contributed to the body of work that made up Jewish social science. As I demonstrate in the following chapters, a shared language, method, and set of categories and concepts united Jewish social scientists one with another, and with non-Jewish colleagues. At the same time, Jewish social scientists were divided by political affiliations and ideological convictions. The representations of modern Jewish life encountered in the texts of Jewish social scientists are products and reflections of these tensions, and in turn contributed to them. It is to these representations that we now turn.

## CHAPTER THREE

# The Wages of Modernity
## Fertility, Intermarriage, and the Debate over Jewish Decline

"The stark decrease in the Jewish birth rate," Arthur Ruppin wrote in 1930, "marks a departure from the great fertility that characterized Jewry over the centuries. It is the most prominent feature of Jewish population statistics in the present period."[1] Ruppin's belief that declining Jewish birth rates lay at the heart of Jewish statistics was widely shared by Jewish social scientists. Indeed, from the start, much of their attention focused on explaining the declining fertility of contemporary Jewry, and on delineating the consequences. "Anyone who wishes to gain a general overview of the level of the health of a *Volk*," one Jewish physician asserted in 1900, "must use, above all else, the population statistics, which provide birth and death rates, and the quotient of increase."[2] And statistics pointed to one undeniable fact: Jewish birth rates over the past few decades had dropped dramatically. The idea of Jewish fecundity, this social scientist noted, was "an almost unquestioned dogma" among Jews and non-Jews. Yet statistics belied this belief in a Jewish numerical advantage. Jews showed uniformly lower birth rates than non-Jews, and this was one indication of national decline.

Lower birth rates served Jewish social scientists as a "master pathology," the main indicator of a host of other social pathologies believed to be plaguing the Jewish community.[3] Chief among these were intermarriage, and, to a lesser extent, conversion, and "disassociation" (*Austritt*) from the official Jewish community. These phenomena were analyzed in terms of their quantitative and qualitative effects upon Jewry. When defined as pathological, low birth rates and increasing numbers of intermarriage and conversion were cast as both symptoms and causes of a dangerous level of assimilation, whose most far-reaching significance was neither religious nor spiritual, but demographic and biophysical.[4] As early as 1904 Ruppin insisted that intermarriage was of particular interest and significance for Jewish social scientists because "one can see in it the most effective means for the quickest absorption [*Aufsaugung*] of the Jews" into Christian society.[5] This quantitative danger was compounded by a qualitative one. Intermarriage and conversion "act as catalysts of the same process: the filtering out and weakening of Jewish blood through [mixing with] the surrounding, numerically superior non-Jewish population."[6] As we shall see, some challenged this thesis that "interracial mixture," either through mixed marriage or conversion, had proven detrimental to the Jews historically or at present. There were those who denied that Jews had intermixed with other nations or races; others minimized the effects of such encounters, and still others offered such mixing as a sign of health and vitality, an invigoration of the race through the introduction of "foreign strains."

Zionist demographers took the statistics on declining birth rates and rising intermarriage and conversion rates as the surest indicators of the crisis modernity presented to the Jewish people. They predicted the imminent disappearance of Western Jewry unless Jewish nationalism succeeded in stemming this tide of dissolution. Immersion in traditional Jewish life, and the concomitant isolation from the surrounding culture, had insured that Jews followed the traditional religious injunction to "be fruitful and multiply."[7] This command was now reinterpreted in biophysical and eugenic terms,[8] and declining birth rates were seen as one of the main indicators of national and racial pathology. Reduced fertility rates, and even sterility, were linked directly to the level of socioeconomic and cultural assimilation of Western Jews into their European milieu.

Qualitatively, the significance of intermarriage and conversion lay in their purported effects upon the purity and strength of the Jewish race.[9] The disciplines of history, anthropology, archaeology, and biology converged in these analyses, as social scientists debated over the extent and significance of Jewish intermarriage and conversion in ancient and modern times. Were the indigenous tribes or "nations" with whom the ancient Israelites intermingled upon arrival in Canaan "Semites" or not? If not, was this grounds for designating the Jews an "impure" or mixed race, and what were the implications of this? From a racial-anthropological standpoint, did the Jews intermarry to any significant extent during the Middle Ages? Did the dramatic increase of intermarriage and conversion in recent times signify a qualitative, as well as a quantitative, change from the past? Were intermarriages between Jews and Christians less fertile, and did they produce offspring of lesser physical or mental quality?

The language with which social scientists approached such questions often echoed that of natural scientists. Hence, social scientists might analyze birth rates, intermarriage, and conversion in terms drawn from biology and animal husbandry. Following general social scientific practices, Jewish social scientists spoke of "inbreeding," "hybridization," and "crossing types"; they drew homologies to plant and animal life, questioning the ability of different races to reproduce, or to create "new types" that would last more than a few generations.[10] In the period under discussion here, biology and medicine—under the rubric of racial hygiene and eugenics—exerted a particularly powerful influence over the social sciences internationally.[11] This meant, in turn, that analyses of fertility, intermarriage, and conversion were shaped by, and infused with, issues of racial identity and purity. These questions were crucial for the construction of a Jewish social science.

Issues such as national strength and racial purity, explored through the categories of fertility and intermarriage, were part of broader debates, conducted in scholarly and popular forums: Jewish identity and difference, tradition and modernity, progress and degeneration, assimilation and nationalism. The intent in this chapter is not to challenge the historical fact of a decline in "pure" Jewish marriages or births, or a rise in the rates of divorce, intermarriage, and conversion during the period under discussion. Rather, it is to explore the various ideas and arguments generated around these phenomena by social scientists, and to analyze the continuities and discontinuities within texts produced for different and opposing ideological purposes.

## The Quantitative Threat

National population numbers were linked closely during the decades under consideration with conceptions of communal, national, and/or racial health and degeneracy. A marked decrease in one's own numbers took on ominous significance when noted alongside the demographic stability or increase of a present or potential "enemy." Significantly, the threat was believed to reside both inside and outside national borders.[12] The debate in France over national health, for example, shifted dramatically in response to the 1870 defeat to Prussia and to the 1871 commune uprising. Both events produced a widespread belief in the "degeneracy" and weakness of the French nation, a belief reinforced and demonstrated by statistics on declining birth rates. For French social scientists, physicians, and social reformers, lower birth rates served as the "master pathology," testifying to a degeneracy whose causes and effects included alcoholism, venereal disease, prostitution, criminality, and suicide.[13] In England, the long-standing concern with the lower and poorer classes intensified after the Boer War, as the concern with the physical fitness of military recruits, combined with concerns about Germany's growing strength as an imperial power, raised questions about the "quality of the nation," and produced fears on the part of many in the British middle class of biological and racial degeneracy.[14] For many German social and racial scientists, external threats to the nation's health could take the form of colonial settlement (the Northern Teuton was not physically and racially equipped, it was argued, to survive and thrive in the tropical climate), or the threat of mass immigration from the "barbaric" Slavic east. Internally, concerns were voiced over the alarming rates of increase of the poor, the disabled, immigrants, and Jews, and the concomitant decline in the number of "healthy German citizens."[15] The Jewish threat to the German social and racial body was cast in terms of a combination of external and internal forces: Eastern European immigration, high rates of natural increase, the "parasitic" influence of Jewish involvement in German life.[16]

A similar politics of numbers also impelled Jewish statistics. For Zionist social scientists, statistics indicating declining birth rates, combined with those showing dramatic increases in intermarriages and conversions since the 1870s, served as further proof of the decline and imminent disappearance of Western Jewry. Like their non-Jewish German, French, and English counterparts, these social scientists framed their arguments in terms of external and internal "enemies." The external threat emanated from two sources. On the one hand, and paradoxically, anti-Semitic propaganda, which insisted upon the cultural and racial worthlessness of Jewry, had been highly effective in the West. It had produced, it was argued, a genuine sense of inferiority among many Jews, leading them to seek a way out of the "Jewish condition" through conversion, intermarriage, or disassociation. On the other hand, the freedom and equality resulting from emancipation produced an unprecedented degree and kind of assimilation, which threatened the future of Jewry to an even greater extent than did religious or racial hostility.

The internal "enemies" of Jewish existence, in this view, were the liberals and reformers within the Jewish community who continued to express their faith in the progressive and meliorative nature of emancipation and integration into Western society. Central European Zionists focused attention, during the years leading up to the 1912 Posen Resolution, on what they labeled "radical assimilation." This served as a means of differentiating themselves from, and radicalizing their attacks upon, the German Jewish liberal mainstream.[17] "The Jewish people is now engaged," Ignaz Zollschan announced in 1912, "in a struggle not only with the world around it, but also within itself; two diverse tendencies are being manifested, from which the continuance or the end of the race must ultimately depend."[18] Assimilationists, whether they intended to or not, were bringing about "the end of Judaism, the absorption and disappearance of the Jews among other peoples." Zionists, Zollschan argued, "are those who desire the continued existence of the race, and wish to defend Judaism against dissolving influences by battling against assimilation."[19]

Intermarriage and conversion, as the clearest manifestations of "radical assimilation," threatened the physical existence of Western Jewry through the diminution of numbers and the loss of racial purity. The sense of a quantitative diminishment and danger was articulated through the publication of statistics and social scientific analysis. *Die Welt*, for instance, which printed excerpts from official government statistical studies on a regular basis, reported in 1904 that according to the Kaiserlichen Statistisches Amt, the Jewish percentage of the population dropped from 1.3 percent to 1 percent between 1871 and 1900. As we shall see, even if one accepted these figures as indicative of a genuine decline, there was no single, clear explanation for this phenomenon. But, in the view of the newspaper's editors, the high rates of intermarriage, and the "fact" that 76 percent of all children born to mixed marriages were raised as Christians, were responsible for Jewish numerical loss. They quoted a Pastor Schneider, who remarked that "Jewry has lost a truly significant number of people due to intermarriage," and concluded: "We hope our Jewish *Kultus* administrators can learn something from the pastor."[20] Figures from the Danish Statistical Office showed that from 1840 to 1901 the Jewish population in Denmark had declined in both absolute and relative terms. "The reason for lower birth rates is to be found in the numerous intermarriages."[21] Nor was this lament over the impact of intermarriage limited to Europe. "We have survived," the American Zionist journal *The Maccabean* declared in 1905, "because our birth rate has always been so well ahead of our death rate. Jewry is dependent, like every other nation, on numerical strength; intermarriage is now endangering that strength."[22]

In some cases Zionists identified emigration as a further cause, together with lower birth rates, of the declining Jewish population within a given country, and the West in general. In 1913, *Die Welt*'s editors wrote: "Hungary has often been called an Eldorado for Jews, a view, however, that does not hold true. Proof of this lies in the statistical data on emigration. This [emigration] has consistently grown, while birth rates have dropped: 1896–1900, 17.8%; 1900–05, 14.8%; 1905–10, 13.3%. We are seeing the same phenomena that have been observed for some time now in Western Europe, and analyzed scientifically."[23]

In his speech on Jewish degeneration delivered to the Fifth Zionist Congress in 1901, the physician and neurasthenist Karl Jeremias warned of the sinking birth rate within Jewry, and blamed this on increasing numbers of conversions and intermarriages, a greater rate of emigration, fewer marriages between Jews, and the older ages of those marrying.[24] Emigration, then, was certainly an important subject for Jewish social scientific research. Yet, at least for scholars working in the West, it did not represent either a quantitative or a qualitative loss to the Jewish people, comparable to sinking births, fewer marriages, and rising rates of intermarriage and conversion. Unlike migration, these latter phenomena touched on matters of reproduction, racial purity, and heredity. As matters of the body, they lent themselves more readily to reinterpretation in terms of biological and anthropological degeneration.

The notion of degeneration—at the individual, social, national, and racial levels—emerged in the latter half of the nineteenth century as one of the dominant models of explanation for the host of "social pathologies" believed to be plaguing societies. The medical model of degeneracy provided a conceptual language by which social problems could be explained. Degeneration, in the sense the term came to have after the work of the French physician Bénédict Augustin Morel, indicated not just variation, but deterioration. The conflation of the individual body with ideas of the social and national body meant that indications of illness within the individual were taken as signs of social and national decline. Mental and nervous diseases, syphilis, consumption, and alcoholism were believed to be both causes and symptoms of national decline, attacks not just upon the health of particular individuals or even classes, but upon the body of the nation as a whole. Decline and degeneracy were also evident, so the argument went, in lower birth rates, and rising rates of crime and suicide.[25]

Degeneration was the obverse of progress, a rejection of the faith in the inevitability of improvement. Yet, even as they bemoaned the present, degeneration theorists also, of course, held open the promise of a brighter future. Regeneration was possible, but it demanded that expert knowledge—produced by these selfsame scientists—be translated into social policy. Like their non-Jewish counterparts, Jewish social scientists committed to the Zionist cause diagnosed the ills of the *Volk* and offered a "cure" rooted in scientific, expert knowledge. The manifestations of disease were lower birth rates and the host of other "pathologies" we will examine; the root cause was assimilation. The cure was a heightened Jewish national consciousness, and ultimately a decoupling of Jewry from modern Gentile society.

In 1906, for instance, Jakob Thon, Ruppin's assistant at the Bureau for Jewish Statistics, published a long article in *Die Welt* on conversion and intermarriage in Austria and Germany. It constituted part of his larger monograph on Austrian Jewry published by the bureau, and appeared in a slightly altered form two years later in the *Zeitschrift für Demographie und Statistik der Juden*.[26] Both conversion and intermarriage, according to Thon, represented the most extreme forms of assimilation, and were the consequences of the ever-increasing freedom and equality Jews enjoyed in the modern world. Thon began with a discussion of conversion, or what he called *Taufseuche*—the "disease" or "plague" of baptism—which "poses a danger to our continued existence."[27] Conversion in both Austria and Germany was a product not of hostility toward the Jew, but "progressive civil equality and *Kultur*." It was a sign, perhaps the ultimate sign, of the success of emancipation, rather than of its failure.

Yet conversion was not as dangerous to Jewry as was intermarriage. The former, according to Thon, was still clearly viewed by most Jews and Christians as an "immoral, dishonorable act"; not so intermarriage. The numbers from Berlin, from the period 1880–1904, indicated a doubling of intermarriages, both in absolute and in relative terms. By 1904 one in every ten Jewish men and one in every eleven Jewish women was married to a non-Jew. The same held true for Bavaria and Hesse.[28] The overwhelming number of children of intermarried couples were raised as Christians.[29]

Thon's statistics on intermarriage came only from Germany, as intermarriage remained forbidden by law in Austria, and was hence unrecorded by the official statistical bureaus. For a Jew to marry a Christian, according to Austrian law, the Christian had to become "*Konfessionslos*"; that is, he or she had to withdraw from the religious community (*Gemeinde*) officially. The Jew, on the other hand, could choose either to leave the community or to remain a Jew.[30] Nonetheless, Thon saw indirect proof of the high rates of intermarriage in Austria in the numbers of Jewish "confessionless" (*Austritte*), which had been consistently rising since the 1868 passage of the Religious Freedom Act.[31]

The danger of intermarriage, Thon wrote, was "the loss of children to Jewry." His remedy was a heightened Jewish national consciousness. Both conversion and intermarriage, as the most extreme forms of assimilation, were products of "rootlessness," of too great a freedom in the modern world. "They [conversions and intermarriages] increase in proportion to the development of urban metropolitan life, where a 'cosmopolitan' type, a world citizen without religious or national ties is formed, and—despite the forces of anti-Semitism—intermarries."[32]

Thon concluded his essay by juxtaposing, in a causal relationship, the rise in intermarriages and conversion in the West with the drop in fertility rates.

Thon's analysis followed that of his teacher Ruppin, whose ideas shaped in a fundamental way the approach of Jewish social scientists, Zionist and non-Zionist alike, to these subjects.[33] Ruppin's interpretation of declining births and rising intermarriages and conversions stressed the nexus between the modernization of Jewish life and the threat to collective Jewish existence. In one of his earliest published pieces on Jewish statistics and demography, Ruppin analyzed the numbers collected and published by official German government offices, and concluded that German Jewry stood in very real danger of being completely absorbed by the surrounding Christian society (*"die Möglichkeit der Aufsaugung der Juden durch die Christen"*).[34] In this article, which was published in the prestigious *Jahrbücher für Nationalökonomie und Statistik*, Ruppin argued that the "remarkable Jewish fertility, which we hear so much about," was a thing of the past. Over the years 1820–97, he wrote, Jewish birth rates had dropped from 37.20 percent to 22.25 percent, while Christian rates climbed to almost double that (38.15 percent). "This fact," Ruppin declared, "has up until now not been sufficiently appreciated, although it is of the greatest significance, and must be decisive for the future of German Jewry."[35]

While he admitted that one could not account for this decrease with any complete certainty, Ruppin offered up "the rise of the standard of living among Jews" as the best possible explanation. Jews, it was true, continued to possess numerical advantages over Christians in terms of mortality rates, especially infant deaths. This was a product of the "Jewish ideal of hygiene." However, Ruppin admonished, improvements in Western health conditions and medical treatment had caused Christian death rates to drop over the last two decades of the nineteenth century as well, so even this advantage was waning. Moreover, Ruppin cast doubt on the real "benefit" of the Jews' traditional advantage in mortality rates. Arguing in social Darwinist and eugenic terms, he claimed that the decrease in deaths of Jews over fifteen years of age had its negative side: Those weak individuals, who had survived through painstaking care, would never have reached adulthood without this intervention. "From the purely economic point of view, one can ask whether the saving of these physically weak individuals is a benefit to the Jews, since these individuals do not live long enough into adulthood, even if they do survive childhood."[36] Rates of marriage between Jews—designated in the literature as pure (*rein*) marriages—had dropped dramatically between the years 1875–99, while divorce rates of both Jews and Christians increased during the same period. The number of intermarriages, on the other hand, had risen sharply.

Two years later, in *Die Juden der Gegenwart*, Ruppin broadened his analysis considerably, offering an historical overview of intermarriage and conversion and incorporating statistics from other Central and Western European countries. He minimized the historical extent and impact of conversion and intermarriage, pointing to the numerous injunctions issued by both Jewish and Christian authorities against intermixture. However, "the social and religious cleft between Christian and Jew was so great that this factor alone acted to prohibit intermarriage."[37] Thus, increasing rates of intermarriage and conversion were clear signs of the modernization process: The dissipation of religious beliefs and practices went hand in hand with the removal of social barriers, so that social, economic, and cultural interaction—assimilation—more and more became the norm. Ruppin's discussion moved from Prussia to Austria, Hungary, Italy, Sweden, Denmark, France, and England. He summed up his findings in the following way:

The conclusion we reach from this data . . . is the following: the best protection against intermarriage as well as conversion is the ghetto (proof: Galicia and East London). In those lands where the Jews take part in public and economic life as equals, intermarriage rises dramatically and reaches a significant percentage of pure Jewish marriages (proof: Prussia, Denmark, Hungary, Italy). Intermarriage is most frequently encountered in the large cities (Berlin, Vienna, Budapest, Copenhagen) because it is here that the cultural level and way of life of Jews most approximates that of cultured Christians, and the avenues of social interaction between the two are greatest.[38]

Ruppin clearly represented intermarriage in a negative light, as a severe threat to the Jewish *Volk*. He nonetheless also viewed its widespread occurrence as counterevidence to one of the mainstays of racial anthropological science: "The strong increase in mixed marriages is an argument against the oft-heard claim from many quarters about the deep instinctive racial antipathy between Christians and Jews."[39] It was precisely because such an instinctive racial revulsion did not exist that the socioeconomic and cultural integration of Jews into Gentile society promised by emancipation had succeeded to such a degree. On the one hand, Zionist social scientists rejected the notion that, historically, Jews and Christians did not intermarry to any significant extent because of a mutual and "natural" racial hostility. Such a claim usually implied a hierarchy of racial worth, and the idea of Christian or Aryan superiority. The high rates of intermarriage in the present, as Ruppin argued, invalidated such an argument. On the other hand, the extent of intermarriage (and, to a lesser degree, of conversion) in the present indicated the unhealthy or abnormal condition of Jewish life in the Diaspora.

The danger to Jewry, according to Ruppin, did not lie in the infertility or lower fertility of intermarried couples; rather, it lay in the fact that only one in ten children born as a result of intermarriage remained Jewish, and not the five out of ten often assumed by statisticians. The overwhelming power of the Christian society acted as a "centripetal force," drawing children to it. These children, Ruppin concluded, were lost not only to the Jewish religion, but to the Jewish race as well. Their "Jewish blood" would disappear after a generation.[40] Significantly, in later studies he softened his objection to the notion of a biological incompatibility between races, which manifested itself in lower fertility rates. While he admitted that sufficient scientific proof still did not exist, "at any rate it is to a certain extent probable that there is a greater frequency of infertility among mixed marriages than pure." For scientific support he pointed to biology, drawing a parallel between the animal and human worlds.[41]

In 1911 Ruppin published a second, highly revised version of *Die Juden der Gegenwart*. Now he stressed the "universality" of intermarriage, conversion, and declining birth rates among Jews, and presented a more inclusive account of these phenomena. Until now one could imagine that conversion, intermarriage, and lower birth rates were "limited to Western and Central Europe. But revolution in Russia, and the high participation of Jews in the process of change there, also threatens traditional *Ostjuden*. They are taking full part in the life of their country."[42] What did this entail? Ruppin noted: 1) the diminished impact of religion among East European Jews; 2) the disappearance of the peculiar position Jews filled within the Russian economy as Christians entered more and more into the world of trade and finance; 3) Jews were being educated in greater numbers with Christians, which necessitated 4) the abandonment of Yiddish for Russian or Polish. As a unified process, these developments "lessen the distance of Jews from Christians and increase the likelihood of conversion and intermarriage, and the raising of Christian children."[43] In a 1930 article entitled "The Spread of Intermarriage Among Jews" Ruppin stressed that Russian Jewry had indeed seen a notable increase in the numbers of intermarriages after the Revolution. According to official Russian statistics on Central Russia, between the years 1924 and 1926, 20.68 percent of all male Jews married non-Jewish women, while 12.47 percent of all female Jews married non-Jewish men. All in all, of every 100 marriages entered into by male or female Jews, 16.77 percent of these would be intermarriages.[44] "These numbers show that the enormous territory of Central Russia, from which the Jews had previously been excluded, and into which the Jews from the overcrowded Ukraine and White Russia are now beginning to storm, is becoming a center of assimilation."[45] In other words, the forces of disintegration that had been acting upon Western and Central European Jewry for decades were now attacking the great mass of Jews in Eastern Europe.

Zionist social scientists took the high rates of both conversion and intermarriage among Jews in the West as signs of the abnormality or "disease" of modern Jewish life. Ignaz Zollschan, building on Ruppin's analysis, noted that until the end of the eighteenth century the abyss between Jew and Christian was as great as that between colonial whites and native blacks in contemporary Africa. And, he added, intermarriage between Jew and

Christian was as "abnormal" as that between black and white.[46] Modernity, unfortunately, was eroding this barrier between Jew and Christian. In his analysis of conversion Zollschan focused on the "deadly" effects of modern education. It "kills tradition," he argued, "kills the particular intellectual/ spiritual life of the Jews [*jüdische Geistesleben*]." *Bildung* must no longer be seen as a force for progress and improvement, either at the individual or at the collective level. Rather it was implicated in the slow but certain destruction of Jewry as a community, precisely because it facilitated the assimilation of large numbers of individual Jews into modern European society. "The more heavily Jews of any particular country take part in the official state-educational system, the greater is their distance and alienation from Jewry as a religion and *Volksgemeinschaft*."[47] Intermarriage, Zollschan wrote, was "the rule" in France, Italy, Germany, Austria, and the United States among the higher social and better-educated classes of Jews.[48] "The following appears to be certain," Zollschan concluded, echoing Ruppin. "[T]he only protection against intermarriage, as with conversion, in the Diaspora is the ghetto. In countries where Jews take part in public and economic life as equals, intermarriage is continuously on the rise. This is most frequently the case in the large cities." In contrast, in those countries or regions where traditional Judaism remained a vital force, such as Russia, Galicia, Bukovina, and Rumania, as well as among the East European immigrants living in France, England, and America, intermarriage and conversion rates remained quite low.[49]

In a 1911 speech before a Zionist group in Basel, Zollschan reiterated Ruppin's views on assimilation, disintegration, and Zionism, using them as a starting point for his own discussion of "the racial problem and the Jewish Question."[50] Invoking both Ruppin and the Zionist social scientist Felix Theilhaber, Zollschan created a scenario of unprecedented crisis. The statistics on conversion and intermarriage, and declining birth rates in the West; the emigration and dispersion of Jewish communities in the East; the "denationalization of Jewry," impelled by social and economic forces and carried out through the "acquisition of cosmopolitan education and manners ("die Akquisition kosmopolitischer Bildung und Sitten"); all had reached such high levels that "the Jews in the Diaspora are faced with complete disappearance [*gänzlichen Untergange*]." "In the contemporary assimilation movement," Zollschan warned, "we are confronted with the most dangerous crisis Jewry has yet encountered since its dispersion."[51]

An equally dramatic warning of Jewish decline was sounded by Felix Theilhaber. In his well-known and controversial work *Der Untergang der deutschen Juden*, and in a series of articles written and published during the first two decades of the twentieth century, Theilhaber sought to demonstrate the baleful impact of modern capitalism and capitalist life on the Jews of Germany. He described his project as "an investigation into the connections between developments in statistics measuring births, conversions, intermarriages, etc. and sociological influences. It examines the significance of numbers, of the curves, with reference to migration, occupational structure, marriage age, and the effects of capitalism."[52] Theilhaber, like Ruppin and others, conceived of Jewry as the most "modern" of nations,[53] whose fate in the urban milieu could be explained as the result of social and biological laws of history and nature.[54] As such, the German Jewish experience with modernity was indicative, *in potentia*, of all of Jewry, as well as of all advanced European nations.[55]

For Theilhaber, urban capitalist and rationalist society—described by him as an "infection"—posed a threat to the existence of Jewry because it undermined the very foundation of Jewish national and racial existence: sexual and family life. Sexual hygiene was, in his view, inextricably bound up with Jewish religious ideals, from the Bible onward. Healthy propagation "is a service to God and *Volk*."[56] Judaism demanded that the sexual life of the individual, like all other aspects of an individual's life, be placed at the "service of the nation."[57]

Theilhaber invoked a number of authorities—anthropologists, racial hygienists, and statisticians—who testified that, until recently, the fertility and vitality of the Jewish people followed traditional patterns. Jews, in other words, were being fruitful and multiplying. Statistics demonstrated, however, that contemporary Jewry faced a "menacing situation," even if the leaders and institutions of German Jewry had "not yet become conscious of the deadly germs that infect it."[58] While he identified a number of pathologies that pointed to the degeneration of the Jews in Germany, his master pathology was declining birth rates. All other "pathologies"—higher mortality rates, fewer marriages between Jews, and increasing numbers of intermarriages; conversion, and higher rates of withdrawal from the community; physical diseases and mental illnesses—all in one way or another led to Jewish men and women producing fewer children, and it was this that above all else signaled the dangers of degeneration and decline.[59] Any growth in the German Jewish population over the past few decades was due solely to Eastern European immigration.

Like other Jewish social scientists, Theilhaber insisted on the environmental over the racial etiology of Jewish degeneration.[60] And like his fellow Zionist social scientists, he explained the pathologies of Jewish life as products of assimilation into the dominant, bourgeois European society and culture. In 1913 Theilhaber entered an essay contest, sponsored by the Society for Racial Hygiene, on the relation between racial hygiene and socioeconomic conditions. He answered the question "Does Material and Social Ascent Produce a Danger to Families in the Racial-Hygienic Sense?"

unequivocally in the affirmative.[61] He insisted emphatically, as he had done in his earlier work, that the degeneration one witnessed among the Jews of Berlin was a product not of racial-biological predispositions, but of the socioeconomic environment, the modernizing process itself. Jews were "victims of their conditions," Theilhaber claimed. He offered numerous statistical tables, charts, and graphs to demonstrate declining Jewish fertility and marriage rates, and rising intermarriage and conversion rates, and he related these causally to the socioeconomic gains made by Jews since the middle of the nineteenth century. The numbers, he argued, indicated that in relation to the non-Jewish German and Eastern European Jewish populations, the condition of German Jewry was "abnormal" and "unhealthy."[62]

Let us put the mosaic together. Given one hundred Jews, one-fourth remained unmarried and a further quarter childless. Of the half of the population that does reproduce, two-thirds have only one or two children, and only a third more than this. This means that one-half of the entire Jewish population does not count when it comes to natural increase; they are completely unproductive. More than a fourth fail to reproduce in sufficient numbers, and only one-fourth reproduces to an extent that can be defined in terms of healthy population increase.[63]

This unproductivity, or un-reproductivity, on the part of a large percentage of Jewry was the result of the absence of those mediating forces required to make sure that the individual Jew look beyond his or her own immediate gratification and toward the welfare and future of the whole of Jewry. A rise in social standing "is no certain guarantee of an improvement in vitality. Communal, national, or religious measures must be in place to guard the socially well-off classes from degeneration. . . . Under contemporary social conditions, material and social ascent—that is, the intensive desire for economic wealth and social standing—is the most significant danger to the family in racial-hygienic terms."[64]

Like Ruppin and Zollschan, Theilhaber clearly and explicitly laid out the wages of modernity for Jewry: urban capitalism produced degeneration, enervation, sterility. He constructed a narrative of decline around the themes of rural and urban, agricultural and mercantile, and judgments of healthy and diseased. The metaphorical sterility of modern forms of life led directly to the biological sterility of the Jews. In *Der Untergang der deutschen Juden*, Theilhaber's language was steeped in Romanticist, *völkish* images. He equated rural village life with physical and moral health: "The influence of physical labor, of life in the small town or village brought Jews into connection with Mother Earth." The "simplicity" and "naturalness" of Jewish life on the land, life "not refined by overcultivation," had resulted in a *"Volksgesundheit."* This "health of the nation" had characterized traditional Jewish existence. Between 1817 and 1910, however, a tremendous shift had occurred, and by 1920 three-quarters of all Jews were living in urban centers. Urbanization, modern *Kultur*, and economic relations destroyed traditional beliefs and practices, which in turn resulted in the increasingly higher rates of biological sterility.

While the causes, then, were environmental, the effects were often biological. So, for instance, in a striking inversion of the older trope on early marriages and degeneration, Theilhaber claimed at one point that later marriages, which he insisted were "a product of modern economic life," brought forth physically and mentally inferior children.[65] He argued a similar point with regard to intermarriage, quoting the German sociologist Werner Sombart, who had argued that while children of intermarriages may appear physically beautiful, they often turn out to be morally and intellectually unbalanced, or "debased," prone to insanity and suicide.[66]

Theilhaber's insistence on the pathology of modern urban capitalist life, and on its negative impact on the Jews, served as refutation of the anti-Semitic theory of biological determinism. The romanticization of the Jewish past as a time of physical and moral health; the juxtaposition of a simple rural and agricultural life—now vanished—with the degenerate present of urban capitalism served to focus the reader toward an ideal Jewish future in Palestine. Theilhaber ended his narrative of decline with a plea for regeneration based on the "return to normalcy." If the Jews were to be a healthy *Volk*, he argued, they required an end to their abnormal conditions. The foundation of normalcy must be a "healthy" (i.e., national/racial) sexual life. This could only emerge in conjunction with the other requisites of a normal or healthy nation: a genuine national consciousness, the unity of land, speech, customs and culture, political and economic interests.

## The Qualitative Threat

For Zionist social scientists, notions of loss and decline were cast in terms not only of numerical quantity but also of physical and bio-racial quality. They accepted, to various degrees, the notion put forth by racial thinkers such as Arthur de Gobineau that "those *Völker* are degenerate in whose veins the blood of the fathers no longer flows as a result of numerous mixings and crossings."[67] The emphasis in debates on racial mixing was placed on the historical and contemporary degrees and effects of intermarriage and proselytism. These phenomena, in the view of Zionist social scientists, posed a danger to Jewish identity insofar as they threatened to efface the differences upon which this identity was based. Racially speaking, conversion out of Judaism was of little or no consequence.[68] The convert and his progeny were lost to Jewry, and the intermixture of Jewish and "foreign blood" would affect only that group to which the Jew had converted. Inter-marriage and proselytism, on the other hand, introduced foreign elements into the Jewish "body," and social scientists took up the question of whether or not this was of real and lasting import.

For those who insisted on the racial purity of the Jews, and on linking purity with strength and racial worth, the historical and contemporary evidence of mixed marriage and proselytism had to be explained (or explained away). This entailed a hermeneutics of biblical and post-biblical Jewish history based on issues of race and biology. The physician Elias Auerbach, for example, equated the "*Rassenfrage*" with the question of the "degree of mixing among a race." He saw in Jewish history proof that the race had maintained and strengthened its purity over one hundred generations.[69] This was the product of a strict adherence to the practice of "inbreeding," or endogamy, and resulted in a fundamental identity of Jewry despite geographic dispersal. "The Jewish race is similar throughout the entire earth. They are not of identical forms, as is no cultural *Volk*, but their differences are not fundamental. . . . Jews are of one general type, and they are excellent proof of the significance of heredity in determining racial fate."[70]

Reviewing the anthropological literature that argued that contemporary Jewry was the product of racial mixing reaching back to the time of the conquest of Canaan, Auerbach granted that the ancient Hebrews mixed with the neighboring tribes they encountered upon entering Palestine. But, he contended, they mixed only with those races identified as Semitic. At the outset of their history Jews possessed a strong "racial instinct," which kept them from intermixing with racially different tribes and peoples. The period of Hellenistic and Roman rule in Palestine, he was forced to admit, witnessed a great deal of racial mixing, but Auerbach argued that "since the destruction of the state by Titus, Jews began a long period of the struggle for self-preservation as a race." The Jewish Middle Ages, extending to the time of the French Revolution, was a period of "purification"; until the nineteenth century, according to Auerbach, the Jews succeeded in remaining "*rassenrein*," or racially pure.[71]

The modern period represented a fundamental change from all that had come before it. True, in certain times and places, such as the "golden age" in Spain, Jews had integrated socially and culturally to a significant degree into the surrounding society. Yet only in the nineteenth century had they willingly renounced their "racial isolation" through intermarriage. Most of Jewish history, Auerbach argued, was characterized by a racial separatism that had been the prerogative of the Jews. The bans on intermarriage and proselytism were sufficient proof of this, acting as they did as effective measures against racial intermixture.[72] Modern Western Jewry, in contrast, abandoned this isolation. Intermarriage rates among contemporary Jews had reached unprecedented heights. German Jewish numbers were so great "one must conclude that the complete disappearance of German Jewry is imminent."[73]

Yet Auerbach minimized the danger this development represented to the racial character of Jewry. Genuine racial mixing occurred only when the blood of non-Jews, carried by the offspring of intermarriages (*Mischlinge*), found its way into the blood of the Jewish *Volk*. But as Ruppin's studies made clear, only 10 percent of *Mischlinge* remained within Jewry, too small a number to exert a racial effect.[74]

For Auerbach the importance of the anthropological investigation into intermarriage and proselytism lay in the evidence supplied about Jewish racial identity and purity. The Jews had succeeded, as Auerbach put it, in preserving their original Semitic genes (*Erbe*) throughout the centuries of dispersion. As racial products of Palestine, their connections with Europe were at best secondary. They were not the *Mischrasse* par excellence, as many were wont to claim, but a "pure, truly inbred race," essentially different from their European Christian neighbors, and morphologically identifiable as a nation and *Volk*.

In his 1902 work *Die Juden als Rasse*, the Polish Jewish anthropologist J. M. Judt undertook an extended investigation of the question of Jewish racial identity and character.[75] A substantial portion of the book was taken up with the question of racial mixing. Judt charted the wanderings of European Jewry from Babylonia to Western Europe and concluded that no justification existed for the claim that modern Jewry was the product of an "amalgamation" with European ethnic or racial groups. The Jews possessed a clearly identifiable "social and racial particularity. The absorption of external elements through proselytism or intermarriage must be thoroughly rejected."[76] Racial mixing had occurred, Judt granted, in ancient Palestine between Hebrews and neighboring tribes such as the Amorites, Hittites, and Kushites. And the Jews were a product, anthropologically, of this ancient mixture. However, by the fifth century B.C.E. intermarriage among Jews had all but disappeared, so that the long history of Jewish exile was characterized by the maintenance of the "original" Jewish racial type. The sole example of mass proselytism in the Diaspora, in Judt's view, was that of the Chazars, members of a kingdom situated near the Caspian Sea whose king and ruling class were said to have converted to Judaism sometime in the early Middle Ages.[77] Yet Judt denied that this constituted an instance of race mixing affecting the makeup of the Jewish type.[78] Judt's anthropological analysis of Jewish history, like Auerbach's, offered proof of the non-European character of Jewry, and the racial ties Jews sustained "in their blood" to their ancient homeland.

Like other social scientists, Judt invoked biology, in addition to history, in order to substantiate his claims about race, arguing that intermarriage resulted in less fertile unions. Others maintained that intermarriage led to infertility and sterility. This biological "fact" indicated the unnaturalness or abnormality of the practice. Nature itself, this position argued, had passed judgment on racial intermixture by condemning couples to a less fertile, or even to an infertile marriage.

Auerbach's and Judt's defense of Jewish racial purity rested on a denial of historical and contemporary racial mixing. Yet the science of race could provide the theoretical framework with which to acknowledge the historical fact of intermarriage and proselytism, and yet to maintain the notion of purity. The racial anthropologist and Zionist Leo Sofer, for instance, granted that Jews had engaged in racial mixing, yet he insisted they had retained their status as a "pure race." In the initial volume of the *Zeitschrift für Demographie und Statistik der Juden*, Sofer maintained that a de-mixing (*Entmischung*) of the races occurred after two or three generations following mixed marriage, and resulted in a "return to original type."[79] He cited Darwin's purported belief in polygenism, or the origins of separate races,[80] and provided analogies to his argument about human races from the plant and animal kingdoms, discussing hybrids, Mendelian genetics, and Ludwig Woltmann's notion of the "de-mixing of the racial germ plasm and return to original type." The Jews, Sofer claimed, constituted just such an original, or primary racial type. They were capable of interbreeding with other races, yet of returning to original type given a few generations of *Entmischung*.

This argument allowed Sofer to grant that, historically, intermarriage had occurred at significant levels, yet to maintain at the same time the idea of the reality of the purity and strength of the Jewish race. After emancipation, Sofer granted, Western Jewry engaged willingly and in great numbers in mixed marriage. This process of racial mixing undeniably threatened the character of Jewry. Yet Sofer remained optimistic, claiming that its effects were reversible "if the foreign racial elements are not too numerous."[81] The isolation promised by Zionism would insure that such foreign elements would cease to pose a threat to the racial character of Jewry.

Other Zionist social scientists were far less sanguine than Sofer, Auerbach, and Judt. In an article entitled "The Jewish Race Problem," published in the Anglo-Jewish journal *The Jewish Review*, Ignaz Zollschan warned that the "high ethnical qualities" of the Jews were in danger of being diminished by "intermarriage with less carefully bred races."[82] In 1911, speaking before the Tenth Zionist Congress, he cautioned that the "assimilation of blood" resulting from the high rates of intermarriage represented "a more difficult, because irreparable, harm to the *Volk* than cultural or emotional assimilation."[83] In a 1914 lecture entitled "The Significance of Mixed Marriage," delivered before an American Zionist audience, Zollschan spelled out in greater detail what he believed to be the inextricable connections between intermarriage, modernity, and the threat to a future Jewish existence.[84] Like Auerbach, he argued that anthropologically the Jews had maintained their racial purity throughout their long history. Although the ancient Hebrews did mingle racially with the tribes encountered upon entering Palestine, all of these, including the Jews, belonged to "one race." And from the time of Ezra, and his legislation banning intermarriage, Jews had succeeded in maintaining this purity. Zollschan minimized the extent and significance of proselytism in Jewish history, arguing that the "admixture of foreign blood must have been infinitely small," and therefore of no real consequence: "The Jewish nation accordingly has propagated itself in an essentially pure manner from the time of Ezra until today, and for more than two thousand years represents an ethnically peculiar race, which was not diluted by foreign blood. . . . And consequently, we can assume with certainty, that the blood which flows to-day in the veins of the Jews, is the same as that of two thousand years ago."[85]

It was the religious proscriptions, acting as social institutions, together with external social and economic isolation, that kept the biological purity of the Jews intact. At present, Zollschan lamented, one found this only in the ghetto environment. In the West, economic, intellectual, and social freedoms estranged the Jew from tradition and faith. Freedom produced crisis and decline, a point borne out by statistics showing numerical losses and a qualitative weakening of the race.

Zollschan employed Ruppin's model of four stages or classes within Jewry to convince his Zionist audience that the fate of Western assimilated Jewry could very well be the fate of world Jewry.[86] At the first stage Ruppin had located "premodern Jews," those culturally and socially "still at the stage of the Middle Ages." These included the vast majority of Russian, Rumanian, Galician, Moroccan, Asian, and Turkish Jewish communities. Stages two through four were defined by degrees of assimilation, ranging from "limited" to "total" (short of conversion). Intermarriages among those belonging to categories three and four reached 10 to 30 and 30 to 50 percent, respectively. Like Ruppin, Zollschan asserted that the progressive changes that exercise their destructive influences upon the Western Jews would come to affect Eastern European Jewry in the same way. "Eastern Jews will after some time apparently find themselves in the same position as the Western Jews are today."[87] While Zollschan granted that the process of disintegration could be discerned in other periods of Jewish history, the modern period was qualitatively different because modern culture—the degenerative agent—was itself now a universal or "world culture."

The unhealthy blurring and mixing of categories represented by modern urban capitalist culture found its natural scientific justification in ideas about crossbreeding. Zollschan made his way through a long list of historical and contemporary examples of nations and civilizations seriously debilitated or destroyed by the practice of racial intermixture. Crossing, he concluded,

is one of the principal causes of the destruction of nations, and . . . the interbreeding of widely different types leads to the reduction of fertility and vitality. The difference of race and character leads, as animal breeders assert, to the formation of discordant, irresolute characters. In history there are many examples of the impossibility for half-breeds, even when their parents did not belong to races very far from each other, to reach a state capable of developing a living culture. This impossibility is also observed in cases where each nationality in itself possessed very great ability. All investigations thus point to the ennobling influences of racial purity, and to the destructive effects of racial chaos.[88]

The destructive effects of intermixture for Jewry would be felt wherever Jews were not constrained by law or religion to refrain from intermarriage. Zollschan posited this as a "social law" of mixed marriage. Modernity was defined by the abolition of such constraints, both legal and religious. The survival of Jewry, therefore, demanded a return to the isolation of the Jews that characterized their premodern existence. This, Zollschan believed, required either the preservation of the ghetto or the abolition of the Diaspora. And "the first alternative can only mean a continued morbid existence."[89]

## Inbreeding and the Health of the Nation

Of correlative interest to Jewish social scientists was the issue of endogamy, or marriage within the clan, tribe, or ethnos. In the period under discussion, as social science more and more took its cues from biology and medicine, endogamy also came to mean "racial inbreeding." In the case of the Jews, what measurable effects had the millennia-long practice of marrying and reproducing mainly among themselves had on their physical and psychological makeup? To what extent did it account for levels of health or disease among Jews in the past and present?

Denunciation of early marriage as a customary practice among Orthodox Jews had been a staple of the discourse of Enlightenment reformers, both Jewish and non-Jewish, since the eighteenth century. Non-Jewish anthropologists and physicians routinely pointed to both early marriage and consanguineous marriage as reasons for Jewish physical and mental degeneration. At the same time, one finds non-Jewish authorities explaining the capacity of Jews to resist a host of infectious diseases as a result, at least in part, of their adherence to the laws of inbreeding. "In the course of its history," according to one German authority, "the [Jewish] race, through its endurance and survival of contagious diseases, acquired hereditary immunizing power, and through inbreeding strengthened it and passed it on."[90]

Zionist social scientists evinced particular interest in the question of inbreeding, seeing in its positive evaluation further evidence for their more general arguments about the benefits of national and racial isolation. Rather than identifying it as a cause of physical and moral degeneration, these scientists represented endogamy as a cause and symptom of strength and vitality. In his 1904 book *Anthropologie und Zionismus*, the physician, racial scientist, and Zionist Aron Sandler quoted approvingly Gobineau's belief that, because of their long history of marrying and breeding only among themselves, the Jews had remained the least degenerate of races.[91] Sandler presented his work as a scientific defense of Zionism, as a response in kind to those opponents who, "armed with the weapons of anthropology," had levied "attacks upon the movement recently." The enemy in this case was not the anti-Semite, but the "assimilationist," who strove to convince the Jews that racial mixing, mainly through the practice of intermarriage, was a beneficial thing. "Some have attempted to create a scientific basis for the assimilatory inclinations through natural scientific material, but I will attempt . . . to demonstrate that this superficial natural scientific coat of armor is merely a shabby short-coat."[92]

One of the most common attacks on Zionism, according to Sandler, concerned the practice of inbreeding. According to its opponents, "Zionism sanctions inbreeding, and inbreeding leads to degeneration."[93] Sandler's analysis of inbreeding, like the analyses of all the social scientists discussed here, must be situated within the broader intellectual and political debate over the racial nature and worth of the Jews, and the effects of emancipation and assimilation. Sandler denied the status of "pure race" to the Jews, dismissing the ongoing debate on the issue as inconsequential. Yet he argued emphatically that the Jews constituted a distinct and unique race, that this manifested itself more in psychological and cultural than in physiological unity, and that inbreeding was a fundamental contributor to this:

No one can deny the enormous worth of inbreeding for the cultural development of a people. The culture bearers of mankind have been predominantly products of inbreeding. The cultures of the ancient inbreeding nations—Indians and Jews—eloquently attest to this. If some Jews today do show signs of degeneration, it is the result of the degenerative effects of unhealthy hygienic conditions under which they have lived for centuries, the one-sided employment in trade and the intellectual professions, the centuries-long effect of a depressed disposition and the almost constant concern over the ability to survive.[94]

Sandler sounds here many of the common themes within Jewish social science that we have attempted to identify. The Jews are both healthy and diseased, showing signs of vitality, yet also of degeneration. For Sandler, positive "racial" attributes were transmitted hereditarily, and must be preserved through a vigilance against intermarriage; negative traits were the product of environment, and could therefore be effaced through nationalist efforts.[95]

Sandler denied that overall the Jews could be defined as a "degenerate" race. Through a combination of inbreeding, acclimatization, natural selection, and "racial purification" the Jews had maintained their racial strength and, most important, their individuality. It was one of Zionism's main tasks, in Sandler's view, to preserve this "racial individuality." Nonetheless, Sandler did refer to the degeneration of the Jews, either as an actual or as a potential condition.[96] We have seen that he spoke of signs of degeneration among Jews and attributed these mainly to environmental factors. He was also willing to entertain the possibility that racial inbreeding, narrowly defined as consanguineous marriage, produced degeneration. Even experts remained divided, he admonished, over the positive or negative impact of marriage and reproduction between close relatives (*Blutverwandtenheirat*). Many believed the positive results outweighed the negative. Yet even those very authorities granted that consanguinity could result in higher rates of physical and mental illness.

If it then proved to be the case (and Sandler reminded readers that statistics remained inconclusive on the entire question) that Jews did suffer the degenerative effects of *Blutverwandtenheiraten*—which he distinguished repeatedly from "racial inbreeding" among Jews as a group—Zionism would prove the solution to this problem as well. Jewish nationalism, dedicated to the physical regeneration of Jewry through mass education in agriculture, hygiene, and sport, would break the cycle of hereditarily transmitted physical and mental deficiencies.[97]

Like Sandler, other Zionist social scientists perceived the importance of inbreeding in terms of the preservation of a distinctive and identifiable Jewish racial type. In Theilhaber's analysis, endogamy was fundamental to the creation and survival of the Jewish nation. It had produced among the Jews a "uniformity of physical type" which, while not a "purity of race," was nonetheless a uniformity that defined the Jewish nation. "Intermarriage is, accordingly, a significant form of dissolution of the Jewish community."[98] For Ruppin, the "racial effects" of conversion and intermarriage upon contemporary Jewry were written on the Jewish body. "The number of Jews today whose facial physiognomy displays none of the traits of the so-called Jewish type," Ruppin wrote in his chapter on intermarriage, "whose morphological type cannot be identified as of Jewish descent is substantial."[99]

The uncertainties of modernity, the blurring of previously clear physical, socioeconomic, and cultural boundaries, were reflected in and amplified by the "racial chaos" intermarriage and conversion represented. The physiological difference between Jew and Christian was in danger of being effaced. Moreover, racial mixing threatened to destroy the last link between Eastern and Western Jewry. The unprecedented rates of intermixture that occurred in the nineteenth century meant that anthropologically the two Jewries were rapidly becoming two distinct types, and an unbridgeable gap was forming. This posed a danger primarily to Western Jewry. In Ruppin's words: "Therewith the last bridge, racial unity, connecting Eastern and Western Jewry, divided as they are already culturally, will be destroyed. And since their bond with Eastern European Jewry has vanished and they stand alone, the absorption of Western European Jewry will happen quite easily."[100]

CHAPTER FOUR

# The Pathological Circle
## Medical Images and Statistics in Jewish Social Science

Issues of health and disease were defining elements of Jewish statistics from its inception as an organized enterprise. The founding documents of the Verein für jüdische Statistik made clear the belief on the part of its organizers that Jewish statistics must make the categories of health and disease central.[1] The *Zeitschrift für Demographie und Statistik der Juden* published vital statistics excerpted from non-Jewish governmental and private sources from around the world; these were supplemented by new studies undertaken by Jewish social scientists. The first annual report of the newly constituted Verein für jüdische Statistik in Munich, for instance, reported that working groups had been established in the fields of medicine and anthropology (among others), and that one of the projects being undertaken by the new *Verein* was a study of "the heredity of Jewish diseases."[2] Jewish social scientists, writing on the subjects of health and disease, published articles in general European and American journals,[3] and, as we shall see, such themes constituted an important category in larger synthetic Jewish social scientific works. Ideas and arguments related to Jewish health and hygiene were also disseminated to the general public through Jewish newspapers, encyclopedias, popular journals, and public lectures.[4]

The issue of Jewish health and disease, like that of birth rates and intermarriage, took on importance, ultimately, because it too became part of ongoing debates over Jewish identity and difference, progress and decline, assimilation and nationalism. This chapter explores the Zionist discourse on Jewish health. It charts the shift in this discourse from its early interest in Eastern European Jewry to the focus on the disease and degeneration of Western Jewry. Constructing a pathological circle that encompassed Diaspora Jewry as a whole, Jewish nationalists were able to argue—and demonstrate scientifically—that the only viable Jewish future lay in a Jewish state and society.

## The Politics of Jewish Health

Jewish immunity from, or susceptibility to, assorted diseases had been the object of analysis on the part of European science since at least the end of the eighteenth century. While there is evidence of Jewish physicians here and there studying Jews in such terms, it was not until the late nineteenth and early twentieth centuries that health and disease emerged as distinct and significant categories of research for Jewish scholars.[5] The language and images of medicine and biology increasingly came to shape the debate on the condition of Jewry. Physical and mental illnesses, fertility and mortality, alcoholism, syphilis, and suicide constituted fundamental categories of investigation and analysis. Physicians and social scientists positioned themselves as authorities on both the Jewish past and present, prepared to take a leading role in diagnosing and remedying assorted "pathologies."

This was, in the first place, a result of broader intellectual, political, and social developments within Europe. Historians of European science and culture speak of an increasing "medicalization" and "biologization" of the human sciences in Europe over the course of the nineteenth century.[6] The emergence of social Darwinian, neo-Lamarckian, and degeneration theories, which offered means of understanding and explaining the mutual influences of heredity and environment, and the creation and impact of public and racial hygiene movements throughout Europe and the United States, testify to the degree to which medicine and biology, and their official representatives, had become a seemingly indispensable part of social theory and policy.[7] More specific political and social forces in the final decades of the nineteenth century also helped shape and give force to the idea of the Jew as diseased and dangerous. Central and Western European anti-Semitism, in its bid to be scientific, appropriated the language of biology and medicine in its analysis of Jews. More and more, the Jew had come to be associated with particular physical and social "diseases" (syphilis and prostitution, for example), and then with the notion of disease itself.[8] The increased immigration into Central Europe of Eastern European Jews, associated as they were in the cultural imagination of both Jewish and non-Jewish Central Europeans with dirt and disease,[9] fueled the anti-Semitic charge of the Jewish attack upon the "body" of the *Volk und Nation*. This idea of the Jews as parasites, as the literal embodiments of disease, is found not only in the rhetoric of German and Austrian anti-Semites, but in the French, English, and American rhetoric as well.[10]

By the last quarter of the nineteenth century a fairly stable and coherent set of ideas and images about Jewish health and disease was firmly in place. These were tied closely to the scientific debate over racial and environmental determinism, and the public debate over anti-Semitism and the "Jewish Question." An essential difference between Jew and Christian, or Jew and European, could purportedly be located at the level of the body. For many, social science offered the tools with which to convincingly demonstrate this difference. "The biological traits of the Jewish race are substantially different from those of the Aryan," wrote the German ethnologist Richard Andree in 1881. "This can be demonstrated statistically, where sufficient evidence for such judgment exists."[11]

These physical and mental differences were, in turn, taken as signs of social and political incompatibility. The deformity or illness that the scientist "discovered" in the individual Jewish body pointed to the deformity of the collective Jewish "body," demonstrating the inability of the Jews to integrate successfully into the European social and political "organism."[12]

Jews suffered, it was argued, in disproportionate numbers from many illnesses, while possessing an immunity or resistance to others. Certain diseases such as diabetes, nearsightedness, and hemorrhoids were so commonly associated with Jews that they came to be known as "Jewish diseases" (*Judenkrankheiten*.)[13] Conversely, Jews were thought to possess an immunity to those infectious diseases such as plague, cholera, and tuberculosis, which had periodically devastated Europe since the Middle Ages, and which by the nineteenth century had obtained such power as metaphor and symbol.[14] Jews were said to be particularly susceptible to nervous disorders and mental illnesses (accounting, among other things, for their high rates of suicide), while they showed a strong resistance to alcoholism and syphilis. In addition, the health of Jews as a group was indicated statistically by their longer life spans, their higher fertility rates, and their lower overall death rates.[15] Positive or advantageous relation to certain diseases and greater susceptibility to certain pathological states were taken as empirical, scientific proof of fundamental difference and identity.

European authorities debated which diseases Jews were either susceptible to or immune from, and argued about the etiology of these conditions. This scholarly disagreement, as well as the underlying contention of identity and difference, is evident, for example, in the following account of French and German opinions: "G. Lagneau states that Jewish women are hardly ever afflicted with goitre [a disease of the thyroid gland], and mentions that the medical society of Metz handed out the question in one of its competitive examinations of 1880: 'Why are Jewesses exempt from goitre?' Bordier also says that this disease is rare among them. On the other hand, G. Buschan states that he finds that Jews are more strongly inclined to this disease than non-Jews."[16]

It is important to emphasize that there were non-Jewish writers who understood the "otherness" of the Jews in non-essentialist terms, as a product of external persecution, or of internal backwardness, or, more likely, of a combination of both. Continuing an Enlightenment line of argument reaching back to Wilhelm Christian Dohm and others, they argued that the physical and mental degeneration of the Jews was reversible, given an end to government hostility and oppression, and given Jewish assimilation into modern society and culture. I will return to these "liberal," or integrationist non-Jewish scholars in the following chapter. What is pertinent here is that they, too, shared the belief that the Jews were, to a significant degree, sick or diseased. Certainly, whether a particular authority adopted a largely racial or environmental explanation for collective Jewish traits was significant. At the same time, it was also important that, in either case, the identity of the Jews as a people, as a race, and their difference from European Christians, were literally "inscribed" on and in the Jewish body through such analyses.[17]

Jewish social scientists inherited this body of scientific opinion and knowledge, built upon it, and set about reinterpreting and transforming it. They did not challenge the notion that comparative statistics about health and disease revealed something significant and real about Jews in relation to other peoples. Many were physicians who had received training in medicine (and related fields such as biology and physical anthropology) at Central and Western European universities. Even those, like Arthur Ruppin, who received no formal university training in medicine or biology, evinced a deep interest in these subjects.[18] Jewish social scientists constructed their own texts out of the paradigmatic language and methods of the time. The developing discourse on social and racial health and hygiene throughout Europe and the United States imposed its own discursive logic upon them.

Yet, while these social scientists accepted the statistics regarding Jewish health and disease, and many of the images and ideas generated around them, they nonetheless set about challenging at least two widespread (though not universal) ideas: the unequivocal association of Jews with disease, and the racial origins of "biostatistical" differences between Jews and Christians. On the one hand, they sought to uncouple the links that had been made in scientific and popular discourse between Jews and disease by constructing counter-narratives of Jewish health. Such counter-narratives stressed the positive hygienic value of traditional Jewish knowledge and practice, the historical role Jews played in the production and transmission of Western medical science, and the conjunction between Jewish and European bourgeois values of cleanliness and purity.[19] On the other hand, Jewish social scientists accepted, to greater or lesser degrees, the "diseased" or pathological nature of the Jew. To be sure, one finds examples of a biological or racial determinism in Jewish social scientific literature. Both positive and negative traits were, at times, explained by reference to "racial peculiarity."[20]

However, Jewish social scientists did not, on the whole, accept the notion that traits such as nervousness were *permanent* racial traits, destined to be passed on hereditarily from generation to generation. They argued that environment rather than biology was responsible for the historical and contemporary condition(s) of Jewry. This emphasis on the environmental over the racial etiology of health and disease was fundamental to the Jewish social scientific endeavor and forms one of the main themes of this chapter. While questions of Jewish racial origin and identity indeed played a significant role in the definition and development of this enterprise, when Jewish social scientists offered an etiology of phenomena, they stressed milieu over biology. They drew a distinction between the causes of particular conditions related to health, and the effects or consequences of these conditions.

Jewish social scientists were united in their conviction that environmental rather than racial factors accounted for Jewish "pathologies." Insistence upon environmental factors or conditions, causes external to the "nature" of the Jews, provided them with the requisite language and ideas with which to argue for the possibility of change and improvement. Conceding a strict bio-racial determinism would have made melioration all but impossible. The powerful attraction for Jewish social scientists of neo-Lamarckian, social Darwinian, and degeneration models of individual and collective transformation lay in the fluidity of boundaries between nature and nurture, society and biology proposed by these theories.[21] Such an emphasis on the determinative role of social and economic factors made reform and amelioration of the Jewish condition theoretically possible, and such a dramatic transformation of Jewish life was one of the central motivating factors behind Jewish social science.[22]

Committed to an environmental model of explanation, Jewish social scientists nonetheless debated among themselves (as well as with non-Jewish writers) about just which "environment" should be identified as pathogenic and which meliorative. Was the isolating experience of the "ghetto"—a code word for a complex set of actions and beliefs governed principally by Jewish religious law and custom, and guaranteeing not only geographic, but also cultural, social, and intellectual isolation—conducive or detrimental to Jewish health? Conversely, what was the relationship between disease and the fundamental transformations in the social, economic, and cultural lives of Jews resulting from their emancipation in the modern West? Embedded in and giving shape to the social scientific texts on health and disease produced by Jews were various and conflicting ideas about tradition and modernity, identity and difference, progress and freedom, and emancipation and assimilation. These divergent interpretations contained within them, as well, expressions of political and ideological differences, reflecting and contributing to broader debates within the Jewish and European communities. Statistics and images of health, including the assumptions about the reality of the racial identity of the Jews, were used by various Jewish social scientists to advocate political and practical positions. These ranged from local communal reform and liberal integrationism to Diaspora nationalism and Zionism.

## Health, Disease, and National Identity

Scientific discussions over social and racial hygiene, disease, and degeneration were to a large degree expressions of concern over national identity and cohesion, and the forces believed to be threatening the unity and health of the nation and race. Zionists embraced the definition of Jewry as a *Volk* and/or race, and conceived of its task as a movement as, inter alia, the "regeneration" of Jewry. This task was to be accomplished through the negation of the "abnormal" conditions in which Jews had lived in Europe for centuries, and the creation of a "healthy" *Volk* in their own land. Social scientific studies of health and disease were instrumental in helping Zionists define contemporary Jewry as unhealthy, abnormal, and degenerate, and in helping it imagine a healthy, normal alternative. Statistics cast the contemporary abnormality of Jewry into bold relief. Already in 1898 *Die Welt* reported that "according to the latest Prussian census of 1895 there are in Prussia 1,889 Jews among the 82,860 mentally ill [*Geisteskranken*]; that is 2 1/4 percent. Jews only constitute 1 1/6 of the total population. Given this ratio, the normal average number of mentally ill Jews should only be 961. Nothing better illustrates the abnormal conditions of life of the Jewish people."[23]

Zionism itself came to be described in medical and biological terms.[24] The social scientist, in turn, came to be regarded as a potential healer, a mediator between the "unhealthy" Jewish present and a regenerated future. "Statistics," wrote Bruno Blau, "will provide the Jewish physicians of the Volk [*jüdische Volksheilkünstlern*] with the means to arrive at a correct diagnosis, and smooth the difficult path toward a successful cure."[25]

The discourse of medicine offered an intellectually and culturally powerful set of categories, concepts, and metaphors with which Zionists could diagnose the Jewish condition, and just as important, prescribe a cure.[26] The conflation and identification of the "deformed" individual Jewish body with the collective Jewish national body, so long a part of European anthropological and medical discourse on the Jews, became a part of Jewish nationalist discourse as it developed in the last two decades of the nineteenth century. Statistics on Jewish health and disease offered a medium by which this conflation could be effected. It produced empirical facts about individual Jewish bodies in the aggregate, which were woven into a narrative—more often than not cautionary—about Jewish identity, and the physical and mental abnormality of the Jewish condition.

Physiological traits or conditions provided Zionists with what they believed to be *objective* markers or signs of nationhood. Anthropology, as the following chapter will show, offered cranial and other bodily measurements as evidence of essential difference; medicine established identity and difference through the discourse on pathology. The Jews "fall prey to mental illnesses four to six times more than other civilized peoples [*Kulturnationen*] in whose midst they live," *Die Welt* reported in 1906.[27] An intensive "struggle for existence" [Kampf ums Dasein] had produced an "extraordinary type," in which "intelligence and racial uniqueness are united." However, inbreeding—consanguineous marriage—had made Jews far more susceptible than other races to physical and mental diseases. "Among the causes, sexual excess plays a great role, while alcoholism plays little. One finds an inferiority and perversion quite often among the youth, and young children suffer from advanced neurasthenia. Neurasthenia is found most often among male Jews, while Jewish women suffer more from hysteria. . . . One seldom encounters epilepsy, but there is softening of the brain in a higher percentage of Jews than in other populations."[28]

In a footnote, the editors of the paper made clear the further significance for Zionism of this psychopathological difference: "What is true of the Jews holds true for ancient Hebrews and Phoenicians."[29] Proof of the Jewish connection to its ancient past, to the land of Palestine and its inhabitants, could be found in something beyond historical or religious consciousness. Here was a sign of Jewish identity or unity, locatable at the physical/racial level, a trait that had purportedly remained unchanged for thousands of years. Medical and anthropological characteristics demonstrated the Jewish nationalist argument that the Jews were a *Volk*, united despite the elapse of thousands of years and physical dispersal around the world.

The corollary of this Jewish national identity was the insistence on the fundamental difference between Jew and Christian. Indeed, at times this difference was drawn in terms of racial particularity. The Munich physician and Zionist Felix Theilhaber, for instance, offered statistics on cervical cancer and menstruation as proof of difference at the racial level. In the case of menstruation, both his own findings for Germany, Theilhaber reported, and those of the prominent Jewish anthropologist Samuel Weissenberg for Russia, confirmed that Jewish women menstruated earlier than did Christian. While rural Christian women began to menstruate on average at the age of sixteen, and urban Christians at fourteen to fifteen, Jewish women, both rural and urban, began at twelve and a half to fourteen. If the dichotomy rural/urban, and other factors linked with urbanization, such as socioeconomic or educational levels, could not help account for this difference, then race was more likely a causal factor. Jewish women also experienced menopause at a later age than did Christian women of the same socioeconomic standing.[30] For Theilhaber, such differences in the realm of pathology were clear evidence of a Jewish "racial unity."

The affirmation by Zionist social scientists of physical and pathological difference attributed to racial peculiarity served to undermine the liberal, emancipationist principle of the universality of fundamental human traits. In this sense, Zionist social scientists shared with conservatives and anti-Semites the conviction that somatic characteristics and conditions signified a basic incompatibility between Jews and Europeans.

Simultaneously, the emphasis upon the mutability of pathological traits through the regenerative efforts of Jewish nationalism denied the anti-Semitic claim of the immutability of Jewish disease. Implicit in the above description offered by *Die Welt* of Jewish propensity, in the past and present, to mental disorders, is the expectation that a return to normalcy—in the political or civic sense—will cure the Jews of their psychological and physical woes. For Alfred Nossig, who conceived of the significance of the Jewish statistical enterprise largely in terms of the meliorative effort aimed at Eastern European Jewry, social and economic improvement accounted for the disadvantageous levels of Jewish health. For instance, in the section on Austria-Hungary in his 1887 work *Materials for a Statistic of the Jewish People*,[31] Nossig explained Jewish demographic and health patterns with reference to the socioeconomic origins of the Jewish condition. He invoked the non-Jewish Austrian statistician Gustav Schimmer, who had demonstrated in an 1873 work that the Jews of Austria displayed a "greater fertility of race," yet also showed at times higher death rates than non-Jews.[32] "Schimmer," Nossig wrote, "is inclined to explain these phenomena less on account of peculiarities of race than through the social and economic conditions of the Jews."[33] In Galicia and Bukovina, for instance, where economic conditions were poor, one encountered correspondingly high mortality rates. In Bohemia, Moravia, and to a lesser extent Silesia, the mortality rates of Jews compared favorably to those of non-Jews. Moreover, living conditions and levels of hygiene differed among Jewish com-

munities within the empire. According to Schimmer, the Jews of Bohemia
and Moravia were "blessed with residences which receive more air and light
than in other regions. In Galicia and Bukovina Jews live in narrow and
dank ghettos, and you cannot say that proper ventilation or cleanliness
exists there."[34] Nossig endorsed Schimmer's analysis of the environmental
determination of Jewish attributes, both negative and positive.

In this early work of Jewish statistics a number of characteristic elements
of later analyses can already be found: language and concepts drawn from
medicine and the natural sciences;[35] the establishment of difference (from
Christians) and identity (among Jews) at the physical level; an environmental etiology of physical traits; and the Zionist impulse at work in the
narrative. Yet Nossig's approach to Western and Central European Jewry
was almost completely positive. He began with a discussion of British
Jewry, which displayed, he claimed, a longer life span than the Anglo-Saxon
race (*Stamm*),[36] a lower death rate, and an immunity to particular diseases.
English Jews seldom intermarried, he argued, and so suffered none of the
consequences of the "unfruitfulness of intermarriage." On account of this,
and also on account of their adherence to the Mosaic dietary laws, Jews in
England had succeeded in maintaining themselves as "a relatively pure
[*reinen*] and refined . . . type [*Typus*]." German Jews had longer life spans
than Christians; they gave birth to more boys than girls (commonly
assumed to be an advantage for the group) and counted fewer illegitimate
births; and they suffered more from color blindness. All of this proved that,
like the Jews of England, the Jews of Germany had maintained their particularity as a tribe or race (*als Stamm*) almost completely unimpaired.[37]
The success of the anti-Semitic movement in Germany, Nossig believed,
was in large measure explained by this "racial particularity" (*Raceneigen-
tümlichkeit*; [*sic*]) of the Jews. Nossig analyzed the Jews along geo-national
lines (i.e., English, French, and German Jewish communities, etc.). Yet the
conclusions he drew, from the numbers he presented, sought to efface the
emancipationist or assimilationist conception of modern Jewish identity.
Despite the markedly different political and social environments in which
English and German Jews lived—the one characterized, according to Nossig, by tolerance, the other by hostility—statistics on health and illness
demonstrated the fundamental difference between Jews and their non-
Jewish neighbors. Simultaneously, it illuminated the similarity, even the
identity of Jews, regardless of geographic boundaries.

For Nossig, who by 1887 had fully identified himself with the nascent
Zionist movement, statistics provided proof of Jewish national and racial
identity by empirically demonstrating a physical, biological unity, despite
any socioeconomic or cultural differences.[38] Yet, in significant ways he
maintained the older, Maskilic dichotomy between the relatively healthy

West and the degenerate East. His work lacked the heightened critical spirit of later Zionist analyses, which insisted on the abnormal nature of modernized Western European Jewish existence.

## The "Degenerate East"

Nossig was not alone in positing this dichotomy of the healthy West and the degenerate East. In 1900 Max Mandelstamm, a prominent Russian Zionist, delivered a speech before the Fourth Zionist Congress in London on "the physical amelioration of Jewry," in which he identified the Jews of the West as healthy and Eastern European Jewry alone as in need of regeneration.[39] Mandelstamm had studied medicine at Khartov University and ophthalmology at the University of Berlin. When he returned to Russia from Germany, he ran an eye clinic in Kiev, and it was there in the 1880s that he became active in Zionism.[40] His speech, as we shall see, would elicit a number of responses, and would act as a catalyst for a concerted shift toward the West in the definition of "degenerate" Jewry.

Mandelstamm would limit himself to an analysis of the "*Ghettojuden*," because it was in the East, he claimed, that one could locate "Jewish degeneration." He began, "I hope to demonstrate that the decrepit, miserable, weak bodily constitution of the Jews of the ghetto is the exclusive result of their wretched social and economic situation. And so I do not consider the Jews of Western lands, since they are no more worse off economically than their Aryan counterparts, and so deserve no special consideration."[41] It was fortuitous, Mandelstamm remarked, that his talk was being delivered in London, for the English, earlier perhaps than any other nation, had recognized the connection between a healthy environment and a healthy body. Exhorting his audience to imagine Jewish Eastern Europe as an "East End without end" (yet reminding them that the misery there was in fact unimaginable), he proceeded to show the literally visible effects this environment had produced on the Jewish body.

In almost every way, he claimed, the Jews compared unfavorably with "normally developed people." On average, Jewish height was lower than that of non-Jews; Jews' limbs were shorter, their chests and muscles more poorly developed. They were susceptible to all sorts of diseases, suffering disproportionately from tuberculosis, numerous skin ailments, and eye diseases such as trachoma and nearsightedness. Jewish women fell victim to particular women's disorders in greater numbers than did their non-Jewish counterparts.

Mandelstamm then made reference to a widely accepted notion, held by Jewish and non-Jewish physicians and social scientists alike. "As far as so-called immunities of Jews against known epidemic diseases, such as pestilence or cholera in the Middle Ages, this is foolish drivel from an earlier time. No one today would seriously try to justify such unfounded claims."[42] However, moments later, he modified and clarified this point, sounding themes that would become central to later Zionist arguments. If Jews did display a marked ability to resist disease (*Widerstandsfähigkeit*), this was due not to any racial peculiarity, but to their moderate intake of food and drink, their adherence to hygienic laws, and their greater willingness to consult a physician. In particular, their general abstinence from alcohol allowed Jews to resist infection to a greater degree than could non-Jews. Yet, sadly, he informed his listeners, this ability to resist disease had been decreasing in recent times, as the "better-off Jews assimilate into the non-Jewish population" and adopt their excessive behavior.[43] The end of Jewish isolation, the integration of Jews into the larger society, would therefore not lead to health, but to the loss of whatever positive attributes Jews already possessed.

In contrast to their poorly developed bodies, Mandelstamm argued, Jews possessed larger than average brains. "Weak muscles, badly developed respiratory organs, weak bone structure, slight physical strength, little capacity for physical labor. Only the skull is highly developed among them; the cranial capacity of the Jew is on average greater than that of the non-Jewish population."[44] In line with nineteenth-century physical anthropology and scientific materialism, Mandelstamm assumed a direct relation between the size and shape of the cranium and mental prowess.[45] The larger cranial capacity of the Jews, established by the numerous craniometric studies of anthropologists, indicated a greater average intelligence among Jews.

There were those who argued that heightened Jewish intelligence was a clear sign of national, even racial superiority.[46] For Mandelstamm, however, the greater mental capacity of the Jews was a sign of pathology. It indicated that they suffered disproportionately from nervous and mental disorders that could be traced back to an "overuse of the brain." Hyper-intelligence had produced the "nervous" or "insane" Jew. It was not a sign of health, nor of equality with or superiority to, the non Jew; rather, it revealed the diseased and inferior condition of Eastern European Jewry.

In Mandelstamm's view the economic and moral impoverishment of Jewish life in the East had produced degeneration (*Entartung*) at the physical level. Regeneration could occur only through a complete transformation of Eastern Jewry's social and economic conditions. He allowed that this could, theoretically, occur in Russia if the 5 million Jews there were given the freedoms of movement, occupation, and residence that Western European Jews enjoyed. However, since this could not be expected, all that could be hoped and worked for were half measures: reforms of the heder, instruction in hygiene, better lighted and ventilated rooms, and the establishment of occupational training centers and gymnastic leagues.[47] Complete regeneration demanded a solution beyond the borders of Europe. In concluding his talk, he spoke as both physician and Zionist:

> Ghetto Jewry cannot become either physically or morally healthy in the ghetto. This can only occur outside of the ghetto, on their own land and soil (applause), and indeed in the only single land where it will be possible to secure this goal patiently and calmly; in a land where new powers and energies can lead to physical and intellectual improvement. Only with a mass emigration to Palestine, carefully planned with great foresight . . . can a new and invigorated generation of Jews arise.[48]

For Mandelstamm, the physical abnormality of the Jews could only be remedied through the political, and consequently the social and economic, normalization of the Jewish condition. The physical, bodily weakness or degeneration of the individual Eastern European Jew both demonstrated and symbolized the degenerative status of the Jews as a collective body. Regeneration of the one necessarily meant the ultimate regeneration of the other.

As he announced at the outset of his talk, Mandelstamm's intent was to analyze Eastern European Jewry alone, believing as he did that Western Jewry was normal and healthy. There was in his approach a fundamental continuity with Enlightenment and emancipationist notions of healthy and diseased, normal and abnormal. The Eastern European ghetto remained the *locus classicus* of degeneration, and the image of the "sick Jew" continued to be constructed out of the twin horrors of Russian and rabbinic oppression. The West continued to signify normalization and health. Assimilation into modern European society, at least at the socioeconomic level, brought about a meliorative rather than a degenerative effect upon the Jews. The significance of the shift represented by Mandelstamm's use of the notion of degeneration in the medical sense—as opposed or in addition to solely the moral sense—should not be underestimated. It points precisely to the transformations in thought under discussion here. Nonetheless, his belief in a trajectory of progress as one moved from East to West placed him squarely in an older Maskilic and emancipationist tradition, and one that many Zionist social scientists were just at this time beginning to undermine.

## The Pathological Circle Widens

During the first decades of the twentieth century, Zionist social scientists focused increasingly on Western Jewry, constructing post-emancipatory and anti-assimilationist narratives of Jewish life in Europe. They rejected the East/West dichotomy represented by Mandelstamm's analysis. The West became the site of a qualitatively different and more serious national degeneration, indicated by comparative statistics on physical and especially mental pathologies. As an interpretive strategy, the representation of Western assimilated Jewry as "sick" and "degenerate" constituted a radical reversal of the Enlightenment and emancipationist narratives of progress. These understood the movement of Jews from East to West, from impoverishment to economic well-being, and from intellectual and social isolation to integration as positive transformative experiences. For the post-emancipatory social scientist, the West was no longer the locus of a welcome security and freedom, but rather of enslavement to urban capitalist culture, whose effects were proving devastating to Jewish survival.

The abnormality of Western Jewish life was a recurrent theme in the Zionist speeches and writings of Max Nordau, whose emphatic insistence upon the need for a regeneration of the "Jewish body" stemmed from his ideas about disease and degeneration. Although he was a physician by training, Nordau cannot properly be categorized as a practicing social scientist; yet, as we have seen, he played an instrumental role in the creation of an institutionalized Jewish statistics. His arguments on the Jewish Question and on Jewish nationalism, infused with the language of medicine and social Darwinism, also helped shape the contours of future Zionist social scientific discourse.

According to Nordau, traditional Jewish culture's neglect or negation of the physical and its overemphasis on intellectual pursuits had over the centuries enervated the body of the Jew. Regeneration, effected through physical exercise and labor, was, in his view, fundamental to the Jewish nationalist enterprise.[49] In his most widely known work, *Degeneration*, Nordau delineated what he perceived to be the cultural and aesthetic manifestations of degeneration. Yet, following his teacher and mentor, the Italian-Jewish physician and anthropologist Cesare Lombroso, Nordau made clear at the outset that he understood degeneration to be a physico-medical condition, manifested in physical and mental abnormality: bodily malformations, nervous disorders, and mental illnesses.[50] Moreover, like other proponents of a degeneration theory, Nordau associated degeneration with increasing rates of crime and madness, alcoholism and suicide, and declining birth rates, as well as with types of genius.[51] Normalcy, for him, was the middle: the moral, cultural, social, and aesthetic area between the heights of genius and the depths of the criminal and insane.[52]

While Nordau did not deal systematically with the Jewish Question in *Degeneration*, nonetheless there was a perceptible continuity between his ideas on the modern European malaise and those on the Jewish condition:

Abnormality, he argued, was the defining characteristic of modern Jewish existence.[53] Physical degeneration, manifested in the deformed and weak Jewish body, was one of the clearest signs of this abnormal condition. Nordau's well-known call for a *Muskeljudentum* stemmed from his belief in the interconnections between the physical, mental, and emotional aspects of the individual condition, and the role this played in the constitution of a "healthy" or "diseased" community or culture. Those who, following Nordau's call for a "new Jew" or a "muscle Jew," established Jewish gymnastic societies as a means to physical and national regeneration, spoke the language of sickness and health, which included the familiar notion of "Jewish nervousness." "A healthy spirit dwells in a healthy body," the Bar-Kochba Gymnastic Society's program announced. "We must battle against the one-sided development of the intellect, which produces such nervousness and mental exhaustion amongst us." The movement's journal, according to the program, would consist of articles on hygiene, as well as on sport, history, and contemporary issues, as a means of inculcating and deepening a sense of national feeling and consciousness.[54]

As we have seen, in his 1901 call for a Jewish statistics, Nordau's list of areas of required research consisted to a large extent of categories related to health. His juxtaposition of physical infirmities such as blindness, deafness, and epilepsy with social "pathologies" such as criminality, together with the indeterminate "insanity," was drawn directly from the contemporary debate over degeneration. These categories were subjects of research that would, almost immediately, become central to the definition of Jewish social science. Perhaps, too, some connection existed between Nordau's identification of "modernism" with psychological and cultural degeneration, and the Zionist social scientific representation of modernity as a corrosive force within Jewish life.

In Nordau's view, both Western and Eastern European Jewry displayed signs of degeneration, and both required the regenerative efforts of nationalism.[55] This shift from East to West was even more evident in the direct responses produced by fellow Zionists to Mandelstamm's congress speech. In a 1901 article entitled "The Physical Inferiority of the Jews," published in *Die Welt*, Karl Jeremias addressed the question of "Jewish degeneration."[56] Citing Mandelstamm's speech, as well as the work of the non-Jewish German anthropologist Bernhard Blechmann,[57] Jeremias asserted that sufficient scientific proof of Jewish degeneration existed. Yet Mandelstamm had not gone far enough—geographically or sociologically—in his analysis:

Mandelstamm seeks the causes of this inferior constitution solely in the economic misery of the proletariat Eastern European Jews, and leaves thereby the physical condition of the Jews of the West completely out of the realm of his analysis. Yet I must emphasize that the physical constitution of Western Jewry is thoroughly abnormal. Deep traces still remain of the misery of the ghetto endured for many centuries, which cannot be completely eliminated through only fifty years of free development. The smaller body shape, the tendency to flat-footedness, varicose veins, hemorrhoids, and hernias; the disposition to diabetes and numerous other internal diseases—these are indications of degeneration which, in the unanimous judgment of all experienced clinicians, Western European Jews experience to a high degree. Furthermore, statistics show that the birth rates of German Jews are constantly declining, compared to both an earlier time and to those of Christians in the present. . . . Statistics unequivocally demonstrate, furthermore, that the number of mentally ill among the German Jews is twice as high as their statistical representation within the overall population.[58]

Jeremias sought to shift the onus of disease from East to West. Yet he maintained, at the same time, that the "deep traces" of "the misery of the ghetto," which remained in the Jews, helped account for their degeneration.

There was no simple inversion here of the models of healthy and diseased. Rather, the circle of pathology and difference now was enlarged to encompass those Jews whose identity hinged on the belief in the transcendence of difference, and on the faith in the integration of Jews into Western society as a progressive, meliorative process. Western Jewry, such an analysis asserted, could no longer seek to define itself as normal and healthy in opposition to Jews in the East.

One year later, at the Fifth Zionist Congress, Jeremias delivered a lecture entitled "Physical Formation and Degeneration of the Jews." He once again called attention to the inadequacy of Mandelstamm's view, and set about demonstrating the pathological identity of both Eastern and Western Jewries.[59] His speech followed Nordau's, in which the latter had called for a Jewish statistics as a nationalist enterprise. Jeremias reiterated Nordau's point about the lack of adequate knowledge of the contemporary Jewish condition, and the need for a concerted and organized effort at gathering and analyzing statistical information on the Jews. He linked this task, as had Nordau, directly to the issue of national health. Jeremias found convincing evidence for degeneration in declining fertility rates, but also in the Jews' diminished body size. He cited military-recruitment statistics from both Russia and Germany. "Every authority recognizes their [the Jews'] lower chest circumference and weakened muscular system; their propensity for flat-footedness and hernias, varicose veins and hemorrhoids." As Sander Gilman has shown, the connection between the underdeveloped Jewish body and statistics on low military recruitment and service among Jews was a well-developed theme in European social scientific literature. It served to demonstrate for many the inability of the Jews as a whole to participate fully in the modern European nation-state.[60] The incomplete integration of the Jews into the European body politic, signaled by their physical inability to serve in the military, offered further justification for anti-emancipationist arguments.

Such an argument also bolstered a post-emancipationist, anti-integrationist position among Jewish nationalists. Zionists agreed with those detractors of the Jews who linked Jewish degeneracy with a failure to serve militarily. Since within the discourse of degeneration, the loss of military strength and numbers was taken as a sure sign of national and social decline, this purported lack of martial talent reinforced more general notions of Diaspora Jewish weakness.[61] Yet Zionists rejected any notion of a racial antipathy on the part of the Jews to fighting. The pathology of the Diaspora, rather, had produced the degenerate Jew, and had made him unable to serve. Arthur Ruppin, for instance, argued that the disproportionate involvement on the part of Jews with trade, industry, and the intellectual professions, together with their high rates of urban settlement, led to their unfavorable physical development; this stood in contrast to the "muscular, free-breathing" Christians. This milieu had produced, inter alia, the smaller chests of Jews, which in all countries signified an unfitness for the military.[62] (The "military Jew" later becomes, of course, one of the primary symbols of the successful regeneration of Jewry achieved by Zionism.)

More than muscular weakness, Jews were said to suffer from an assortment of nervous and mental disorders. Like Mandelstamm, Jeremias attributed this in part to their "intellectual overactivity." Yet, since Jeremias's focus was on modern, that is, Western, Jewry the category was in need of redefinition. Intellectual activity was no longer the study of Torah and Talmud, as in the East. Mental and nervous disorders were now the product of too great an engagement with modern, secular learning (as well as with the institutions of capitalism, or "the life of trade" as Jeremias put it). Jews "sacrifice their youth to the 'Moloch' of science and learning." As proof Jeremias presented educational statistics on the overrepresentation of Jews at German and Austrian universities. In 1890, for instance, among the total German student population, 9.6 percent were Jews, sevenfold more than the percentage of Jews in the general population. Between 1860 and 1880, the number of Jews in Austrian universities doubled. Little wonder, he concluded from this, that there existed extraordinary levels among Jews of degeneration of the nervous system. The numbers of Jews suffering from neurasthenia, blindness, deafness, muteness, and assorted mental illnesses—hysteria, idiocy, madness—far surpassed the number of Christians who fell prey to such things.[63]

Education was only one component of the "assimilation complex" that Zionists had identified as disintegrative of Jewish collective identity. In Jeremias's view the prime cause of degeneration among Jews was their propensity for "intellectual overcultivation" (*geistige Überkultur*). He contrasted the intellectual etiology of Jewish degeneration with the alcoholism and syphilis prevalent among the Christian populations of Europe.[64] Significantly, though, in a piece published in 1902, entitled "The Hygiene of Jewish Nerves," he amended this, noting that while Jews continued to abuse alcohol relatively infrequently, syphilis was unfortunately attacking the Jews of the West more often than in the past. This, he made clear, was a direct result of the assimilatory process.[65] As we shall see in a moment, other Jewish social scientists working at the same time would insist that the Jews were also succumbing to the lures of alcohol, and with the same devastating effects felt by the rest of the population.

The propensity to mental and nervous illness characterized both Eastern and Western Jewry, uniting them, and setting them apart from Christian Europe. Statistics on mental health from Italy, Denmark, Prussia, Bavaria, Austria, and Russia "demonstrated objectively," Jeremias argued, that "[t]he nervous system of the Jew on the average is less resistant, more disposed to illness than the non-Jew. . . . There exists, then, no doubt that the Jews of all lands and cultures display in the same way an unusually high proclivity to mental illness, that the Jews tend to a particularly severe alteration of the nerves and mind."[66] Jeremias's indication here of a "proclivity" to nervous and mental disorders suggests a bio-racial rather than a strictly environmental causality to Jewish pathology. Indeed, in a public exchange of letters in 1902 with Alphons Levy, general secretary of the leading liberal German Jewish organization, the CV, Jeremias argued explicitly for a biological, hereditary component to Jewish disease.[67] Levy, responding to an article on "Jewish Nervousness and Degeneracy" written by Jeremias, and published in the *Allgemeine Zeitung des Judentums*, accused him of providing the enemies of the Jews with "pure capital." "At a time when anti-Semites are so eager to rebuild the walls of the ghetto, which have only recently come down, it is disconcerting to find a Jewish physician claiming that this current generation of Jews bears the unmistakable stamp of nervous degeneration."[68] Levy's counterargument bears witness to the impact the discourse on Jewish degeneration and modernity had on the thinking of Jews from across the political and ideological spectrum:

The indisputable fact that the number of mentally ill Jews in Prussia exceeds that of mentally ill Christians should not be mentioned on the Jewish side, without also pointing out that the Jews in a more predominant way are dependent on forms of livelihood that are particularly detrimental to the nerves. If one looks not at the total population numbers, but only at the number of mentally ill businessmen, then it would become clear that in relative terms there are fewer insane Jews than Christians, and having recourse to the occupational statistics, it would be difficult to claim an unfavorable condition of Jews with regard to mental illness.[69]

Levy appears to have both accepted and rejected the idea of disproportion-

ate Jewish mental illness. Reacting to Jeremias's claims regarding the biological element to Jewish nervousness, he admitted that Jews do suffer from
these pathologies, but stressed their "forms of livelihood" as the causal factor. In his reply Jeremias granted that the environmental element required
further study. Yet he maintained that the number of Jews "born feeble-
minded" (*schwachsinnig*) was significantly higher than the number born
among non-Jews. "We have unimpeachable statistics from Germany, Austria, and France to support this, and to show that the basis for this is a
hereditary-degenerative condition." He then invoked numerous recognized
authorities—Charcot, Krafft-Ebing, Erb, Wernicke, Oppenheim—who had
demonstrated in their own work a "Jewish neuropathological
disposition."[70]

Jeremias concluded his letter with an attack upon the CV (referring to
them as "Janus-faced" and a "Mischmaschverein"), and a declaration that
questions of politics should have no bearing upon the scientific inquiry
into the Jews. "What in the world does this biological problem have to do
with what the anti-Semites say?!", he asked. Yet this question was clearly
disingenuous. Throughout his speeches and writings he made explicit the
Zionist impetus to his own statistical inquiries into Jewish health. He called
for a national regeneration, and designated his suggestions for the "rebuild-
ing of the Jewish national organism," *Gegenwartsarbeit*, the cultural Zionist
term for present-centered work undertaken in the Diaspora. This would
entail, he argued, a combination of a renunciation of urban capitalist culture and society, and a reinvigoration through a complete reworking of
Jewish public and private life. The family and schools had to be made principal targets for direct intervention and reform on the part of Jewish physicians and administrators;[71] both, he concluded, had the responsibility for
Jewish children, "who are our future."[72] Thus, Jeremias too stepped back
from an unmitigated racial determinism. As a Jewish social scientist he
ended up embracing the idea of melioration through reform; as a Zionist
he pinned these hopes on nationalist-oriented efforts.

## Imagining a Healthy Future

By medicalizing both the Jewish past and its present, the social scientist
appropriated for himself, as the possessor of a highly valued and specialized
body of knowledge, the task of directing the behavior (and in some cases
the beliefs) of the Jewish masses. For Zionists, this conjunction of knowledge and power, statistics and social policy, was conceived in terms of both
the present and the future. A statistical analysis of Jewish health identified
"problems" within contemporary Jewish life upon which Zionists could
focus and act. It helped define the condition of Diaspora Jewry as "sick"

and "abnormal," and it helped suggest appropriate means for improvement. Statistics also appeared to reveal the impossibility of a viable future for Jews in Europe.

Social scientific work on Jewish vitality prescribed measures that could be undertaken in Europe in the present, while simultaneously pointing to Palestine as the sole space within which complete national regeneration and health could occur. Even as they went about redefining Western Jewry as diseased, many Zionists continued to argue that Eastern European Jewry remained degenerate—either at the physical or at both the physical and the mental levels—and hence were equally in need of nationalist regenerative efforts. Formulating the impossibility of a Jewish future in the Diaspora, the Viennese physician and Zionist Martin Engländer wrote in 1902:

> In the East the fundamental root of evil is the ghetto, with its oppressive poverty, filth and misery; in the West, it is the nerve-shattering competitive struggle for material and intellectual existence. Neither in the East nor the West is there within sight an improvement of these conditions. Prophylactic measures for individuals can make some bit of difference. However, the regeneration of the great masses through the means of a nerve-strengthening agriculture and farming; the education of an indigenous and strong *Landvolk*, which can serve as a regenerator for the city dwellers whose nerves are exhausted, these are things which require political means and measures. The Jews need, for their physical regeneration, land, light, and air![73]

Engländer's work, labeled by its author "a sociological study," was another direct response to Mandelstamm's lecture on Jewish health. Engländer acknowledged his debt to Mandelstamm, who, he emphasized, was one of the first Jewish physicians to speak scientifically on the subject of "Jewish illnesses." The subject was heretofore "a province mostly of non-Jews." Yet Engländer, too, sought to challenge Mandelstamm's notion of the fundamental health of Western European Jewry. "Despite the better living conditions of Western European Jewry," Engländer wrote, "despite their physical development, and their nourishment, they find themselves at a precarious level of degeneration."[74]

Engländer had no interest in denying the degrading conditions in which Eastern European Jews lived. His analysis in this regard echoed much of Mandelstamm's own. Heredity and environment together "bring about two grotesque, interrelated facts: the cranial capacity of Jews is greater, on the average, than non-Jews, and their chest capacity is both in absolute and relative terms much less than their neighbors."[75] As a result, Jews in Eastern Europe suffered to a far greater degree from particular diseases. They were more prone to tuberculosis, as a result of their smaller lung capacity, insufficient diet, and lack of exercise. Trachoma "is nowhere as prevalent as in the poor and dirty ghetto"; shortsightedness, which was caused by poor lighting, was a widespread affliction. Gynecologists reported on particular diseases that afflicted predominantly Jewish women. And the degeneration of the central nervous system, a consequence of "over-striving" and "overuse of the brain," was more common among Jews than among their non-Jewish neighbors.[76]

Eastern European Jews, in Engländer's account, did demonstrate some positive traits. They were not given over to alcoholism; overall they led moderate or temperate lives (*"züchtiges Leben"*), so that syphilis was not a problem. In fact, at the end of his summary of the condition of Eastern European Jewry Engländer sounded a positive, hopeful note: the Jews were halfway to overcoming the negative influence of their anti-hygienic living conditions through their "virtuous home life," "moderation in food and drink," "tenderness and care for wife and child," adherence to the traditional hygienic laws of sexual purity and the practice of domestic preventive medicine.[77]

The Jews of the West, on the other hand, who resided in the most advanced countries economically and socially, found themselves in an advanced state of degeneration and decline. Engländer agreed with Mandelstamm that Jews in the West had benefited from improved health and hygiene conditions. They no longer suffered to any greater degree than did their non-Jewish neighbors from tuberculosis, skin disorders, eye ailments, or "bodily degeneration." "In industrial Bohemia/Moravia and in agricultural Hungary Jews are as robust as Aryans."[78]

However, modernity had taken its toll on the mental and emotional life of the Jews. They suffered in disproportionate numbers from nervousness, neurasthenia, hysteria, and insanity. Engländer cast his explanation for this in social Darwinian terms. The protective walls of the ghetto had shielded the Jews from the struggles occurring in the outside world, and from their debilitating consequences: "With the fall of the ghetto walls, the Jews were tossed out of their little rooms into the great arena of battle. . . . Now they suddenly found themselves in a competitive struggle, not only as individuals, but as a people, in the economic sphere."[79] Jews were at the forefront of the great economic transformations of the recent past—changes in production and distribution, the shift to large industries, imperialism—but their material success came at a heavy price: "The cost of *Nervenkapital*." The Jews, Engländer was quick to point out, were not alone in suffering the effects of modern urban and industrial life. Statistics demonstrated that year by year the successful classes of Europe suffered in increasingly greater numbers from nervous and mental disorders, and that an ever-higher percentage of them committed suicide. Significantly, though, "authorities agree that Jews lose more individuals in this battle than non-Jews."[80]

In his discussion of mental and nervous disorders, Engländer drew on the work of one of the leading psychiatric authorities of the period,

Richard von Krafft-Ebing, who had argued for a direct link between nervous disorders and industrialized urban centers, and, conversely, agriculture and health.[81] In Krafft-Ebing's view, the Jews, "uprooted from the land" (*Bodenentwurzelten*) and urbanized en masse, suffered to an extraordinary degree from nervousness. Krafft-Ebing, in turn, had referred approvingly to the work of Wilhelm Erb, who explained the overrepresentation of Jews among neurasthenics in terms of their "Semitic racial origins." The Jews, Erb argued, possessed an "indomitable acquisitive spirit, which has characterized their way of life for centuries." The racial propensity on the part of the Jews for capitalism, in this analysis, produced a biological, hereditary predisposition to nervous disorders.[82]

This nexus between Jews, modernity, and nervous disorders was a familiar component of nineteenth- and early-twentieth-century racial and social scientific literature. The "sickness" of industrial capitalism and urban society, many authorities claimed, had inscribed itself on the bodies and minds of its most identifiable representatives. Pathological traits and diseases were signs or stigmata of the "curse" of capitalism, and the culture it produced. The Jews were offered up as both agents and effects of these maladies. As such, they suffered the consequences to a greater degree than did other peoples.

Zionist social scientists embraced this nexus of Jewry, modernity, and degeneration. They, too, understood what they perceived to be the "sickness" of Western Jewry in terms of "the modern condition": industrialization, urbanization, and the high degree of social, cultural, and intellectual integration or assimilation into the dominant society that capitalism and the metropolis made possible. Felix Theilhaber, for instance, appropriated the language of *völkish* romanticism to describe the negative impact of modern urban capitalist life upon German Jewry. He contrasted the "simplicity," "naturalness," and "health" of rural agricultural life, and the Jew who had not been "refined by overcultivation" (*von keinerlei 'Überkultur' beleckt*), to the Jew who "with his nervous character seeks out the excitements of the city."[83] The modern city, characterized as it was by intense intellectual and economic struggle (the "infection of modern capitalism"), became the space within which the process of Jewish degeneration unfolded. "Jewry is the most urbanized, capitalistic, rationalistic sector of the population"; hence, the higher rates within that sector of every sort of physical and social pathology. This pathology directly reflected the very condition of modernity.[84]

What Theilhaber and other social scientists found so appealing about the category "modernity" was that it provided the framework within which to undermine an explanation of Jewish abnormality based principally upon biology, with its implications of racial determinism. Theilhaber, as we saw above, believed he had identified manifestations of Jewish degeneration (and difference) at the racial, biological level; yet he assigned blame for this unequivocally to the modernizing, emancipatory process.

The way from full fertility to a poverty of reproduction, from inbreeding to mixing, from a martyrlike willingness to sacrifice for the community to the cowardly disavowal of this duty and an irresolute negligence, are symptoms and stigmata of a larger process. . . . Emancipation opened the gates and allowed the storm of new ideals into the ghettos. Modern economic life, the period of interlocking capital, factories and technology produced transformations in every realm of life . . . [and led to] all forms of pathological phenomena.[85]

Like Theilhaber, Engländer, too, insisted that the greater susceptibility among Jews to mental and nervous diseases (in addition to other illnesses such as diabetes and glaucoma) was due directly to their social and economic pursuits. Jews were highly concentrated in urban, "unhealthy," "nerve-shattering vocations." They spent "too little time relaxing, too little time in nature, too much time in coffee houses, at lectures, at the theater, concerts, ballets." After sketching out the definition and symptoms of diabetes, Engländer explained the Jewish predisposition to the disease with reference to occupation: "One finds among diabetics primarily many academics, musicians, poets, schoolteachers, politicians, big businessmen and stockbrockers."[86] As Engländer's list makes clear, the Jewish academic appears as one of the more likely candidates for degeneration. Arthur Ruppin referred approvingly to the argument put forth by another Zionist social scientist, Hugo Hoppe (whose work shall be dealt with shortly), who claimed that Western Jewish academics in particular had taken to assimilating the harmful drinking habits of their non-Jewish environment, thereby forfeiting the healthy traits that accompanied moderation.[87]

The historian of European degeneration Daniel Pick has pointed out that scientists, not surprisingly, rarely if ever appeared on the lists of degenerate groups so often compiled by scientists (although they did appear on the lists made by novelists).[88] They escaped the taint of degeneration, at least in terms of the internal logic of their own discourse, by identifying other groups or segments within society—the lower classes, criminals, prostitutes, the insane, women, Jews—as the diseased. Male, white, and Christian, social scientists who were largely middle class in origin and sensibilities, defined "normal," "healthy," and "fit" along these lines. Yet they universalized these judgments through scientific discourse. In this way they naturalized socially and ideologically constructed categories and hierarchies.

For the Jewish social scientist such a process was far less easily accomplished. They identified themselves (and were identified by others) as both

Jews and as European scientists. As such, they stood at one and the same time within the community that had been identified as "diseased," and outside of it, claiming the ability to understand and analyze it objectively. How could they identify the Jews as pathological, and yet fall outside this circle of condemnation, thereby rendering themselves fit to analyze and cure?[89] Science—as the purported means for arriving at objective truth—offered Jewish social scientists an "island of normalcy,"[90] a separate and elevated sphere from which they could observe the pathologies of their own community, nation, "race," and remain, nonetheless "uncontaminated" by them.

The remedy for these illnesses, according to Zionist social scientists, was recognition on the part of Jewry of the negative effects of modern urban life, and a (re)turn to the regenerative model offered by nationalism. The solution lay, in Theilhaber's words, in the "return to normalcy." The Jews, if they were once again to be a "healthy *Volk*," needed to return to "the land of their fathers," to a condition of "unity of land, speech, customs and culture, political and economic interests."[91]

By locating the etiology of Jewish degeneration in environmental conditions rather than in permanent racial traits, Zionist social scientists were able to argue theoretically and practically for meliorative, regenerative efforts. In broadening out the domain of pathology to include the West as well as the East, Zionists could make a more cogent and forceful claim that the only "space" within which such a regenerative effort could fully occur would be Palestine.

## The Ghetto and the Jewish "Struggle for Existence"

One year after the appearance of Martin Engländer's work, Hugo Hoppe, a Berlin physician, Zionist, and frequent contributor to the *Zeitschrift für Demographie und Statistik der Juden*, published his comparative study, *Diseases and Mortality among Jews and Non-Jews*.[92] Hoppe was recognized in the broader scientific community as an authority on alcoholism and its relation to criminality, and he brought this interest and knowledge to his studies of modern Jewry. He set out to explain the greater "tenacity of life" or "capability for survival" (*Lebenszähigkeit*) that Jews were said to have traditionally enjoyed. This was an advantage, he wrote, which had been acknowledged and asserted for centuries, but for which only the modern science of statistics could offer numerical and therefore certain proof.[93]

Jews, on average, lived longer than non-Jews; they showed more favorable mortality rates, particularly in the case of children; and they suffered fewer stillbirths. All of this, Hoppe continued, pointed to the fact that Jews possessed greater immunity from infectious and life-threatening diseases: tuberculosis, pneumonia, typhus, malaria, cholera, plague, and so forth. "Already during the devastating epidemics of the Middle Ages, it was generally observed that Jews possessed a greater immunity than Christians," Hoppe wrote, echoing that widely held belief among medical writers encountered earlier.[94]

Above all else, Hoppe called attention to the role of moderation in the Jews' resistance to disease. Following European social and racial hygienists, Jewish social scientists as a whole extolled the virtue of moderation in matters of both body (food, drink, and sexuality) and mind (culture and education). There was a strong middle-class, even conservative impulse to much of the Jewish—including Zionist—social scientific analyses of Jewish health. The conjunction of traditional Jewish and European bourgeois values and practices related to marriage, family, and "normal" sexuality was celebrated, while the deleterious effects of modern urban culture were denounced.[95]

Throughout his numerous writings Hoppe stressed the positive effects he believed that abstaining from alcohol use, or using alcohol moderately, had on Jewish health. All major diseases, he claimed, appeared in higher percentages among peoples with a greater relative number of drinkers.[96] In a 1907 article dealing with Jews, criminality, and alcoholism, Hoppe drew connections—common to medical writers on degeneration—between alcohol and physical degeneration, mental illness, apathy, poverty and prostitution, venereal disease, and criminality.[97] Alcoholism, in his view, was the crucial link in a chain of social pathologies plaguing modern society. Moreover, it adversely affected not only individuals and contemporary society, but future generations. "The children of alcoholics are seldom normal. Most are weak, nervous, psychopathic, given to irritability, impulsive, tending to mental deficiency, idiocy, epilepsy, moral and sexual perversity, also tending to drunkenness, insanity, and criminality."[98]

Significantly, within the context of his discussion of Jewry, Hoppe unlinked alcoholism, crime, and illness from poverty. Impoverished Jews, in both the East and the West, showed far less tendency, in his view, to criminal activity and disease than did their poor non-Jewish neighbors. The key to this, Hoppe maintained, was Jewish resistance to alcoholism. And what was the origin or cause of this moderation? The most common answer pointed to the notion of moderation or immunity among Jews as an immutable racial trait. Hoppe quoted one German anthropologist as representative of this view: "There seems to be in their (the Jews') nervous system, in their constitution, a particular quality that makes them immune to the enticement of alcohol." While Hoppe did argue that moderation had become, over the centuries, an acquired, inherited characteristic, he rejected an explanation based on a rigid racial determinism. Rather, he asserted that moderation among Jews was an effect, ultimately, of adherence to the religious sanitary and dietary laws and customs.[99] It was precisely among the impoverished religious Jews, isolated physically, intellectually, and socially in the ghetto, where one found an absence of alcohol abuse, and hence a greater degree of vitality and health.

Hoppe's work would appear to be rather positive and optimistic about the Jewish condition, and seemingly at odds with the analyses of Jeremias, Engländer, and others. Yet this paean to Jewish health (which was also a slightly veiled attack upon Christians) was directed at a set of conditions and circumstances that Hoppe feared was already passing. The advantage the Jews had enjoyed for centuries, he warned, was now in danger of disappearing. Jewish resistance to infectious disease was waning; Jewish birth rates were declining, while alcoholism, syphilis, criminality, and suicide were on the rise. Jewish mortality rates were higher, so that since the 1860s the statistical advantage Jews could once claim in overall population increase had been reversed.[100]

Hoppe linked these reversals directly to emancipation and assimilation into Western Gentile society. As Jews moved from East to West, from isolated communities where traditional laws and customs had been preserved and practiced, they lost the ability to resist those physical and social pathologies associated with degeneration. One observed this in Germany, where Jews had adopted more and more the drinking habits of the Gentiles, and in the United States, where Jewish birth rates were dropping, while alcoholism, venereal disease, and suicide were on the rise.[101] Like others writing on the subject, Hoppe noted the high incidence of mental and nervous degeneration among Jews. Significantly, of all nervous disorders, Jews were afflicted to the greatest degree with the "modern" ones—neurasthenia and hysteria.[102] Yet he stressed that in this regard no distinction between Eastern and Western Jewry could be made. The number of Jews in Russia and Poland suffering from neurasthenia and hysteria, as well as diabetes (which Hoppe saw as a result of nervous disorders), idiocy, and insanity, was statistically as significant as was the number of those suffering from these ailments in the West.

Hoppe was confronted with numbers showing significant levels of mental and nervous degeneracy among Eastern European Jews who had not assimilated the drinking habits of their Gentile neighbors. He was forced, therefore, to modify his explanatory model. In doing so, he drew upon both social Darwinian and neo-Lamarckian ideas of evolution and selection. As we have seen, Hoppe contemptuously rejected any explanation for Jewish differences based on racial determinism. He also refused to accept the argument, put forth by Ruppin and others, that differences in standards of living between Jews and non-Jews could account for differences in levels of health. Rather, he argued that Jewish health and disease were products, first of all, of the two-thousand-year-old "struggle for existence," the "tools" for which were provided by orthodox Jewish law. During this "natural-selection process" Jews had developed great powers of resistance to infectious disease, a resistance their offspring then inherited. At the same time, he added, the "weakest and most unfit" (*die Schwächster und die Untauglichsten*) had been eliminated.

Yet this centuries-long struggle, experienced most intensely by East European Jewry, also explained the "second biological peculiarity of the Jews": their tendency toward nervous and degenerative diseases.[103] Thousands of years of persecution, which provided the Jews with extraordinary mechanisms of survival, also produced great anxiety. Over generations, these effects of environmental (i.e., political and social) conditions and causes became acquired traits, passed on to descendants hereditarily.

Moreover, these acquired characteristics were reinforced by two more factors: urban dwelling and inbreeding. Drawing on a commonplace in the social scientific literature of the day, Hoppe located Jewish pathology, in part, in the Jews' nonagricultural status. The numbers of other urban-dwelling peoples were constantly infused with the "healthy fresh blood of those who dwell on the land." Jews, however, were prohibited from owning landed property, and so could not reap this benefit. "They have always reproduced among themselves, urban men and women, and so the nervous disposition is passed along to the offspring."[104] Hoppe also accepted the oft-repeated charge about the high incidence of Jewish inbreeding, or consanguineous marriage, and the harmful role it played in degenerative nerve disorders:

It is without doubt, then, that the thousand-year-old persecutions, the persistent and harsh struggle for existence, and particularly the over-execution of intellect have produced the nervousness of the Jews. This has increased and spread because of urban dwelling and inbreeding. So we see the extraordinary frequency of neurasthenia and hysteria, the extreme mental agitation, and idiocy; deaf-muteness, which is particularly common among inbreeders; shortsightedness, due in large part to the emphasis on "learning" Torah and Talmud; constitutional diseases, particularly diabetes, and the other hereditary and degenerative diseases among the Jews.[105]

Clearly, this was no simple romanticization of East European Jewish life. The ghetto and orthodox religiosity produced the conditions for Jewish vitality, yet the same environment was also responsible for degeneration.

As the analyses we have examined thus far reveal, the older Maskilic, or Enlightenment, notion of the physical and moral degeneracy of Eastern European Jewry was not entirely abandoned by social scientists. It was, however, modified to varying degrees. If Jewish social scientists were not willing to discard completely the image of the impoverished and debilitated Eastern Jew, who stood in need of reform and regeneration, Eastern European Jewry nonetheless came to be seen increasingly as the embodiment of "national health," particularly psychological or mental health.[106] This image developed in tandem with, and to an extent as a result of, that of Western Jewry as increasingly prone to psychological disorders. For a number of Zionist social scientists the tendency of Western Jews to display signs of mental and nervous illness served as the surest indication of the qualitative difference between Eastern and Western European Jewries. Statistics, as well as anecdotal evidence, served as the means by which to demonstrate that precisely those conditions that integrationists had hailed as signs of progress were, in fact, causes of disease and decline. The increasing distance of the Jews from the "ghetto" had produced among them ever-increasing numbers of physically and mentally ill, in addition to proportionally higher rates of alcoholism, syphilis, and suicide, and dramatically greater numbers of intermarriage and conversion.

The reevaluation of Western Jewry and the transformation of the image and understanding of Eastern European Jewry were intimately connected. The continuing physical impoverishment of Eastern Jewry was not denied; it remained a source of intense interest to Zionist social scientists. Their research was impelled to a significant degree by the conviction that knowledge of the negative aspects of Eastern European material culture and life was necessary for the successful Zionist effort at national regeneration. At the same time, material poverty and suffering were decoupled from intellectual and cultural "impoverishment," and the isolation of the ghetto was transformed into an historical mechanism of national vitality and health. The ghetto became the locus, in social Darwinian terms, of the thousand-year-old Jewish "struggle for existence." Both positive and negative, healthy and unhealthy Jewish traits were understood to be products of environmental or historical forces associated with the "ghetto experience."[107]

The use of the Darwinian notion of "struggle for existence" was a commonplace among Jewish and non-Jewish social scientists analyzing the Jewish past and present. Both the ghetto and the post-ghetto experiences were interpreted explicitly in such terms. As we have seen, at least according to Zionists, Jews appeared to be losing the post-ghetto, emancipatory-era struggle for survival. Increasingly, pre-emancipation Jewish life was represented in positive terms, even as the notion of an actual return to the ghetto was derided. The centuries-long experience of "oppression and persecution" was portrayed as a "selection process," during which, in the words of one influential non-Jewish authority, "all that proved too weak, bodily and spiritually, was eliminated from the race, either by death or baptism."[108] However, this positive reading of the ghetto remained one side of a complex, ambivalent attitude toward the East and Eastern European Jewry on the part of Central and Western European Jewish social scientists. The ghetto, both in the past and in the present, remained a site of both health and disease, physical degeneration yet mental and spiritual vitality.[109]

The romanticization and idealization of Eastern European Jewish life and culture within central European Zionist circles beginning in the last decade of the nineteenth century helps account in part for this reevaluation.[110] Accompanying this romantic view of the ghetto was an animus of antimodernism, a "politics of Jewish cultural despair," to play upon Fritz Stern's well-known phrase.[111] This was an antimodernism not at all hostile to technology or science, but rather to those social, economic, and cultural forms of modern life that were viewed as the necessary result and expression of urbanization and capitalism.[112] For Zionist social scientists, the categories of urban and rural, commercial and agricultural were intimately linked with the categories of abnormal and normal, diseased and healthy. In their analyses of modernity and its effects on the "Jewish body"—both individual and collective—these scientists sought to demonstrate the essential interconnection between the processes of modernization and degeneration. The one produced, in near mechanistic fashion, the conditions for the other.

The factors that Zionist social scientists pointed to as causes for the degeneration of Western Jewry were, in fact, mirror opposites of those identified, by earlier analysts, as having produced similar results within Eastern European Jewry. In the East: poverty, ignorance (defined as the insularity produced by the maintenance of traditional education and the resistance to secular knowledge), the oppression of anti-Semitism, and the absence or failure of emancipation. In the West: material success and higher social standing, too great a degree of participation in and enthusiasm for modern Western education and culture (*Bildung*)[113], civil equality, and freedom—the success, more or less, of emancipation—leading to unprecedented levels of integration and assimilation.

However, in the texts under discussion here, the significance of the ghetto and the tradition it served to maintain was as much their assured disappearance in the imminent future as their powerful effect in the past. In Eastern European Jewry the Zionist social scientist believed he saw Western Jewry as it appeared 150 years before, in the condition of pre-emancipation. And the fate of Western Jewry in this scheme awaited Eastern European Jewry, as millions of immigrants moved from East to West and assimilated into the modern culture of urban capitalism.

Central European Jewry, and particularly Prussian and Austrian Jewry (i.e., the Jewries of Berlin and Vienna) played such an important role in

Jewish social science in part because it represented the inevitable result of the modernization process in Europe.[114] This was a schema somewhat akin to the nineteenth-century anthropological theory of stages, in which contemporary primitives were taken as living models of civilized Europe's past. The Jewish social scientist, in other words, imagined the Eastern European Jew as Western European Jewry's past incarnate. Moreover, Western Jewry's present represented Eastern European Jewry's future. Statistics demonstrated the consequences of modernity for contemporary Western Jewry, as well as for the Jews of the East *in potentia*. Arthur Ruppin, for instance, argued that differences between Eastern and Western European Jews (and between modernized Jews and Christians) should be understood as "temporal." The effects of "modernization," he claimed, which began for Western European Jewry in the 1860s and 1870s, would likewise affect Eastern European and Oriental Jewish communities (as well as Western Christians) at the point when they reproduced the socioeconomic conditions of Western Jewry.[115]

The image of the healthy, albeit potentially endangered, *Ostjude*, and the "insane" or "neurasthenic" Western Jew, persisted into the 1920s and 1930s, as did the belief that the very conditions of Jewish modernity produced these higher rates of disease. Studies by Zionist anthropologists and psychiatrists such as Leo Sofer, Max Besser, Max Sichel, and Raphael Becker all posited the "West" as a locus of mental pathology and the "East" as the site of Jewish health.[116] Yet, as we have seen, other Zionist social scientists resisted this dichotomy between a healthy East and a diseased West, and constructed an image of a European Jewry united, despite their differences of geography or culture, through physical and/or mental pathologies.

Neither East nor West, then, could be viewed as potential loci of health and regeneration at the national level. Only in a place beyond Europe could a milieu necessary for regeneration be created. Concluding his analysis, Hugo Hoppe asked "What can the Jews do to free themselves of the danger posed by nervousness and degeneration?" His answer, like that of other Zionist social scientists, was a plea for a dramatic transformation in Jewish economic, political, and social life. The "dance around the golden calf," the constant striving after wealth—so much a part of Jewish life in the metropolis, he argued—must come to an end. The Jews, he instructed his readers, must "return to the land," to a life of colonization and agriculture. They must engage more in bodily activities, in sports of all kinds, in order to offset their "mental overactivity."[117] Hoppe's demonstration, like Engländer's, of the physical degenerative effects of assimilation upon Western Jewry; the ability to link a complex political and socioeconomic development with a medical and biological condition in a causal relationship, and thereby define both as pathological and abnormal, was intended as scientific proof and support of Zionist claims regarding the necessity of a regenerative national effort.

## "Crumbling Stone by Stone": Assimilation and Decline in the Work of Arthur Ruppin

The nexus of modernization, assimilation, and decline found one of its clearest and most influential expressions in the work of Arthur Ruppin. An examination of his evolving ideas about Jewish health and disease illuminates forcefully the political and ideological impulses to Zionist social scientific work. In his seminal book *Die Juden der Gegenwart*, published in 1904, Ruppin presented an ambiguous, even contradictory evaluation of the Jewish condition in Europe, which mirrored his own ambivalence toward the Zionist movement. In the years that followed, the solidification of his personal commitment to the idea of Zionism found clear expression in his social scientific writing. The possibility, present in his early work, of a collective Jewish future in the Diaspora vanished, to be replaced by an unambiguous equation of vitality and normality with Palestine-centered Jewish nationalism.

Ruppin began his chapter on Jewish "bio-statistics" in the 1904 edition of *Die Juden der Gegenwart* with a comparative analysis of Jewish and non-Jewish births. He noted that Jews showed fewer stillbirths than did Christians, presenting statistics from Prussia, Austria, and Budapest. (Statistics from Algeria indicated that Jewish women gave birth to more stillborn babies than did Muslim women.) Overall, this indicated an advantageous condition for Jews within Europe. Ruppin then proceeded to compare the statistics regarding Jews among themselves, and to draw conclusions about the different rates observed. The significance of these numbers lay in the revelation of a paradox: The lower rates of stillbirths among Jews were to be found in the poorer Jewish communities, while among the wealthier Western Jews, rates were higher. Ruppin linked this phenomenon directly to modernity:

It is noteworthy that precisely in Algeria and Austria—with its poor and culturally backward Galician Jews—the number of stillbirths is lower than in Prussia, while general experience tells us that stillbirths should decline given a higher standard of living (which permits the woman a greater indulgence and ease during the period of pregnancy) and a more advanced level of hygiene. In Prussia the rates of stillbirths sank among the general population from 4.1% during the years 1861–70 to 3.2% between 1891–1900. Since we cannot trace this phenomenon [of higher Jewish stillbirths] back to incomplete registration practices, . . . it can only be explained in

Prussia with reference to other factors, particularly the greater frequency of sexual diseases among the men, and the greater difficulty of delivery among the women. In addition, the greater disposition to certain diseases (anemia, nervous disorders) are the consequence of modern culture.[118]

The pathological, abnormal state of Western Jewry was revealed in the paradox of a rising standard of living coupled with a rise in stillbirths. Statistics on the Jewish handicapped or infirm (*Gebrechlichen*) from Prussia indicated a similar condition. Jewish rates exceeded those of Christians in this case in all categories: blind; deaf/mute; blind and deaf/mute; blind and insane; blind, insane, and deaf/mute; deaf/mute and mentally ill; mentally ill. According to the Hungarian census of 1890, Jewish rates were higher in each of the above categories, save for blindness.[119]

It was important, Ruppin was quick to note, that the statistics on mental illness distinguished between madness (*Irrsinnige*) and imbecility (*Blödsinnige*). The latter was congenital, the former the result of the "dissolution of a previously normal condition," and hence a product not of race but of environment. Both the Hungarian and the Prussian statistics revealed that Jews suffered to a far greater degree from madness than from imbecility, that is, from an environmentally rather than a hereditarily determined illness. The Prussian statistics also showed that 84 percent of blind Jews became so after birth. Only the percentage of congenital deaf/muteness exceeded the number of noncongenital deaf/muteness.[120]

Ruppin offered three possible explanations for the higher rates of mentally and physically infirm Jews: 1) Jews possessed a greater sense of the value and sanctity of life. They would therefore be more likely to preserve the life of handicapped children, and would hence count more handicapped within their population; 2) Jews entered into a greater number of consanguineous marriages; and 3) Jews exerted more intellectual exertion and agitation, which in Western Europe resulted from their higher degree of participation in the learned professions, trade, and speculation, as well as from their physical concentration in urban centers, particularly big cities.

Present in this early work was the idea of socioeconomic and cultural modernization—assimilation into the West—as a force of dissolution and degeneration within the Jewish *Volk*, and the exclusive identification of Eastern European Jewry with a vital Jewish *Volkstum*. Ruppin conceded that in Eastern Europe Jews, too, suffered from "infirmities." Like Hoppe, he explained this with reference to the extraordinarily difficult "struggle for existence," combined with intense intellectual activity. Nonetheless, Eastern European Jewry alone continued to possess those attributes that constituted a nation or *Volk*: linguistic unity, historical consciousness, and above all "unity of race and descent."[121] Western Jewry, in contrast, had succeeded, albeit incompletely, in integrating far enough into European society to cast their identity as Jews into doubt. "One can still not identify Western European Jewry with the English, German, French or Italian nations; yet neither can one identify them with the Jewish *Volk*."[122]

It was precisely in those lands where Jews enjoyed the greatest degree of legal equality and respect that their connection to the Jewish *Volkstum* declined, while their feeling of belonging to the *Volkstum* of their homeland rose:

The areas of contact between Jews and Christians are becoming ever greater. This has occurred because of the rising living standard of the Jews; on account of their ascent to the better-educated classes and their strong attraction to the big cities, which, characterized as they are by a high degree of interconfessional interaction, constitute the dynamic centers of assimilation; and through their ever more intense participation in the modern economy, science and art, and at the same time their sinking birth rates.[123]

Ruppin appeared emphatic in his belief that the assimilation of Western Jewry had proceeded far enough to insure the disappearance of those communities altogether. He argued that Eastern Jewry, although displaying signs of degeneration, represented the sole hope for the future of Jewry.

Yet he claimed, at the same time, that a physical regeneration of both Western and Eastern European Jewries had indeed taken place over the course of the nineteenth century, and that the twentieth would witness a continuation and furtherance of this regenerative process:

We are of the opinion that the nineteenth century signified progress for the Jews in terms of physical degeneration, that Western European Jewry improved during this time with regard to health and physical strength, even if at the same time they also became more nervous and excitable on account of urbanization and intensive involvement in the intellectual and economic life of the West. Nonetheless, the health conditions of the immigrant Russian Jews to England and America have undoubtedly improved, although there still remains much to hope for in this regard. In eastern Europe itself the obligation of military duty proved to have salutary effects with regard to physical regeneration. And so we believe, as well, that the twentieth century will witness the progressive entry of Western European culture into the East, and we can predict that this will produce a regeneration rather than physiological degeneration among Eastern European Jewry.[124]

Ruppin certainly appeared to be highly optimistic in this passage about the Jewish future in both Eastern and Western Europe. However, earlier we saw that he insisted on a causal connection between higher levels of cultural and socioeconomic standing, and the dissolution of Jewry. This would seem to suggest that physical regeneration need not imply national or racial vitalization. This certainly appeared to be valid, in Ruppin's view, in the case of Western Jewry.

In the end, Ruppin appeared ambivalent about the impact of Western culture upon Eastern European Jewry. He acknowledged its destructive influence, yet posited it as an essential ingredient for Jewry's survival as a *Volk*. Ruppin still believed in 1904 that Eastern European Jewry could successfully meet the "challenge from the West." He held out the possibility that a cultural as well as a physical regeneration of Jewry might yet take place in Eastern Europe if a successful integration of modern Western with traditional Jewish culture could be achieved. He judged Zionism to be a noble, yet utopian and illusionary enterprise. The great challenge for the Jews in the twentieth century, he concluded, will remain in Europe.

The fate of the Jewish people in the future hangs less on if and when the Zionists obtain a charter from the sultan, as it does on how East European Jewry conducts itself under the influence of the economic and cultural conditions invading from the West. In Eastern Europe it will be decided whether or not the Jewish people will continue to exist, and if and what part they will take in the culture of humanity.[125]

"Zion" for Ruppin remained metaphorical, a space in which particularity and universality meet: "Zion will be that place where a strong Jewish *Volkstum*, conscious of its worth and goals, pulsates in close contact with the general culture of humanity."[126]

Over the next few years Ruppin changed his mind about the possible future of Jewish life in Europe. He came to embrace Zionism unambivalently as the only viable remedy to the danger he believed the Diaspora posed. This shift would be fully evident in the revised edition of *Die Juden der Gegenwart*, published in 1911, and to which we will turn in a moment. But something of this change in his political thinking was already evident in his 1906 study of Russian Jewry, a work undertaken with the financial support of the Zionist Actions Committee and published by the Bureau for Jewish Statistics.[127] In a chapter entitled "Physical Deformities and Mental Illnesses" Ruppin argued that the ultimate significance of comparative statistics of diseases among the national groups in Russia lay in what they revealed about the development of Western Jewry. Russian statistics, he wrote, show us a Jewry in a state of backward social conditions, akin to Western European Jewry—no longer directly observable—one-half or a full century ago. Statistics on blindness (both congenital and noncongenital), deafness, muteness, and a variety of mental diseases among Jews, Russians, Lithuanians, Poles, and Germans demonstrated that the Jews showed no greater proclivity to degeneration than did other populations. Russian Jews counted the smallest percentage of blind, save for Germans and Poles, and they counted fewer deaf and dumb than all other nationalities. Furthermore, Ruppin noted that Germans, but not Russians or Poles, displayed higher percentages of mentally ill than Jews ("yet no one speaks of 'German degeneration,'" he was quick to note). This last statistical fact indicated, in Ruppin's opinion, that it was a combination of urbanization and socioeco-nomic and intellectual stratification, rather than any inherent racial degen-eration, which accounted for mental disease. And these were conditions far more characteristic of Western than of Eastern European Jewish existence.[128]

By 1911, and the publication of the revised edition of *Die Juden der Gegenwart*, Ruppin had arrived at the same conclusion about contemporary Western Jewry, and the potential fate of Jews in the East. He now pre-sented his position in sharp and unambiguous terms. "Before our eyes," he wrote at the outset, "the solidly constructed edifice of Jewry is crumbling stone by stone."[129] Until now one could imagine that this process was lim-ited to Western and Central Europe. But the 1905 Revolution, and the higher participation of Russian Jews in the processes of transformation there ("They are taking full part in the life of their country") now threat-ened traditional East European Jewish life. The end of the social and cul-tural isolation of the ghetto—an isolation that had guaranteed Jewish par-ticularity—and the concomitant rise in wealth, social standing, and cultural and intellectual integration (i.e., assimilation), meant dissolution and decline. In those sections of the book devoted to Jewish biostatistics, Rup-pin again noted the pathogenic nature of increased wealth and education. Jews remaining in Eastern Europe could expect their people to be charac-terized by more sterility, neurasthenia, sexual diseases, and overall "physi-cal unfitness."[130]

The overall prognosis for Jewry's present and future was bleak. The emergence of what Ruppin referred to as "world capitalism," accompanied as it was by the triumph of Western culture, insured the ever-increasing integration of the Jews into the dominant Christian society. In the statis-tics on relatively lower birth rates, Ruppin believed he had found the evi-dence that Eastern European Jewry was already moving in the direction of Western European and American Jewry. The process "seems unavoidable. The fate of the Jews is sealed." And he offered an organic metaphor for the death of the Jewish community: "Like the tree whose roots are dead, but which continues to stand for years although its death must come, so too the Jews. They will survive for some time, but as a community [*Gemein-schaft*] they are declining, not ascending."[131]

Ruppin warned against a "false optimism," against the facile belief that "we have survived all of this before." True, Jewish history was punctuated by periods of intensified assimilation. But the past, he admonished, could tell us nothing of the present, for all the fundamental external conditions had changed. The inevitable spread of international capitalism, and the pro-found transformations in social relations produced by it, made contemporary assimilation into a qualitatively different process. Modernity was upon the Jews, affecting them in unprecedented ways, yet they remained, for the most part, unaware of the changes or dangers. In terms reminiscent of Salo Baron's later well-known lamentation of the "lachrymose" approach to Jewish historical writing, Ruppin argued that Jewish historiography bore much of the responsibility for this ignorance. Bemoaning this, he made a plea for the social scientific approach. "Jewish historical writing concerns itself, unfortunately, far too much with the great events and with persecutions [*grossen Ereignissen und Verfolgungen*]. The much more important, yet far more difficult phenomenon of the undermining work accomplished by assimilation still awaits representation."[132] Social science was now placed directly and explicitly at the service of Zionism. The purpose of his work, Ruppin wrote, was "to examine how far the danger has spread, what the future will bring, and to what extent the defense of the Jewish nationalist movement against assimilation may succeed."[133] In contrast to his earlier estimation, Ruppin now pronounced Palestine "healthy," the only "choice" place for the Jews. He conceded that the commitment within segments of Jewry to territorialism or autonomous nationalism in Eastern Europe was evidence of the "manifestation of the will to life" (*Willens zum Leben*) on the part of the Jewish *Volk*. Still, he insisted that Palestine alone offered the possibility of the territorial, linguistic, economic, and intellectual isolation required for "the revival of the whole of Jewry."[134]

## *Suicide, Criminality, and the Disease of Western Society*

Ruppin's conviction of a modernized, assimilated Jewry in the throes of decline and dissolution found further support in the statistics on suicide and crime. Linked with other social pathologies such as syphilis, alcoholism, sterility, and mental illness in the discourse of degeneration, suicide and criminality were distinct and identifiable categories of research within the general European and Jewish social sciences. Both figured prominently in discussions of national and social health. Increasing rates of crime and suicide were read as further indicators of pathology and decline at the collective level.[135]

For sociologists and statisticians, suicide was a social phenomenon (rather than purely a matter of individual morality or psychology) requiring a social explanation.[136] Many European authorities had linked the rise in suicide rates to the decline of religious faith and traditional communal structures, in conjunction with urbanization, industrialization, and the resulting mental and nervous strain brought on by modern life. There were those, however, who accounted for either low or high rates of suicide within a group by reference to racial differences. The Jews, as a religious and/or racial group, constituted a category of research and analysis within this scientific literature.

Until the beginning of the twentieth century the dominant judgment among scientific observers was that the Jews were indisposed to suicide. In 1881 Tomáš G. Masaryk, the Czech sociologist (and future president of the Republic) explained the low rates of suicide among Jews as a product of their strong religious faith and their "great moderation." "Persecuted and despised, the Jewish people cling to the religion of their fathers and have distinguished themselves by a joy in life and a practical optimism which does not allow the development of the morbid suicide tendency. Their great moderation also has a favorable effect in the same sense."[137]

Emile Durkheim, writing in 1897, believed this to be the case as well. He acknowledged that recent statistics from Germany indicated that suicide rates for Jews had been rising,[138] yet it was the low rate of suicide among Jews that he sought to understand within his broader analytical framework.

Durkheim rejected explanations of suicide based on notions of race, climate, "mental alienation," or "imitation"—all commonly accepted explanations in the nineteenth century. He argued instead that changes in suicide rates were related to social structural transformations. More specifically, Durkheim posited a direct relation between suicide rates and relative degrees of social solidarity within particular communities. Religion played a fundamental role in his analysis in this regard, for different religions, by their nature, produced either greater or lesser levels of social cohesion or solidarity among members. Protestantism, for example, was characterized in Durkheim's view by a high degree of individualism. It held to fewer common beliefs and practices, encouraging instead a greater intellectual and social freedom. The bonds of community, which had offered individuals meaning and purpose, were therefore weaker, and suicide among Protestants occurred more frequently than it did among people of other faiths.

Catholicism and Judaism, on the other hand, were paradigmatic religions of community, and so Catholics and Jews lived in a "higher state of social solidarity."[139] Indeed, any sense of individuality within the Jewish community was absent from Durkheim's analysis: "Everyone thought and lived alike;" "Individual divergencies were almost impossible." Yet the Jews posed a particular problem in this regard. Statistics on the presence of different religious groups in institutions of higher learning showed that Jews attended secondary schools and universities at far higher rates proportionately than did either Catholics or Protestants.[140] For Durkheim, education—the search for knowledge—was antithetical to, and destructive of, tradition. It weakened those "collective customs and prejudices" that defined the traditional religious community. How, then, could Jews expose themselves to the disintegrative forces of modern learning and yet retain their traditional religious beliefs and customs? Durkheim resolved this by arguing that, as members of a religious minority, Jews acquired secular knowledge for solely functional reasons. They utilized it as a weapon in the social battle for survival. This meant that knowledge was "superimposed" upon tradition; it did not destroy it. "The Jew, therefore, seeks to learn not in order to replace his collective prejudices by reflective thought, but merely to be better armed for the struggle. For him it is a means of offsetting the unfavorable position imposed on him by opinion and sometimes by laws."[141]

Zionist social scientists, in contrast, posited an inextricable link between higher suicide rates among Jews—demonstrated by official governmental statistics from the first decade of the twentieth century—and their assimilation into Western culture.[142] For them suicide served as a powerful sign and symptom of the more all-encompassing abnormality of modern Jewish life. Like Durkheim and others, they acknowledged the significance of the abandonment of traditional religious belief in accounting for this phenomenon. In addition, they rejected the explanation, still being offered well into the twentieth century, based on racial predisposition. Yet they maintained that the Western Jew, above all others, was identified with modernity, and hence susceptible to its degenerative effects. In a discussion of Jews and suicide, Ruppin identified "lack of despair" as a characteristic Jewish trait. However, unlike Durkheim, who had made no distinction in this regard between Eastern and Western Jewry, Ruppin made this an indication of difference:

According to our personal experience and the scattered testimony found in literature—statistical data is not at our disposal—suicide among the Orthodox Jews of Eastern Europe is very infrequent, in contrast to Western European Jewry. The orthodox Jew, despite all the adversities of fate, is an optimist, an affirmer of life. In addition, the religious injunction against suicide still possesses real meaning for him. Pessimism has only become a common accessory of cultured/educated West European Jews [*der Weltschmerz ist erst in Westeuropa ein häufiges Zubehör der gebildeten Juden geworden*].[143]

The "Orthodox Jew"—an ideal type in sociological terms—remained enveloped in a vital community, where the Jewish religion served as a force for cohesion and meaning. Divorced from this environment through the modernization process, the Western Jew exhibited the pathological symptoms of the modern condition. In his 1930 study *Die Soziologie der Juden*, Ruppin argued that Jews were "given over" to those depressive and melancholic diseases that led to suicide. Moreover, they were highly concentrated in urban and metropolitan areas, and more highly represented in those professions from whose ranks suicide most often occurs, namely commerce and the free professions. "The types of economic exchanges involved in commerce, and the heightened emotional reactions that come with unwanted occurrences in the free professions, with a higher level of education, and with a refined sense of honor, make it understandable that these occupations produce fertile ground for suicide."[144] This analysis was based on the work of the Berlin psychiatrist and Zionist Max Sichel, who had argued a few years earlier that the heightened nervousness and insanity of Jews in the West, together with their greater susceptibility to depression and melancholy, were largely responsible for increased rates of suicide.[145] Felix Theilhaber linked suicide to other symptoms of the abnormal Jewish condition in the West, such as high rates of intermarriage, prostitution, and sexual diseases. He quoted approvingly the opinion of the German sociologist Werner Sombart, who had argued that while the children of Jewish/Christian intermarriages often appeared physically beautiful, they nonetheless ended up morally debased and insane, and committed suicide in greater numbers.[146]

The impression that suicide among Jews in the West had reached epidemic proportions, and ought to be considered a sign of the serious threat facing Jewry, was also provided by the statistics collected from the various official government sources and published regularly in the *Zeitschrift für Demographie und Statistik der Juden*. The numbers were more often than not accompanied by a brief analysis, written by the editor, stressing the connections between urbanization, economic modernization, psychopathological conditions, and the rise in suicide rates.[147]

Criminality, like suicide, constituted a recognizable category of theory and research within the general European and Jewish social sciences during the late nineteenth and early twentieth centuries. And it, too, formed part of the discourse on race, medicine, degeneration and the place of the Jews within modern society.[148] If Jews suffered from particular physical and/or mental illnesses at higher or lower rates than non-Jews, if their rates of fertility, mortality, alcoholism, and suicide marked them off as different from, and even inferior to, Christians, then would not their essential particularity reveal itself as well through statistics on crime?

The image of the Jew as criminal, like that of the Jew as diseased, reaches back, of course, to before the nineteenth century. The Jew as the perpetrator of deicide, who then re-created this original criminal act by introducing plague into Christian society, was a central theme in medieval Christian myth, and highlights the deep connection between disease, criminality, and the Jew in European discourse. In the late nineteenth and early twentieth centuries, Jewish criminality had become an issue of race and biology (as well as of theology).[149] In 1907, for instance, the eminent German crimi-

nologist Franz von Liszt published an essay, "On the Problem of the Criminality of the Jews," in which he posed the "problem" as one of etiology. It
has long been recognized, Liszt wrote, that the criminality of the Jewish
population in Germany is different and distinct from that of the Christians.
The dilemma for social scientists was how to account for this difference.[150]

Jewish social scientists addressed themselves to the same issues and questions. "Is the criminality of the Jew a racial criminality?" the Zionist social
scientist Rudolf Wassermann asked in a 1911 article published in the
*Zeitschrift für Demographie und Statistik der Juden.* Or is it an "occupational
criminality," a product of particular historical and contemporary socioeconomic forces and conditions? Wassermann rejected the arguments of those
who believed that the Jews were racially predisposed toward crime. Rather,
Jewish crime was a result of the Jews' historical role as "pioneers" of capitalism, and of their current overrepresentation in the capitalist economy. In
an earlier article devoted to Jews and criminality, Wassermann quoted at
length from an article by Welly Helpach on "Berufspsychose," or "occupational psychosis." According to Helpach, the urge for wealth, when it succeeded in dominating everything in a culture, produced mental as well as
moral illness. This had happened to the Jews in the West, and accounted for
their high rates of criminality and insanity.[151] The medicalization of crime
was explicitly linked with the "sickness" of the modern capitalist ethos. The
abnormality of Jewish economic life, in Wassermann's view, was reproduced in abnormal rates of crime. He also linked this abnormality with two
other pathologies of modern Jewish life: higher suicide rates and lower
birth rates.

The environmental argument for Jewish criminality was made most
forcefully by Ruppin.[152] In his view, variations between Jews and Christians
in social standing, occupation, and education meant that these two groups
engaged in different types of crimes in different degrees. Christians committed far more crimes against the person, particularly violent physical
crimes and robbery. Jews, on the other hand, committed more "abstract"
crimes, involving trade and big business, or violations of moral codes and
public order. Their average higher standard of living in Germany
accounted, according to Ruppin, for the infrequency of crimes committed
by Jews against property. The overrepresentation of Jews in higher education explained the negligible involvement of Jews in "brutal" crimes involving physical force (although it also accounted for their higher participation
in the crime of dueling). Differences in occupational structure and
urban/rural concentration accounted for higher rates among Jews of crimes
involving business and the free professions (for instance, libel, or laws
against work on Sundays).[153]

In their analyses of criminality, Zionist social scientists relied heavily on the well-established "fact" of a heavy Jewish representation in modern finance and industry. As such, the connections they drew between Western Jewry, capitalism, and degeneration appear—perhaps uncomfortably—to parallel anti-Semitic characterizations of the time, and have led some to see in this an expression of "self-hatred" or "Jewish anti-Semitism."[154] Regardless of whether or not such judgments are germane, it should be made clear that, at least for Jewish social scientists, Jewish criminality provided evidence not only of degeneration, but also of Jewish intelligence, and hence of a "moral equality" with Christians. Analysis of Jewish criminality, like that of Jewish health and disease as a whole, functioned, therefore, not only as a means of critique, but also as *apologia*. Nossig, for instance, argued in his work of 1887 that Jews mainly commit "crimes of property," while Christians commit them "against the person." He saw this as proof of the injustice of the reproach of the Jews in connection with criminality, and as the "best evidence of their moral qualities."[155] In *Die Juden der Gegenwart* (1911), Ruppin placed his discussion of criminality within a chapter entitled "The Racial Worth of the Jews," in which he sought to justify the continued existence of Jewry as a separate nation and race.[156] The future of the Jews as a *Sondervolk*, or distinct and particular nation, depended in Ruppin's view upon their "worth." What did the Jews have to offer humanity that could justify their continued existence? Could the effort to preserve them as a separate *Volk*, through the means of Zionism, be defended? Here the particular and the universal met in Ruppin's thought, for the Zionist goal of a distinct and separate Jewish nation and race could only be justified if the Jews continued to contribute something unique to general human culture. In line with the Herderian stream in German nationalist thought, Ruppin conceived of the cultivation of a distinct Jewish national culture as a fulfillment of universal ideals and goals. This, however, depended upon the "worth" or "value" of Jewry. In other words, were the Jews an "inferior" people, as their critics claimed?

Ruppin first established that the Jews were indeed intellectually and artistically equal, if not superior, to Aryans.[157] He then turned to the question of "moral worth." Are the Jews, he asked, truly less worthy in terms of morals and character? "One cannot say anything with any certainty by observing individuals. Only observation of the mass offers the possibility of arriving at an objective judgment."[158] *Kriminalstatistik* offered this possibility. Clearly reacting to those who claimed that Jewish crime was both quantitatively greater and qualitatively different than that of Christians, Ruppin argued that "the result of all investigations is that Jewish crime is different, but no greater than Christian."[159]

Ruppin rejected the Italian (and Jewish) social scientist Cesare Lombroso's influential idea of the *delinquento nato*, or born criminal, as irrelevant in this case. Jews committed "occupational crimes," and the cause of this was surely socioeconomic, and not biological. He pointed to the higher standard of living enjoyed by Jews, their greater representation in higher education, greater concentration in trade and commerce, and greater settlement in urban areas.[160] Once established as environmentally determined, Jewish criminality could be effaced—at least theoretically—through nationalist regenerative efforts.

As a *Volk*, then, the Jews were different, but no less worthy than Christian Aryans. Jewish criminality, because its causes lay outside the nature of the Jews, should not impinge on the world's judgment of the Jews as a nation. At certain junctures, though, Ruppin was willing to entertain the idea that racial traits did play some small part in determining the differences in Jewish and Christian criminal behavior. Following Hoppe, he posited alcoholism as a racial, hereditary trait of Christians, and connected this etiologically with their proneness to brutality and violence. Jews, in turn, counted "greater cunning" as a racial characteristic, which made fraud on their part easier and more likely.[161] Yet this attribution of a negative racial trait to the Jews also carried within it a positive valuation. For even an analysis of Jewish criminality, bound up as it was with ideas about greater Jewish intelligence and learning, served at some level to raise and celebrate Jewry. Despite his stated distaste for the apologetic tendencies in Jewish *Wissenschaft*, Ruppin too seized the opportunity to use social science for just such purposes. Both the negative and the positive aspects of Jewish criminality served, therefore, to justify Zionist efforts of regeneration. Criminal statistics reinforced medical and anthropological statistics that demonstrated the underdevelopment of the Jewish body and the hyperdevelopment of the Jewish mind. On the one hand the Jewish body and mind were identified as diseased, and hence in need of the "cure" Zionism offered. At the same time, Jewish intelligence was interpreted as a sign of national and racial worth, and hence as justification for Jewish nationalist efforts.

The social scientific representation of Jewish crime, then, built upon more general assumptions about both Jewish and Christian character. The overcultivated Jewish mind or intelligence was the counterpart of the overdeveloped Christian body. Much of the Jewish social scientific literature, in fact, reproduced negative images of Christians—particularly lower-class or peasant Christians. The idea of the Gentile as "alcoholic" was a mainstay of popular and scholarly Jewish literature, and Jewish social scientists readily accepted this image, juxtaposing it, as we have seen, with the proverbial sobriety and moderation of Jews. The counterpart of the image of a traditional Jewish sexual propriety was an image of a Christian society characterized by high degrees of syphilis, prostitution, adultery, and illegitimate marriages and births. Statistics on lower child mortality rates among Jews were taken as proof that Jewish mothers loved their children more than did Christian mothers. Jewish women, it was argued, were better able and more willing to suckle their young; Jewish infants hence survived at greater rates.[162] Just as common was the more general argument that Jews as a whole valued and sanctified life to a greater degree than did Christians. Ruppin, for instance, offered the higher regard among Jews for the sanctity of life as a reason for the statistically higher rates of handicapped children found among them.[163] Unlike Christians, who traditionally did away with unwanted infants, Jews kept their children, healthy and unhealthy alike.

Significantly, the Zionist social scientific discourse on Jewish health and disease constructed a narrative of Jewish degeneration in which the dominant Christian society itself was diseased. Hence, assimilation into this society on the part of Jewry produced pathology and abnormality. In shifting the onus of blame from "inside" the Jewish body to external conditions, from "race" to the environment, Zionist social scientists identified Europe as pathogenic. In their encounter with the European discourse on Jewish health, these social scientists reproduced the image of the Jew as diseased and degenerate, yet, at the same time, they asserted that this pathological Jew was the creation of a pathological modern society and culture. Unlike Leo Pinsker and Theodor Herzl, for whom the "sickness" of European society had to do with the continuing presence of anti-Semitism (a "ghost" or remnant of a premodern sensibility), Zionist social scientists identified modern Europe itself as diseased. They demonstrated the impossibility of making the Jews normal within an abnormal environment. Neither isolation in the ghetto nor freedom in the West offered the chance of regeneration. Hence, only Zionism provided "a third way, an alternative to the degeneration and disappearance of European Jewry" (*Auflösung der Rasse oder physische Degeneration, als—den Zionismus*).[164]

By the first decade of the twentieth century, the "sickness of Jewry" had become, for many Jews as well as non-Jews, more than a metaphor. The "Jewish body," both individual and collective, was something that *was* diseased and degenerate, an entity that literally had to be healed. The anxious concern of Jewish statisticians and social scientists over the health of the "Jewish body" mirrored anxieties felt by social scientists, reformers, and social critics in almost every major European nation during this period. For Jewish social scientists, and for Zionists in particular, this discourse on social and racial degeneracy presented both challenge and opportunity. As scientists they "inherited" a body of literature that identified the Jewish body and mind as diseased, and that took physical and mental pathologies as signs of difference, abnormality, and incompatibility at the social, national, and racial levels. Jewish social scientists accepted, in different degrees, the conjunction of "Jewish" and "diseased." Yet science did not speak about the Jews univocally. Jewish social scientists constructed their own narratives of Jewish health and disease around the fundamental debate over causality. They emphasized the contingent historical and environmental origins of Jewish pathologies, and rejected the idea of either health or disease as a product of immutable racial traits. In so doing they opened up the possibility of progressive, meliorative change.

Thus far I have focused on this social scientific vision as it came to be conceived in Zionist terms, and for Zionist purposes. I want to now turn to those scholars who formulated an alternative vision, one rooted in the belief in the Diaspora as a still-viable space within which to reform and regenerate the Jews.

## CHAPTER FIVE

# The Diaspora as Cure
## Non-Zionist Uses of Social Science

In her *Reflections on Gender and Science*, the historian of science Evelyn Fox Keller has written that "science is the name we give to a set of practices and a body of knowledge delineated by a community, not simply defined by the exigencies of logical proof and experimental verification."[1] The social scientists with whom the present study deals were just such a community, united by a set of practices and a body of knowledge. These practices and this knowledge were "universal" insofar as they were not circumscribed by geographic, linguistic, or ideological boundaries. Without minimizing the significance of contextual differences—clearly, as I argue throughout, the work of Zionist and non-Zionist social scientists, or a German and an American Jewish social scientist, differed in important ways—I do nonetheless treat Jewish social scientists as a community. Despite such varying contexts, they shared a common set of practices and a body of knowledge.

As members of an interpretive community, Jewish social scientists were united by methodology, but also by certain key assumptions and notions: A faith in numbers and a belief in objective characteristics as signs of collective identity and status;[2] an environmentalist explanation for Jewish traits; a reformist, regenerationist agenda. They drew extensively on each other's research, as well as on the international literature produced about Jews by non-Jewish authorities. Many of them published in more than one language, in journals and books produced in countries other than their own.

At the same time, there were important differences and divisions within this community of scholars. Even if the numbers themselves—generated as they often were by outside, governmental agencies—were stable, and rarely open to contestation, their interpretation was not. The meanings or morals that could be derived from the statistics were many. It was the numbers, and the methods utilized to analyze them, that allowed an identifiable Jewish social scientific community to constitute itself, an intellectual community that transcended geographic and political boundaries. It was the various meanings derived from the numbers that differentiated members of this community ideologically.

Thus far I have focused on Zionist social scientists, who took a particular and conspicuous interest in the social scientific discourse generated about Jewry. Zionists, however, were not alone among Jews in actively engaging with the social sciences, or with making this knowledge serve particular political and social ends. In this chapter I turn to what I call "Diasporist" Jewish social scientists, to those who remained committed to the idea of a viable collective Jewish life in the Diaspora.

Despite this shared commitment, Diasporists were not uniform in their visions of the Jewish future in the Diaspora. There were those who believed that a return to health and normalcy could be obtained through a return to traditional forms or aspects of Jewish life: the nuclear family, religious law and custom, a modification of contemporary occupational patterns. Others insisted on health and normalcy as a product of the integration or assimilation on the part of Jewry into the surrounding Gentile society. Still others argued that integration, while a noble goal, ought to be rooted not in assimilation, but in the recognition and preservation of an already existing positive, even superior, status of Jewry as a people or race. We will deal with each in turn, in this and following chapters. Yet, as different as these visions were, they shared, to varying degrees, the belief in the continuing viability of the Diaspora. Whether Jews as a collective would be better served by a sort of retrenchment, a return to traditional Orthodox Jewish patterns of life, or by continuing on the path of assimilation that most everyone agreed was the dominant trend of the last century and a half, there existed a consensus that the future of the Jews lay in Europe and America (and not in Palestine).

## Visions of European Normalcy and Renewal

In an earlier chapter I discussed Felix Theilhaber's analysis of purported negative demographic trends within German—and by implication European—Jewry, and the lessons about the Jewish future he drew from the statistics. Theilhaber's arguments about the future of Jewry, as he himself related in the second edition of *Der Untergang der deutschen Juden* (1921), were not well received within the Jewish community, although they did receive favorable reviews in general scientific journals.[3] One of Theilhaber's severest critics was the demographer Jacob Segall. From 1908 onward Segall was codirector of the Bureau for Jewish Statistics in Berlin, and a prominent member of the leading liberal Jewish organization in Germany, the CV. If we examine Segall's objections more closely we can see the way in which a liberal, counter-Zionist position on the condition of Jewry could be staked out. Segall accused Theilhaber of carelessly employing statistics in order to prove a conclusion reached a priori, and of not fully comprehending the science of statistics.[4] Theilhaber, Segall argued, had based his thesis of Jewish decline on fertility statistics produced by a method recently proven incorrect. The older method of calculating Jewish fertility rates, upon which Theilhaber, Ruppin, and other Jewish social scientists continued to rely, had assumed a direct relation between the number of marriages in any single year and the number of births. Yet no such simple relation existed. Any given number of births in one year may be, and most likely was, the product of marriages entered into in the years before.[5]

Segall granted that German Jewry had experienced a decline in birth rates since the 1870s. But he denied that Jewish social scientists had the requisite knowledge to adequately explain this decline, and cast doubt on the ability of Jewish social scientists in general to say anything meaningful yet about Jewish demography:

We stand at the beginning of scientific research into the development and contemporary condition of German Jewry. Individual regions and communities are still unexamined. We know nothing about the impact of the migrations of German Jewry in the 1880s and 1890s on natural population increase, and the effect of immigrants on birth rates. And we are only now beginning to analyze, thanks to the recent census, the effects of the last thirty years of socioeconomic revolution on Jewish life. This certainly had much to do with decline in rates. Without the requisite preparatory work, it is senseless and irresponsible to speak of a loss of fertility among Jewry, or of the "decline of German Jewry."[6]

At the same time Segall did offer an alternative explanation for declining birth rates based on migration patterns. Theilhaber, he argued, mistakenly looked only at the beginning and end of the span of time designated for study. But a statistician, Segall declared, must pay attention to interim developments. Had Theilhaber studied the fluctuations in Jewish demographics during the interim decades, he would never have argued that the decline in Jewish population relative to non-Jews was a "natural" development, attributable to biophysical factors. Above all, he would not have argued that declining birth rates were the product of such natural causes.[7]

For Segall, migration best explained the drop in Jewish fertility. Economic depression and the rise in anti-Semitism during the 1870s and 1880s produced large-scale emigration. Jews lost significant numbers in terms of real loss, and in lower birth rates. "All German states witnessed a significant loss from emigration in the 1880s. . . . In Prussia alone approximately 40,000 Jews emigrated, among them many who were at the age of initial reproductive power."[8]

Segall's critique of Theilhaber shifted the focus of the discussion of declining birth rates onto factors other than the Jewish body itself: onto patterns of migration, and the limitations of the social scientific enterprise. On the one hand, this constituted a contribution to the further methodological refinement of Jewish statistics. In his own books and articles dealing with German Jewry, Segall incorporated both his epistemological skepticism about Jewish demography, and his insistence upon migration and socioeconomic patterns as fundamental factors in Jewish fertility rates.[9] On the other hand, one can locate a particular ideological impetus to Segall's debate with Theilhaber. German Jewry, in the former's view, was not, as Zionists claimed, unhealthy, abnormal, or degenerate. The relative youth of Jewish social science, combined with methodological difficulties, made Theilhaber's dramatic assertions about Jewish fertility highly questionable. Enough, however, was known, according to Segall, to comfortably assert that declining birth rates were the product of a variety of factors and were a complex historical and socioeconomic development. Moreover, the modern German Jewish experience was "normal" insofar as it paralleled developments among every other civilized society, within which heightened economic struggle led those within the middle and upper-middle classes to choose to produce fewer children in order to improve the chances of the children they had.

Thus Segall was intent on explaining trends in Jewish demography and economy along strictly sociological lines, thereby "normalizing" them. This included, as I have said, an attention to methodological questions not always evinced by fellow Jewish social scientists. In a 1913 article on the Munich census of 1907, for example, Segall sought to explain the following trend: between 1880 and 1895 the general Jewish population of Munich rose by 47.65 percent; the "Berufsbevölkerung," that is, the wage-earning population (save for servants), rose by 91 percent. This dramatic increase saw a reversal in the years 1895–1907, when the general population rose by 40 percent, but the wage-earning by only 32 percent. Segall was quick to point out that this decline is easily explicable once the categories of age and gender are factored in. In the earlier period there were large numbers of immigrants who were young, and of prime working age. They therefore accounted for the precipitous rise in the number of wage earners. The latter period witnessed a saturation of the employment market, and the immigrant population was made up to a greater extent of women, children, and the elderly.[10] What is of import here is Segall's choice of explanation. As he did elsewhere, Segall invoked reasons or causes for Jewish "decline" that shifted the burden away from the nature of the Jews, away from their purported character (i.e., Theilhaber), or some fundamental condition or component of modern Jewish life such as assimilation (Ruppin, Zollschan, and others). For Segall, explanations lay elsewhere: in transitory conditions such as migration patterns, or in larger European or global trends.

There were other Jewish social scientists who shared Segall's Diasporist vision, but who were less sanguine about contemporary Jewry's "health" or well-being, less willing to explain "decline" with reference to external trends or methodological inadequacies. Like many others, for instance, Louis Maretzki, a *Sanitätsrat* and the head of B'nai Brith in Berlin, believed that the Jews suffered from certain degenerative illnesses, particularly nervous and mental disorders. The Jewish past and present combined to bring about the fact that "in almost every land in the world the Jews suffer from nervousness" (*fast im allen Ländern der Erde sind die Juden nervös*).

Jewish history is filled with persecutions, expulsions of the Jewish masses from countries and cities. Hate, contempt, disdain, insult and setbacks of all types were suffered by the Jews until most recent times. The eternal *Angst* and uncertainty have exercised a significant impact on their nervous systems, and produced constant unrest. Two thousand years of such treatment have inflicted deep wounds on the soul of the Jew; these scars of the soul have made him markedly nervous. . . . Hand in hand goes aggravation in occupational relations.[11]

Maretzki had been an early advocate of Jewish statistics, a member of the Verein für jüdische Statistik planning committee, and of the initial research working group in Berlin. He shared a faith in statistics and social science, and in the power of environment to transform the Jews. Yet for Maretzki the key to a renewal of Jewish collective health lay not in the ideal of the nation, but in the family. He saw no signs of a "revolutionary transformation" occurring within Jewish life; change, he argued, would necessarily come slowly.

The best immediate measure to effect a positive transformation would be "the acceleration of the sanitation/renovation process" (*Sanierungsprozeß*). This would be, above all, a matter of education (*Bildung*), which had to proceed from the family. "The family is the foundation of humanity. It is our entire communal life; it is essential not only to economic unity but also to the foundation of the total social body."[12]

Over the past few decades, Maretzki wrote, the Jewish family had suffered through a process of degeneration and disintegration. Here, too, modernity itself was to blame. ("Our age is merciless in destroying what our fathers held dear.") However, for Maretzki "modernity" meant the abandonment and destruction of the middle-class European values of hard work, obedience, and *Bildung*. Above all, modernity had destroyed the healthy patriarchal family structure, the "sacred hearth" from which "morality, the charm of veneration (*Zauber der Ehrwürdigkeit*), and a deeply ingrained *Gemütsfülle* emanate."[13] A return to the traditional organization of the family would serve as a catalyst for Jewish health: "The patriarchal family structure brings tranquillity, contentment, and sedateness into the family circle. It is an important and expedient means of battling against agitation of the nerves."[14] In full agreement with those who viewed the city or metropolis as a source of nervous illness, Maretzki argued that "it would be an improvement of the greatest kind to settle more Jews in small towns and villages." The "quiet life" there, the lack of stimulus, was a proven means for combating neurasthenia. However, Jewry was so tightly bound up with metropolitan urban life that meliorative efforts had to be taken there. Enumerating the many positive effects upon the health of working in the civil service, Maretzki argued for an increase in the number of Jews serving as lower- and middle-level government employees.[15]

Maretzki's analysis of Jewish health and disease served to legitimate Jewish life at the local, communal level. "Social" problems, he urged, were to be solved through "personal *Bildung* and communal reform." These, in turn, would produce a transformation of objective Jewish mental and physical conditions. Although he agreed with Zionist social scientists on many points, he nonetheless maintained a faith in the liberal, emancipationist ideal of Jewish integration and progress. Jewish "health," in his view, was attainable within German (and European) society.

Maretzki, like many other Jewish social scientists, insisted on a causal connection between aspects of modernity and Jewish communal decline. Others, however, insisted that the blame for Jewish degeneration could be assigned to a failure to modernize, to an incomplete accommodation to Western norms. The West was equated with health and normalcy; this was contrasted with the persistent image of the *Ostjude* as the "diseased Jew," whose "environment" produced a wide variety of psychopathologies.[16] Moritz Benedikt, a Viennese neurologist, attributed the high rates of Jewish mental disease mainly to the continued dominance of orthodox Judaism. Steeped in traditional religious modes of thought and behavior, the East European Jew was literally made ill by his adherence to orthodoxy. "From childhood on," he wrote in 1918, "especially in religious circles, the dialectics of the Talmud are forced on capable and incapable brains, whereby paralysis is actually bred."[17] For Hermann Oppenheim, a Berlin neurologist, the combination of poverty and oppression, and the overemphasis on traditional religious study explained the high incidence of mental and nervous disorders. Both analyses represented a continuity with Maskilic, or Jewish Enlightenment, critiques of traditional Jewish life in Eastern Europe, and both sought to reinforce the notion of Western European Jewry as the embodiment of health and normalcy. Assimilation into modern Western society and culture in this case represented the best hope for a healthy, regenerated Jewry in the future. Difference, judged as a negative condition, was defined as a nonessential state of being, to be overcome through the positive work of integration.

Still other Jewish social scientists held up the model of the Eastern European ghetto as the environment most conducive to Jewish health, while identifying the forces of secularization as corrosive. The prominent Russian Jewish anthropologist and physician Samuel Weissenberg summarized and reformulated this approach in his writings on Jewish health and disease. Weissenberg, although sympathetic to the cause of Zionism, remained committed throughout his career to the idea of the viability of Jewish life in the Diaspora, and to the goal of political and cultural autonomy for the Jews of Eastern Europe.[18] In his articles on Judaism and health, Weissenberg presented both a counterargument to anti-Semitic theories of Jewish biological degeneration and an affirmation of a continued Jewish existence in Europe.[19] He stressed the ability of the Jews—as a community, nation, and race—to survive and flourish in numerous and diverse places, despite historical and contemporary oppression.

Weissenberg defined Jewish social biology as a set of "social hygienic practices and rules that over the centuries have contributed to the survival of the Jewish people."[20] He traced its origins back to the Bible, where one could find "the commandments for a cultivation [*Züchtung*] of racial purity, the laws regarding resistance to infectious diseases, the rules of waging successful war, and so forth." The Talmud reinterpreted and strengthened these rules and customs so as to meet the new and changing conditions of Diaspora life. Physical health, in his view, was inextricably bound up with Jewish religious tradition and community.

Weissenberg sought through the medicalization of the Jewish past to assign social and racial hygienic significance to traditional religious practices, and thereby to make Judaism relevant to the modern scientific world. (Although he also insisted that not everything modern culture and science found meaningless or useless was necessarily so.)[21] This was a desire shared by many Jews throughout Europe and America during this period. Already in 1894 Alfred Nossig had published a study on social hygiene and Judaism in which he sought to demonstrate that the classical Jewish texts—Bible, Talmud, Mishneh Torah, Shulhan Aruch, and so forth—were, first and foremost, guides to individual and collective health and hygiene.[22] In 1911 and again in 1926 German Jewish communities officially took part in public hygiene exhibitions held in Germany. Jewish representatives stressed the hygienic and eugenic import of biblical and Talmudic laws, and the conjunction between ancient Jewish and modern European notions of health and purity.[23] An abundant literature was produced, by both Jews and non-Jews, during the years 1880–1930 on the subject of modern medicine and ancient Judaism, much of it seeking to establish an equivalence of knowledge and value between contemporary science and biblical/Talmudic law.[24]

Weissenberg did feel compelled to discount explicitly the rhetoric of such an equivalence. "One can believe that Moses saw God," he wrote; "however, he never saw trichina." Nonetheless, in his opinion the effects of Jewish religious law were wholly beneficial, and akin in this respect to those produced by modern medicine and hygiene. The rules of *kashrut*, circumcision, ritual hand-washing, Passover cleaning, and rest on the Sabbath all possessed social hygienic value. For example, concerns over purity demanded that Jews defecate daily, Weissenberg explained. Yet he added that this was not an easy thing for many Jews to accomplish given their highly sedentary lives. Religious tradition, then, became the source of both health and illness. "It may be that this forced defecation is one of the causes for the fact that Jews suffer to such a degree from hemorrhoids . . . and hernias."[25]

Like other Jewish social scientists before him, Weissenberg stressed the causal connection between religious orthodoxy and abstinence or moderation in dietary, sexual, and familial matters; these, he asserted, bore directly upon Jewish health. "The Jews who are true to their faith and people" insured that a strong sexual ethic was passed on to their children. Evidence of this could be found in the extraordinarily low rates of illegitimate births among East European Jews, as well as in the low rates of venereal disease. (Like Hugo Hoppe and others discussed above, Weissenberg simply asserted that Jews were moderate when it came to alcohol; it was a social scientific truism he felt no compunction to prove.) This moderation, in conjunction with moderation in matters of diet and "familial morality," helped account for the lower incidence of tuberculosis among Jews.

The hygiene of women, according to Weissenberg, had been of signal importance to Jewish sociobiology since ancient times. The biblical laws of purity regarding menstruation, pregnancy, and the ritual bath each produced a heightened concern for the level of health among Jewish women. The conservative impulse in Weissenberg's thought emerged clearly when he wrote about women, and what he understood as their correct place within the Jewish family and community, and within society as a whole.[26] Like Maretzki, Theilhaber, and many others, he believed Jewish health to be tightly bound up with a strong sense of family and moral purity. He therefore declared himself strongly opposed to the "weakening of the inurement to the passion of the erotic." He linked this weakening of moral

purity within the Jewish community to a rise in physical and social pathologies: "I am therefore against coeducation, and against all unrestricted
relations between the sexes. Observations made of my large clientele indicate that since the emergence of feminism (*Frauenfreiheiten*), premature
births among Jewish women have become more common, and abortions
among unmarried girls more frequent."[27]

Weissenberg found comfort, nonetheless, in the fact that Jewish women
were not employed outside the home. "I am not ashamed of this," he
announced, "either as a Jew or a human being, since all gynecologists are
united in this: that work on the part of women can only be damaging."
Jews, he continued, have long understood that the only rightful place for a
woman was in the home. Support for these contentions could be found in
the "remarkable fact" that Jews in Russia showed a lesser mortality rate
than any other national group (one-half of the average rate). This, Weissenberg concluded, indicated that Jewish women defined themselves, first
and foremost, as mothers; hence the greater love and care they gave their
children resulted in lower death rates.[28]

Noting the ongoing debate in scientific circles over Jewish immunity to
particular infectious and acute diseases, Weissenberg stated the definitive
conclusions he believed could be derived from the data: 1) Jews were not
naturally immune to any particular diseases; 2) the relation of Jews to a disease differed according to the particular disease. They suffered less from epidemic diseases, while their relation to endemic illnesses was akin to that of
Christians; 3) the death rate was in all cases lower; 4) the causes for 2) and 3)
were external rather than internal; 5) the relation of Jews to disease was not
constant, but changed from place to place. This was proof, again, that scientists were dealing not with racial but with environmental phenomena.[29]

All of the statistical and observational material gleaned from an investigation into Jewish social hygiene indicated, according to Weissenberg, that
the Jews "suffer no inferiority" relative to other nations or peoples. Yet, he
added, "despite this shining image, the general demographic picture of
Jewry is anything but radiant." He called attention to the "terribly low
birth rates still plaguing Jewry," referring to Theilhaber's study of German
Jewry, and his own statistics on Elisavetgrad—which he argued reflected
the condition of Russian Jewry as a whole. The population increase within
Jewry, during the years 1901–15, was negligible. The postwar period had
shown some improvement, but this was short-lived. "Whether or not the
anti-Semites, and many Semites, whose rest has been disturbed by the
threat of a possible invasion of Europe by *Ostjuden*, will find reassurance in
this remains open to question."[30]

Weissenberg also argued that Russian Jewry, while "normal" physically,
suffered disproportionately from neuropsychiatric disorders. He rejected

the notion of a "neuropathic predisposition" to insanity among Jews. But there existed "a definite excitability, and a tendency to neurosis." The question of whether or not this was a degenerative condition or the consequence of specific exhausting undertakings, combined with living in the city, required, in his opinion, further investigation.

For Weissenberg, the promise of Jewish mental and physical health resided neither in the modern West nor in Palestine. Although a nationalist, he did not share the Zionist belief in a non-European solution to the Jewish Question. Nor did he share the antimodernist sentiments that characterized so much of the Zionist social scientific analysis. Rather, he envisioned a reconciliation in Europe of modernity and religion, moderated by social hygiene. He placed great emphasis, as did Zionists, on "Jewish culture," but defined culture predominantly in terms of religion and tradition. Jewry's future existence depended in his view upon the reinvigoration of the definition of the Jewish religion as the core of Jewish social hygiene. This was necessary because "fundamentally, social hygiene and religion in Judaism can hardly be separated, and modern life demands a modernization of religious deeds appropriate to general cultural progress."[31] Although he believed in the possibility of a "healthy" Jewish future in Eastern Europe, Weissenberg shared with Zionist social scientists the conviction that "assimilation" into modern European life had proven detrimental. The Jewish encounter with modernity had to be mediated through a return to traditional Judaism, and this demanded a degree of separation, even isolation from the surrounding culture and society.

## Assimilation and the Virtues of America

By the last quarter of the nineteenth century concerns over national identity and health were being voiced not only in Europe but also in the United States. North American social scientists and medical authorities played a crucial role in the developing debate over national identity, a debate that was framed increasingly in the language of racial biology and medicine. While concern over the "racial" identity and health of the American nation continued to focus on black Americans, the impact of Jews and Italians was also of interest and concern. The focal point of anthropological and medical investigations into the Jewish body was the Eastern European immigrant population, which had begun arriving in massive numbers in the 1880s. In the Gilded Age, and after, "the traditional fear of decay often centered on the new immigrants, presumably primitive and unassimilable."[32]

The historian of American social science Dorothy Ross is certainly correct in insisting that we understand the growth of American social science mainly within the context of American history and thought. In her words, "American social science bears the distinctive mark of its national origin."[33] Nonetheless, as Ross herself points out, there were also important similarities and continuities between American and European social sciences. By the end of the nineteenth century at the latest, the major forces that had acted as an impetus to social scientific research in Europe—industrialization, and a bit later immigration—were also at work in the United States. Moreover, science itself was "universal," insofar as the categories, methods, and assumptions "traveled" across national and linguistic boundaries. Hence, the contours of the debate over "the social question," the "immigrant question," and "the Jewish Question," in the United States paralleled but also intersected with those in Europe.

Thus, for example, in America, as in Europe, the census statistics provided evidence, so it was claimed, of a dramatic decline in native (i.e., Anglo-Saxon) birth rates, and a concomitant rise in the immigration of "strange peoples." This demographic imbalance was taken as a crucial indicator of a broader threat to traditional American values and society. Anti-Jewish and nativist forces railed at the impoverishment, uncleanliness, and "strange" social and cultural customs of the immigrants. In 1890 the Federal Census Office in Washington, D.C., published a supplement to the decennial census entitled "Vital Statistics of the Jews in the U.S." John Shaw Billings, the director of the study, and the author of the report, was officially attached to the U.S. Army, and acted as a special agent for the Census Bureau.[34] Billings began his report by situating its findings within the ongoing debate over European immigrants, their vital statistics, and the extent to which these were or might be modified by the new conditions in the United States. To what extent, Billings asked, have "any special influences" in the United States exerted an appreciable impact on members of "the Jewish race"? A separate census was necessary, as Billings himself related, because the U.S. government did not ask about religious affiliation on the regular census. The Jews, as Billings well knew, were regarded at least officially as a religious group. His categorization of the Jews as a race is therefore revealing.

It is clear that his intent was to construct a portrait of Jewish difference through the statistical findings, a difference that extended beyond the religious. For instance, he noted that Jews in America fall into different social classes. Of the families responding, 3,996, or about one-third, reported "keeping no servants," while the remainder, or 6,622, "kept one or more servants, and may, therefore, be presumed to have been in easy circumstances." Billings then continued: "It is somewhat remarkable that there should be so little difference of the vital statistics of these two classes, and this difference is for the most part in the opposite direction from that which usually occurs under such circumstances, the average death and birth rates being somewhat less in the poorer classes than those keeping servants." The statistics showed such a notable divergence of the Jewish pattern from "other races in this country" that for a moment Billings wondered about the accuracy of the data. But he quickly reaffirmed its general accuracy. So the divergence must have lain with the Jews themselves, in an identity or nature that belies social or class stratification.[35]

Billings sought to establish identity and difference chiefly through statistical tables. His report lacked the sort of biological or racial determinist language that had gained greater prominence already by the end of the nineteenth century, and that characterized the much fiercer rhetoric of anti-Semitic nativists. Jews came to be described more and more as "parasites," "germs," and in similar terms drawn from biology and medicine. These metaphors were given enormous power by the very real dangers posed by contagious diseases such as typhus and cholera, diseases associated with Southern and Eastern European immigrants.[36] Yet, as the historian of medicine Howard Markel has suggested, the episodic nature of these diseases, and the fact that the panic they engendered passed rather quickly, meant that they were less than fully effective as metaphors of long-term racial and medical danger. Far more effective was the danger associated with genetic inheritance of negative traits. This provided "a stronger and more permanent metaphor of disease" with which to characterize the danger posed by immigration, and by extension all "alien" groups. Inheritable diseases and defective genes were passed on from generation to generation; hence, they were a threat not only to the present, but also to the future of the American social body.[37]

Informed as it was by this eugenic impulse, American anti-Semitism, like its European counterpart, had a "clearly identifiable genetic component inextricably linked with the restriction of the 'new' immigration of white ethnics from southern and eastern Europe prior to 1924."[38] Clearly influenced by European racialist thinkers such as Joseph-Arthur Comte de Gobineau, Georges Vacher de Lapouge, and Houston Stewart Chamberlain, American racialists identified the Jews as an "asiatic" or "oriental" race. The Jews were, therefore, deemed incompatible with, and unassimilable to, the Anglo-Saxon race, which, it was argued, created and continued to define the United States.

Evidence of this unassimilability was found in the Jewish anatomy and physiology, in Jews' deformed and disease-prone bodies. This physical deformation—attributed variously to Jewish "inbreeding" (i.e., endogamy) born of racial pride, or historical intermixture with inferior Eastern or Oriental breeds (e.g., the medieval Chazars)—was genetic or biological, and hence presented a grave threat to the racial purity and health of America.

Restrictionists in the decades prior to 1924, the year in which the U.S. Congress succeeded in passing highly restrictionist legislation, referred repeatedly to the physical and moral degeneration of Jewry, and to the threat this posed.[39] In sum, American nativists and anti-Semites, in the words of Alan Kraut, "sought to sketch the Jew as a public health menace, one who might end up on the public relief roles in droves, deficient in the physical vitality to stand the test of the rugged American environment, as did the pioneer forbears of the native-born and the sturdier stock that had emigrated to the United States from Northern and Western Europe."[40]

The emergence in the last half of the nineteenth century of an "international" anti-Jewish discourse that employed the methods and categories of the social sciences meant that those Jews trained in these disciplines were particularly well equipped to respond. It was the task of social scientists sympathetic to the goals of immigration and integration to provide the empirical, scientific evidence for the viability of assimilation, and to thereby counter the nativist and anti-Semitic position. The best-known example of such an attempt was the work on immigrant anatomies published by the eminent German Jewish anthropologist Franz Boas.[41] Boas sought to influence directly, through science, the shape of political debate and social policy, which bore directly on the future of Jewish immigration into the United States. Nor is it difficult to see the personal component to his professional and political commitment. He was himself a Jewish immigrant to the United States, having settled in New York City permanently in 1897, ten years after marrying Marie Krackowizer, who was born and had been raised in New York. Without lapsing into reductionism here, it seems clear that Boas's positive formulation of immigration and assimilation, as a process that would result in a "new type of American," was at least in part motivated by his own personal experience.[42]

Boas's earliest forays into the study of headforms included the Jews. In 1903 he published "Heredity in Headform" in the *American Anthropologist*, in which he examined the relationship between inheritance and headform in light of Mendel's recently rediscovered work.[43] He included data on 49 Jewish families, data compiled by the New York physician and anthropologist Maurice Fishberg, with whom we shall deal at length in a moment. Fishberg's research also found its way into Boas's best-known study of race, immigration, and assimilation, *Changes in Bodily Form of Descendants of Immigrants*.[44] This work on the relation between immigration and anatomical formation constituted part of a much larger study undertaken by numerous social scientists on behalf of the U.S. Congress Immigration Commission. Published in 1911, in 40 volumes, the study "symbolized the high point of political propaganda for immigration restriction before the immigration laws were enacted in the twenties."[45]

The political impulse behind Boas's contribution, however, was anti-restrictionist. He granted, as he put it in a 1908 letter, that the new immigrants coming into the country, from East, Central, and South Europe, were different from the "tall blonde Northwestern type of European." "And the question has justly been raised, whether this change of physical type will influence the marvelous power of amalgamation that our nation has exhibited for so long a time."[46]

Boas suggested that the investigation "be directed toward an inquiry into 1) the assimilation or stability of type, and 2) changes in the characteristics of the development of the individual." Intensive anthropometric investigations would reveal the extent to which forces such as "selection" in the immigration process, intermarriage, and environmental changes affect bodily form over generations.[47] If, as Boas had indeed come to believe, environmental factors significantly influenced the typology of immigrants, then "all fear of an unfavorable influence of South European immigrants upon the body of our people should be dismissed."[48]

Boas focused his research into "changes in bodily form" on the shape of the head, since this was taken by almost every anthropologist at the time to be the most "stable" of anatomical traits. In 1908 he studied Russian-Jewish boys in City College and two public high schools. As George Stocking writes, this anthropometric investigation yielded unexpected results. Rather than the stability of headform that anthropologists took as a given, Boas found significant modification in immigrant children's head shape. This divergence between generations indicated that the American physical and social environment exerted a marked impact on the anatomy of these new Americans. Further anthropometric studies of Italian and Jewish immigrant skulls revealed a plasticity of head shape that, Boas argued, demonstrated the powerful impact of environment and culture on anatomy.

The investigation has shown much more than was anticipated. There are not only decided changes in the rate of development of immigrants, but there is also a far-reaching change in the type—a change which cannot be ascribed to selection or mixture, but which can only be explained as due directly to the influence of environment. . . . It has been stated before that, according to all our experiences, the bodily traits which have been observed to undergo a change under American environment belong to those characteristics of the human body which are considered the most stable. We are therefore compelled to draw the conclusion that if these traits change under the influence of environment, presumably none of the characteristics of the human types that come to America remain stable. The adaptability of the immigrant seems to be very much greater than we had a right to suppose before our investigations were instituted.[49]

As Elazar Barkan and George Stocking make clear, Boas well understood the political implications of his results, and was not at all reticent about directly using them to fight against immigration restrictions.[50]

Boas presented these same findings, albeit in a greatly abbreviated form, in a paper delivered to the First Universal Race Congress, held in London in 1911. The European Jewish immigrant figured prominently here as well. "Thus, among the East European Jews the head of the European-born is shorter than the head of the American-born. It is wider among the European-born than it is among the American-born. At the same time the American-born is taller."[51] Significantly, Boas did not sever the purported link between bodily form, and particularly headform, and mental or moral characteristics or abilities. This link was central to racial anthropology, and racial science in general. A good deal of the power of racial thought derived, of course, from this notion that nonphysical traits, or an individual's internal life, could be deduced from external or physical traits. But Boas did argue that the instability or plasticity of human type meant that one could expect a plasticity of mind or character as well. If environmental forces worked to transform the physical, they would do the same for the mental and the spiritual.

American Jewish psychiatrists took a particular interest, of course, in the question of purported Jewish mental and nervous disorders. Like their European counterparts, these scientists conceded that modern Jews suffered from a host of mental and physiological maladies. The psychiatrist and Freud translator A. A. Brill, for instance, argued in a number of articles published in the 1910s that the rates of insanity and nervous disorders among Jews decreased in direct proportion to the rates of assimilation.[52] Brill explained the high rates of mental and nervous disorders among Jews as a product of two main factors: a strong racial and religious identity and sensibility, which manifested itself historically in separation from the non-Jewish environment; and the persecution and oppression suffered by Jews throughout the ages, which also led Jews to live alone, "apart from other humans."

This isolation, in turn, produced in the Jew a far stronger sense of, and reliance on, the family (*Familiensinn*). Unlike Maretzki, Brill linked this emphasis on family with pathology: "No race shows so much attachment to family and racial ties as the Jew. . . . My own observation convinces me that the *Familiensinn* among Jews is so strong that it savors of the abnormal. . . . My feeling about the abnormal character of the Jewish family attachments was forced upon me by years of psychiatrical observation among Jews of all classes."[53]

Brill's solution to this problem of Jewish neurosis was freedom from the constraints and demands of the Jewish past, especially the oppression of religious orthodoxy. "Freedom of environment undoubtedly begets free individuals," he wrote; emancipation and assimilation are essential to mental health. Of course, too rapid an assimilation could also produce mental disease. "The sensitive Hebrew nature, formed throughout the centuries, cannot be transformed into that of a well-adjusted western individual without being subjected thereby to profound and even dangerous modification."[54] Making the biblical/rabbinical Jew into the modern Jew is a very difficult process. Moreover, "even in the most modern Jew one can observe the manifestations of maladjustment." In this case, neurosis stems from the assimilation process. There is a too-powerful desire to belong, to make oneself into a non-Jew in everything but name, and there are barriers to this.

In the end, Brill asserted that all Jews go through this "great struggle" between the past and the present, the old religion and the new world. "[A] great many succumb in this conflict either in the form of a nervous or mental breakdown or in some criminal act. Almost all of them become alienated from their religion. They do not seem to realize that they can become thoroughly Americanized and still remain Jews." The best means of prevention or cure is "a gradual process of Americanization, or assimilation."[55] Brill stressed education, and the role of the teacher in this process. If the young Jew is taught by an assimilated Jewish teacher at school, but an orthodox Jew at home, in private lessons, then this continues the classic tension. Orthodox teachers must therefore be replaced by "thoroughly Americanized Jewish ones who could harmonize Judaism with American ideals."[56]

Much the same sort of analysis can be found in the work of the Boston physician and professor of neurology, Abraham Myerson. Myerson insisted that "there is no difference of opinion about the liability of the Jews to psychoneuroses. Step into any clinic for nervous diseases in any large city in Europe and America and the Jew is unduly represented amongst the patients."[57] Like Brill, Myerson argued that the nervousness of the Jew could be traced back to the external persecution and internal isolation that characterized so much of Jewish history in Europe; that is, to environmental, not biological, factors. The oppression and isolation imposed on the Jews produced a particular anthropological and sociological type: physically weak but intellectually overdeveloped. Legally excluded from landed, agricultural pursuits, the Jews became an "exclusively" urban people, and this produced the ideal conditions for nervousness. "That urban life develops neurasthenia and the like conditions is an old story." Moreover, the Jews grew increasingly "clannish" and isolated, eventually living in ghettos. The ghetto life "was not only unwholesome physically, but unwholesome mentally, emotionally, and spiritually. . . ." As a result, "the bulk of the race was undernourished, underdeveloped, and overstimulated mentally and emotionally."[58]

The remedy to these ills lies in greater integration into the general environment. This demands, on the one hand, a desire on the part of the Jews to assimilate, and, on the other hand, an openness on the part of the non-Jewish society that allows this to occur. "How quickly racial characters can be changed under a fostering environment may be exemplified by the development of the last generation in Jewish life in the free countries of Europe and America. Intermarriage, especially in Germany, Scandinavia, and France, is so extraordinarily prevalent that, unless checked, the Jew will disappear in these countries, to be merged into the general population."[59]

Clearly, Myerson viewed assimilation as a double-edged sword. The conditions of freedom allowed for greater social interaction, and for intermarriage, and hence produced the sort of concern over demographic decline and disappearance voiced by social scientists in Europe. "What persecution could not do throughout the centuries, toleration does in a generation." At the same time, the positive results of assimilation were undeniable. The negative qualities historically attributed to the Jews vanished: stinginess and miserliness, dislike for physical sport and combat, excessive intensity in matters intellectual and financial. Myerson touted the Jewish prizefighter in America, "who in the weights, from the lowest up to the light heavy-weight, outclasses proportionately to his numbers any race. The race that produces so many Phi Beta Kappa scholars likewise produces the champion prize fighter."[60]

Ultimately, then, assimilation into the American environment was a necessary and healthy process. Myerson, again like Brill, granted that the dissolution of traditional Jewish modes of thought and behavior produced its own psychoneuroses among first-generation American Jews. A radical shift in ideals and "life-governing notions" destabilized many. However, the second generation, "brought up in American methods, learning early to fight physically, taking part in athletics in ever-increasing numbers, discarding the intensely communal life of the past, coming into contact with the less emotional, more controlled life of the neighboring Gentile, is being changed in character, has much less liability to the psychoneuroses."[61]

Boas, Brill, and Myerson provide clear evidence of the assimilatory impetus to the social scientific discourse on Jewry, and vividly illustrate the way in which issues of personal identity, scholarly activity, and politics came together in research on Jews. (Indeed, at the beginning of his article on the "nervous Jew," Myerson stated explicitly that his interest and expertise in these matters derived not only from his training as a neurologist, but also from his identity as a Jew, as one "familiar with the intimate life and history of his people.")[62]

This sort of advocacy of melioration through assimilation could be found in the work of sociologists as well as of anthropologists and psychologists. The sociologist Charles Bernheimer, writing on Jewish health

conditions in Philadelphia, conceded that nearly all medical authorities—
including Mandelstamm, Engländer, Richard Krafft-Ebing, and Jean-Mar-
tin Charcot—recognized that the Jews are prone to nervous and mental disorders; it is a "medical axiom." This predisposition is hereditary, a "racial
predisposition transmitted through generations."[63] Bernheimer, like Myerson and Brill, spoke of a Jewish race, and of Jewish racial traits. Yet he
insisted that these traits were mutable, a product of history and environment. A combination of the will to adapt and assimilate, and a healthy environment, will cure the nervous Jew. "With all his proverbial tenacity of
character, the Jew, and especially the Eastern Jew, is physically and psychi-
cally extremely plastic, and only needs a reasonably favorable environment
to develop into a noble specimen of man. His energy, intelligence, and
integrity will solve many of the perplexing economic problems, and in that
way the sanitary and hygienic questions will, partly at least, be answered."[64]

In his well-known 1928 study *The Ghetto*,[65] the American Jewish sociologist Louis Wirth set out to discover "the extent to which the isolation [of
the ghetto] has shaped the character of the Jew and the nature of his social
life. What are the forces that maintain his isolation, and in what ways has it
become modified by contact?" After tracing the origins and development
of the Jewish ghetto over the centuries, and then analyzing the institutional
structures of the ghetto, Wirth turned to "the Jewish type." He referred to
the debate among anthropologists and sociologists over the definition of
Jews: Are they a race, a nation, a religious or cultural group? Have they
maintained their "purity," or are they a mixture of different races and peoples? Wirth argued that the Jews lack any real physical trait that can identify them. "Among modern anthropologists the notion of 'pure' races is no
longer seriously entertained. The Jews are apparently a hybrid people, like
all the rest."[66]

Nonetheless, there is an argument that "their peculiar historical experiences have contributed to maintaining a fairly close adherence to the characteristics which they displayed when they first appeared on the European
scene, nearly two thousand years ago. . . . Ever since Darwin, isolation has
been recognized as one of the basic factors in the development of biological variations. The Jews therefore furnish a crucial experiment."[67] To the
factor of physical isolation must be added the practice of inbreeding, which
has "tended to develop a physical type."[68] Wirth conceded that inbreeding,
together with other factors, has produced an increased number of "defec-
tives" in the Jewish population. Jewish authorities, Wirth was quick to
point out, have convincingly demonstrated this.[69] The ghetto here is an
unwholesome environment in biological terms. It has produced a weakened, pathological organism. In these passages the Jews are a race, acquir-
ing and genetically passing along over generations particular characteristics.

But in the end Wirth returned to a repudiation of a racial definition of Jewry. The "Jewish type" is "less than skin deep."[70] Ultimately, it is the externals—dress, side-curls, hat, and so forth—that define the "look" of the Jew. Wirth acknowledged that there is such a thing as a distinct physical shape to the Jew, a bend of the body, a look in the eyes, that is the product of the ghetto. But it is an acquired characteristic, and therefore not immutable. Wirth's analysis, like that of other integrationists, allowed him to argue that Jewish identity was fluid or permeable. That the isolation of the ghetto had produced a distinct Jewish "type," more or less uniform despite geographic dispersion, was granted. However, this "type" was mutable, given a transformation in environment. Writing in the last half of the 1920s, which witnessed the increasingly public presence of Nazism in Germany, and a successful anti-immigration campaign in the United States, Wirth's scientific assertions about Jewish adaptability possessed a clear political resonance.

A similar faith in the powers of assimilation can be found in the work of the American Jewish sociologist Julius Drachsler. In 1920 Drachsler, who at the time was an assistant professor of Economics and Sociology at Smith College, published *Democracy and Assimilation*.[71] Drachsler's main purpose in the book was to offer a defense for immigrant assimilation and cultural pluralism. Moreover, his work offers an excellent example of the way in which the scholarship of European Zionist social scientists could be appropriated by an American Jewish social scientist and used to support an integrationist position.

Drachsler believed that the key to a much-needed rational social policy on immigration and assimilation lay with intermarriage statistics. "These furnish concrete, measurable quantities and can be made to serve as an index of ethnic fusion."[72] The Jews furnished, in his view, a happy example of the meliorative effects of assimilation, including intermarriage. Following the analyses of Ruppin, Zollschan, and others, Drachsler argued that emancipation had engendered among the Jews "an increasing tendency to amalgamate with the peoples among whom the Jews happened to live. This holds especially of the western European countries." He then reproduced Ruppin's "four classes of Jews" and quoted his conclusion: "the more Jews and Christians mix with one another in economic and social life, the more likely is it that they will intermarry with one another." As Ruppin and others insisted, it is social and cultural, not biological or racial, differences that prevented and continue to prevent Jews and Christians from intermarrying.

Unlike Ruppin, Drachsler believed the increase in intermarriage among Jews to be a positive phenomenon. Assimilation and amalgamation were for him the greatest balms to American democracy. So even the relatively low rate of Jewish intermarriage in New York City and America in general was for him a cause for celebration, since—as Jewish social scientists demonstrated—it was due to social, not racial, factors.

## Maurice Fishberg and the Jewish Politics of Jewish Assimilation

The most comprehensive and systematic social scientific justification for Jewish assimilation can be found in the writings of Maurice Fishberg, a Jewish physician and physical anthropologist. Fishberg emigrated to the United States from Russia in 1889. By the early 1900s he had established himself, through his writings and professional work, as an authority on contemporary Jewry.[73] In particular, his position as chief medical examiner for the United Hebrew Charities of New York offered him direct access, as both physician and physical anthropologist, to Eastern European Jewish immigrants. He conducted anthropometric measurements, and examinations for physical and mental disorders.[74] These empirical studies were supplemented with the extensive physical anthropological and medical literature on the Jews produced by European and American authorities.

Fishberg was the integrationist counterpart of Arthur Ruppin. His books and articles published during the first two decades of the twentieth century contain the most comprehensive and systematic social scientific justification for Jewish assimilation. Fishberg's analysis was impelled, on the one hand, by specific developments within the United States: the mass immigration of Eastern European Jews into New York and elsewhere, beginning in the last quarter of the nineteenth century; the extreme poverty of these immigrants, as well as their high rates of disease; and the racial anti-Semitism that took hold in important quarters, and that pushed for far tighter immigration restrictions.[75] In 1905 and again in 1907 Fishberg had traveled to Eastern Europe as anthropological consultant to the U.S. Bureau of Immigration. He had done so at the behest of the congressional committee investigating the immigration question. As noted above, his findings, together with earlier anthropometric investigations he had undertaken, were incorporated into Franz Boas's studies of immigrant headforms. Fishberg, in turn, incorporated Boas's research into headforms into his own writings on Jews.[76]

While his social scientific work on the Jews clearly grew out of the American context, Fishberg's work also owed a great deal to intellectual and political developments in Europe.[77] As a member of an international scientific community, he drew heavily on research conducted about Jews throughout Europe, and published in Russian, German, and other European journals. Writing in German as well as in English,[78] Fishberg addressed his work to an audience both within and beyond the United

States. His social scientific work must be understood as a product not only of the particular American political and social context, but also of the intellectual and political debates occurring mainly in Europe among Jewish elites. His analysis of modern Jewish life was driven in part by particular national (American) and local (New York) concerns. Yet it was also impelled by his antagonism to European Zionism, to what he believed to be the dangerously mistaken racial definition of Jewry advanced by some Jewish nationalists, and the "separatist" conclusions they drew from it. In the penultimate chapter of his magnum opus, *The Jews: A Study of Race and Environment*, published in 1911, Fishberg set forth in bold terms the ideological stakes of the social scientific debate over contemporary Jewry. The raison d'être of the Zionist movement, a movement he adamantly opposed,

is not only their sympathy with their suffering co-religionists in Eastern Europe, where they are being discriminated against politically, but is a sense of fear, of apprehension for the future of Judaism. In other words, although they maintain that the modern Jews are a race quite distinct from other racial elements in Europe and America; although they claim that they are a separate nation . . . ; and although they state a Jew can never become entirely a German, Frenchman, Englishman, or Italian in feeling and thought, they also confess that the most important fear they entertain is that the Jews are becoming estranged from the religion of their forefathers, discard their traditions, ideals, and aspirations as soon as they come in intimate social contact with the Christians.[79]

The Zionists' ardent efforts were aimed at preventing "the impending assimilation and perhaps fusion with the non-Jews." In pointing to the fear of decline and disappearance through the mechanism of assimilation, Fishberg identified a central concern of Zionist social scientists, if not of the Zionist movement as a whole. He also, insightfully, pointed to a chief paradox in Zionist thinking in this regard: Even as they insisted that the Jews, for religious, racial, or national reasons, could never successfully integrate into Gentile society, they decried that this was precisely what was rapidly occurring. Thus, "the assimilation of the Jews is not only possible, but has been going on since they have been emancipated in Western Europe."[80]

For Fishberg, Jewish assimilation—particularly into the United States— was not only possible but also highly desirable. It represented the remedy to Eastern European Jewish physical and mental disease. During a period of heightened hostility to immigration of East European Jews (among others) into the United States, Fishberg sought to counter the claims advanced by American nativists of a Jewish racial pathology that posed a physical and moral threat to the American nation. Utilizing European and American anthropological and medical statistical studies, he stressed the social and economic etiology of disease, and posited a direct correlation between the degree of assimilation into American society and the positive level of Jew-ish health.

In a 1903 work entitled *Health Problems of the Jewish Poor*, which origi-nated as a lecture to the United Hebrew Charities, Fishberg noted that "[t]he Jews, as is well known to every physician, are notorious sufferers of the functional disorders of the nervous system."[81] Jewish women com-monly suffered from "psychic injuries" associated with hysteria, men from neurasthenia. Both of these illnesses, and particularly the latter, were believed to be common and widespread among Americans (as well as Euro-peans) in general at this time. One might expect Fishberg, therefore, to have seen their spread among Jews as the sign of that successful assimila-tion he so desired. This, however, was not the case. While nervous disor-ders were more often than not associated in the medical literature with the middle classes, and the anxiety-ridden culture of capitalism, Fishberg denied any necessary connection between socioeconomic standing and ner-vousness.[82] In his speech before the Hebrew Charities, he linked Jewish nervousness with Jewish impoverishment and with an incomplete acclima-tization to the American work ethic. His concern, shared by his audience, was with Eastern European immigrant Jews, and the "pathology" of their incomplete assimilation.

Given his audience, it was not surprising that Fishberg's discussion of health revolved around the question "Is the Jewish condition an impedi-ment to productive labor?" Hebrew charities, he proposed, impeded rather than furthered the attainment of health by offering the poor an alternative to work. "The best cure for these people is to convince them that the char-ity organization society can do nothing for them. This brings them to their senses."[83]

Toward the end of the work Fishberg made clear the meliorative effects upon the Jewish body he believed inhered in a change in environment. The "small stature, the weak chest, the fragile skeleton" of the East European Jew were acquired traits, he insisted, and so were not necessarily passed on hereditarily through the generations. Like other Jewish social scientists who appropriated an Enlightenment model, he connected ill health in East-ern Europe with tradition (although he also gave credence to the vitalizing effects of religious laws and practices). In Russia the child was placed immediately into the heder, or elementary religious school: "The unsani-tary and unhygienic surroundings of those schools are well known to everybody, and it is rather surprising that any child is able to visit them daily for several years and come out alive."[84] There was no outdoor activity, he continued, only Bible and Talmud study. The healthy body was invari-ably "retarded" by such an experience. "Now contrast this with the condi-tion obtained in the United States," where Jewish children exercised out of doors, and schools were "models of hygiene." Even first-generation Jews were in far better physical condition than were their Eastern European counterparts:

They are taller, their chests and muscular systems are in better condition than those of their less happy brothers and sisters in Eastern Europe. They prove by this that the shortcomings of the Jews in European ghettos are more the result of cruel and malignant abuse, persecution and unjust oppression than a racial characteristic. Wherever he is given a chance to recuperate the Jew at once manifests a more remarkable regeneration of his physical self; he is becoming an entirely new man.[85]

This reference to the Jew becoming a "new man" through assimilation into American life paralleled, and in all likelihood consciously responded to, the well-known Zionist image of the "new Jew" or "new man."[86] The Zionist "new man" would come about, as we have seen, through the regenerative efforts of Jewish nationalism, including a return to the land and agricultural labor, and the creation of a majority Jewish polity and culture. Fishberg's vision of regeneration, in contrast, hinged on integration into the already healthy American environment, structured around just those values inimical to the Russian Czarist regime: freedom and tolerance. The social sciences, particularly physical anthropology and social medicine or hygiene, provided him with the tools to demonstrate scientifically that Jews could successfully assimilate, and when they did, this both contributed to and was reflected in their physical and mental health.

The interrelation between physical anthropology and assimilationism is just as evident in his 1905 study of Eastern European Jewry.[87] Working with comparative statistics on the stature, girth of the chest, headform, nose shape, and pigmentation of Jews and non-Jews throughout various regions in Eastern Europe, and among immigrant Jews in the United States, he set out to prove that 1) somatically, Jews differed little from the ethnic groups among whom they lived; 2) one finds a consistent variation, rather than a uniformity, between individual Jewish communities over geographic boundaries; and 3) physical traits were environmentally, not racially, determined acquired characteristics, and assimilation into a new milieu produced a transformation at the biophysical level.[88]

Jews were, on average, slightly deficient in stature, Fishberg claimed, compared with non-Jews. Yet they were always so in ratio to their neighbors, so that in environments where Christians were, for instance, taller on average, so too were Jews; this remained so even though Jews remained shorter relative to their neighbors. "It is of scientific interest to inquire into the reasons why the stature of the Jews depends to a great extent upon the stature of their neighbors: wherever the latter are short of stature the Jews display the same characteristic, and the reverse; but what is most remarkable, they are always somewhat shorter than the Gentiles."[89] This last fact, Fishberg explained, was due in part to the Jews having dwelled for centuries predominantly in towns and cities. "The general rule in Europe seems to be that the urban type is physically degenerate," he wrote, quoting the eminent American racial scientist William Ripley.[90]

In addition, "the wretched social, economic and sanitary conditions under which the Jews labor in Eastern European ghettoes will also account for the deficiency they display in bodily height when compared with their gentile neighbors." In Galicia, where conditions were worst, Jews were shortest; in Poland, they were somewhat taller, and in Southern Russia Jews were "quite tall." In each case, physical stature mirrored economic conditions. "Another indirect proof of this theory is the increase of stature of the first generation of Jews in New York City, where the social and economic conditions are much improved. . . . The superior stature of the native American Jews is thus seen to be a result of superior social conditions and environment."[91]

Fishberg proceeded in the remainder of the work to demonstrate the same point with reference to girth of chest, size and shape of the head, face and nose, and color of skin. Each of these categories allowed him to prove his point about physical traits, environment, and the assimilation process, and to respond to scientific anti-Semitic "truths."[92]

In contrast to Zionist and other Jewish nationalist social scientists, Fishberg offered his analysis as a scientific demonstration of assimilation as the agent of health and normalcy. It facilitated positive transformation at the physical and biological levels, and this transformation in turn was the sign or indication of assimilation's success. Despite the claims of opponents of Eastern European immigration that this "new breed" of immigrant represented a threat to the biological and physical health of the nation, Jews in the United States could be expected literally to "measure up" to native-born Americans.

One year later Fishberg made the same argument, only this time he broadened his analysis to include non-European Jews. In an article entitled "North African Jews," published in a volume dedicated to Franz Boas, Fishberg compared the anthropometric data on European and non-European Jews. He found that "[c]ontrary to the generally accepted theory that they have maintained their racial purity for centuries, research by modern anthropological methods has shown that the physical type of the Jews bears a striking resemblance to the ethnic types encountered in the indigenous races and peoples among whom they happen to live."[93] Fishberg appeared uninterested here in the mechanisms responsible for this resemblance. We are not told if it was due to intermarriage and interbreeding, to environmental factors, or to some other set of causes. Rather, Fishberg was interested in the results. Using data collected during a 1905 trip to North Africa, he compared statistics on height, hair and eye color, and cranial and facial shapes. The Jews of North Africa, he concluded, are far closer somatologically to Berbers, Arabs, and Kabyles than to Jews in Germany, France, or the United States. The Jews in Morocco and Tunis, for instance, are distinctly dolichocephalic, or long-headed, as are their non-Jewish neighbors. Jews in Europe, on the other hand, are overwhelmingly brachycephalic, or broad headed. Measurements of noses also proved the nonuniformity of the Jews as a race. Relying on his own observations as well as on the numbers, Fishberg discovered that the noses of North African Jews are "somewhat longer and narrower than in European Jews."

It is a striking fact, however, that while the idea that the Jews have a very large number of hooked noses is erroneous as regards Europe, only from about 10% to 15% having such noses, among the North African Jews such noses are still more rarely encountered. Only 5 of the 77 had such form of nose. While walking around the Jewish district in Algiers, Constantine, and Tunis, I was also struck with the rarity of hooked noses.[94]

The response to a scientific and popular anti-Semitic image of the Jew is clear here. Equally clear is the extent to which Fishberg relied on the racial anthropological framework to counter particular racialist arguments. Races or ethnic groups were dolichocephalic or brachycephalic; there did exist some relation between the shape of a nose and racial identity. Indeed, Fishberg went looking for the "Jewish" or hooked nose; that he was unable to find it in a majority of Jews he took as significant. While he sought, therefore, to discredit specific arguments about Jewish identity constructed out of racial language, Fishberg nonetheless accepted and used this language himself. In so doing, he justified and reinforced the very system of thought and images he was struggling with and against.

Less explicit in Fishberg's analysis of North African Jews is the way in which this text could function, indirectly, as further proof of the ability of Jews to assimilate physically into North American society. If the Jews of Europe and the United States resembled to a far greater degree non-Jewish Europeans and Americans than their "brethren" in Asia and Africa, then the argument of nativists about the racial unassimilability of Eastern Europeans was scientifically unfounded.

By 1911, and the publication of his magnum opus *The Jews: A Study of Race and Environment*, Fishberg was offering a more complex and ambivalent reading of Jewish identity, and on the questions of assimilation, modernity, and health. In three lengthy chapters devoted to "Jewish pathologies," for instance, Fishberg emphasized, as he had in his previous writings, the overriding importance of contingent, historical conditions in the genesis of disease. He reiterated his belief that the attempt to identify race as a causal factor of Jewish health and/or disease was a mistake, as was the notion that one could establish an essential difference between Jews and Aryans through pathologies.[95] He stressed that no uniformity existed among Jews of different countries or locales when it came to either immunity or susceptibility to disease. "In some places the Jews appear to suffer less from these diseases, while in others the contrary is true."[96] He repeated as well the arguments made in his earlier writings about the heterogeneity of Jewish bodily shapes and sizes, and the evidence this offered about the historical assimilation of Jews into their non-Jewish environments.[97]

On the whole, Fishberg sought environmental explanations for Jewish traits, and especially "Jewish pathologies." This was so in part because his personal experience as a physician to the Jewish poor exposed him on a regular basis to the debilitating conditions in which these Jews lived and worked. Yet it was also part of a developing intellectual strategy aimed at advancing the twin goals of a liberal American immigration policy, and the integration of immigrant Jews into American society. Nonetheless, in places Fishberg did analyze Jewish health and disease in terms of biological, rather than strictly environmental, adaptation or natural selection.[98] The lower rates of tuberculosis among Jews, for instance, could be explained by the fact that Jews lived for so long in urban, overcrowded environments where TB was most likely to spread. Those Jews who were weak and vulnerable were slowly but surely killed off by the disease; the strongest and fittest survived and reproduced. In modern times, therefore, the Jews display a greater resistance on the whole to the disease, a resistance born of environmental conditions, but which over time developed into an acquired, inheritable trait.

In his extended analysis of conversion and intermarriage, and of the question of "the purity of the Jewish race"—which he identified as "the crucial point in the anthropology of the Jews"—Fishberg emphasized to a far greater degree than he had in his earlier work the significance of heredity in the makeup of the Jews.[99] He reproduced earlier arguments he had made on the connections between environment and somatological traits, yet voiced some reservations about the conclusiveness of these theories. At one point he went so far as to deny altogether the influence of milieu on bodily traits.[100] This stress on heredity was significant in that it indicated, according to Fishberg, that the heterogeneity of Jewish bodily forms could have only occurred as a result of a long process of racial mixture on the part of Jews through intermarriage and conversion.

In the first of the two chapters devoted to the subjects of intermarriage and conversion, entitled "Proselytism and Intermarriage among Jews," Fishberg set out to disprove the theory of Jewish racial purity and homogeneity of physical type. Beginning his discussion in the biblical period and moving through the Babylonian exile, the reforms of Ezra, Greco-Roman times, and the Christian era, Fishberg showed that throughout their long history Jews had intermarried and accepted converts as a matter of course, and to such a high degree that this "infusion of non-Jewish blood into the veins of the Chosen People" had markedly transformed the Jews as a race. While some parts or traits of the body, such as stature and girth of chest, were capable of being changed by milieu, others, such as head shape and skin and eye color, were wholly the product of heredity. And the fact, Fishberg maintained, that Jewry possessed statistically significant numbers of individuals with blonde or red hair, blue eyes, and black skin signified that throughout their history Jews had mixed with other races.[101]

In contrast to Zionist social scientists, he made a great deal of the conversion of the Chazars, and of their subsequent significance in both historical and racial terms.[102] According to Fishberg, this racial intermixture went a long way in explaining the mystery of how Jews came to be present in such large numbers in southeastern Europe:

The most important infusion of non-Jewish racial elements into the veins of Eastern European Jews took place in the eighth century when the Chozars [*sic*] adopted Judaism. . . . The history of the Jews in Russia furnishes ample evidence that in the south of the Empire, especially in Kief [*sic*], there were Jews long before the Jews came thither from Poland and Germany. Some historians even say that during the eighth century the majority of the population of Kief was made up of Jews of Chozar descent. Many of these Jews, after the fall of the Chozar kingdom and their subjugation by the Russians during the eleventh century, have spread all over the country, and made up the nucleus of the future Jewry of Eastern Europe. Later, when the German Jews came, both these classes commingled, and their descendants constitute the millions of Jews living to-day in Eastern Europe. History thus confirms the observations made by anthropologists to the effect that many of the types of the Jews in that region are hardly distinguishable from the types of mankind met with among the Christians in Eastern Europe, and that this is due to intermarriage and proselytism.[103]

In a chapter devoted to mixed marriages, Fishberg reviewed the literature, most of it produced by Jewish social scientists and published in the *Zeitschrift für Demographie und Statistik der Juden*, and affirmed that throughout those countries where statistics were available, intermarriage had been rising steadily. In a number of major European cities the number of mixed marriages approached or surpassed 50 percent of "pure marriages." In the case of Copenhagen there were reportedly as many mixed as pure marriages during the years 1901–05. Statistics on Berlin showed that from 1875 to 1906 the ratio of mixed to pure marriages rose from 36.07 percent to 44.05 percent. In Hamburg it reached 61.19 percent in 1905–06, and so on. "From the facts and figures just presented, it appears that the Jews do intermarry with people of other faiths in every country where the law permits such unions."[104]

For Fishberg, as for Ruppin before him, the significance of such a high degree of intermarriage lay in part in its refutation of "the assumption of many authors that the Jew and Christian refrain from intermarriage because of an inherent racial antipathy existing between the Aryan and the Semite." When one encounters such refrainment or resistance, it is due to the continuing influence of religion, and/or the legal sanction of the state.[105] Again, like Ruppin and others, Fishberg argued that the ghetto was "the best preventative of intermarriages of Jews." Statistics and empirical observation in the cases of Galicia, Russia, London's East End, and the Lower East Side of New York proved that. And like Ruppin, Fishberg linked intermarriage rates to levels of socioeconomic assimilation, urbanization, and secularization.

Not surprisingly, Fishberg's analysis of intermarriage and conversion lacked the apocalyptic-like references to decline and imminent disappearance that punctuated the narratives of Zionist social scientists. Nor did he accept the idea that intermarriage produced degeneration or its effects. Such unions, he argued, do not produce lower fecundity, infertility, or sterility; they do not result in greater numbers of stillbirths; nor do mixed marriages produce physical or mental deterioration and degeneration in offspring. Fishberg even reproduced a list of intellectually "extraordinary people" who were products of intermarriage. "This can hardly be called intellectual degeneration," he concluded.

At the same time Fishberg presented in clear and forceful terms the detrimental impact emancipation and modernity had upon Jewry. Oftentimes in his narrative he sounded themes associated more closely with Zionist social scientists. "It is evident from all available facts that Judaism thrives best when its faithful sons are isolated from the surrounding people, segregated in Ghettos or Pales of Settlement, excluded from educational institutions frequented by people of the dominant faith, and thus prevented from coming into contact with their non-Jewish neighbors."[106]

It was precisely in those countries, like Russia and Romania, where Jews were politically, socially, and economically most isolated, that their birth rates were highest, and their intermarriage and conversion rates lowest. In the West, where the Jews enjoyed freedom and equality, just the opposite was the case. "Indeed, the Western Jews display a striking retrogression and decadence, which is by no means accidental."[107] The only "redeeming factors" for Western Jewry were their low mortality rate and East European immigration. But neither of these, Fishberg was quick to point out, could offer "indefinite help." Death rates could not realistically be expected to drop much lower, and immigration from the East was not an inexhaustible resource. Moreover, Eastern European Jewry would surely follow the Western pattern of integration and assimilation as their political conditions improved. Echoing Ruppin, Theilhaber, Zollschan, and numerous other Zionist social scientists of the time, Fishberg spoke of "race suicide" among the Jews of both East and West.[108]

In the end, however, Fishberg reaffirmed his faith in assimilation as the only "normal" and "natural" course for Jews to take. He denied that the statistics concerning fertility, intermarriage, and conversion indicated any genuine pathology: "We do not want to be misunderstood on this point. In showing the tendency to retrogression of the Jews we do not at all mean to imply that this is a sign of a physical degeneration of a physiological or pathological nature." Indeed, Fishberg proceeded to normalize the condition of modern Western Jewry by universalizing it. "[The Jews] are not unique. The same phenomena are to be observed among all civilized peoples in varying degrees of intensity. 'Prudential foresight' goes hand-in-hand with an improved standard of life, with greater ambition to raise children who are fortified with a proper education, the best weapon in the fierce struggle for existence which has been going on in modern commercial and industrial life."[109]

Zionism, in fact, was identified by Fishberg as abnormal and pathological. It was an ideological movement "born of negatives": the "rejection of emancipation" and fear of assimilation; the adoption of "the chauvinistic ideas of their [the Jews'] Christian neighbors" in order to "revive a racial and national spirit;" and "apprehension for the future of Judaism."[111]

"To the Zionists the Jews are a distinct, non-European race which has preserved itself in its original purity in spite of the Jews' wanderings all over the globe. They hold that the Jews can never merge with the European races, and are bound to remain distinct from their Christian or Mohammedan neighbors."[110] Fishberg rejected this, arguing that modern Jewry was neither a race nor a nation. "[I]t is thus evident that Zionism, based as it is on the erroneous notion that the Jews are a nation, fails at the outset, because it is founded on false premises."[112]

Both the Jewish past and its present demonstrated that Jewry was a product of intermixture, at all different levels, between Jews and the surrounding peoples and races. Moreover, Jewry—although not necessarily Judaism—was "healthiest" when it acted on these impulses. Isolation, whether imposed by external regimes or internal ideologies, was an "unnatural," abnormal condition for Jewry. In the nineteenth century European Jewry proved "there is nothing within the Jew that keeps him back from assimilating with his neighbors of other creeds; that as soon as the political and civil laws which previously kept him apart from the general population are abrogated, he begins to adapt himself to the new surroundings in a wonderful manner."[113]

*

If Jewish scientists were united in their desire to appropriate the discourse that had traditionally evaluated their people negatively, and labor to reverse the condition of Jewry, they were divided over how, more precisely, to interpret the social scientific data, and what practical conclusions to draw from it. Zionist social scientists saw in the data generated about the Jewish body and mind evidence of a Jewish national/racial identity that transcended geographic boundaries, and they understood both Jewish health and disease as proof that "modernity," in the guise of emancipation and assimilation into non-Jewish society, posed an unprecedented danger to Jewry. Integrationists shared with Zionist social scientists the desire to counter the negative image of Jewry that formed a part of much of the modern social scientific literature. In this sense, there was a unity of purpose impelling the analyses of Jewish social scientists, a unity that transcended the political commitments that divided them. At the same time, Fishberg, Maretzki, and others engaged with Jewish nationalists at the intellectual and ideological levels, offering a spirited scientific defense of Jewish integration. Both assimilationist and Zionist social scientists, therefore, recognized the reality of Jewish assimilation in the present at the physical as well as the social and cultural levels. What they debated were the effects of assimilation, and how, ultimately, Jewish identity ought to be defined.

## CHAPTER SIX

# Measuring and Picturing Jews
## Racial Anthropology and Iconography

Beginning in the last decades of the nineteenth century, Jewish social scientists in Europe and the United States became engaged in the public debate over Jewish racial identity and difference. Their ideas and images were shaped by the general discourse on race, and in many cases their writings helped shape the work of non-Jewish scientists in turn.[1] Many, probably most, Jewish social scientists took this racial identity for granted, though as we saw in the previous chapter there were those like Fishberg who challenged it in significant ways. Certainly, few disputed that the category of race was a legitimate and crucial one for scientific inquiry, and that racial differences played an important part in shaping society and culture. "Almost all inquiries," Arthur Ruppin wrote in 1906,

into the social, intellectual, and physical differences between Jews and Christians address the question of whether these differences have their root in the particular racial makeup, or in the unique economic and political conditions of the Jews over the past two thousand years. One might designate this question, in fact, as the fundamental problem or issue of social scientific research of the Jews. Just as it is quite easy now for authors of polemical literature to express their opinions on this one way or another, so it is difficult to arrive at an answer to the problem grounded in exact knowledge.[2]

Exact knowledge could only be derived by employing the tools of social science: the language, categories, and images developed over the course of the past century and a half, and defined as scientific.

From the eighteenth century onward, a number of sciences concerned with measuring and representing the human body emerged, contributing to the production of knowledge about racial identity and difference. Craniometry, physiognomy, and phrenology were all, at one time or another, regarded as indispensable tools in the science of race. By the beginning of the twentieth century, at the latest, anthropology, biology, statistics, medicine, and archaeology were considered central; all shaped, and were in turn shaped by, the concept of race.[3] These disciplines provided much of the interpretive and conceptual language of the developing scientific discourse about ethnic and racial differences.

Historical analyses of racial thought have, for the most part, focused on the written narrative component of texts on race. This is true as well for works on Jewish racial scientists.[4] And thus far in this study my concern has been exclusively with the written narratives produced by and about Jews. Less attention has been paid by scholars to the role of iconography in social scientific texts, and to the ways in which visual images supplied "evidence" for scientific claims about racial identity and difference.[5] Yet this mode of interpretation appears consistently throughout the scientific racial literature produced over the course of more than a century. This chapter explores the Jewish social scientific engagement with the discourse of race, and its ideological impetus, through an analysis of iconographic representation and interpretation. Focusing on the role of visual images in social scientific texts, and on their relation to the written narratives, highlights the crucial position occupied by representations of the Jewish body in Jewish social scientific discourse. Moreover, such an analysis illuminates fundamental aspects of social scientific epistemology and ideology.

Representation of the body was a central element in the construction of narratives about race and ethnicity in the nineteenth and early twentieth centuries. The shapes of heads and noses; the colors of eyes, hair, and skin; the length of a jaw or girth of a chest all aided researchers in their task of defining and classifying individuals and groups. Somatological traits, as much as, or even more than, language or history, were understood as constitutive of a given type, and typological thinking was fundamental to the science of race. Furthermore, the body pointed beyond the physical self, offering insight, it was believed, into moral and intellectual capacities. The volume of the cranium and the weight of the brain, to offer only two of the best-known examples, were taken as indicative of intellectual prowess or retardation.[6] Visual images of the body, and particularly of the face, supplemented arguments adduced from statistics. Pictures made the abstract argument of numbers concrete. The reader could see the "thick lips" or "prognathous chin" of the black, the "thick and fleshy" nose of the Jew. Images, however, were more than supplemental. They offered a unique sort of evidence of their own, which in the case of the Jews became a central motif in racial narratives.

Both Jewish and non-Jewish scientists interested in the Jews as a race used visual representation as an analytical tool. These scientists shared fundamental epistemological assumptions about images and the kind of knowledge they offer. Images, whether they be ancient bas-reliefs, medieval paintings, or modern photographs, provided direct access, it was believed, to the reality they purported to represent. Moreover, all images were created equal in the eyes of these racial theorists. An ancient illustration found on a tomb or at the base of a monument was no less valid a source for determining racial traits than a photograph was. The hierarchy of images, so pronounced a part of discussions about art and representation during this period, seemed to find little echo in the literature on race.

We can speak of a coherent tradition of racial iconographic narrative, lasting into the 1930s, from which Jewish and non-Jewish scientists drew, and to which their works contributed. These social scientists all seemed to agree that visual imagery had something important to say about racial identity. Yet they disagreed over the conclusions to be drawn from this knowledge. This interpretive tradition, in other words, lent itself to diverse political and social ideologies.

## The Visual Image of the Jew

The iconography of Jews acquired meaning within the context of the century-long debate over the identity and purity of the Jews as a race, and in the struggles over emancipation, assimilation, and national identity that came to be identified as the Jewish Question. The issue of Jewish racial identity was itself part of the larger debate within the sciences over the relative importance of heredity or environment, nature or nurture, in the formation of individual and group traits. The debate hinged on the issue of continuity of somatological characteristics over time and space.[7] In the case of the Jews, did contemporary Jewry retain the same features as the ancient Hebrews, or Semites, despite the elapse of thousands of years and their dispersion over the entire globe? If so, this racial continuity demanded explication.

For advocates of the racial purity, or at least the racial distinctiveness of the Jews, the images preserved on the ancient monuments in Egypt and Mesopotamia were believed to offer some of the best empirical evidence. In his 1873 work *The Inequality of Human Races*, Arthur Comte de Gobineau, for example, argued the case for Jewish racial continuity as part of a broader polygenist position. Racial differences, he wrote, are permanent;

neither geography, climate, nor custom can affect them in any meaningful way. The Jews, he believed, offer an excellent example of this. Despite having "settled in lands with very different climates from that of Palestine, and [having] given up their ancient mode of life," the Jews have maintained their unity and particularity as a race.[8] Gobineau granted that modifications or changes in Jewish life occurred over time. They have, however, never been of sufficient importance or degree "to change the general character of the race." "The warlike Rechabites of the Arabian desert, the peaceful Portuguese, French, German, and Polish Jews—they all look alike." For proof of this identity Gobineau turned to ancient illustrations: "The Semitic face looks exactly the same, in its main characteristics, as it appears on the Egyptian paintings of three or four thousand years ago, and more; and we find it also, in an equally striking and recognizable form, under the most varied and disparate conditions of climate."[9]

The "identity of descendant and ancestor," according to Gobineau, went beyond facial features. The "shape of the limbs" and "temperament" also pointed to the essential identity of Jews, and their difference from the peoples around them.

Gobineau was not the first to argue along polygenist lines that the Jews offer proof of the fundamental physical differences of the races. In 1839 Samuel George Morton, the eminent American scientist, included the Jews—along with "Arabians, Hindoos, and Negroes"—in his list of racial groups that have remained unchanged over time. As for Gobineau's, ancient visual images provided evidence for Morton's claims: "In like manner the characteristic features of the Jews may be recognized in the sculpture of the temples of Luxor and Karnak, in Egypt, where they have been depicted for nearly thirty centuries."[10] Similar arguments appear in the works of leading British and French anthropologists.[11]

Examples drawn from the literature produced in France, England, and the United States are reminders that questions and debates about Jewish racial identity engaged social scientists (as well as other political and cultural elites) in a variety of countries. As Michael Marrus argued nearly thirty years ago about the case of France, issues of racial identity and difference were assigned urgent significance precisely in the post-emancipatory period at the end of the nineteenth century. Racial science sought to reestablish clearly recognizable distinctions between Jews and non-Jews at just the time when such distinctions were widely perceived to be disappearing. Biology and anthropology provided a language with which to establish differences that could no longer be sanctioned legally.[12] For those intellectuals and cultural critics concerned—even obsessed—with questions about national identity, the Jew who presented himself as a real German or Frenchman in all but religion constituted a palpable threat.[13]

The geographer and anthropologist Richard Andree's *On the Ethnography of the Jews*, published in 1881, offers an excellent example of the counter-emancipatory impetus to German racial science.[14] The work, and in particular Andree's use of ancient images, quickly became standard reference material for many of those, Jewish and non-Jewish, addressing the issue of Jewish racial purity.[15] In his introductory remarks, Andree declared environmental factors meaningless in matters of race, and argued for the permanence and stability of racial traits over time. He then turned to the "Semites and Aryans." These two distinct tribes or races, both categorized as Caucasian, are together responsible for all of civilization and culture. However, moral and intellectual differences do exist, and these are linked in Andree's analysis to physiological traits. The Semites, predictably, possess more negative than positive traits, chief among them egoism, intolerance, and fanaticism. This discussion of the Semites served as an introduction to Andree's arguments about Jews.

The Jews are fascinating anthropologically, Andree wrote, because "one can trace them with certainty over thousands of years, and no other racial type has maintained such constant form and remained as immune to time and space." Semitic blood has remained the dominant biological force, and "the ancient Jewish physical and mental structures have remained constant."[16] While he introduced into his narrative on racial stability ancient and modern texts, including the works of the Jewish historians Leopold Zunz, Isaac Marcus Jost, and Heinrich Graetz, it was the ancient monuments upon which Andree chiefly relied for "empirical" evidence.

Whoever takes a look at Egyptian and Assyrian monuments, upon which Jews were represented with masterful certainty over two thousand years ago, will be assured of the unchangeability of the Jewish type, and will be stimulated by the comparison between the portraits of people he sees and the flesh and blood wandering amongst us today. . . . They stand before us unchanged in body and spirit despite numerous accommodations, which time and the nations amongst whom they have lived have forced upon them. . . . Undoubtedly, we encounter here in the type and in the gestures the actual Jew, who is present among us even today.[17]

The polemical thrust of Andree's thesis is evident here. Despite the concerted efforts of those committed to emancipation and assimilation, in Germany and throughout Europe since the late eighteenth century, the Jew remains essentially unchanged. And regardless of liberal claims to the contrary, Jews in Germany share a fundamental identity with all other Jews—despite geography, national affiliation, and social status; concomitantly, they differ from the nations and *Völker* among whom they live.

This use of iconography to help establish an unchanging identity among Jews, and the message of a fundamental difference between European

("Aryan," "Teuton," etc.) and Jew reappears in a variety of German texts dealing with the race question. Houston Stewart Chamberlain, in his *Die Grundlagen des neunzehnten Jahrhunderts*, included crudely drawn outlines of Hittite and Amorite profiles—copied, as he noted, "from well-known Egyptian monuments"—to bolster his argument about the Semitic and Syriac racial origins of the Jews. These illustrations helped establish Chamberlain's thesis that the ancient Hittites, like the Jews of today, were wide- and round-headed (brachycephalic), and that "the so-called 'Jewish nose' is a Hittite legacy."[18] In his 1911 study on *Jews and Modern Capitalism*, Werner Sombart used similar ancient images to support his thesis about the "Jewish spirit" and the capitalist ethos.[19] In response to Max Weber's theory about the relationship between capitalism and the Protestant spirit, Sombart posited the "Jewish spirit" as most highly akin to that of modern capitalism, and the Jews as primarily responsible for the tenor of modern economic life.

According to Sombart, the entrepreneurial ethos had been the central trait of Jewry since biblical times. It is an intellectual and moral characteristic that has remained constant over time and place. Following a commonly held belief in the relationship between physical and moral or intellectual traits, Sombart argued that this continuity of "spirit" was reflected in the continuity of bodily characteristics.[20] The anthropological or racial continuity of Jews, for which Sombart found evidence in ancient illustrations, is an external sign of an internal essence. The Jews, in Sombart's view, were biologically, as well as intellectually and morally, "programmed" for the capitalist enterprise.

As a prelude to his section "How the Jewish Genius Remained Constant," Sombart presented his proof for the constancy of the Jewish physiognomy:

> To consider the Jewish physiognomy as an expression of decadence, or to account for it, as [the American authority William] Ripley does, as a result of ghetto life, is not very conclusive in face of the undeniable Jewish types depicted on the monuments of ancient Egypt and Babylonia. Look at the picture of Jewish captives in the epoch of Shishak (973 B.C.), or of the Jewish ambassadors at the court of Salmanasar (884 B.C.), and you will be convinced that from those days to our own, a period of nearly three thousand years, few changes have marked the Jewish type of countenance. This is but another proof of the proposition that the Jewish stock is an anthropological entity, and that its characteristics have been constant through the ages in a most extraordinary fashion.[21]

Sombart rejected arguments that the Jewish penchant for commerce and trade was a late development, a product of historical or environmental factors. Just as the Jews have remained true to form, as it were, in the physical sense over thousands of years, so too have they retained their original intellectual traits. Linking the Jews with capitalism, and with modernity in general, Sombart cast German and Jew, *Deutschtum* and *Judentum*, as fundamentally antithetical. The modern assimilated Jew, no less than the ancient Semite, was not and could not be truly at home in Europe.

By no means, however, was this interpretive device limited to the anti-Semites among non-Jewish scholars and writers. Nor were the proponents of Jewish racial unity and purity the only ones to make use of iconographic evidence. The initial issue of the *Zeitschrift für Demographie und Statistik*, for example, began with an article by the chair of anthropology at the University of Berlin (and one of Arthur Ruppin's teachers), Felix von Luschan, entitled "On the Physical Anthropology of the Jews."[22] An earlier extended version of this essay had been highly influential in directing the debate among anthropologists over the designation of the Jews, anthropologically, as "Semites."[23] Luschan was one of several important German scientists, among them the renowned pathologist and anthropologist Rudolf Virchow, who challenged the notion of a unified "Aryan race," and concomitantly the purported racial link between the Jews and the "Semites."[24] The challenge to the notion of distinct "Aryan" and "Semitic" races, each endowed with essential spiritual and cultural, in addition to physical characteristics, was also a challenge to the moral hierarchy that accompanied these taxonomies. The assertion of Jewish inferiority vis-à-vis European, and particularly Germanic, peoples rested in large part on the connection—well established in racial discourse since the 1870s—that the Jews were "Semites," and on the image of "Semites" as barbaric or uncivilized. As a physical anthropologist, Luschan worked within the bounds of the racial paradigm. In arguing for the disassociation of Jews with "Semites," he sought to distance anthropology from the judgments about "superiority" and "inferiority," which were a dominant, though by no means essential, element of the discipline.

In Luschan's view, the assertion that linguistic unity indicated racial origin and affinity was mistaken. One could argue plausibly, as many did over the course of the nineteenth century, for a common Indo-Germanic family of languages; it was foolish to move from there, again as so many had, to the assertion that all of the "Indo-Germanic nations" were united anthropologically.[25]

Neither Aryans nor Semites could be grouped together somatologically. Craniology, physiognomy, and iconography provided evidence for this. The racial continuity and purity of the Bedouins, for instance, could be seen from the Egyptian monuments. "Long and narrow heads are a prominent characteristic of contemporary Bedouins, and we can observe on ancient Egyptian monuments that the Bedouins of those days appear just as they do today." Bedouins represented the "racially pure Semite," in comparison to whom the Jews emerged as anatomically distinct. "Above all we see that the racially pure Semite always has a short, small, and slightly curved nose, which is in fact the opposite of what laymen today like to designate as a 'genuine Jewish nose.' We find such genuine Jewish noses, together with extremely short, high, and broad skulls, already in earliest antiquity in the Near East represented on monuments belonging to the Hittite cultural realm."[26]

Ancient iconographic evidence revealed the racially pure Semites to be dolichocephalic (long- and narrow-headed), with short, small noses. The Jews, on the other hand, evinced precisely the opposite traits. The Jews, then, were not a pure and distinct race, but rather the historical product of three different races. Their heterogeneity, in Luschan's view, was a strength, demonstrating as it did their ability to intermingle and assimilate successfully with other *Völker*.

## The Nature of Iconography and the Nature of the Jews

Scientific studies of racial character and continuity that utilized visual imagery as evidence rested on a fundamental assumption about the nature of iconography: images offer direct, unmediated access to objective reality. Gazing at a two- or three-thousand-year-old painting or bas-relief, the scientist believed he could learn something real and concrete about the figures represented, and that this in turn offered insight into group or racial identity. In this crude positivist approach the artist all but disappeared. The image was equivalent to the numerical measurement in that both provided the scientist with a body of facts with which he could then construct a narrative about race.

Even more striking, though, was the equivalence assumed in these texts between formally and technologically different modes of representation. Just as time was made irrelevant by the assumed continuity of racial essence, so too artistic and technological developments became meaningless in these texts. Ancient images were set side by side with photographs, and these were seen as equally valid sources of knowledge about racial groups. Iconography, in fact, could only be made to demonstrate the main thesis of racial continuity over time if hierarchies in modes of visual representation were denied.

Yet it was precisely during the last half of the nineteenth century that such a hierarchy of images developed.[27] Photography, it came to be widely believed, had replaced painting as the "mirror of nature." The "objective" nature of the medium was acknowledged, regardless of on which side of the highly charged debate over the artistic or social value of photography one stood.[28] In painting, it was argued, the artist mediated between reality and its representation. No such mediating process occurred with photography. Mechanical reproduction assured a "true" and objective representation of reality; human subjectivity vanished as the camera faithfully recorded what was "out there." The power of the photograph derived (and continues to derive, of course) in large part from its presumed ability to reproduce reality in all its details. The social scientist was a beneficiary of this power, of the notion of the photograph—and not the painting—as a mirror. At the same time, social scientists continued to treat older forms of representation, such as ancient illustrations, and Renaissance and early modern paintings, as sources of knowledge no less valid than photographs.

Epistemologically and methodologically Jewish social scientists inhabited the same world as their non-Jewish counterparts, invoking the same authorities and utilizing the same technologies. Jewish scholars adopted the interpretive model that offered ancient visual imagery as evidence about modern Jewish identity, utilized modern technologies of representation, and appeared as little inclined to draw distinctions between these forms as their Gentile counterparts. At the same time, of course, Jewish social scientists often had their own, very different political and social agendas. For example, in an 1885 paper entitled "On the Racial Characteristics of Modern Jews," presented at the Royal Anthropological Institute in London, the Anglo-Jewish social scientist Joseph Jacobs called upon photography, as well as statistics, to demonstrate "the purity of the Jewish Race."[29] His explanation for the use of photographic images of Jews illuminates the interdependence of non-Jewish and Jewish social scientific scholarship, and the ways in which mechanical reproduction came to be seen at the end of the century as offering a type of objective evidence of which statistical measurement was incapable.[30] After an extended discussion of the physiological and anatomical traits of Jews, Jacobs turned to what he called the typical "Jewish expression," which was the result of the peculiar combination of Jewish features. Yet, unlike individual anatomical features such as the cranium or nose, this "expression" could not be measured statistically. "[I]t might seem impossible to give anything more than subjective impressions. Thanks, however, to Mr. Galton, science has been enabled to call in the aid of photography to obtain those averages which no measurement can supply."[31] In a series of articles and lectures in the late 1870s, the English statistician and eugenicist Francis Galton developed the idea of the composite photograph as part of his ongoing exploration of physiognomic "types" and "averages."[32] Galton sought through composite photographs to provide a "visual analogue of the binomial curve" of statistics, a more accurate representation of "the average man" (*l'homme moyen*).[33] This, he believed, would facilitate in turn the eugenics project. Galton produced composite photographs of what he defined as "fit" and "unfit," "healthy" and "degenerate"—this included members of the royal family, men of science, criminals, consumptives, the working-class poor—as a means of better identifying individuals somatologically and classifying them eugenically.

Galton made his composite portraitures of Jews in 1883 at the behest of Jacobs.[34] Both men agreed that these visual images revealed something fundamental, even essential about the nature of modern Jewry. For Galton, however, the Jewish faces confirmed his negative appraisal of Jewry. "The feature that struck me most, as I drove through . . . the Jewish quarter, was the cold scanning gaze of man, woman, and child. . . . I felt, rightly or wrongly, that every one of them was coolly appraising me at market-value, without the slightest interest of any kind."[35] Here the "Jewish expression" as it was captured through photography blends into Galton's own impressions of individual Jews encountered in the East End. The composite image and the individual Jew become one, and the "average Jew" revealed as "economic Jew" through reference to the market.

Jacobs responded directly to the anti-Semitic implications of Galton's commentary. Referring to the first three of the four composite photos, Jacobs wrote that "I fail to see any of the cold calculation which Mr. Galton noticed in the boys at the school in the composites A, B, and C. There is something more like the dreamer and thinker than the merchant in A."[36] The overall significance of these photographs for Jacobs lay in the fact that they demonstrated that "there actually exists a definite and well-defined organic type of modern Jews. Photographic science thus seems to confirm the conclusion I have drawn from history, that there has been scarcely any admixture of alien blood amongst the Jews since their dispersion."[37] Jacobs also found evidence for this purity, and continuity of type, in ancient iconography. "At the same time something like it [the Jewish expression] may be traced throughout the history of Art, and I may refer to one of the earliest representations of the Jews in Art, the Assyrian bas-relief of the captive Jews of Lachish. . . . The subject is undoubted and well-known, and the persistency of the Jewish type for the last 2,600 years is conclusively proved by it."[38]

Yet, despite this assertion of Jewish racial purity and identity, Jacobs's arguments nonetheless aimed at reinforcing the political and social position of English Jewry. As such, he provides an excellent example of the way in which racial notions could be employed for liberal (i.e., integrationist) purposes. In the first place, while Jacobs asserted the continuity or persistence of the Jewish type, he also stressed throughout his writings the primary significance of environmental factors in shaping and reshaping racial traits. This meant that, despite an insistence on Jewish difference, assimilation at the physical as well as cultural levels was possible. The "typical" Jewish expression, for example, was due in large part to "long residence in ghetti and the accompanying social isolation. I fancy at least that it disappears to a large extent in Jews who pass very much of their life among Gentiles."[39]

Yet, even in his emphasis on the anthropological distinctiveness of Jewry, and its racial heritage, Jacobs was not denying the ability of Jews to assimilate into society. Quite the contrary. Working within the broad interpretive and methodological framework constructed by Galton in his work *Hereditary Genius*, which posited a direct correlation between the intellectual abilities of a group and its worthiness as a class or race, Jacobs set out to demonstrate that the Jews' racial purity made them ideally suited for survival and success in Victorian Britain. Statistics showed, according to Jacobs, that Jews counted a higher percentage of "illustrious" and "eminent" individuals than the English—two of the three categories Galton had offered in analyzing "hereditary genius." On the one hand, counting such a disproportionate number of intellectually and artistically gifted individuals among them, Jews must be considered a sort of racial aristocracy, a model of the hereditarily fit held up by Galton and other eugenicists. On the other hand, Jacobs's explanation for the failure of Jewry to produce as many "distinguished" individuals (the third of Galton's categories) also supported the idea that Jewry benefits from assimilation into the broader society in which it lives. Jacobs attributed the relative dearth of "distinguished" Jews not to biological, but to social and political causes. In short, the persecution of Jews in Eastern and Western Europe kept the numbers of talented Jews from developing. Social scientific research, then, illuminated a direct correspondence between emancipation, integration, and eugenic health.[40]

A few years earlier Jacobs had argued much the same thing, explaining the high numbers of brachycephalic, or broad-headed, Jews counted by anthropologists with reference to the Jews' heightened mental abilities.[41] Jacobs invoked the famed English statistician and eugenicist Karl Pearson, who had "demonstrated" that brachycephaly implied superior intelligence. The enlarged Jewish head was a product of historical adaptation in a Darwinian struggle for survival. In order to compete successfully, Jews were forced to develop their intellectual capacities, which included involvement in trade and finance, beyond average or "normal" levels. Their skulls grew bigger in order to accommodate their oversized brains. For Jacobs this morphological adaptation was significant because it demonstrated, in his opinion, the racial purity of Jewry, as well as Jews' extraordinary mental powers.[42] Arguing in a liberal or integrationist mode, he viewed both Jewish racial purity and Jewish intelligence as proof that as an elite and highly cultured group, the Jews were perfectly capable of integrating into and contributing to English society. In his racial hierarchy, the Jews were either equal to or superior to the English, Scotch, and "Teutons."[43]

Maurice Fishberg made extensive use of photographs, as well as of paintings and ancient iconography, to reinforce his general argument about Jewish identity, difference, and the powers of assimilation. Fishberg reproduced 142 illustrations in his work on race and environment.[44] These ranged from "Ancient Races portrayed on the Egyptian Monuments," through paintings by Rembrandt, to photographs, including the composite photos created by Galton and Jacobs. The images reproduced and lent power to the arguments made in the written narrative: Jewish racial purity and unity is a myth; there are, rather, different Jewish typologies, characterized by diversity and heterogeneity; and the Jews in any given country or region are firmly embedded in the surrounding society and culture. The latter point was made through the dress or costumes Jews were shown wearing. Dagestan mountain Jews, a Spanish Jewess, a Syrian Jewess—each is presented in the traditional dress of the nation or region in which he or she resides. A photograph of a "Fat Jewess in Tunis in Native Costume" makes the point a bit more explicitly.[45] These images of non-Western, "exotic" Jews provide a vivid contrast to the portraits of the American Jew and Jewess, he dressed in some sort of military (perhaps police) uniform, she in a fancy dress and hat. Both are the epitome of turn-of-the-century bourgeois respectability.[46]

Fishberg took pains to deny that those physical features that anthropologists and others insisted on categorizing as "Jewish"—the hooked nose, thick lips, dark hair and eyes, and so forth—could be used to identify Jews, or to distinguish Jews from their non-Jewish neighbors, in any essentialist way. The face of a "White Jew" from Cochin, East India, is juxtaposed with one of a "Black Jew" from the same place. When the reader turns the page she encounters Chinese Jews, then Tunisian, Algerian, and Falashan Jews. As in their dress, so too in their physiognomies: they differ little from the non-Jews in whose midst they live. The point is made emphatically through the juxtaposition of Jews labeled "Teutonic Type, United States," with a "Polish Jew in Jerusalem."[47] Fishberg's assertion of the racial disunity of the Jews, and of the historical and anatomical legacy of their assimilation, is also demonstrated by the numerous photos of non-Jews who possessed so-called "Jewish traits." There are photos of Tartars and Georgians, each of whom has a "Jewish physigonomy"; a "Bakairi Indian with Jewish Cast of Countenance"; and "Japanese with Jewish Physiognomy."[48] Thus, iconography demonstrated that non-Jews can and do possess "Jewish" features. At the same time, Fishberg was compelled to admit that such a thing as a "Jewish look" and a "Jewish bend" or posture did exist. There is a "ghetto face," though experts are divided over its essential components. What was clear for Fishberg is that it was the product of historical and environmental forces, and that it vanished once the Jew was permitted to live in freedom, as an equal. In the end, then, it was a "psychic" trait, which manifested itself in the physiognomy, and which was born of the oppressive conditions under which Jews had been forced to live. This notion is demonstrated through two photographs, inhabiting the same page, of the "Jewish Lad's Brigade, London." The first photo is of a group of 21 boys, dressed somewhat shabbily in coats and caps. It evokes the East End of London, and the figure of the immigrant street urchin. This photo is labeled "The Raw Material." Below it is a photo labeled "What Became of Them." Thirteen young men are dressed smartly in military-like uniforms. Their clothing, their posture, their serious stares all suggest that these young Jews are as fit as any Englishman to take on the duties of a free citizen. The caption at the bottom, which brings the two photos together, reads "Showing the Effects of the Environment on the Type of the Jew."[49] Fishberg's written narratives demonstrated the heterogeneity of Jewish identity, and told the story of the meliorative effects of integration into a broader liberal society. It did so through statistics and through the interpretive tools of the social sciences. Visual images supplemented this written narrative, but also provided a distinct type of evidence, more visceral, and thus perhaps more convincing.

## Nationalism and the Jewish Image

In an article published in 1905 on the cultural Zionist goal of "Gegenwartsarbeit," Arthur Ruppin argued that the notions of "racial unity" and "racial fitness" constitute part of the Zionist arsenal for reconstituting Jews the world over as a *Volk* and nation. If the weakening of orthodoxy today threatens the dissolution of group identity, Ruppin wrote, then Zionists need to stress other binding elements: racial unity (*Rassenzusammengehörigkeit*), linguistic unity, a common national past, and common expectations for the future. "The knowledge of the racial unity and racial fitness [*Rassentüchtigkeit*] of the Jews must be broadened, the common language . . . advanced, and every potential for Jewish literature and art lovingly encouraged."[50]

Ruppin's conviction about the relevance of race for the Zionist movement was widely, though by no means universally, shared. To be sure, not all Zionists accepted the legitimacy of approaching the critical issue of Jewish collective identity through an exploration of a racial or biological definition of Jewry. For those who did, however—and they were a sizable and vocal number—ideas about race provided a powerful tool for responding to anti-Semitic critics, who themselves had appropriated science, and for addressing purported faults in the contemporary, "assimilated" Jewish character. As Ignaz Zollschan phrased it, "Racial anthropology and biology have established the intellectual, moral, aesthetic and physical inferiority of the Jews as a race. This is a result of practical and political needs. Sanction of Jew hatred, on the one hand, lack of pride and sense of self on the other. Even though we know the theory of Aryan/non-Aryan is nonsense, still it is a strongly held theory."[51]

It is important to note that in describing the theory of Aryanism as "nonsense," Zollschan by no means meant to condemn racial thought in toto.[52] Aryanism was nonsense not because it was derived in large part—though, significantly, not entirely—from racial science. Nor did Zollschan condemn hierarchies constructed along racial lines per se. Rather, it was the claim of Aryan superiority and Jewish inferiority to which he, and other Jewish social scientists, objected. The science of race provided Zionists, just as it provided non-Jewish racial thinkers, with the tools for establishing, or at least reinforcing, Jewish identity and difference.

If, as Zionism claimed, Jews were united by more than a common faith, and yet lacked many of the attributes associated with nationhood—common territory, language, manners and customs—then on what basis could the Jews be said to constitute a *Volk*? Jewish racial unity and particularity provided scientific proof for Zionist claims that despite apparent differences between Jews around the world, they nonetheless constituted a people or nation. In other words, geographic disunity was transcended, and temporal unity established through the social scientific narrative. Moreover, the racial continuity posited by Zionist social scientists between modern Jewry and the ancient Near East reinforced Zionist claims on Palestine. Just as iconographic representations demonstrated that Jews were not part of Germany and Europe, so, too, these images provided evidence that the Jews did in fact *belong*, in a fundamental way, in Palestine.

As early as 1862, the German Jewish writer Moses Hess argued along these lines in his work *Rome and Jerusalem*. Hess was not a social scientist per se; nor does his writing fall within the time frame of this study. Nonetheless, it is clear that Hess was familiar with the anthropological and archaeological literature being produced about the Jews, and that he incorporated some of this into his own work. A consideration of his ideas is therefore helpful in arriving at a notion of the continuity of these themes in social scientific and Jewish nationalist literatures. Hess adopted a quasi-polygenist position, claiming that "the Jewish race is one of the primary races of mankind that has retained its integrity, in spite of the continual change of its climatic environment, and the Jewish type has conserved its purity through the centuries."[53] It has exhibited, as anthropologists recognize, the same "physiological and psychical characteristics" over the course of thousands of years. Ancient Egyptian monuments, "depict Negroes as well as Indo-Germanic and Semitic types, races which have lived from time immemorial in the same land and which were likewise scattered in different countries and climates, yet their primal types have not undergone any perceptible changes."[54]

The main theme of Hess's work was the failure of Jewish emancipation, the impossibility of successful assimilation, and the need for a renewed Jewish nationalism and national home. Appropriating the language of race, he posited an "inborn racial antagonism" of Germans for Jews, an antagonism that made normal life for Jews in Germany an impossibility. Physiognomy, for Hess, played a crucial role in German racial antipathy, as well as in Jewish "self-hatred" and delusion. The German "hates the Jewish religion less than the race; he objects less to the Jews' peculiar beliefs than to their particular noses." And the Jew, on the other hand, fools himself into believing he can alter his appearance, thereby transforming himself into what he most wishes to be—a German. Hess linked this futile attempt on the part of some Jews "to deny their racial descent" with the Reform movement, which "lays the ax at the root of Judaism and its national historical cult. . . . Jewish noses cannot be reformed, and the black, wavy hair of the Jews will not change through conversion into blond, nor can its curves be straightened out by constant combing."[55]

According to Hess, it was this Jewish racial particularity, and the hatred it elicited among Germans, that rendered false the liberal promise of integration. Shlomo Avineri is correct in pointing out that Hess viewed this racial struggle as a product of an historical dialectic, and envisioned a time in the future when it would give way to a longed-for universalism.[56] However, considered within the context of his attacks on emancipation, assimilation, and reform, along with his call for a return of the Jews to Palestine, the implications of his notions about race seem clear. The Jews are not, as liberals and reformers claimed, "Germans of the Mosaic faith." Hess condemned the hatred between groups brought about by racialism, and predicted the eventual disappearance of this antagonism; nonetheless, he wrote about race in essentialist terms, positing it as an objective factor in history. The Jews were not and could never be Germans, for *Judentum* and *Deutschtum* stamped individual members with immutable traits, physical signs of racial identity and difference. In order to demonstrate this racial identity of the Jews, Hess turned to the visual images found on ancient monuments:

On the western mountain slope which encloses the City of the Dead, at Thebes, in Egypt, there still exists the tomb of one of the ancient architects, who supervised the construction of the king's buildings, on which are depicted reliefs of all the works constructed under his direction. Here we can see how the obelisks were erected, the sphinxes hewn out of the rock, the palaces built, as well as how all the preliminary labor was performed. Here are scenes representing white Asiatic slaves making bricks, many of which are piled up near the building, while other slaves are carrying stones away. At a little distance from the group of laboring slaves stands the overseer with raised whip in his hand. The tomb was built, according to the inscription, about the time of Moses, and in the reliefs of the Asiatic slaves there is a resemblance to the present Jewish type. Later Egyptian monuments, likewise, show Jewish reliefs which strikingly resemble our modern Jews."[57]

These images established the identity of ancient and modern Jews, and, by implication, the differences between Jews and Germans. Furthermore, within the context of Hess's plea for a Jewish return to Palestine, this passage suggests that the "proper place" for Jews is not Europe but Palestine, to which Jews remain connected racially as well as historically.

This mode of argument became a commonplace among Zionist social scientists in the first decades of the twentieth century. The physician and racial scientist Elias Auerbach argued for the "racial unity" of Jews and other Semitic peoples on the strength of iconographic evidence in an article published in the prestigious scientific journal *Archiv für Rassen- und Gesellschaftsbiologie*. Auerbach challenged the prevalent notion in racial science that the ancient Semites were long-headed, or dolichocephalic, and that the round-headedness of Jews proved that no racial unity existed between Arabs and Jews.

One would be justified in protesting against this interpretation (Semitic longheadedness). In contrast to it, there is the true unity of character of the Babylonians, Assyrians, Phoenicians, Arabs and Jews. It is a unity that is made known in their illustrations, their language, their legends, their architecture, and frequently their original religious forms, down to the smallest details. The pictorial representations of the Assyrians and Babylonians that we have show not only a great conformity with the ancient representation of Jews, but also a surprising similarity with today's Jewish type. We are also justified in speaking of a general Semitic type, to which Jews belong.[58]

Whereas Joseph Jacobs had argued for a disunity between Jews and other Semitic nations, thus allowing him to represent broad-headed Jews as European (albeit, not as a result of racial mixing), Auerbach insisted on the unity of Jews and other Near Eastern peoples. This unity, and the categorization of the Jews as Semites, were aspects of Auerbach's attempt to provide a scientific basis to the Zionist claim of an intimate and inextricable Jewish connection to Palestine. A similar sort of argument can be found in the anthropologist J. M. Judt's 1902 work, *Die Juden als Rasse*.[59] Judt denied that the racial formation of the Jews occurred during their wanderings in

Europe, and that variations in geography and environment produced any meaningful changes. Rather, the Jews were a product of "distant primary wanderings during the period of political independence," in which the ancient Hebrews intermingled with numerous Semitic nations—Amorites, Hittites, Kushites, and so forth. One could not, therefore, speak of the Jews as a "pure" race. Racial formation was a dynamic process. And although he disagreed with the contention of the prominent American racial scientist William Ripley that the ghetto experience had formed the Jews racially, he granted that this had produced a particular type of emotional, social, and economic sensibility. Nonetheless, all of these were "secondary characteristics." Primary traits, he maintained, had remained stable over time. "In view of the fact that antiquity produced the Jewish physiognomy, we find a striking resemblance between the Jews of then and now. One has only to remember the images of Jewish prisoners of war in the epoch of Schischaks, or the settlers of Lachish in the time of Sennacherib. One has the impression that these are a collection of images of contemporary Jews."[60]

Judt reproduced dozens of plates drawn from works of archaeology and ethnology, as well as line drawings of ancient reliefs, exhibited in the British Museum in London. Photographs of contemporary Jews, mostly inhabitants of regions in the Near East and Eastern Europe, were also reproduced. The profiles of ancient Hittites, Amorites and Canaanites, labeled "Semitic" or "Jewish" types, and the profiles of modern-day Jews also labeled according to type, provided Judt with an iconographic narrative of race.

This mode of thought and the utilization of iconography was by no means limited to Central European Zionist scholars. We can find it, for instance, in the writings of the Anglo-Jewish geneticist and Zionist Redcliffe Nathan Salaman, who argued for a racial identity of Jewry and a biological link to Palestine, and sought support for such arguments in genetics, history, and iconography. As a geneticist Salaman was unequivocally committed to Mendelism, and this led him to embrace more fully than did most of the other social scientists we have encountered a biological definition of Jewish identity. He was not a thoroughgoing racial determinist, but Salaman did seek to minimize the effects of environmental factors. Environment "may call forth that which is latent both in spiritual and physical realms, [however] it does not of itself modify the physical type of the human race in a directly causative sense, at any rate within the compass of historic times."[61] In a series of articles published during the first two decades of the twentieth century, Salaman applied this principle to the case of the Jews, and set out to demonstrate the physical identity of Jewry.[62] He argued for the relative purity of "Jewish blood," and for the physiognomic and anatomical distinctiveness, if not uniformity, of the Jews. Salaman granted that in ancient times the Jews mixed with other nations and peoples. However, he rejected the evidence brought by Fishberg and others about the extensive mixing of Jews and others in Europe. "Fishberg would see intermixture everywhere. . . . [However] there is very little solid fact to substantiate the view that the Jewish type varies directly and in accordance with the non-Jewish physical type of the district, or that European Jews are infiltrated with non-Jewish local blood."[63] Rather, there is "a typical Jewish facial physiognomy and expression" which survived despite centuries of dispersion.

In addition to the proof provided by Mendelian genetics, evidence of this physical uniformity could be found in the iconography of the ancient Near East and in artistic works of the West:

> The peculiar facial expression is at least not the outcome of recent times. We have evidence of the greatest antiquity. In the Assyrian sculptures, 800 B.C., are depicted Jewish prisoners who are thoroughly Jewish . . . and Petrie[64] has brought home from Memphis terra-cotta heads dating from 500 B.C. of Jews at once recognizable by the Jewishness. On a forest roll of the pre-expulsion times in England, is a pen and ink sketch, or one might rather say a caricature of a certain Aaron, "Son of the Devil," dated 1277 which, crude though it is, hits off a distinctly Jewish type. . . . The great master Rembrandt has given us numerous drawings of Jews."[65]

Thus, despite the elapse of a millennium and extensive geographic dispersion, the Jews remain more or less the same.

The racial origins of the Jews can be found in the ancient Near East, in the mixture of the Hebrews with other indigenous peoples: the Hittites (known in modern times as the Armenian people), the Amorites, and the Philistines. Salaman was adamant on the point that these ancient groups were white, and that at least in the case of the Philistines, their features corresponded with what European racial science had long identified as superior physical characteristics. The Hittites were a "white people, with black hair and eyes, and the aquiline, strongly Jewish nose, and the Amorites [were] . . . probably light skinned and had amongst them a number of fair-haired persons."[66]

Ancient iconography played a crucial role in Salaman's reconstruction of the Philistines' racial profile. The Philistines display "delicate classical features." Taking a page straight out of eighteenth-century physiognomic texts, Salaman extolled the facial and cranial proportions of the race: "The nose and brow are in one more or less vertical line, the chin is small but well-formed, the mouth and lips delicate, the head is clearly a long one." He then linked the Philistines to the ancient Greeks, the embodiment of perfection for eighteenth- and nineteenth-century racial thinkers,[67] and assured his readers that the Philistines were a "white skinned people."

Without doubt, Salaman's interest in and interpretation of Jewish racial origins, like Joseph Jacobs's before him, owed much to the particular British context. The insistence on the nobility, purity, and "whiteness" of Jewry must be understood within the broader context of the Anglo-Jewish concern with what Todd Endelman has called "uncertain gentility." The status of elite Jewry within respectable British society was "a vexing, unresolved question."[68] Establishing the nobility, the respectability of Jewry was therefore an ongoing process. It entailed not only the reform and relief efforts of communal institutions, but also the intellectual work of scholars such as Salaman. Moreover, since in Great Britain "definitions of the nation did not rest on notions of organic solidarity or racial homogeneity to the extent they did elsewhere," Jews could assert their collective difference or distinctiveness with less fear of doing harm to their claims to being British.[69]

At the same time, Salaman's work on Jews and race must be understood within the context of his developing commitment to Zionism, and to his engagement with social scientific debates that transcended the British context. As Endelman has argued, Salaman's belief in the racial identity of the Jews "spurred or reinforced his interest in Zionism."[70] His commitment to the "hard" genetics of Mendelism allowed him to argue for the constancy of physical traits, and thus to maintain that despite the millennium-long sojourn in Europe, the Jews remained "Israelites," essentially unchanged from their ancient Hebrew ancestors.[71] Like Auerbach and Judt, Salaman maintained that there had been "no modification in physical types" of European or American Jewry in racial terms since commencement of the Christian era. And he believed that knowledge of the racial origins and nature of the Jews could shed valuable light on modern Jewry. The classical Greek features of the Philistines, for instance, account for the 20 or so percent of Jews today who have "pseudo-Gentile" features. One cannot explain this, as Fishberg and others are wont to do, by "teutonic intermixture" in the Diaspora, but by Philistine stock.[72] In an article from 1925, published in *The Palestine Exploration Fund Quarterly*, Salaman made the connection between genetics and politics explicit. The "recessive Pseudo-Gentile type asserts itself as the laws of Mendel would lead us to expect, and gives us today Jews who are physically indistinguishable from the Philistine enemy of old." Salaman then went on to relate how, serving in the British Army in Palestine during the war, he had observed the young Jewish colonists. He commented favorably on their muscular development and on their greater than average height.

It was, however, the facial type of the younger generation that was most interesting. The outstanding fact was that the Palestinian youths presented a very considerably higher proportion of Pseudo-Gentile faces than did their foreign brethren of the other batallione. Indeed it would appear that some force was at work which was bringing into existence again the old Philistine type in the land of the Philistines. . . . It may therefore be forgiven the writer if, when looking at the young home-born Palestinian Jews as they were marshalled under their Zionist banner on the plain of Sharon, and noticing the prevalence of the Pseudo-Gentile type of face he fancied that here, too, perhaps was evidence of another correlation, a correlation between the spirit of adventure and the Pseudo-Gentile type of face.[73]

Here was persuasive "empirical" proof, offered less than a decade after the Balfour Declaration and the assumption of British control over Palestine, that Jews remained essentially the same despite the myriad transformations throughout their history. The racial origins of the Jews in Palestine, and the uniformity of type maintained in exile, meant that the Jewish people "belonged" in a biological sense *to* the Land of Israel—even if many Jews in Britain and the West, Salaman included, could not quite see themselves living *in* the Land of Israel.

Is there not a contradiction, then, between this assertion of a stable Jewish physiognomy, pointing to a racial identity, and the fear of Jewish physical "decline," including a transformation at the anatomical level? On the one hand, anthropological and iconographic evidence suggested that the Jews were racially united, if not unified; that this racial identity was constituted at the beginnings of their history, and that the exigencies of exile had done little to alter this fact. Nature seems to have trumped nurture when Zionists came to write about racial identity; environmental forces appear to have had little substantive impact. On the other hand, the danger of assimilation lay with the qualitative as well as the quantitative changes it purportedly wrought. As the earlier discussion of intermarriage demonstrated, Zionist social scientists feared the negative impact of Jewish and Christian mixing; it threatened the physiological or "racial" character of the Jews. The contradiction, however, is only apparent. Stability did not necessarily mean immutability. Surely, most Zionists were unwilling to grant, as Fishberg had, for instance, that Jewish history was indeed characterized by such intermixture; they certainly were unwilling to embrace this as a positive phenomenon. But they did believe that such intermixture was possible, and that its significance for collective Jewish life ought not to be underestimated. And this was the import, for most Zionists at least, of the radical, unprecedented nature of modern assimilation. It threatened to efface Jewish identity to a degree hitherto unimagined. In focusing on the continuity of the Jewish physiognomy Zionists believed they could provide further evidence for the unity of the Jewish People. Simultaneously, assimilation—

as their analyses made clear—severely threatened this unity and identity. This identity could only be maintained, or regained, through the successful effort of Jewish national regeneration in Palestine.

In *Die Juden der Gegenwart*, Arthur Ruppin argued that the Jews had maintained a high degree of racial unity (which he distinguished from racial purity), and exhibited a continuity of clearly recognizable physical and moral characteristics.[74] And, like other Zionist social scientists, he made a case for the racial affinity of the Jews with what he termed other *"vorderasiatische,"* or Near-Eastern races, particularly the Armenians. In a footnote Ruppin referred to Richard Andree's use of ancient bas-reliefs and his rejection of the idea that Jews were related racially with Armenians. He countered with examples from different bas-reliefs, arguing that indeed Jews and Armenians were related. Interestingly, in the same note Ruppin cited photographic evidence found in Andree's work to prove the somatological unity of modern Jewry:

It is well known just how great remains the similarity of morphological type among the Jews of all lands. One finds among the Jews in Galicia and Russia oftentimes precisely the same face as among those in Germany, France and Holland. A well-trained anthropologist will in only a very few instances not recognize a Jew as such. In any case, the morphological similarity (and its cause: the unity of descent, that is—race) among the Jews is far greater than among other European nations. Despite the greatest distance and remoteness, Jews of East and West resemble one another, although between them no contact has taken place for centuries. . . . So, for example, von Brandt (*33 Jahre in Ostasien*, Bd. I, p. 39, Leipzig 1901) could speak of a remarkable similarity between the Jews of Aden (Arabia) and the Jews of Galicia and Russia/Poland, while Andree commented that photographs of southern Arabian Jews . . . could easily have been made from originals taken [of Jews] in Leipzig. In Egypt and Persia, in Samarkand as in Palestine the similarity of the Jews with those in Europe is extraordinary.[75]

The "morphological similarity" of the Jews indicated a number of things to Ruppin. As this passage makes clear, it united the Jews both temporally and spatially. Authorities acknowledged that "despite the greatest distance and remoteness, Jews of East and West resemble one another." Moreover, this physical unity, or at least similarity, allowed Ruppin to maintain that a "spiritual" or intellectual (*geistliche*) unity existed among Jews. Evidence for such a unity could be found in particular Jewish "talents," including economic and intellectual overachievement. In turn, this maintenance of the characteristic talents of the race, strengthened over time through a Darwinian selection process, proved the "racial worth" of the Jews. This, then, demonstrated the necessity of preserving the Jews as a culture and a race. Since Ruppin believed that the continued assimilation of Jews into advanced Western civilization and culture posed an imminent threat of "race suicide," racial and cultural preservation could only be accomplished through the Zionist goal of a separate state and society. In Ruppin's view, the great physiological and intellectual similarities of the Jews and those groups indigenous to the Near East (Semites and *Vorderasiatischen*) provided racio-historical evidence for national Jewish claims to Palestine.

Increasingly convinced of the value of racial iconographic evidence, Ruppin amassed a considerable collection of such material, and incorporated it into his scientific studies.[76] Living and working in Palestine from 1907, he traveled widely throughout the region, photographing members of the various Jewish ethnic communities. In addition, he clipped hundreds of pictures of Jews from international newspapers, collected ethnographic postcards, and familiarized himself with the scholarship of others who had included pictures of Jews in their works. In diary entries from the mid-1920s Ruppin clarified the relationship he believed existed between Zionism, racial science, and iconography, and the need to make this a central theme of his own work:

I think that Zionism is tenable only if it is provided with a completely different scientific foundation. Herzl's view was naïve and only makes sense in the light of his complete ignorance of the conditions in Palestine. We will once more have to take our place among the Oriental peoples and create a new cultural community in the Near East, together with our racial cousins, the Arabs (and the Armenians). I think that Zionism is less than ever justifiable now except by the fact that the Jews belong racially to the peoples of the Near East. I am now collecting material for a book on the Jews to be based on the problem of race. I want to include illustrations showing the ancient peoples of the Orient and the contemporary population and describe the types that used to and still predominate among the peoples living in Syria and Asia Minor. I want to demonstrate that these same types still exist among the Jews of today.[77]

During the years 1924–26 Ruppin undertook the research for this planned book on "the Jewish race," and photography played a significant part in his conceptualization of the work.[78]

However, he never published this separate work on race. Rather, he included the material in his comprehensive two-volume study *Die Soziologie der Juden*, published in 1930.[79] Ruppin opened the work with a section entitled "Origins and Race of the Jews," and devoted a subsection to "pictorial representations of the Jews from antiquity." The Jews, he wrote, have left us no representations of themselves, their religion having forbidden the making of images. We do find, however, representations of Jews on monuments left by their neighbors:

The Salmanassar Obelisk, dating from the ninth century B.C. and now in the British

Museum, gives us a representation of Jews in Palestine. It shows us the emissaries of King Jehu of Israel bringing tribute to Salmanassar. A. H. Sayce [*The Races of the Old Testament*, London: The Religious Tract Society, 1879] remarks that these Jews display the characteristic features of Jews of today. "No modern painter could portray them more accurately," writes Sayce.[80]

The conjunction of racial continuity, Palestine, and iconography appears again here. The Jews of Palestine, as represented on the ancient monuments, "display the characteristic features of Jews of today."

At the end of the first volume of his work Ruppin appended 32 pages of reproductions and photographs of ancient images and of Jews from various countries and communities around the world. The ancient images were the same as had appeared in scores of archaeological and anthropological texts, some of which have been analyzed here. Most of the photographs had been taken by Ruppin in his years of traveling in Palestine and the surrounding regions. The remainder were taken from other published texts. Ruppin's collage of images tells the story of Jewish racial unity and continuity over time, while also making clear the geographic as well as the racial origins of contemporary Diaspora Jewry. Setting ancient images of "Semites" together with photographs of contemporary Jews would serve to illustrate the truth of the Zionist claim that the Jews belonged in Palestine, while the photographs of contemporary Jews—from Eastern and Western Europe, England and the United States, Palestine, Morocco, Yemen, Algeria, and elsewhere—purportedly demonstrated, as Herzl had put it, that "the Jews are one people."

Strategically organized on the page, the photographs made a number of subtle points about national identity. For example, Albert Einstein's face is placed on the same page as those of the British diplomats Lord Reading and Herbert Samuel, and an anonymous Jewish woman from Palestine. Einstein is classified typologically as "mediterranean." Reading and Samuel are not classified; the woman, we are informed, comes from a Sephardic mother and an Ashkenazic father.[81] The captions inform the reader that these are Jews from different countries, from varying environments and climates. The faces themselves, grouped as they are together on the page, invite the reader to identify these individuals as typologically similar and related. That is, differences in what might be termed subjective identity— one's own sense of national identity—are obviated by a deeper, more fundamental "objective" reality, rooted in biology as well as history.

The individual qua individual is meaningless in this context. It is not Einstein's genius, his unique personality or scientific contributions, which are of significance and interest here. Precisely the opposite. It is as a representative of a type, as a Jew with recognizably "typical" features, that he has meaning. In fact, Einstein—the genius—proves the point that, regardless of intelligence, status, or class, the Jew is above all else a member of a particular and identifiable nation and race. The photo "montage" provides an immediacy and power that the written narrative, with its statistical tables, does not possess. It makes the Zionist argument tangible and concrete: the German Jew, the English Jew, and the Palestinian Jew are "identical," and a reconfiguration of Jewish national identity along social scientific and raciohistorical lines is "empirically" validated. At the same time, when viewed in the context of Ruppin's social scientific narrative about the imminent threat to Jewish identity posed by assimilation, the visual narrative offers further proof of what Jewry stands to lose if the nationalist project does not succeed.

An analysis of the role of iconographic representation within social scientific texts demonstrates the way in which a highly coherent and routinized discourse about the Jews as a race developed, and the extent to which it was accepted and reproduced by Jewish as well as non-Jewish writers for particular ideological purposes. The combination of ancient illustration and contemporary photography became a common hermeneutic and analytic device by which meta-individual identities and differences were discovered and reconstructed.[82] The same images from ancient Egypt and Assyria appeared time and again in the works of racial and social scientists, as did many of the same photographs. Iconography, like statistics, offered scientists a sustained tradition of interpretation into which they could place their own works. Judt, for example, referred at the outset of his book to the 1829 study of the French ethnologist Edwards, who argued for the racial purity of Jews and pointed to the pictures from Egypt in the tombs of the pharaohs, as well as to Leonardo da Vinci's "The Last Supper" as proof of Jewish physiognomic continuity.[83] Judt's analysis, including the evidence iconography offered, served as one of Sombart's primary sources in his study on Jews and modern capitalism. And Ruppin, in turn, was motivated in his work by Sombart's analysis, as well as by the extreme racialist Hans F. K. Günther.

This proliferation of images was due in part to turn-of-the-century technological developments that made reproducing photographs cheaper and easier.[84] More important, it testified to the degree to which the visual image had, during the last half of the nineteenth century, come to be accepted as an almost unimpeachable source of scientific truth, as well as a tool for political persuasion and social change. Social reformers, criminologists, eugenicists, and racial scientists attempted to harness the power of the photograph to the body of statistical facts as a means of advancing one or another political or social agenda.[85]

The conflation of older, more traditional forms of visual representation with photography sought the advantage or power of mechanical reproduction while at the same time denying its uniqueness. Racial and social scientists displayed a faith in images *as such*, believing them to be unmediated reflections of the reality science sought to understand and control. For racial scientists, both Jewish and non-Jewish, ancient and modern iconographic representations of Jews demonstrated the assumed continuity of the Jews as a race over time, and their essential difference from European races and peoples. Zionist social scientists accepted this tenet of continuity and difference. Jews, they argued, were united by more than a common faith and a shared history; their identity was rooted in a fundamental physical, biological "Jewishness," which bound them—despite time and space—to one another and to their ancestral homeland.

## CHAPTER SEVEN

# National Economy and the Debate over Jewish Regeneration

"Until the middle of the previous century," Jacob Segall wrote in 1911, "the economy developed only slowly. The transition from one form of economy to another, for example from the natural [i.e., agricultural] to a money economy, proceeded gradually. This meant that the need to gain a knowledge of developments was limited. In the last few decades, because of revolutionary transformations in political economy, technology, and social relations, a more exact knowledge of economic and social conditions became necessary."[1] Segall's explanation for the heightened interest in political economy situated his own work, and by implication that of other Jewish social scientists, within the context of general German and European developments. Indeed, these developments do account in part for the emergence of a systematic study of Jewish economic life beginning at the end of the nineteenth century. The "revolutionary transformations" of which Segall wrote—industrialization, urbanization, mass migration, and class tensions—exerted no less profound an impact upon Jews, and impelled investigations into the effects of these changes.

Together with this, developments that might be termed "internal" to Jewry, yet that directly related to the broader structural changes mentioned above, further highlighted the need for social scientific research. The persecution and misery of the Jews in Eastern Europe, and their large-scale immigration to the West in the last decades of the nineteenth century, fueled interest in a social scientific approach. This was initially part of programmatic efforts at relief and regeneration aimed at the poor and working-class sectors, mainly of Eastern European origin. By the first decade of the twentieth century Jewish social scientists had also turned their attention to the Jewish middle class of Central and Western Europe. The prominence of economic themes in scientific and popular anti-Semitic discourse imbued these tasks with an added political and social urgency.[2]

The impetus to Jewish social scientific research into economic issues, among both liberal integrationists and Zionists, was both apologetic and self-critical. Jewish statistics, as the organizers of the Verein für jüdische Statistik explained it, was motivated by the "psychological" need to answer anti-Semitic accusations ("Is what the anti-Semites say correct? Are we corrupt and corrupting as a whole? Are we really greedy and wealthy, hoarding riches?") and the practical desire to "create the foundations for the alleviation of Jewish mass misery."[3]

Shaping the analyses of these descriptive statistics was a set of assumptions and questions regarding the value of particular types of economic labor: agriculture, crafts, trade and industry, and the free professions; the nature and value of capitalism; the role of the Jews in capitalism's origins and development; and the effects capitalism exerted upon Jewry. To what extent could the present-day occupational distribution of Jewry be ascribed to a Jewish penchant or predisposition to trade and commerce reaching back to biblical times? Were the Jews the embodiment of the capitalist ethos, and could this be a national and/or racial attribute? Could one discover, through historical analysis, a pattern or "law" of Jewish economic life, and what implications did this have for the Jewish present and future?

As with the other categories of research discussed thus far, Jewish economic activities and conditions were assigned meaning and significance within the broader debate, held among Jews and non-Jews, over the status and character of Jewry as a whole. Questions of identity and difference, normalcy and abnormality, progress and degeneration, assimilation and nationalism were addressed through an analysis of economic issues. The socioeconomic conditions of Eastern and Western European Jewries were conceived as fundamental determinants of other phenomena such as birth and death rates, physical and mental health, educational levels, criminality and suicide. Economic analyses shaped in fundamental ways the interpretive framework within which these other "facts" of Jewish life were explained.

Economic research was understood to have direct import for practical instrumental goals. Investigations into current levels of poverty or occupational distribution, for instance, aided in the conceptualization of what had thus far been accomplished, and what still needed to be done to reform Jewry. Or, to take another example: research by Zionists into the status of the ICA's projects of economic retraining and resettlement in Palestine and elsewhere pointed up the "failure" of the colonization efforts, while at the same time providing needed guidelines for Jewish nationalist policy and activity. However, as significant as the practical side to social science was, it is not the focus of this analysis.[4] My interest, rather, is in exploring the central themes of the discussion and debate over Jews and modern economic life, and in showing the ways in which the representation of the socioeconomic status of Jewry functioned ideologically. This chapter places such analyses within the context of a European, and particularly a German, historical and social scientific interpretive framework, and it traces the discursive interconnections between the economic and social, and other categories and themes of Jewish social science.

## Relief and Regeneration in the Diaspora

Jewish social scientific studies of economic issues were shaped from the outset by the need to comprehend, and if possible to alter, the actual conditions of Jewry, and to respond to the anti-Semitic discourse that linked Jewish economic activity with corruption and disease.[5] Beginning in the late 1880s integrationist organizations such as the Deutsch-Israelitische Gemeindebund, the B'nai Brith, the Österreichische-Israelitische Union, and the ICA sponsored statistical surveys of conditions in Eastern and Western Europe in an effort to acquire requisite knowledge for philanthropic and economic retraining programs.[6] These studies, together with governmental censuses and surveys, were the main sources for later Jewish social scientific analyses.[7] They stressed the overwhelming poverty of much of Jewry, the concentration of Jews in what were considered "unproductive" occupations—primarily petty trade and commerce—and their alienation from agriculture and craftswork.

On the one hand, it was believed, social scientific analyses of Jews and the economy would serve to counter anti-Semitic characterizations of Jewry as a "nation of millionaires." On the other, the demands of philanthropic activity and the urge to reform and restructure Jewish economic life demanded the sort of knowledge provided by social scientific inquiries.[8] The philanthropic and reformist impulses were wedded into a social policy designed to meliorate poverty and suffering, and to facilitate the *embourgeoisement* of lower-class Jews. For liberal Jewish social scientists the imbalance in Jewish economic pursuits was ultimately a sign of the incomplete course of Jewish integration. The occupational redistribution of Jewry, and its increasing bourgeoisification, were conceived in terms of progress, or, as one B'nai Brith official put it, as movement toward "the true and final emancipation of the Jews in the ethical and social realms."[9]

Within the liberal paradigm of progress, positive change occurred as a result of subjective will and broader transformations within the European economy and society. Both of these assumed an environmental determinism of Jewish economic conditions and activities. These determinants were both external and internal; that is, they derived from forces emanating from without and within the Jewish community. On the one hand, historical and contemporary political and legal restrictions forced Jews into a limited number of professions or occupations. On the other hand, atavistic religious and social beliefs and practices inhibited any significant material or occupational improvement.

At work here was the East/West, traditional/modern moral valuation that reached back at least as far as the eighteenth-century debates over the improvement or the regeneration of Jewry.[10] Maurice Fishberg argued that "the Western European Jews, who, but seventy five years ago, lived in a condition of poverty and want, due to legal degradation, have recuperated within the last five decades, after their disabilities have been removed. The same process is repeated at present with the Jewish immigrants in the United States and England." On the one hand, according to Fishberg, "the social and economic conditions of the Jews are thus seen to depend on their political status."[11] Where Jews were allowed the freedom of choice in residence, occupation, and so forth, they thrived. On the other hand, degeneration was not merely the result of "external," that is, political or legal, causes. Jews would also, in Fishberg's opinion, need to make a constant effort to assimilate. "For wherever they did so successfully, they were prosperous. When they refused to do this, or were forbidden from doing so, they [were] generally poor and destitute."[12]

Socioeconomic progress among Jewry was the product of increasing liberalization and modernization on the part of state, society, and the Jews themselves. The overt political context for Fishberg's analysis was the Anglo-American debate over immigration. "This capacity for regeneration is of immense importance for those who are troubled about the problem of immigration in England and the United States, and who are horrified by the thought of the invasion of the 'alien pauper' and the resulting consequences."[13] Just as Fishberg had argued that anthropologically and biologically the Jews were transformed for the better through a change in milieu, so too their socioeconomic progress led to similar improvements.

For liberal social scientists, economic regeneration was linked causally with the social and cultural modernization or Westernization of Jewry. "The economic deprivation and the low cultural level of the [Jewish] masses are inextricably bound," the Austrian communal leader Siegfried Fleischer wrote in an article published in *Jüdische Statistik*. "The 'standard of life' rises with the penetration of culture, and greater conditions for earning a livelihood. The two depend upon each other. This is demonstrated when we compare the way of life of contemporary Central and Western European Jews with those of the past times of the ghetto (in the West)."[14] Regeneration, in this view, was the overcoming of the barriers sustained by premodern beliefs and practices, whether they be those erected by government, guild, or religion.

In the first decades of the twentieth century liberal Jewish social scientists were already documenting such a positive economic redistribution of Jewry. The most systematic and sustained analysis of Jewish economic conditions along liberal lines came from Jacob Segall. In a 1908 monograph Segall analyzed the occupational statistics of German Jewry, drawing his data primarily from official German occupational censuses published in 1882 and 1895.[15] The numbers, he claimed, reflected the reality not merely in Germany, but throughout Central and Western Europe. Segall concluded that

three-quarters of all income-earning Jews [*Erwerbstätigen*] in the German Empire are occupied in trade and industry. . . . This occupational distribution is so pronounced, it has become so much a component of Jewry itself, that not only throughout the Empire or in individual states, but everywhere [in the West] where a great number of Jews collect, this occupational distribution reproduces itself.[16]

In 1911–12 Segall published far more extensive and detailed accounts of the economic and social condition of German Jewry in the *Zeitschrift für Demographie und Statistik der Juden*.[17] Once again he based his analysis on the occupational censuses of the German government, this time including the years 1895–1907. In these latest figures he discerned a notable shift in the occupational distribution of German Jewry. The percentage of Jews involved in trade had decreased dramatically, while the numbers of wage-earning Jews in industry and the free professions had risen.

This shift in occupational distribution was, in Segall's view, a product both of structural changes in the German economy and of the Jews' free will. Objective and subjective factors together were responsible for the progress, as he put it, observable in Jewish economic life. Segall acknowledged that this process of redistribution remained incomplete. Jews were still too little represented in civil-service positions and in the state educational system. And they were still too heavily concentrated in urban areas, a fact that he decried as "dangerous."[18] But the causes of this were wholly external. Political and legal restrictions continued to limit Jews' access to the full range of occupations and professions. Concomitantly, occupational restrictions forced Jews into urban areas. Trade and industry have their centers, he wrote, so Jews had to settle in cities. In line with the Enlightenment vision of regeneration, Segall argued that further progress would come as a result of a willed effort on the part of both government and Jewry. "One must note their [the Jews'] deep interest in occupying these positions once they have been truly opened. It is within the power of the state and community to recognize the quality and potential of Jewry," and to respond accordingly.[19] Jews for their part were encouraged to move into rural areas and to take up local civil service positions. In this way they would contribute to the geographic and occupational redistribution of Jewry, and would serve as a model to Jewish youth.[20]

Segall viewed those changes that had already occurred, and that were indicated by the government's own statistics, as an unambiguous refutation of anti-Semitic accusations about Jewish economic activities and, more important, about the Jewish character. Jews did not constitute a *Schachervolk*, a nation of hagglers, nor were they "marked by a distinctive '*Handelsgeist*,'" or intellectual/spiritual predisposition to trade. He thereby made explicit his awareness of the ideological and polemical import of social scientific discussions of Jews and the economy, and his own insistence on normalizing the case of German and by implication all of Western Jewry.[21]

This impulse to normalize was clearly evident in Segall's analysis of the interrelationship between demography, social structure, and occupational distribution. Segall granted the relative decline in the Jewish population between the years 1871–1905. Yet he explained this with reference to the particular socioeconomic structure of Western Jewry, a variable that allowed him to cast this development in a more positive light. "When we consider that the Jews, unlike the general population, lack a real working class—and it is this class that contributes to such a considerable degree to the natural increase of a population—then we describe the development of the Jewish population in the Reich as not unsatisfactory."[22]

Demographic differences also needed to be understood, in Segall's view, as a product of German Jewish migration patterns, which in turn were linked with socioeconomic developments. Beginning in the 1880s Jews moved in massive numbers from the eastern provinces westward, from rural agricultural lands to urban industrial centers. This process of urbanization and industrialization, according to Segall, transformed not only the economic but also the intellectual and social structures of Jewry. It imposed "a type of rationalist thinking with regard to reproduction, which took hold first among the upper classes, and then gradually gained an even greater hold." It became an idea of decisive importance among Jews that children were to receive the best education so as to equip them for the economic and social struggle that defined modern life.[23] This "striving after *Bildung*" was part of the broader economic competition in which Jews now necessarily found themselves engaged. This competition engendered a new "family sensibility" and led to smaller families. "The enormous demands which parents placed upon themselves to insure economic success led to diminished procreation."[24]

This sort of analysis was not so different from the analyses of Zionists like Ruppin and Theilhaber. Yet Segall, while acknowledging a decrease in German Jewish birth rates, sought to portray this as a normal and natural development. It was a by-product of social and economic transformations that impacted not just the Jews, but every modern, civilized population. One ought to comprehend not only birth rates, but each and every social phenomenon within this broader framework. The migration pattern of Jews in the present, for instance, "is not one that defines Jews alone. The general population is taking it upon itself to migrate, and the numbers indicate that this is the largest movement of populations in history." The shift from agriculture to industry, from rural to urban centers, defined Germany and much of Western Europe as a whole over the latter half of the nineteenth and the first decade of the twentieth centuries.[25] Segall's de-emphasis of the issue of Jewry's "alienation" from agricultural pursuits was particularly significant, given that this alienation was a prime focus of those who would argue for Jewry's degenerate character and condition. For Segall, German Jewry's economic path mirrored that of Germany as a whole, and pointed to the conjunction of the Jewish and German economic present: "The German Jew recognized earlier the direction of modernity, which now expresses itself economically in Germany's development. He willingly follows this direction, and thereby takes an even stronger part in the industrial flowering of Germany."[26] Segall achieved here a rhetorical reconciliation of the differences and tensions he himself had noted throughout his article. In the above passage, as in others, the twin forces of objective structural development and subjective will converged to bring about a substantive change in Jewish economic life, and to facilitate the ongoing integration of Jewry into German society.

Segall moved back and forth in his analysis between acknowledging and rejecting any causal connection between the economic and the demographic. Even as he utilized the statistics generated about birth rates and occupational distribution, he challenged their validity on methodological grounds. This challenge constituted yet one more strategy for delegitimizing the arguments about modern Jewry's declining state. To do this, Segall invoked the concept of incommensurability (*Incommensurabilität*), or the incompatibility of categories.

Social scientists, he argued, were accustomed to comparing Jewish birth rates with those of the general Christian population. Yet they neglected to factor in the differential of age, and the effect of this on reproduction. Due to their lower rates of mortality, Segall maintained, Jews counted more individuals among the age group of fifty and above; hence, the Jewish population contained a greater number of "unproductive" individuals. They also possessed a higher number of urban dwellers, whose social conditions differed from those of the general population. Therefore, "a comparison in usual statistical terms is mistaken." To gain an exact comparison "one would require a special fertility statistics that is now lacking."[27]

As we have seen, the notion of Jewish "unproductivity" in terms of natural increase was central to social scientific narratives of contemporary Jewish life. As a result of numerous forces, Jewry—and Western Jewry in particular—had forfeited its traditional advantage vis-à-vis the Christian population. This decline in fertility had been linked to Jewish "unproductivity" in the economic realm.[28] Segall rejected this link between demography and economy, arguing that imprecision in statistical categorization and comparison had led social scientists to misrepresent the reasons for the slower rate of increase in the number of Jewish wage-earners (*Erwerbstätigen*). This had led scientists to conclude mistakenly that "the Jewish population represents occupationally a completely different mass than the general population."[29] He granted that there were relatively fewer wage earners (17.2 percent) among Jews than among Christians (29.1 percent). In order to explain this difference one needed to examine more carefully the categories, and their effect on the overall numbers.

Agriculture and industry were both economic realms in which youth and women could participate. Industry in particular, Segall noted, was now heavily populated by women. Yet these were not sectors in which Jews had been highly represented. Only recently had they become involved in industry in any appreciable numbers, and their negligible representation in agriculture, a result of their settling overwhelmingly in cities, was well established. In contrast to industry and agriculture, both trade and the free professions tended to exclude women and youth. And the latter were precisely the economic areas in which Jews had been concentrated. It was not the case, therefore, that Jews showed fewer wage earners because they produced fewer "dependents"—women and youth. Rather, occupational distribution and the nature of these occupations dictated a lower statistical level of wage earners among German Jewry. This was so "not because the Jews are less capable of earning a wage . . . but because numerically they constitute less of a contingent."[30]

Argued to its logical conclusion, the concept of incommensurability would have undercut the entire Jewish statistical enterprise, for which comparison between Jew and non-Jew had been fundamental. Yet this was clearly not Segall's purpose. Rather, he wished, on the one hand, to advance an argument for a more nuanced methodology. Differences due to age and gender needed to be factored in before valid numbers pertaining to fertility or economic activity could be produced. On the other hand, this was also a means by which to defuse or counter the claims, to which Segall made explicit reference, about decline and degeneration. Pointing to the uncertainty of the numbers, and to the inadequacy of the method of their production, cast doubt on arguments, including those made by Zionists, about the pathological or abnormal condition of Western Jewry.

A liberal integrationist interpretive framework did acknowledge the difference between Jewish and general non-Jewish economic life. "What allows us," Segall asked, "to discuss as a particular phenomenon the economic and social condition of Jewry in Germany? Simply this, that the social structure and the occupational distribution of Jews departs in many significant respects from that of the general population."[31] Yet this difference was a condition to be transcended within Germany itself (and by extension within other modern nations), through willed efforts at self-reform and through objective changes in the structure of economy and society. The difference was never pathologized, never made to reflect something unhealthy or unnatural in either the Jewish condition or character. True, philanthropy and social reform, which took economic difference as a given, may have reinforced the Jewish identities of the elite involved in such projects.[32] Yet these liberal elites did not interpret Jewish economic activity in terms of Jewish character, and hence, of Jewish identity. Jewish economic activity, in other words, did not serve as a sign or referent to something beyond itself, to some more fundamental truth about the collective Jewish character.

For Zionists, on the other hand, Jewish collective identity emerged, in part, out of the apperception and representation of economic difference. In particular, the purported penchant and talent Jews had historically evinced for capitalist forms of enterprise pointed beyond the limited economic realm, and to a more fundamental Jewish nature or "spirit." Just as Jewish identity could be demonstrated from the research of anthropologists and physicians, so too an analysis of the relationship between Jews and capitalism, in the past and present, proved the existence of a distinct Jewish national character.

This analysis, and the construction of Jewish identity that emerged from it, owed a great deal to the interpretations of Jews and capitalism that had become, by the end of the nineteenth century, a fixed part of European social scientific (as well as popular) discourse. The interpretations offered by German national economists exerted the most profound influence in this regard.[33]

## The Jews and Capitalism in German Scholarship

The writings of two historical economists in particular, Wilhelm Roscher and Werner Sombart, played an especially crucial role in the thinking of

Zionist social scientists.[34] Roscher's 1875 essay, "Die Stellung der Juden im Mittelalter, betrachtet vom Standpunkt der allgemeinen Handelspolitik" (The Position of the Jews in the Middle Ages Considered from the Standpoint of the General Political Economy), focused on the economic function of the Jewish presence in Europe. It provided an analytical framework within which to comprehend the pattern of settlement and expulsion that appeared to define the history of the Jews in the Middle Ages.[35] According to Roscher, the Jews had settled in Western Europe upon the invitation of Christian kings and princes, who, lacking an indigenous Christian commercial class, were anxious to take advantage of Jewish knowledge and experience in trade and commerce. The disintegration of the Roman Empire in this scheme signaled the disappearance of the ancient capitalist economy and society, and the emergence of a "natural economy" rooted in agriculture among the new "barbarian nations." The Jews, alone among the ancient nations, had survived the downfall of Rome, and they became the repositories or carriers (*Träger*) of ancient commercial knowledge and practice.

As such, the Jews fulfilled a vital economic role or function during the early Middle Ages. Settling in a particular country or region, they would take up the business of trade and commerce. Gradually, however, a Christian middle class would emerge, forged out of an interaction with Jewish merchants. This Christian middle class would now compete with the Jews economically and socially. Supported politically and legally by both church and state, this new Christian middle class would eventually succeed in marginalizing the Jews, forcing them into those limited areas of commerce—particularly moneylending and petty trading—deemed onerous and unfit for Christians. No longer in need of their economic services, the Christian authorities were free to expropriate Jewish wealth, and to persecute—and eventually expel—the Jewish population. "Wherever a middle class developed and established itself earlier or later, there the persecutions of the Jews regularly took place correspondingly early or late."[36] In Roscher's view this cycle had been disrupted by the advent of modern capitalism, which enabled the Christian middle classes to begin to succeed economically without requiring the displacement of the Jews.

The historical economist and sociologist Werner Sombart developed many of Roscher's main themes, adding a pronounced racial and psychological element to his analysis of the relationship between Jewry and capitalism.[37] Moreover, he emphasized, more than had earlier writers, the fundamental role Jews had played in the formation of modern capitalism. Sombart accepted the importance of historical developments and environmental conditions for an understanding and explanation of the nexus of Jewry and capitalism. Yet, in the end, this nexus was an expression of something more fundamental about the nature of Jews and Judaism. Only if one took biology into account could the phenomenon in question be adequately explained.

In brief, capitalism for Sombart was the embodiment of the nature or spirit (*Geist*) of Jewry. The abstract, mechanical way of thinking and acting that characterized capitalist relations, and that made industrial capitalism possible, also characterized Judaism and Jewry. The intellectualism and rationalism that lay at the heart of Judaism, with its stress on the legalistic, contractual relations between God and man ("Jewish prayer is a bargain," i.e., a transaction), found its secular counterpart in capitalist social and economic relations. Sombart accepted, as we have shown in an earlier chapter, the popular materialist notion of an essential connection between the physical and the psychological. Thus, he found evidence for the genetic link between Jews and capitalism in the continuity of Jewish somatological traits over the millennia. From ancient to modern times, one could establish a clear continuity and identity of physical and mental characteristics. Moreover, the strong somatological similarities between the Jews and other ancient Oriental trading peoples such as the Phoenicians, Syrians, and Armenians further established the biological roots of the Jewish/capitalist conjunction. The Jewish racial type and the Jewish economic type—the Semite and the capitalist—converged to reinforce and validate one another.[38]

It was around the work of Sombart, more than any other single figure, that the debate among Jewish social scientists and historians over Jews and economy centered during the years 1902–30.[39] What accounts for this intense interest in Sombart's work, and for the legitimacy granted by many Jewish scholars at the time to his theories about the relationship of Jews and capitalism? Certainly, Sombart's status as one of the leading national economists and sociologists in Imperial Germany gave his work the imprimatur of scientific authority. This may explain in part the seriousness with which his ideas were discussed, even by those who disagreed with or challenged them. Yet more than this was at work, at least in the case of the reception Sombart's ideas received among Zionists. Unlike Roscher, who was a vocal advocate of Jewish emancipation and integration, Sombart spoke openly about what he considered to be the harms imposed upon German public life by the assimilation of the Jews. Zionists embraced him as a powerful advocate of their position.[40] Moreover, Sombart's scholarly work, together with Roscher's thesis on competition and displacement, offered Zionists another set of facts and theories with which to construct arguments about Jewish identity and national/racial worth, assimilation and integration, and the overall abnormality and impossibility of a viable Jewish life in the Diaspora.

At the same time, it must be stressed that in their historical and statistical analyses of contemporary Jewish life, Zionists challenged and refuted a number of Sombart's chief points about the nature of the relationship between Jews, capitalism, and modern life. In so doing they undermined the moral economy Sombart and numerous other European writers had constructed around the Jews and capitalism: Jewry and capitalism were implicated in the creation of a modern society and culture antithetical to all that was healthy and noble in the German *Volk* and *Kultur*. For Zionists, the Jews were ultimately the *victims* of capitalism and the culture it brought about. Emancipation and assimilation were direct consequences of the shift in social relations produced by the emergence of modern capitalism. And it was assimilation, defined as the end of isolation, which Zionists of course identified as the chief agent of dissolution within modern Jewry. We shall return to this point after a consideration of the relationship between capitalism and Jewish identity in Jewish nationalist discourse.

## Capitalism, National Identity, and "Racial Worth"

"All national economists agree," Arthur Ruppin wrote in 1911, "that the Jews were predisposed to their role as businessmen. Sombart's opinion can stand for the general: the Jewish race is the incarnation of the capitalist-business spirit."[41] This predisposition was traced back to biblical times, and explained with reference to the relationship between the Hebrews and the ancient maritime and trading people, the Phoenicians. Capitalism, it was asserted, could not be limited to the modern period.[42] Rather, both capitalism and Jewry's particular relationship to it were present already in the ancient world. The equivalencies drawn between ancient and modern capitalism, and ancient and modern Jewry, like those derived from the iconographic evidence, suggested a Jewish identity that transcended historical contingency.

Felix Pinkus, for example, who headed the Bern section of the Verein für jüdische Statistik, argued in two extended essays that a fully developed capitalist economy existed in the ancient world, and that the Jews were its foremost representatives.[43] Invoking Roscher and Sombart, whom he identified as the most profound interpreters of this aspect of Jewish history, Pinkus traced the Jewish involvement in capitalism through the Middle Ages and into the modern period. The Jewish economic past and present, linked through capitalism, provided proof of the identity and unity of the Jewish *Volk*, despite temporal and spatial distance.

Yet Zionist social scientists rejected the biological determinism propounded by Sombart and others. The millennia-long involvement in capitalism was indeed taken as a sign or marker of Jewish racial identity. However, any insistence on a causal connection would have made the occupational reformation of Jewry impossible. Hence, Zionists stressed historical and environmental forces as formative. According to Pinkus, the abnormality of Jewish life, including the economic, was a product of the loss of political independence during the Roman period.[44] Writing in the Zionist-oriented newspaper *Ost und West* on "the origins of Jewish capitalism," the sociologist Franz Oppenheimer argued that "the Jews were not always a people of trade. . . . On the contrary . . . their 'trading spirit' or inclination (*Handelsgeist*) is completely a product of their history."[45] This insistence on the historically conditioned nature of the Jewish "trading spirit" allowed Zionists to identify a Jewish characteristic that reached beyond the epiphenomenal, and yet was not essential or unmalleable. The ability to assert, as Oppenheimer and others did, that in their earliest history the Jews were mainly an agricultural people, and that biblical evidence pointed to an "estrangement" of Jews from trade and commerce, offered Zionists a conceptual opening onto a future in which their agricultural past would, again in Palestine, be re-created. At the same time, the "ancient" connection between Jewry and commerce was acknowledged and made to serve specific ends of Jewish nationalism.

Ruppin formulated the notion of a Jewish national or racial identity manifested in economic proclivity in more explicit terms than most. Analyzing the racial history of Jewry, he linked the Jews anthropologically to the Western and Southern Asian peoples, whose typical representatives were the Armenians and Persians, and whose "*geistliche*" anthropological affinities manifested themselves in economic similarities. "The resemblance [of the Jews] to the Armenians," Ruppin noted, "is striking."

The *Völkergruppe* to which the Jews stand most closely related [racially] have demonstrated up to the present, in all their branches, a high level of intellectual nimbleness. This makes them dangerous opponents in the economic competitive struggle. The Armenians are known as the most capable and agile businessmen in the whole Orient, and the Persians as well are praised for their great business talents and high intellectual character. . . . It is, however, this similarity [of a talent for business] with the *vorderasiatischen* nations from which Jews have been spatially separated for two thousand years, that proves that the Jews have remained unchanged, and that we have before us in today's Jews, in racial terms, the same beings who did battle under King David, who repented under Ezra and Nechemiah, who died for freedom under Bar Kochba, who ruled in the earlier Middle Ages as great tradesmen, moving between Europe and the Orient, and finally at the end of the Middle Ages, were secondhand dealers and money lenders in the isolation and misery of the ghetto.[46]

Just as physical anthropological traits bound Jews with other Oriental peoples, and with the Orient (i.e., Palestine) itself, so too did the Jews' talent for trade and commerce. Nonetheless, Ruppin modified this analysis, and backed away from the implications of this racial argument by asserting that the talent was not in itself a racial trait. Rather, it was one manifestation of an essential Jewish intelligence, a mental dexterity that explained a host of Jewish characteristics (including the disproportionate number of Jewish chess players, writers, and white-collar criminals).[47]

As a positive trait this intelligence was not something requiring reformation or regeneration. On the contrary, it served not only as proof of the national/racial identity of Jewry, but of their worth as a *Volk*. Hence, it demonstrated the value and feasibility of the nationalist project of regeneration. Ruppin identified this intelligence and the economic talent it spawned as key factors in the social Darwinian "selection process" (*Auslese-prozeß*) in which the Jews had been highly successful. "The extraordinarily unfavorable conditions under which Jews lived for the last five hundred years have had the effect of strengthening the struggle for existence, in which only the most intelligent and economically talented survive." The premodern *Gemeinschaft* became the site of collective strength and vitality, as it had in the analyses of demography, physiology, and health and disease. Traditional cultural forms were not necessarily barriers to economic success and progress. Rather, a "type" of Jew had evolved in the ghetto who could lay claim to being superior to the modern, Westernized Jew. "The high evaluation of knowledge, and particularly Talmudic study, has worked in a selective way to produce the most capable. The wealthiest in the ghetto married their daughters to the brightest, and thereby carried out a higher breeding of the race. . . . So it happens," Ruppin concluded, "that we see in the contemporary Jew a particularly worthwhile human type, marked by unequaled and unprecedented intellectual ability. It is this fact that justifies the existence of the Jews as a *Sondergemeinschaft*."[48]

Yet the "contemporary Jew" to whom Ruppin referred here was not the equivalent of the modern Jew. We will return to the significance of this distinction in a moment. What is of importance at this point is the validation of Jewish national and racial worth that Zionists extrapolated from the interpretations of Sombart, Roscher, and others.

Like Ruppin, Zollschan framed his discussions of Jews and capitalism around the question of "Jewish cultural and racial worth." He took as a given that the creation of all European trade in the first half of the Middle Ages was a Jewish accomplishment. Trade and commerce were positive and necessary activities; they made (and make) civilization and culture possible. Hence, capitalism ennobled the Jews, and the Jews in turn ennobled the West. The Christians, according to Zollschan, comprehended this, and therefore assented to both the economic and the cultural necessity of trade, and the Jewish presence in Europe:

Instinctively the blonde barbarians recognized that the trading activities of the Jews were aimed at a higher good. And this feeling was correct. Their [the Jews'] trade fulfilled one of the most elevated of tasks. The beginning of the Middle Ages represented, in contrast to the ancient Roman Empire—which culturally can only be compared to the eighteenth century—a marked lapse into barbarism. *The trade of the Jews was above all else the preservation of ancient elements of culture, which made possible the planting of new seeds.*[49] (emphasis in the original)

The inversion here of the anti-Semitic theme, found in Sombart's work, among the work of numerous others, of the Jew as barbarian, as destroyer of culture and community through a pernicious economic and intellectual influence, is clear. Zollschan accepted that the Jews were "the trading people" par excellence. Yet he identified trade with progress, and with the transmission of high culture. The Christian "blonde barbarians" owed whatever was of greatest value in their culture and economy to the Jews. This, in turn, demonstrated the value of the Jews as a *Volk* and justified their continued existence.

The Zionist interest in the subject of the Jews and capitalism, and especially in Sombart's views, extended beyond academic social scientific circles. Summarizing Sombart's 1909 Berlin public lecture series on Jews and capitalism, *Die Welt* exulted in the importance assigned to the Jews by the well-known national economist. The Jews had been responsible for the most significant development in the early history of capitalism: the shift in economic power during the sixteenth and seventeenth centuries from the Southern and Southwestern nations (Italy, Spain, and Portugal) to those of the Northwest (Holland, England, and the Americas). The Jews financed Columbus, settled en masse in South America, and then moved northward to settle what would become the United States. "Jews were indeed the actual founders of modern colonialist economies, as they played a major role in the management of the East-India Company and in the discovery of America. America was conquered by Jews both externally and internally."[50] From here it was but a short leap to the claim that Jews were also responsible for the modern state, a leap *Die Welt* enthusiastically took. Equating Jewry with both unequaled financial resources and power, as well as with the "spirit" of rationalism and capitalism, *Die Welt* followed Sombart in situating Judaism and Jewry at the core of modernity.

The celebratory tenor of this sort of representation, like the narratives produced by Ruppin, Zollschan, and others, emerged out of a particular interpretive paradigm of capitalism and colonialism, and out of a type of culture brought about by these modern economic forms. Capitalism, and economic activity in general, was represented as healthy and vital, the prerequisite for civilization's development and progress. And the Jews were the crucial component in this process.

Yet this triumphalism was only one side of a more complex equation. An analysis of the writings of Zionist social scientists reveals an ambivalence toward capitalism and its myriad effects, an ambivalence shared with many social scientists (and of course others) during this period. This ambivalence about, even antagonism toward, industrial capitalism found its counterpart in an idealization of agricultural life. The familiar set of images associated with conservative Romanticism—the robust peasant or agricultural laborer, the healthy rural setting, the traditional society and culture where bonds of family and fellowship remain intact—these can be found, too, in early Zionist writings.[51]

Yet, whereas the anti-Semitic discourse identified the Jews as the embodiment of an abstract, rationalized modernity, agents of dissolution and decline, Zionists sought to describe the negative effects of capitalism, and by implication modernity, upon Jewry. Paradoxically, Zionists could accept that the Jews embodied the spirit of capitalism, and could adduce positive value from the Jewish role in the creation of the modern industrial economy, while at the same time casting capitalism as the principal causal agent of the assimilatory process they sought to reverse. If historical analyses of Jews and capitalism helped to prove the racial worth of Jewry, they also proved, when combined with contemporary economic statistics, the fundamental abnormality and impossibility of Jewish Diaspora life.

## The Abnormality of Jewish Economic Life

For Zionist social scientists there were numerous signs and symptoms of this abnormality. According to Felix Pinkus, the abnormal status of Jewish economic life began in 70 C.E., with the loss of political sovereignty and the advent of mass exile. For it was in exile, as a minority population, that Jewry developed a *Zwischenwirtschaft*, or dual system of economic and moral relations. Throughout their history in the Diaspora Jews behaved one way toward one another, within the *Gemeinde* or Jewish community, and differently toward the outside Christian world. This moral and economic duality, identified as pathological, and explained by exile, would be undone by the Jewish return to Palestine and the construction of an organic economy and society.[52]

Signs of abnormality were to be found in the present as well as in the past. The Jews remained settled overwhelmingly in urban areas, and were hence alienated from the land and agriculture. Their chief occupations were still those traditionally identified as "Jewish."[53] "The economic foundation for the existence of every *Volk* is agriculture," the Russian-born Zionist Daniel Pasmanik wrote in 1905, "which does not possess merely economic, but also biological significance. Only the introduction of fresh elements from the village renews the blood of city dwellers."[54] The 1897 Russian census showed only 3 percent of Russian Jewry living on the land. Even these were not farmers, according to Pasmanik, but were involved in some business aspect of agriculture. Even granting that 3 percent of Russian Jewry was involved in a positive way with agriculture, this was still "abnormally low." "Unfortunately," Pasmanik concluded, "we cannot foresee any improvement in the future." The "spring" or revolution would not change anything in this regard; it would not make Jewish mass agriculture any more likely. "The cultivation of a quantitatively and qualitatively normal class of farmers among Jewry in Russia is absolutely impossible."[55]

In one of his earliest social scientific articles the socialist Zionist Jacob Lestschinsky found evidence of abnormality in the anomalous manner in which Jewish emigrants resettled economically. The Jewish emigrant, unable to take up "productive labor" because of a lack of training, discipline, and physical strength, "carries his occupational pathology with him and re-creates it in his new home."[56] Felix Theilhaber offered the following statistics to demonstrate what he called—following the Marxist Zionist Ber Borochov—the "historical pathology" of Jewish economic life. In 1907, 29 percent of the total Prussian population was involved in agriculture, while only 1 percent of Jewry made their living off the land. In contrast, 55 percent of Jews were to be found in trade and commerce, while only 13 percent of Christians were involved in these economic sectors.

Of greatest import, according to Theilhaber, was the dramatic rise in the numbers of Jews in the free professions. "In other words: The Jew is pushed above all to the free professions, that is to mental and intellectual labor (*Kopfarbeit*)."[57] On the one hand, as we have seen, the intellectualism of the Jews—as a positive attribute—could be traced back to ancient times, and made to serve as a sign of national/racial identity and value. The powers of rational abstraction had allowed the Jews to play a significant role, through their involvement with capitalism, in the development of Western civilization. On the other hand, the overdevelopment of mental capacity signified the abnormal condition of Jewry in the present. Occupational maldistributions reflected a more fundamental imbalance within the Jew: overrepresented in mental rather than physical labor, alienated from his own body, divorced from the land and from nature, the Jew was physically as well as economically diseased and degenerate. In Ruppin's formulation,

The Jews of the ancient Jewish kingdom were religious through and through; they had courage and a deep sense for myth and the works of nature. That is, they were farmers. Since the Jews have stopped pushing the plow, they have become degenerate; they have for the most part lost a natural, human outlook and have become a reflexive people (*Reflexionisten*). Only a people engaged in agriculture can be healthy, only a state with the majority of its people engaged in agriculture constitutes a firmly bound, organized whole.[58]

The distorted occupational structure of Jewry was both a symptom and a cause of Jewish abnormality. In and of itself, it was proof of the pathological. Yet it was also responsible for the broader decline and degeneration that Zionists detected within modern Jewish life. Echoing the German sociologist Ferdinand Tönnies's widely known formulation, capitalism was conceived as a disintegrative force, dissolving the traditional forms and structures of "community" (*Gemeinschaft*) and reconfiguring them into a "society" (*Gesellschaft*).[59] Ruppin, for instance, posited capitalism as the causal mechanism of the emancipation and assimilation of modern Jewry. He developed a sophisticated sociological model that charted the influence of economic changes on the social relations between Jews and Christians, and the impact of this, in turn, on Jewish intellectual and cultural life. "The fundamental ground for the so-called emancipation of the Jews was not laid by individual Jews, but by the rapid revolution in technology and economy during the 18th century."[60] Writing decades before Jewish social historians such as Jacob Katz, Raphael Mahler, and Salo Baron, Ruppin argued that changes in economic relations "breached the wall" between Jews and Christians socially. This made it possible for Jews to participate more fully in, and identify with, European intellectual and cultural life.

According to Ruppin, the Enlightenment did not produce emancipation; on the contrary, the Jewish Enlightenment was the result of structural transformations in the socioeconomic realm. The world of the Enlightenment—materialism, positivism, scientism—stood in direct contrast to the Jewish world, and "Christian *Bildung*" demanded "the complete or partial rejection of Judaism." This *Auflösungsprozeß*, as Ruppin called it, consisted of the alienation of modern Jews from Jewry (*Judentum*), their "de-nationalization" through *Bildung*. Ruppin offered an analogy drawn from the natural sciences as a way of explanation: "Just as in the fermentation process, when numerous bodies, once united, break up into different elements and then reconstitute themselves in new relations, so too the Jews, who in the ghetto were one homogeneous group, through fermenting *Bildung*, now break up and recombine in various different cultural classes with Christians."[61] For Ruppin there existed an inextricable connection between economic dependence, and social and cultural assimilation and national disintegration. Zionism, therefore, represented the only viable means for the reestablishment of an economic isolation and independence of the Jews. Such independence would, in turn, make possible the existence of a vital Jewish society and culture.

Description and explanation of the historical process of modernization was interlaced with moral judgment, as the social problems associated with modern urban life were traced back in one way or another to capitalism's disruptive influence. The Munich social scientist Rudolf Wassermann, in an article entitled "The Jews in Contemporary German Economic Life," argued that the *Judenfrage* was not about anti-Semitic fears of Jewish control of Germany, but rather about "when will German Jewry diminish to such a point that it will cease to be a factor in German cultural life."[62] The decline of German Jewry was evident, first of all, in lower birth rates. Declining fertility, as we saw in an earlier chapter, was the "master pathology," the chief sign of collective decline and eventual disappearance. Like others, Wassermann understood lower birth rates as a product of the increasing secularization and rationalization of modern Jewish life. The traditional religious impulse to procreate disappeared in the last half of the nineteenth century; rationalism, the antithesis of religion, initiated a process of "denationalization" of Jewry. "Modern, free-spirited Western Jewry no longer possesses the God-induced will to reproduce."[63] This "lack of will to reproduce," in Wassermann's view, was found chiefly among those of higher socioeconomic standing, and among urban dwellers. Since Jews were disproportionately represented among these categories, it was not surprising that Jewish birth rates were in decline.[64]

According to Felix Theilhaber, "rationalism," "capitalism," and "Americanization" were all components of the "*neue Zeit*," and Jews were victims of this modern period. In support of his equation "capitalism plus rationalism equals the destruction of the family," Theilhaber provided statistics from income and tax levels showing the correlation between higher socioeconomic standing and lower rates of fertility. In addition, this "destruction of family," and of traditional Jewish communal structures in general, could be seen in the increasing numbers of Jewish women in the workforce. Economic survival demanded that Jewish women work, Theilhaber maintained, but this represented a revolutionary transformation in their lives, and in the life of the community. It would "take its toll on Jewry," resulting in later marriages and fewer children. As such, it was one more cause and symptom of the pathology of modern Jewish existence.

Ruppin, as we saw above, posited the existence of a healthy "contemporary Jew," made vital by hundreds of years of Darwinian-like struggle in the ghetto. Yet this sociological ideal type was not the equivalent of the modern Jew described by Zionists. Rather, the modern Jew was the product of the distancing from traditional Jewish belief and praxis that had taken place as a result of emancipation and assimilation. In Theilhaber's words,

The way from full fertility to a poverty of reproduction, from inbreeding to mixing, from a martyrlike willingness to sacrifice for the community to the cowardly disavowal of this duty and an irresolute negligence, are symptoms and stigmata of a larger process. . . . Emancipation opened the gates and allowed the storm of new ideals into the ghettos. Modern economic life, the period of interlocking capital, factories and technology produced transformations in every realm of life . . . [and led to] all forms of pathological phenomena.[65]

One encounters the themes of fertility and infertility, productivity and unproductivity throughout social scientific texts on health and disease, intermarriage and the family, and economic conditions and activities. For Zionists, the pathological status of the Jewish body, both individual and collective, manifested itself in this condition of unproductivity. Lower birth rates, infertility (due to intermarriage), concentration in trade and commerce, and the concomitant alienation from agriculture, were all signs of an *inability to produce* at normal levels. These phenomena converged to create an image of the diseased contemporary Jew.

Social scientists granted that this sort of decline and degeneration was not without precedent in Jewish history. Yet the challenge posed to Jewish survival at present was altogether unique because of the nature of modernity. The process of assimilation, as Ruppin, Theilhaber, Zollschan, and others envisioned it, was now a universal one, made so primarily by the emergence of global capitalism. As the key to the mechanism of assimilation, capitalism's universal nature meant that the degenerative effects upon Jewry were inevitable. Regeneration could only occur through the cultural and economic isolation of Jewry in its own land, in its own society apart from—yet still a part of—the larger non-Jewish world.[66]

The language and ideas used to describe the pathology of modern Jewry—infertility and unproductivity—were, moreover, also used to describe the contemporary condition of Palestine. The image of the "dead" land, unproductive physically, economically, and culturally, pervaded early Zionist (and European) literature and iconography.[67] The Jewish nationalist project, in fact, was conceived as a double cure: The Jewish body (and the body of Jewry), and the land of Palestine would both be regenerated. The editors of *Palästina*, for instance, the official journal of the Zionist-oriented Committee for Research into the Economy of Palestine, identified the journal's task as demonstrating "what Palestine can do for the Jews and what the Jews can do for Palestine."[68] Mediated through Zionism, the Jews and Palestine would regenerate one another, bring one another back to a condition of normalcy. The present conditions of "barrenness" were counterposed to a future "blossoming" of the land and the *Volk*.

## Economic Decline and the Impossibility of Diaspora Existence

The historical models advanced by Roscher and Sombart provided Zionist social scientists with an interpretive framework within which to explain not only the Jewish past but also the Jewish present in terms of instability and decline. Central to this analysis were the notions of economic and social competition and displacement. The heyday of Jewish economic success during the period of modern capitalist development, it was argued, had been the eras of early and middle capitalism, or what national economists had termed high capitalism. For it was during these phases that Jews fulfilled the roles for which Christians—still largely settled in rural agricultural areas—were unsuited. As the possessors of mobile capital, Jews were able to act as financiers for kings and princes, as well as to play a major role in the initial stages of modern banking and finance.

Yet, "we are again standing," in Zollschan's words, "at the beginning of an historical stage in which the Jews will be forced out from and dispossessed of their economic position."[69] According to Ruppin, all of the advantages Jews enjoyed in the socioeconomic realm "are at present weakening or disappearing." Christians possessed more and more mobile capital because immobile capital was being made mobile through the development of mortgages; the urbanization of non-Jews led to greater numbers of Christians attaining higher education, which in turn allowed them to compete more successfully in business; and the "occupational selection," which before had led Jews mainly into trade, was now doing the same for Christians. "So Jews and Christians are now engaged in ever-increasing economic struggle or competition."[70]

Moreover, the changing nature of capitalism dictated that the Jews would find less and less of a place in the new economic culture. The emergence of trusts, syndicates, price fixing, big banks, and warehouses—in short, monopolization and bureaucratization—had limited or reduced individuals' chances to succeed.

Whereas Sombart had argued that the Jewish "spirit" was antithetical to the entrepreneurial, "productive" side of capitalism, Zionists asserted that it was precisely this aspect that accounted for the Jews' earlier success. The "de-personalization" of the economy in its late capitalist phase meant, in Ruppin's words, that "the personal flair and pioneering spirit that the Jews exhibit" were no longer in demand. Roscher had believed that the pattern of competition and displacement that had characterized the Middle Ages was not relevant for the modern period. Modern capitalism, in his view, would produce the conditions for Jewish emancipation and integration. Zionists, on the other hand, saw in Roscher's model of the medieval past an accurate guide to the Jewish present: "This [contemporary] displacement [*Verdrängung*] of the Jews from capitalist life echoes and reenacts their displacement from trade at the outset of the Middle Ages. At that time as well the Jews were displaced by Christians when new economic forms or organizations (guilds) replaced free competition."[71]

In the first years of the century the political economist Chaim Dov Horowitz, who headed the Warsaw branch of the Verein für jüdische Statistik, published a series of essays in Hebrew, applying Roscher's thesis to contemporary Eastern European Jewry. Horowitz used Roscher's model to argue for a Zionist solution to the Jewish Question.[72] The demographer and political economist Jacob Lestschinsky also appropriated Roscher's model of displacement and applied it to both Eastern and Western European Jewry. Lestschinsky was one of the leading figures of Jewish social science in the 1930s and after World War II, and this argument of displacement continued to inform his work in the postwar period.[73]

Rudolf Wassermann, referring to the "bureaucratization of capitalism," produced statistics to demonstrate that in all those areas usually associated with Jewish "dominance" the distribution of Jews had actually diminished. In banking, finance, trade, and the free professions the numbers revealed that between 1895 and 1907 the Jews had lost ground to Christians. "Capitalism is like a beast devouring its own children," Wassermann concluded. It was only in industry that Jews continued to thrive, since industry alone had thus far escaped total bureaucratization.[74]

This process of competition and displacement, according to Zionist social scientists, was occurring throughout Eastern and Western Europe, and the United States. It represented a "permanent crisis" for Jewry, in Ruppin's words. Nor would emigration or internal migration serve to ease the pressure. The mass movement of Eastern European Jews westward caused governments to enact restrictive immigration policies, and had begun to re-create the social and economic conditions that would make competition and displacement inevitable in the West.

This hermeneutic circle of decline was closed by the analysis of the consequences of socioeconomic improvement among Western Jews. For even if this predicted social and economic displacement did not materialize, Jewry was nevertheless caught in a double bind from which only Zionism offered escape. The phenomenon of proletarianization and displacement was envisioned as moving from East to West; that is, the fate of Eastern European Jewry—a large Jewish mass made up predominantly of a marginalized proletariat and an unemployed underclass—would in the near future characterize the Jews of the West. Yet, as we saw in a previous chapter, Zionists also constructed a model of development in which improving economic and social conditions among Western Jews produced degeneracy and decline. In this scheme, it was not impoverishment but wealth and status that created a milieu conducive to pathology. And this model was then posited as predictive of the future of Eastern European Jewry, should they succeed in reproducing the experience of the Jews in the West.

This scenario, in which the continued economic and social existence of Jews in the Diaspora was presented as impossible, paralleled and reinforced that found in analyses of Jewish health and disease. In both cases, a complex set of external or environmental factors had come together to shape the Jewish character and condition, producing an abnormal, pathological present. This present stood in direct contrast to the idealized image of a healthy future, in which the imbalance of Jewish economic life would be remedied by a return to the land and involvement in the regenerative labor of agriculture. "For it is only commercial nations," Zollschan wrote, "that are liable to be driven away and dispossessed; but nations who maintain themselves by cultivating the ground, cannot be dispossessed unless they are violently annihilated."[75] Zollschan drew the analogy between Jewry and the Phoenicians, who ruled over the ancient commercial world, and then, on account of competition and displacement, disappeared. Removed from their own soil, "no longer devoted to its cultivation," the Phoenicians were victims of the socioeconomic law of dispossession. "[This] shows the necessity of bringing the great masses of the Jews back to their original occupation as a ground-tilling people."[76]

For Zionists the results of an economic analysis of Jewry pointed to the impossibility of Jewish life in the Diaspora. Studies of occupational trends of East European Jews, within the context of broader structural economic and social changes in Eastern European states, indicated increasing impoverishment. The historical theories of Roscher, Sombart, and others, which outlined the course of Jewish economic and social development in Europe in nomothetic terms, were taken up and offered as guides to the Jewish present and future. As long as Jews lacked their own territory, with their own isolated economy and culture, the traditional pattern of settlement, economic success, Christian competition and resentment, marginalization, expropriation, and expulsion would repeat itself.

# Conclusion
## A Usable Knowledge

The practical applicability of social scientific knowledge was axiomatic for Jewish social scientists. Regardless of ideological predilection, research and reform went hand in hand. This is not to say that some ideas and arguments were not intended, or did not function, to defend a particular status quo, or to serve as apologia. But at the core of the Jewish social scientific enterprise was a critical appraisal of the modern Jewish condition, and the conviction that a more exact, scientific knowledge of Jewry was necessary if a positive transformation in that condition was going to occur.

The research produced by Jewish social scientists was also "usable" by others. The numbers and some of the major themes and arguments were taken up and utilized by other scholars, Jewish and non-Jewish, and by particular political and social agencies. Jewish social scientific research was incorporated into, and had an impact on, contemporaneous and subsequent scholarship, an impact that has more or less gone unremarked by scholars. Moreover, it played a role in practical, political, and administrative realms, including Jewish social work, and debates about Jewish settlement in Mandatory Palestine.

This concluding chapter traces the utilization of Jewish social science, both during the period covered by this study and after. As we shall see, statistics about Jewry found their way into a host of different, oftentimes ideologically antagonistic, studies produced over the past half century or more. By no means is the discussion here intended to be comprehensive; piling up examples toward that end would very quickly become tedious. The purpose, rather, is to indicate the extent to which Jewish social scientific research was appropriated by others, for both intellectual and political reasons, and in the course of this to illuminate some of the more general points about the nature of this sort of research.

Two points are particularly salient. Tracing the way in which others at the time and after uncritically made use of the statistics found in Jewish social science illustrates the power of, and trust in, numbers.[1] Second, Jewish social science provided general scholars, that is, those who were not specialists in Jewish Studies or *jüdische Wissenschaft*, with an ability to speak with authority about the contemporary condition of Jewry and to draw practical, political conclusions from it. The "Jewishness" of the social scientific texts, in other words, lent a special authority to the arguments produced about Jewry. The statistics, for instance, may have been generated by non-Jewish authorities. Once they had appeared in an article or book identified as "Jewish," these numbers assumed a different power and legitimacy.

## The Impact of Jewish Social Science on Contemporaneous Scholarship

In their seminal article "Appropriating the Idioms of Science," Nancy Leys Stepan and Sander Gilman remarked that the scientific studies produced by Jews and African Americans, in response to the dominant scientific discourse, "made relatively little difference to mainstream science. The white, male academy usually ignored the contributions of minorities to the sciences themselves." In the case of Jewish social scientists, "writing on the Jewish race and self-identity was more important to Jews themselves than to the establishment circles of science."[2] Certainly, Stepan and Gilman are correct in asserting that minority scientific writings were of greatest import and meaning for those producing them (and for their constituent communities). Their immediate power, as this study has tried to show, lay in the way in which representations of collective identity, framed in scientific language, could offer alternative explanations for this identity, and could serve the political as well as the intellectual and emotional needs of the relatively powerless.

Given the neglect of Jewish social science by later Jewish intellectual and cultural historians, it would be tempting to conclude that the impact of Jewish social scientific research has been negligible. However, the work of Jewish social scientists was neither ignored nor judged meaningless by the broader, established scientific community. Jewish social scientists published articles in leading scientific journals of the time, and delivered their research at professional meetings and congresses.[3] Jewish social scientific works were also reviewed by general professional journals.[4]

More important, the information and knowledge produced about Jewry by Jewish social scientists was taken up and used by members of the dominant community. Rather than ignoring what Jewish scientists said, non-Jews integrated the arguments of Jews into their own work, thereby gaining greater credence and legitimacy for the assertions made about Jews and Judaism. Such assertions, of course, were not necessarily "friendly" or philosemitic. The German Catholic social thinker Hans Rost, for instance, asserted that modern Jewry had degenerated from a premodern condition of relative health and vitality, and he cited the works of Jacob Segall, Maurice Fishberg, Felix Theilhaber, and other Jewish authorities to prove it.[5] The majority of scientific sources used by Werner Sombart on the question of the Jews as a race were in fact produced by Jews. Indeed, if one examines the footnotes to the chapter "The Race Problem," in *The Jews and Modern Capitalism*, it is evident that Sombart was very familiar with the writings of Jewish anthropologists and demographers, and in particular with the articles found in the *Zeitschrift für Demographie und Statistik der Juden*.[6] The same holds true for the extremely influential work on human biology and genetics, *Grundriss der menschlichen Erblichkeitslehre und Rassenhygiene*, by Erwin Baur, Eugen Fischer, and Fritz Lenz, and published by a leading anti-Semitic publishing house, Lehmann.[7] In his section on "Racial Differences in Mankind," Fischer—who was trained as an anthropologist—discussed the question of "the Jewish race" and made extensive use of research produced by Jewish authorities. In a discussion of Jewish physiognomy, and of the impact of racial mixing on the shape and structure of the eye, Fischer invoked the work of the British-Jewish geneticist Redcliffe Nathan Salaman, the American Maurice Fishberg, and the Russian Samuel Weissenberg.[8] In his essay, Fritz Lenz, one of Germany's leading racial hygienists during the Weimar and Nazi periods, also utilized the work of Salaman and Fishberg, and added that of Felix Theilhaber and the physician M. J. Gutmann. All of these Jewish authorities provided extensive evidence, in Lenz's view, of the physical and psychological difference between Jews and Aryans. True, Lenz insisted that he was not an anti-Semite, and berated the anti-Semitic movement as a waste of energy.[9] He "celebrated" the Jewish acumen, and the Jewish geniuses from Spinoza to Einstein who had contributed so much to the building of Western Civilization. At one point he called attention to, and seemed to endorse, Maurice Fishberg's assertion about the favorable effects of intermarriage between Aryans and Jews.[10]

In the end, however, it was the physical and especially mental "peculiarities" of the Jews that Lenz emphasized. While he called upon non-Jewish authorities such as Sombart and Günther, he also invoked Jewish social scientists. So, for instance, Redcliffe Nathan Salaman had proven in 1923 that Jewish soldiers in World War I had suffered from a higher percentage of flatfootedness; Theilhaber's findings indicated that Berlin Jewry suffered to a greater degree from diabetes; and Gutmann, in his 1920 study *Die Rasse-und Krankheitsfrage der Juden*, had shown that Jews suffered to a greater extent from *paralysis agitans*.

Jewish social scientific research also found its way into general works in the United States. William Z. Ripley's *Races of Europe*, published in 1900, was acknowledged at the time as the preeminent synthetic work on race and physical anthropology. Chapter 14 was devoted to "Jews and Semites." Ripley thanked Joseph Jacobs and Samuel Weissenberg at the outset, acknowledging them as authorities; he relied heavily, he wrote, on their works for his own analysis, even if he did not agree with many of their interpretations.[11] And, he added, they provided him with photographs of "Jewish types." Since *Races of Europe* appeared before the bulk of Jewish social scientific research was carried out—the Verein für jüdische Statistik would be founded two years later—the paucity of references is understandable. Still, the presence of these early authorities in a work as widely disseminated as Ripley's testifies to the fact that the "minority voice" was present in the dominant scientific narratives, and is an early illustration of the importance assigned in texts by non-Jews to the Jewish authoritative voice. Nearly four decades later another extraordinarily influential anthropological textbook, Carleton Coon's *The Races of Europe*, would also make extensive use of Jewish social scientific research.[12] In Great Britain the work of Franz Boas and Maurice Fishberg was critically engaged by the eminent statistician and eugenics advocate Karl Pearson. A student of Pearson's, G. M. Morant, together with Otto Samson, a German Jewish refugee from Nazi Germany, challenged Fishberg's and Boas's findings about the instability of the human form. Ultimately, the goals of Pearson and Morant in engaging with Boas and Fishberg were to fight a rearguard battle for the legitimacy of a biological interpretation of history and society. Attacking the best-known examples of the environmental determinist view of physical anthropological data seemed a good way to go about it. For our purposes what is of significance is the simple fact that Jewish social scientific research was engaged in a leading British journal, even if the goal was its refutation.[13]

Jewish social scientific data also found its way into the work of contemporary Jewish writers, academic and popular, who were not social scientists. A few examples drawn from works produced in the first three decades of the century suggest the wider dissemination and influence of this material. In the introduction to volume two of his *Neuste Geschichte des jüdischen Volkes*, the historian Martin Philippson made special mention of the Bureau for Jewish Statistics, and of the significance of its publications for the treatment of the "economic and biological aspects" of modern Jewish life.[14] He incorporated into his work the categories, themes, numbers, and many of the arguments of Jewish social science.

Jonas Kreppel's *Juden und Judentum von Heute*, published in 1925, made extensive use of Jewish statistics. Kreppel, a lawyer and an Austrian political figure, intended the work as a handbook on Jewry—a source of reliable information for policy makers and anyone else interested in the *Judenfrage*. He began with a chapter titled "Jewry Before the War, 1900–1914," and moved from there to a statistical representation of worldwide Jewry, and then to numbers and conditions of individual countries and communities. One might call this contemporary history, akin in nature, if not in quality, to the final volumes of Graetz, Dubnow, and others who took their histories up to their own times. The work produced by Jewish statistical bureaus, and the monographs of Jewish social scientists, occupy an important place in these contemporary histories. Kreppel explicitly acknowledged this debt in the book's foreword,[15] and he titled part IV of the book "Die Juden der Gegenwart (Statistik)," an unmistakable echo of, and tribute to, Ruppin's well-known study of the same name.

In the preface to his 1914 survey *Jewish Life in Modern Times,* Israel Cohen acknowledged the special debt he too owed to the work of the Bureau for Jewish Statistics.

I have brought within the covers of a single book the fullest description yet attempted of all the main aspects and problems of Jewish life in the present day. References are given in footnotes to the more important sources that have been consulted, of which the *Zeitschrift für Demographie und Statistik der Juden* and other publications of the Berlin Bureau for Jewish Statistics deserve a special need of acknowledgment, as without them the collation of the latest vital statistics of Jews in different countries would have involved considerable labor.[16]

Indeed, Cohen did not exaggerate his reliance on the work published by the *Verein*, as well as on monographs by Jewish social scientists published elsewhere. Chapter 1, "Dispersion and Distribution," and an appendix on "Statistics of the World's Jewish Population," are based largely on statistics culled from the *Zeitschrift* and other *Verein* studies.

## Jewish Social Science and Jewish Social Work

Professional Jewish social work, which came of age during the Weimar period, was tied at a number of levels to Jewish social science.[17] Jewish social welfare in Germany was "Jewish" according to its leading theorists and practitioners first and foremost because of the distinctive social traits of the Jews. "Jewish leaders reasoned that Jews' unique social, physical, economic and cultural characteristics required social measures geared particularly to them."[18] It made sense, then, for Jewish social workers to rely on Jewish social scientific work that established such distinctiveness at all levels.

This connection can be clearly seen in the work of the main social welfare agency in the German Jewish community, the Zentralwohlfahrtsstelle der deutschen Juden.[19] The *Zentralwohlfahrtsstelle*, founded in 1917, was the brainchild of Bertha Pappenheim, who wanted to centralize and systematize the various independent efforts at social work among Jewish organizations and individuals in Germany. A number of the most prominent Jewish social scientists working in Germany, and attached in one way or another to the Verein für jüdische Statistik and/or to YIVO, were also directly involved in the *Zentral*: Felix Theilhaber, Jacob Lestschinsky, I. Koralnik, and Jacob Segall.[20]

Jewish social scientific research set the agenda for a Jewish *Sozialpolitik*. Already in 1910 Segall had argued in the pages of the *Zeitschrift für Demographie und Statistik* that the main task of Jewish statistics ought to be administrative: welfare and care for the poor and disadvantaged.[21] It is undoubtedly true that the concerns of Jewish social workers mirrored those of the broader society and culture, yet, as this study has shown, Jewish social science had translated the general developments and concerns, and the terms of analysis and debate, into a body of knowledge immediately relevant to Jewish life. In other words, Jewish social science produced Jewish knowledge about contemporary Jewish conditions, and this was a chief impetus for practical social work. By the late 1920s the perceived "crisis" in Jewish demographics—the fears surrounding lower birth rates, high intermarriage rates, and the attendant concerns over Jewish health and disease—were producing concerted action on the part of the Jewish community.[22] The discourse on Jewish health and disease also influenced working physicians who had a measure of power over policy, but also direct access to Jewish patients. For example, Dr. Heinrich Stahl, a pediatrician at the *Jüdische Kinderhilfe* (Jewish Children's Clinic) in Berlin, "restated the idea that a distinctive Jewish physiology required medical services geared specifically for Jews. Jews' nervous system [*sic*] bore a relationship to the body that was different from the Gentiles' to theirs." Stahl, like other physicians and Jewish social scientists, insisted on Jewish sports organizations as a means for regenerating the "Jewish body." Jewish physicians, like their non-Jewish counterparts, were also expected to act as educators and counselors at Jewish youth, marriage, and sexual counseling centers. They were to offer advice "in order to promote a[n] understanding of eugenic considerations in marriage."[23]

The practical or political uses of social science became especially salient in debates over Palestine in the decades preceding the founding of the State of Israel. Social scientific research played an increasingly important role in the politics of immigration and settlement of Palestine in the 1930s and 1940s. Both American and European scholars became more and more involved in studying with social scientific methods the past and present "capacities" of Palestine, and both Zionists and Arabs used this material to argue their cause.[24] Yet the "re-imagining" of Palestine along social scientific lines had already begun in the late nineteenth century.[25] One finds proof of this in the reports sent back from Palestine about demographic, economic, and health/sanitation conditions. These reports found their way into Zionist newspapers and journals, and were also taken up by other Jewish social scientists who incorporated them into their own academic and popular representations.[26]

As Derek Penslar has demonstrated, the Zionist vision of Jewish immigration and settlement in the pre-State period was profoundly influenced by European models of social engineering, which included a strong social scientific component. "There took place a wide-ranging transfer of technology from Europe to Palestine; Jews in the Yishuv took an active part in the production and dissemination of scientific knowledge."[27] Social scientific research figured in political debates over the "nature of Palestine," and, just as important, on the "nature" of the Jewish immigrant into the Yishuv. While Zionist technocrats evinced the keenest interest in questions of national or political economy, nonetheless there is evidence that other social scientific categories and themes also played a part in their practical work. For our more limited purposes here, the clearest example of this sort of application of social scientific knowledge to the practical problems of Jewish immigration and settlement can be found, not surprisingly perhaps, in the work of Arthur Ruppin. As Penslar writes, Ruppin's "legitimacy as a settlement engineer rested not on natural but on social-scientific knowledge. Like the academic reformers whom he had emulated as a young man, Ruppin laid claim to an expert knowledge of political economy and social pathology."[28]

In a series of articles and speeches, dating from the start of his tenure as director of the World Zionist Organization's Palestine Office, Ruppin employed this social scientific knowledge to analyze contemporary issues of immigration and settlement with an eye to practical policy.[29] So, for instance, in an article titled "The Selection of the Fittest," Ruppin brought the social Darwinian categories of "fitness," "struggle," and "survival" to bear on the issue of Jewish immigration into Palestine. In speeches delivered in the 1920s, to both Zionist and non-Zionist audiences, he continued to infuse his arguments about Jewish immigration and the economic absorptive capacity of Palestine with social scientific—including Darwinian and racial—language.[30] Throughout his speeches and popular journalistic writings, from 1907 onwards, it is evident that Ruppin was drawing on the assumptions and notions of early-twentieth-century social science, and that there was—not surprisingly—a clear continuity between his academic and his practical, policy-oriented work.

## The Use of Jewish Social Science by National Socialist Researchers

Jewish social scientific research was taken up and utilized by scholars not only from varying fields or disciplines, but with different, even opposing, political or ideological agendas. Zionists and integrationists used one another's research, and placed it in the service of their own political ends. Nor was the use or appropriation of Jewish social scientific knowledge limited to Jews. As we have seen, non-Jews were not only fundamental to the emergence and development of a Jewish social science discourse, but many also incorporated the work of Jewish experts into their own writings on the subject.

Nor, interestingly enough, were authors hostile to Jewry reluctant to utilize Jewish social scientific knowledge. We have seen that scholars such as Werner Sombart, Fritz Lenz, Francis Galton, and Karl Pearson, among others, incorporated elements of this scholarship into their own work. This engagement and exploitation of Jewish research continued into the 1930s and 1940s, and included intellectual work undertaken in the Third Reich. In addition to Fischer and Lenz, prominent statisticians such as Friedrich Burgdörfer and biologists such as Otmar von Verschuer made extensive use of studies produced by Jewish social scientists.[31] Even a cursory glance at the research produced by the five institutes set up in Nazi Germany to study Judaism and Jewry reveals the profound extent to which Jewish knowledge was appropriated.[32] In 1935, for example, the Institut zum Studium der Judenfrage (Institute for the Study of the Jewish Question) in Berlin published a volume entitled *Die Juden in Deutschland*. The work, a collective effort, utilized to a significant extent the research and writings of Jews, ranging from Martin Buber to Walter Rathenau, from Arnold Zweig to the *Jüdisches Lexicon*, an encyclopedia of Jewish knowledge published in 1930. Jewish demographers and social scientists also appear, together with official government studies, as authoritative sources of knowledge and evidence. The chapters follow the lines or categories of inquiry set down by the social scientific discourse on the Jews that had developed over the past half century or more. There are chapters devoted to the demography and vitality of Jewry, to Jews in the economy, in the free professions, to the "criminality and racial degeneration of the Jews"

("Die Kriminalität und rassische Degeneration der Juden") and so forth. The findings of Theilhaber, Philipstahl, Georg Halpern, and other Jewish social scientists are repeatedly invoked; a detailed presentation of Ruppin and Wassermann's argument that explains the purported predilection of Jews for particular types of crime—in particular, white-collar crimes—and Jewish economic and occupational distribution, forms the basis for the discussion of "Jewish criminality." Ruppin and Wassermann's findings on the propensity of Jews for *Handelsdelikten*, or crimes related to trade and finance, found their way as well into numerous other studies, including Karl Friedrich Wiebe's *Deutschland und die Judenfrage*, Friedrich Hermann Zander's *Die Verbreitung der Juden in der Welt*, and the Institut zum Studium von Judentum und Bolshewismus's *Die Wanderung und Verbreitung der Juden in der Welt*.[33]

This use of knowledge produced by Jews, or of Jewish knowledge, by Nazi researchers raises significant and intriguing questions about the nature of scholarship, its production and utilization, and the nature of evidence and proof. A full treatment of these questions, as necessary as it is, would be beyond the scope of this work.[34] Here I want to limit my analysis to a few points that illustrate more general arguments made throughout this chapter. In the first place, it is clear, as the Nazi researchers themselves said, that they believed that by featuring the research of Jewish authorities prominently in their own work, they freed themselves of any charges of bias or anti-Semitism. When the discussion moved to the demography of Jewry since the beginning of the nineteenth century, the authors of *Die Juden in Deutschland* explicitly remark on the importance of this: "We have the very good fortune of having the statistical work of the Jews to rely on. This provides a barrier to any anti-Semitic tendentiousness."[35]

But the continuities and interdependencies between the National Socialist and Jewish social scientists illuminate more than the merely functional. They speak to the power of science, and particularly to the power of numbers. For Nazi researchers seem to have had little problem relying on information and evidence produced by Jews, and invoking these Jews as authorities in their own work. Given the Nazi belief about the nature of the Jew, we might expect that there would have been great reluctance on the part of Nazi scholars to accept and use knowledge produced by Jews. "Deception and fraud are essential traits of Jewry" (Täuschung und Betrug sind dem Juden wesenseigentümlich)," asserted the anonymous author of the 1938 study *Die Wanderung und Verbreitung der Juden in der Welt*. Yet the author relies heavily, as he himself admits at the outset, on statistics and social scientific studies produced by "Jewish officials."[36]

The Nazis' use of Jewish research and knowledge can only partly be explained by the aforementioned desire on the part of the Nazis to avoid appearing anti-Semitic by invoking the research of Jews. It seems that at least some Nazi academics also possessed a faith in the notion of objectivity. Not only did they share the desire to *appear* objective in their scholarship, but they also assumed that there exists, in fact, some gap or difference between the knowledge produced and its producer. That is, despite the fact that knowledge about Jewish history and contemporary life was produced by Jewish scholars, this knowledge was valid as evidence about a reality apart from the individual who produced it.

It is of course vitally important to point out the discontinuities between Jewish and Nazi interpretations and intentions. Nazi researchers took the earlier Jewish self-critique, which, as I hope this study has demonstrated, was an integral part of this Jewish scholarship, and turned it against the Jews. Obviously, this was no longer "jüdische Wissenschaft"; that is, in the hands of the Nazis it ceased to be Jewish scholarship produced in the main by Jews, with an aim toward reform and regeneration, as well as self-knowledge and understanding. Context in this case is almost everything. But it was also important that the apparatus of legitimate scholarship could be found in these Jewish texts. Nazi researchers could thereby have it both ways: the Jewish provenance could be highlighted, and could serve its polemical purpose, while the objective status of the evidence, a status that came in large part through the presence of numbers, could at the same time be assumed.

While there were those who believed that the content of these Jewish texts confirmed the diseased and degenerate nature of the Jew, there were other Nazi researchers who believed that the form of Jewish scholarship was contaminated by this very same degenerate nature. In 1938 the University of Königsberg economist Peter-Heinz Seraphim published a study of over 700 pages titled *Das Judentum im osteuropäischen Raum* (Jewry in the Eastern European Realm). The work was sponsored by the University of Königsberg's Institute for Eastern European Economy, and it brought together in one volume Seraphim's expertise in general Eastern European economic issues and the more specific Jewish Question in the East. What is of particular interest here is not the content of his book, but Seraphim's scholarly apparatus. As Alan Steinweis recently noted, "one of the hallmarks of Seraphim's book is its extensive exploitation of Jewish scholarship."[37] In his extended discussions of demography, migration, and occupational distribution Seraphim relied heavily on the research of Jewish social scientists, including Ruppin, Nossig, Lestschinsky, Kaplun-Kogan, Tartakower, and others. Throughout, Seraphim used the phrase "according to Jewish sources." Yet he insisted that there was a substantive, qualitative difference between Jewish and non-Jewish treatments of contemporary Jewish life. In his extensive bibliography he placed a "J" before those names he had identified as Jewish; of the 563 sources, 346 have the mark. In his introduction Seraphim made clear the implications of this difference.

It is undeniable that the Jewish authority working on issues of a Jewish theme, will analyze relationships and connections differently than will a non-Jew. It is therefore doubly necessary that non-Jewish scholars concern themselves with the analysis of Jewish issues. Only in this way will we finally escape from the old interpretive rut [*eingefahrenen Gleis*] made by Jewish writers, from the schematic view of historical, cultural, political and economic questions, and arrive at a new, different, and more correct understanding.[38]

The Jewish interpretation of Jewish life was, in Seraphim's view, fundamentally, we might say inevitably, flawed, given that Jews are analyzing the evidence. Hence, non-Jewish, and more specifically "Aryan" analyses were called for. This was a common assertion, unsurprisingly, within the German academic community in the Weimar and Nazi periods. Increasingly, the political or ideological impetus to scholarship was not only acknowledged but also demanded as "healthy" and normal. The needs of the Volk, Nation, Race ought to be reflected in, and give impetus to, the nation's scholars and scientists.[39] The striving toward "objectivity" or neutrality that had so preoccupied German scholars such as Max Weber and Ernst Troeltsch a generation before came to be associated with values inimical to the interests of the *Volk* and nation. Indeed, the very urge for "objectivity" was now identified as a Jewish trait, and therefore as supremely un-German. Seraphim endorsed this politicized view of scholarship at the conclusion of his introductory remarks. Veracity and reality in representation were guaranteed to German science (*deutsche Wissenschaft*) only when it was infused with the sensibility and goals of the Volk ("*völkischen Ziele und Sinnes*").

It seems all the more remarkable, then, that Seraphim relied to the extent that he did on Jewish sources, on knowledge produced by Jews. Why did he trust the sources, given their Jewish provenance and his own deeply held belief in the inextricability of *völkish* interests and scholarly production? Were the three hundred and fifty or so works that appear in his own bibliography marked with a "J" not corrupt, and therefore useless as avenues to the reality of Jewish life? And certainly Seraphim, like other Nazi scholars, was concerned with the reality of Jewish life, in no small measure because they sought to exert some influence on German policy vis-à-vis the Jews. In 1937–38, when Seraphim was writing, the German conquest of Poland and the Soviet Union, and control over millions of Jews there, were still of course only a future possibility. In his own mind at least, Seraphim intended his massive work on Jews in the Eastern territories to serve as a guide to practical decision making. It was, then, quite important that the most reliable facts about contemporary Jewish life be obtained and disseminated.

Clearly, the urge to appear neutral, to distance one's work from accusations of "anti-Semitic tendentiousness" cannot help explain every case of Nazi use of Jewish scholarship. Nazi academics, as I argue above, also possessed a faith in the notion of objectivity, even if they explicitly rejected such a notion on political grounds. In the case of the authors of *Die Juden in Deutschland*, there did exist the desire to *appear* objective in their scholarship; in the case of Seraphim, this desire did not exist. Yet in both cases there was the assumption that there does in fact exist some gap or difference between the knowledge produced and those who produced it.

We can see this not only in the volumes emanating from Nazi academic institutes, but also in the actual planning and implementation of anti-Jewish policy. How, for instance, did Nazi bureaucrats arrive at the number of Jews in any particular country or region under their control? As scholars such as Raul Hilberg, Götz Aly, and Karl Roth have demonstrated, the enumeration of Jewry was of enormous significance not only for the Nazi conception of the "Jewish Problem," but for the process of identification and concentration.[40] Bureaucrats relied, first and foremost, on the statistics compiled by the Reich Statistical Office, which conducted two official censuses during the Third Reich—in 1933 and 1939. Yet they also at times relied for their information about Jewry on figures produced by Jewish scholars. For instance, in April 1935, State Secretary Hans Pfundtner, of the Reich Ministry of the Interior in Berlin, circulated a memo regarding the number of "full, half, and quarter Jews in the German Reich."[41] According to the census of June 16, 1933, there were just under 500,000 "mosaische Juden," or Jews of the Mosaic faith, in the German Reich (if one added the Jews from the Saar Region, the number rose to just under 504,000). The number of full "racial Jews" and "Mischlinge" (offspring of mixed marriages) could only be estimated, since the census had not, interestingly enough, incorporated racial categories. There were an estimated three hundred thousand "full Jews, not of the Mosaic faith," and seven hundred and fifty thousand "Mischlinge."

Pfundtner also wanted to note how the total number of Jews broke down statistically along the lines of gender and age. And for this he turned to a book entitled *Die Bevölkerungs- und Berufsverhältnisse der Juden im deutschen Reich* (Population and Occupational Patterns of the Jews in the

German Reich) published in 1930. Pfundtner did not identify the author; it would not matter in the context of the memo. Yet he must have known, or at least suspected, that Professor Heinrich Silbergleit, who was well known as the director of the statistical office of the city of Berlin in the last years of the Weimar Republic, was a Jew. Pfundtner did note in the memo that the work was published by the Akademieverlag Berlin. Yet, at the top of the title page it also states that the book is a publication of the *Akademie für die Wissenschaft des Judentums, Sektion für Statistik und Wirtschaftskunde* (Academy for the Science of Judaism, the Statistical and Economic Section). And the foreword begins by stating that the book was commissioned by the academy. Like his academic counterparts, Pfundtner trusted in numbers, and in the science that generated them, even when they were to be found in texts clearly written by Jews, and published by Jewish institutions.

## *Jewish Social Science and Postwar Jewish Scholarship: The Question of Race*

There are discernible and important continuities between Jewish social science, as it developed between 1880 and 1930, and post–World War II Jewish scholarship. Most obvious is the survival of those categories of research that were amenable to redefinition within the newly emerging social scientific paradigm: Jewish demography, migration, intermarriage, and occupational distribution. Scholars such as Bruno Blau, Jacob Lestschinsky, and Arieh Tartakower, writing in Israel and the United States in the late 1940s and 1950s, facilitated this sort of intellectual transition and continuity. Tartakower, for instance, began his 1956 sociological work, *Ha-Chevrah ha-Yehudit* (The Jewish Community), by placing his own contribution in a long line of social scientific research stretching back to Ruppin and others at the start of the century.[42] Of course, as Tartakower went on to write, recent developments—the catastrophe in Europe, and "the miracle of the birth of the State of Israel" chief among them—demanded new research and writing. At the same time, Tartakower, like other postwar Jewish scholars, was deeply indebted to the writings of earlier Jewish social scientists.

Surely one of the most obvious discontinuities between early Jewish social science and postwar Jewish scholarship was the status of "race" as a legitimate or normative category of analysis. As Elazar Barkan has shown, racial science—at least in Great Britain and the United States—was already under attack from influential anthropologists, geneticists, and biologists in the 1920s.[43] Jewish social scientists played a role in the intellectual and political struggles against scientific racism. In the 1920s and 1930s Maurice Fishberg joined with Franz Boas to publish and lecture about the dangers of racism.[44] Ignaz Zollschan labored in Europe, and then in England and the United States, to create an international anthropological research center to combat racism scientifically.[45]

This does not mean, however, that Jewish social scientists necessarily stopped invoking racial categories altogether—only that there was a more vigorous denunciation of the sort of biological determinism associated with the Nazi regime. This can be seen, for example, in Arthur Ruppin's final book, *The Jewish Fate and Future* (1940). Like his previous works, the first chapter of this one included an extended discussion of the racial nature of Jewry. He now emphasized to a greater degree than in earlier works the mixed, nonhomogeneous nature of the Jews historically, and his value judgment about such "racial intermixture" was far more tempered. At the same time, Ruppin still ended with a discussion of the "racial differences of mentality" between Jews and non-Jews.[46]

While a serious challenge to racial science was launched in the 1920s, it is nonetheless true that the revelations of the death camps, and the growing realization of the integral part played by racial scientists in the genocidal process, delegitimized the sorts of racial and social Darwinian analyses that had been so ubiquitous in previous decades. Surprisingly, though, analyses of Jewry along racio-anthropological lines did continue to appear in works of Jewish scholarship in the immediate post-Holocaust period. There was a lag time between the Holocaust and the delegitimization, at least in mainstream scholarly circles, of the categorization and analysis of Jews in the sorts of racial or biophysical terms that had become so commonplace during the previous half century. One finds bio-anthropological and medical analyses in both specialized and popular scholarly forums. In both cases much of the literature produced by early Jewish as well as non-Jewish social scientific authorities informed and shaped this later work. There was a continuity, therefore, in both form and content between pre- and post-Holocaust anthropological literature on Jewish identity. Perhaps it is not terribly surprising to find Bruno Blau writing in such terms in the postwar period, given his training and career as a social scientist during the first decades of the century. Blau's continuing interest in the Jewish racial question can be seen in an appendix he included in his unpublished manuscript on German Jewry now held at the Leo Baeck Archives in New York City.[47] The text, titled "Die Rassejuden und jüdischen Mischlinge," is a statistical investigation of the categories "racial Jews" and "Jewish Mischlinge" (offspring of mixed marriages), utilizing, inter alia, the 1939 census undertaken by Nazi authorities. Blau's purpose is not to question or undermine the categories, but rather to arrive at more exact figures.

In 1951 Blau published an article entitled "The Jew as Sexual Criminal" in *Jewish Social Studies*, one of the leading Jewish academic journals in the

United States.[48] Blau's particular argument is of less interest here than is the fact that the article appeared where and when it did. For, as in his unpublished manuscript cited above, Blau did not take the opportunity to reject the very terms of the debate, nor was there any indication that the journal's editors (the well-known Jewish historian Salo Baron was the chief editor of the journal) felt it necessary to distance themselves from this type of material. Rather, Blau used Jewish and Christian criminal statistics to demonstrate, once again, that those—such as the Nazis—who argued for the racial-biological nature of Jewish criminality were wrong. From Bulgaria to Canada, according to Blau, when it came to bigamy, incest, rape, seduction, sodomy, and bestiality, the Jews were statistically underrepresented.

This persistence of a racial anthropological approach to the question of Jewish identity is evident in scholarship more widely disseminated and read than was Blau's. It was alive, for example, in a massive sourcebook of Jewish social scientific writing published in Israel in 1954, and edited by the distinguished historian Benzion Dinur, and by Arieh Tartakower and Jacob Lestschinsky.[49] Part II is devoted to the issue of "the Jews as a race" ("ha-Yehudim ke-Geza"). To be sure, the enormous problems posed by the political uses to which racial science had been placed were acknowledged at the outset. But the questions of Jewish racial identity and history, as they had been formulated over the past century and more, remained open. The editors reproduced selections from Ruppin, Fishberg, Fritz Kahn (the author of *Die Juden als Rasse und Kulturvolk*), Franz Boas, and others. Not surprisingly, the selections were antiracist, intended to point up the progressive, that is, environmentalist thrust to Jewish writings on the subject. Yet it is illuminating that the question of Jewish racial identity remained, in 1954, a theme or problem for Jewish sociology. At least for Dinur, Tartakower, and Lestschinsky, the category had not yet been fully historicized; it remained an issue open to discussion within the social sciences. Nor had these issues been fully historicized in American-Jewish scholarship in the two decades after World War II. For instance, an entire section of volume 2 of Louis Finkelstein's monumental anthology *The Jews: Their History, Culture, and Religion* is devoted to "The Sociology and Demography of the Jews." The first article in this section, "Who Are the Jews?", was written by the prominent anthropologist Melville Herskovits, who was himself Jewish, and who had been a student of Franz Boas at Columbia University.[50] While Herskovits seems to have wanted to move away from older analyses of the Jews as a racial entity, he ended up summarizing the earlier literature, and in the process validating the questions and categories. In the end, Herskovits denied the racial unity and identity of the Jews, arguing for a multiplicity of Jewish types rooted in local variation. Yet his article is a fascinating illustration of the way older Jewish (and non-Jewish) social scientific research continued to function in post-Holocaust Jewish scholarship, and of how older categories and questions, as well as the particular measurements, continued to shape analyses of Jewish identity even after the paradigm of racial anthropology—certainly in the case of the Jews—had been made highly problematic, to say the least. Thus Herskovits finished his survey by addressing the question of "nasality" and the "Jewish look." Again, he ended up dismissing these categories. But it is instructive that he felt obliged to spend three pages representing the varying opinions and arguments about a peculiar Jewish physiognomy.[51] While his point, in the end, is that the "Jewish look" is a highly questionable proposition, he had to establish that through scientific means, including statistical anthropometric studies.

## Critical Reassessments: Jewish Social Science and Jewish Social History

Finally, Jewish statistical studies undertaken in the decades prior to World War II continue to be a rich source for Jewish social historians interested in reconstructing the reality of nineteenth- and early-twentieth-century Jewish communal life. Population numbers, occupational distributions, migration rates, levels of intermarriage and conversion, health and disease, and other categories drawn from early social scientific work are utilized, as positive knowledge, by contemporary historians of Jewry.

The impact of Jewish social science on postwar Jewish scholarship is evident in the writings of Jewish historians whose work emphasized demographic, social, and economic forces. One can, for instance, find strong echoes of the "sociological" approach to Jewish history, with its elucidation of the causal relationship between industrial capitalism and the revolutionary change in Jewish-Christian social relations in the work of more recent Jewish social historians. Simon Dubnow, of course, was the major driving force in this direction, having identified his own work as sociological. Still, Jewish social scientists, most prominently Ruppin, had earlier on identified transformations in the socioeconomic, rather than in the intellectual and political, realm as being of primary importance in Jewish emancipation and integration. A later generation of historians such as Jacob Katz, Salo Baron, Raphael Mahler, and others have developed and refined this theme.[52]

It is interesting to note, though, that historians such as Katz and Baron did not acknowledge any continuity between their own work and earlier social scientists. On the contrary, they emphasized the discontinuities, or denied any real progenitors; they thereby staked out a more striking claim to originality of method or approach. For example, in the 1939 inaugural issue of *Jewish Social Studies*, Salo Baron published a review of approaches to Jewish history, and offered suggestions for new or underexplored avenues of research.[53] At a certain point he called attention to the need for applying sociological, biological, anthropological, and especially statistical methods and insights to Jewish history.

The rates of Jewish natality and mortality in different periods; the varying age and sex distribution in each generation; the numerical division between urban and rural groups, the extent and the biological effects of polygamy in various Jewish settlements; the frequency and effects of intermarriage, whether officially more or less tolerated or outlawed—are all problems of vital significance for the understanding of the economic structure, the social relationships, and even of certain cultural and religious developments of the Jewish, as of any other, people.[54]

But, according to Baron, little work had as yet been done by Jewish scholars in this promising direction. He mentioned Dubnow's effort, which he found deeply problematic—hardly a real improvement over Graetz's "*Leidens- und Gelehrtengeschichte*"—and his own intention of publishing at some point a "Jewish History in the Light of Numbers."[55] But there is no mention in his writing of the efforts of Jewish social scientists who had been at work in Europe and the United States for four decades. The collective work of the Bureau of Jewish statistics, the articles and monographs of Ruppin, Fishberg, and the others, have vanished. A social scientific approach to Jewry remains a future task: "In any case the time seems overdue for the marshalling of all the available information and for its utmost exploitation by statisticians, sociologists, and historians."[56]

Nearly four decades later, at the end of his career, Baron's account of modern Jewish scholarship, and his own intellectual genealogy, had hardly changed. In *The Contemporary Relevance of History* he reflected on the contemporary state of Jewish historical scholarship, and on the various intellectual and disciplinary strains that had contributed to its development. Early in the book he mentioned the studies of Ruppin and Lestschinsky in passing, but only to dismiss them as insufficient. "In the Jewish field, in particular," Baron concluded, "many sociological studies have suffered from the meagerness or lopsided nature of the evidence on which the conclusions were based."[57] In his discussion of anthropology Baron included ethnology, which also embraced "racial studies"; these, he insisted, were of "special significance to Jewish history." But he neglected to mention any work on ethnology, or on racial and physical anthropology (which he singled out for mention at the outset) by Jewish social scientists or historians. There was only the link between racial anti-Semitism and Nazism; the enormous corpus of scholarly work produced by Jews on the "racial" character of Jewry had vanished.[58]

If one were to expect a discussion of previous attempts by Jewish scholars to work with statistics, it would be in Baron's chapter on "quantitative
methods." Yet, again, there is nothing to indicate that Baron's efforts at
such work emerged out of an established trend within Jewish *Wissenschaft*.
"It so happens that I have always (at times unwittingly) been in favor of
some such quantitative approach. Throughout my career as an historian I
have constantly evinced great interest especially in population figures and
quantitative economic data." He wrote again of his plan—unrealized—to
write a "Jewish History in the Light of Numbers." We are then told that 40
years later he remained "amazed at the paucity of research in this field." Little work had been done in the field of what might be termed biblical
demography. This had to do with the relative lack of data. Baron then generalized from the biblical to other periods of Jewish history: "In most other
areas and periods we are confined to a few, more or less fragmentary, data
and must supplement them with numerous hypotheses from various angles
and degrees of plausibility."[59] Since Baron made no effort to inform his
readers that the situation with regard to demographic sources was any different for other periods of Jewish history, we are left to conclude that work
in the areas of demography and related disciplines by Jewish scholars is
equally lacking.

In a book such as Baron's, one of the goals of which certainly seems to
be to integrate Jewish and general scholarship, to demonstrate that Jewish
scholars have grappled with many, if not all, of the methods and issues
occupying general, non-Jewish scholars, it is fascinating that Jewish social
scientists vanish almost without a trace. How might we account for Baron's
unwillingness, even inability, perhaps, to acknowledge the existence of this
body of scholarship, and his own indebtedness to it? Perhaps we have an
instance here of what the literary critic Harold Bloom has called the "anxiety of influence."[60] It is indeed striking that Baron focused exclusively on
the ancient and medieval periods in his discussions of methodologies, even
though he himself did a great deal of important work on modern Jewish
history. But this served his purpose, since it allowed him to elide the existence of social scientific scholarship, most of which—for reasons Baron
himself made clear through his discussion of the lack of adequate materials
from earlier periods—concerns itself with the last two centuries.

Almost certainly Baron was aware of this scholarship, if not at the time
he wrote his 1939 piece, then shortly thereafter. For if one returns to his earlier writings, there is evidence not only that he was quite familiar with this
body of social scientific research, but that he had incorporated it into his
own work. For instance, in his well-known article "Modern Capitalism and
Jewish Fate," published in *The Menorah Journal* in 1942, Baron made reference to a body of Jewish statistical data that revealed a demographic crisis

within German Jewry.[61] He cited Felix Theilhaber's 1911 work *Der Unter-gang der deutschen Juden*, and though Baron believed that Theilhaber over-stated the imminent danger to Western Jewry, he did conclude that "when the basic trend [of demographic decline] began to spread to more and more countries, gradually penetrating even the east-European fountain of Jewish biological strength, a real menace to world Jewry was revealed."[62]

Baron was aware, then, of the research and writing of earlier Jewish social scientists; he utilized it in his own work. His own representation of his intellectual genealogy, therefore, needs to be amended. At any rate, given Baron's stature in the world of twentieth-century Jewish scholarship, he provides an important example of the influence exerted by early Jewish social science. There is further evidence for the engagement with prewar Jewish social science in the critical reassessments of this research on the part of later scholars that began appearing in the 1940s and 1950s. By 1940 *Jewish Social Studies* had already published an article, "On the Use of the Term 'Non-Jewish' in Jewish statistics," which seemed to call into question the enterprise of Jewish statistics itself. The author, H. L. Lurie, argued that the category "non-Jew," which Jewish social scientists employed as a mat-ter of course, was meaningless, since "an assumed homogeneous 'non-Jew-ish' or general population . . . is obviously non-existent."[63] The upshot of this is that the claim, touted so often by Jewish demographers and others, about the existence of "major differences" between Jews and non-Jews is unsupportable.[64] Other critiques were less all-encompassing, focusing on particular realms or categories of earlier Jewish social scientific work. In an article titled "Some Reflections on the Jewish Participation in German Eco-nomic Life," published in the first volume of the *Leo Baeck Institute Year-book*, Eduard Rosenbaum called into question the category of "Jewish eco-nomic life in Germany."[65] Rosenbaum examined the arguments of Felix Theilhaber, Alfred Marcus, Arthur Ruppin, and Jacob Lestschinksy, in addition to those of select non-Jewish authors. For reasons of methodol-ogy and ideology, these authorities had maintained that such a thing as a "Jewish economy" existed, and could be analyzed scientifically. Some, like Marcus and Lestschinsky, recognized that the sorts of sociological general-izations they relied on were problematic, and that the economic fate of Jews in Germany, or anywhere else for that matter, could not be separated from the general economic trends. Upswings or downturns in the economy would affect Jews and non-Jews alike; such general forces made talk of a distinct Jewish economic life all but meaningless. Jewish and non-Jewish social scientists, nonetheless, treated the Jews as a separate entity. More-over, Rosenbaum perceptively noted that Jewish social scientists tended "to accept almost unconsciously Gentile reproaches and somehow to apologize for the Jewish part played in commerce and retail trade."[66]

In the end, Rosenbaum called for a turning away from the older, statistically based analyses of the economic activities of Jews in Germany and elsewhere. What was required was "a kind of differential sociology and a more intimate analysis of group life than the preponderantly statistical method. And from this starting point we become deeply interested in biographical studies of outstanding personalities even in the field of economic life." Such a biographical approach would avoid the pitfall of treating the Jews as a "*Volkskörper*," as a biological or racial entity distinct from the German *Volk*.[67]

More recently, Jack Wertheimer, an historian of German and American Jewry, offered an extensive analysis of the difficulties posed by the statistics produced by early Jewish social scientists. Wertheimer's interest is in the use historians of Jewry might make of these numbers. A discussion of his insights and reservations provides entry into the broader issue of how contemporary Jewish social historians have used this older research, and the difficulties posed by doing so. In an appendix to his 1978 dissertation on East European Jewish immigration in Germany, Wertheimer noted that "the demographic figures at our disposal pose numerous difficulties."[68] These include general methodological problems in German census taking, as well as problems of "categories," which often varied from state to state or region to region, and so prevented the production of consistent tables. For example, Wertheimer raised the crucial question of how to determine the origins of Jews—in this case, Eastern European immigrant Jews residing in Germany—when the census taker was only counting those present in a particular place at a particular time, that is, when the "population was defined as the total of those present in the location at the time of the census."[69] How is it possible to determine the number of *Ostjuden* in Berlin during any given period, when the census simply records the number of "Juden" without inquiring about origins? As Wertheimer shows, a number of earlier historians devised or relied upon highly dubious methods for determining the numbers of Eastern European Jews. Some, most prominently Shalom Adler-Rudel, at times pulled numbers out of thin air.[70] In the case of a work such as Adler-Rudel's, the problem of statistical methods becomes even more pronounced, since his book—including the numbers—was, and remains, a central secondary text in the field.[71]

What is of primary import and interest, at least in the context of this chapter, is not the fact that Jewish social scientists relied on problematic numbers, or even that they produced such numbers themselves. Rather, it is the fact that later scholars relied to a significant extent on these numbers. This demonstrates, again, the two points I want to emphasize here. First, early Jewish social scientific research was taken up and utilized by other scholars, both before and after World War II. Hence, the impact of this body of work was, and is, far greater than historians of Jewish scholarship have recognized. Secondly, the ability of this research, and particularly of the statistics, to "travel" is due in large measure to more universal assumptions about the nature of numbers. This, in turn, reveals a great deal about historians' unquestioned assumptions about critical issues like evidence and proof. Numbers, it seems, enjoy an immunity from critical scrutiny not vouchsafed to other types of historical evidence. The trust in numbers referred to throughout this study thus extends into the present. This issue is made more forceful when we recall that in many cases the numbers Jewish historians today are drawing from early works of Jewish social science were themselves derived from highly questionable sources.[72] It is worth noting, for instance, that Jewish social scientists working in the first decades of the twentieth century made extensive use of the censuses conducted by the Russian authorities. Given what was known of the Czarist regime and its relationship with its Jewish population—indeed, a number of Jewish social scientists had firsthand knowledge of the regime, having been born in the Russian Empire, and having fled Russia in order to attend universities in the West—it is striking that the Russian census data regularly appears, often unattributed, in the studies produced by Jews. Despite the character of the regime, Jewish social scientists possessed a faith in the statistical data generated about Jews by the Russian government.[73] Surely Wertheimer's cautionary statement regarding the utilization of German numbers ought to be extended to Russia, Poland, and elsewhere.

Other historians of Jewry, however, have been far less cautious than Wertheimer in utilizing the statistics produced in the half decade before World War II. Ismar Schorsch's influential work on Jewish reactions to German anti-Semitism incorporates statistical works from the same period he analyzes. He reproduced the statistics found in Bernhard Breslauer's studies of Jews in the professions and the universities, and Ruppin's table on Jewish university attendance compared to that of Christians.[74] Whether or not these numbers are correct, or whether or not they tell the "truth" about the past in the way they were intended to, is not of primary import here (although it is not, or should not be, a nugatory issue, particularly for working social historians). What I find illuminating about examples such as these is what they reveal about our approach to numbers, our faith in numbers. Schorsch's work is in large measure built on a critical examination of the primary literature, an intellectual-cultural study of newspapers, articles, and books, and the political impetuses to these. In all of his writings—on Jewish historiography, and on German and German Jewish politics—his critical attention to the ideological elements and motives embedded in texts is evident.[75]

Yet when it comes to the numbers, this critical approach seems to be absent. The statistics appear contextless; they can be lifted out of the narrative and used again, regardless of when, why, how, or by whom they were produced. It is difficult to imagine other elements within texts from fifty or one hundred years ago being approached this uncritically. This does not mean that historians cannot and do not use older texts to reconstruct not only subjective beliefs and ideological positions, but also past material and social realities. But the sort of critical skepticism about data, found in texts that, with the passage of time, have moved from being secondary to primary sources, oftentimes seems absent in the case of numbers.

Another even more striking example of this faith or trust in numbers, as well as of the direct influence of early Jewish social scientific work on later Jewish scholarship, can be found in Marsha Rozenblit's seminal study on Jewish assimilation in Vienna.[76] As Rozenblit makes clear in her introduction, her study is in fact a response to, and a test of, Arthur Ruppin's contention about the effects of urbanization on modern Jewish identity. Ultimately, her work refutes Ruppin's formulation that urbanization led to acculturation, which in turn led to an assimilation that threatened to destroy collective Jewish identity. Rather, Rozenblit demonstrated that Jews underwent the process of modernization in a distinctly Jewish way. In the social and economic spheres Jews remained distinct, even as they sought to acculturate. Ruppin's position, she wrote in the introduction, was "overly pessimistic."

It is instructive, then, to proceed through the body of Rozenblit's book and see that she relied on Ruppin's as well as on a number of other early Jewish social scientists' statistics. In her chapter on the "Creation of Viennese Jewry," the statistics on Jewish urbanization are derived from Ruppin.[77] The research of Jakob Thon, Jacob Lestschinsky, and Leo Goldhammer (as well as the 1873 work of the non-Jewish statistician Gustav Schimmer) also figure prominently. The research of these authorities appears in the analyses of occupational patterns, education, and intermarriage and conversion. At certain points Rozenblit made it clear that she understood that the numbers were inexact, that there were methodological problems inherent in their production and compilation. Nonetheless, these qualifications are overwhelmed and in the end obscured by the presentation of the numbers—the numerous charts and tables, and the statistics that occupy a crucial place and serve an important function, in the narrative. Any hesitations all but disappear in the sea of graphs and numbers.

Equally illustrative is Peter Honigmann's recent analysis of Jewish conversion in Central Europe.[78] Honigmann set out to challenge the notion that the numbers of conversions can be used to determine levels of assimilation. While he did not deny that assimilation was linked to conversion, he found that there were significant variations in numbers of conversions in cities in which the degree of assimilation of Jewry was not markedly different. Jewish conversions in the late nineteenth and early twentieth centuries depended increasingly on political pressures. Conversions were a product of not just assimilation, but of a combination of assimilation and political pressure.

What is of interest here is Honigmann's approach to the statistical sources. He began with a discussion of the problems involved in obtaining reliable numbers on Jewish conversion and secessions (*Austritte*). Ideally, one would like to have what Honigmann called a "snapshot" of the situation: figures from particular locales regarding the total number of Jews living in the community, and the number of baptized and seceded Jews residing there. These are not, however, available for most of the period covered by Honigmann's study. "It was only the National Socialist regime which actually initiated such 'snapshots' through the German census of 1939 and the Hungarian census of 1941."[79] Honigmann provided the statistics on Berlin, Vienna, and Budapest. But he was quick to warn us that "these figures have to be regarded with caution." Why? Remarkably, it was not that these numbers were produced by the Nazis about Jews. Honigmann offered no indication that the numbers might be questionable because of the context(s) in which they were produced. Rather, the problem was that it was impossible to determine the demographic impact of the emigration of Berlin Jews from that city. This made any comparison of the Jewish populations of Vienna, Budapest, and Berlin difficult. Honigmann then qualified this and said that the 1939 census might offer, at best, a sense of the cumulative effect of conversions over the previous five or six decades. So, in the end, his skepticism about these statistics was muted, and the numbers seem to be usable after all.

Honigmann then proceeded to establish a sounder means of arriving at an accurate statistical portrait of conversion, a process that uncritically utilized Jewish social science research. This entailed, first of all, establishing the total number of Jews settled in a particular place. For that he relied on Bruno Blau's 1950 above-cited unpublished manuscript, a synthetic study constructed out of earlier studies.[80] According to Blau, the Berlin Jewish community counted seventy-three thousand members in 1941. This is the base point for Honigmann's working out of the statistical equation that he then used to determine the number of Jews lost to conversion between 1873 and 1941. This number, he concluded, was only half of what it was believed to be earlier.

Now Honigmann was highly attuned to the political implications of the conversion statistics. He began his essay with just this point, and examined the point at a number of junctures. Conversion statistics were interpreted, he reminded us, as a sign of Jewish assimilation, and ultimately, disappearance. This was judged desirable or undesirable, depending on one's point of view. Yet because Honigmann was offering his own alternative explanation as a Jewish social historian, he was obliged to rely on these numbers himself. He told us that we needed to take care with the numbers, yet he then went on to use them for his own purposes.

There is no doubt that Honigmann's statistical methodology is highly sophisticated. Nonetheless, he relied on figures produced over fifty to seventy years ago. His trust in numbers is apparent in the fact that he nowhere seemed to acknowledge the history of statistical methods itself; this would have thrown open to doubt his own use of the numbers, and by implication his arguments and conclusions. The problem was therefore elided by de-contextualizing the statistics. At certain junctures this is a methodological de-contextualization, so that the reader is unaware of the myriad number of problems and difficulties raised by the production of statistics. At other points it is a political or sociocultural de-contextualization, so that the ideological impetuses to both the production and interpretation of such data disappears.

Neither Rozenblit's nor Honigmann's work is necessarily any less convincing or worthy if the numbers are challenged. Nor is the issue that the numbers are even necessarily "wrong." The question of the truth or validity of the numbers may, in the end, be meaningless and impossible to answer. For it is difficult to see how we might arrive at any sort of independent verification of the matter. What is illuminating, however, is that the numbers take on a life of their own. They circulate from text to text, gaining an increasing influence and power to shape the evaluations made of Jewish life. Statistics are given an authority or pride of place that few if any other types of knowledge, at least in the discipline of history, are allowed. It would be difficult to find a professional historian who would approach a text from 1904 or 1930 uncritically, reproducing the images and ideas, arguments and conclusions as simple, unmediated reflections of reality. We are, of course, trained to approach texts critically, to interrogate them, to ask about the author's reason for writing, about her own complex identity and position within a particular society and culture. Thus, Rozenblit herself understands Ruppin's narrative, his interpretation of Jewish urbanization and assimilation, in just such ideological terms: hers is an interpretation that reveals as much, if not more, about Ruppin—social scientist, Zionist, German Jew—as it does about the reality of European Jewish life in the nineteenth and early twentieth centuries.

It testifies to the power of statistics as "objective" or neutral facts that social scientists, Jewish and non-Jewish, of different and competing political orientations oftentimes utilized one another's numbers, and the interpretations within which they were embedded. Perhaps an even more potent testament to statistics' force is the unproblematic use of these numbers, produced over half a century ago, by scholars working today. The faith that in statistics we possess a type of knowledge impervious to external or extra-scientific influence, that numbers offer direct, unmediated access to social and economic reality is evident in the way statistics are commonly lifted out of the larger narrative of which they form a part, and are offered as evidence. This separation of statistics from their context attests to the continuing significance of this older body of scholarship, a significance that has gone largely unappreciated.

It bears emphasizing that pointing out the unself-conscious use of statistics by no means necessarily calls into question the validity of the works under discussion. It does, however, point to the need for a more critical approach to this material. When the numerous problems involved in the statistical project have begun to be identified, and the ideological impetus to much of the work drawn out, what, if anything, will be the effect? I am not suggesting a facile dismissal of statistical evidence produced in the past, only a more critical and self-reflexive approach to the material.

*

Within the social scientific literature discussed in this book, we find a sustained and serious effort on the part of Jews to begin to understand and explain the enormous effects the transformations of nineteenth-century society and culture worked on European Jewry. The phenomena of mass migration, industrialization and urbanization; technological and medical developments; and the social, economic, and cultural effects brought about by these changes necessitated, according to the proponents of Jewish social science, new methods and categories of scholarly analysis. This marked a significant shift within modern Jewish scholarship, a broadening of the definition of "Jewish science" to include demography, anthropology, social biology, sociology, and political economy. I have emphasized the nexus between nationalism and social science because Zionists were instrumental in creating and shaping the enterprise at both the institutional and the intellectual level. Simultaneously, I have tried to provide a sense that Zionists were not alone in engaging with the social sciences, and seeking to identify and remedy problems within contemporary Jewish communities.

The question that lay at the heart of the Jewish social scientific enterprise, and that preoccupied Jewish social scientists, as well as other Jewish elites at the time—the impact of integration, or assimilation, on Jews and Jewry—continues to preoccupy many within the established Jewish community. Fears of demographic decline, and of the ultimate disappearance of the Jews in the Diaspora in the not-so-distant future, have not abated. In some cases, those warning of the imminent disappearance of the Jews openly link their own work to that of early Jewish, mainly Zionist, social scientists, acknowledging it as a model and inspiration. Others construct arguments that echo those of earlier Zionist social scientists without being aware of or acknowledging the striking parallels.[81] Like their progenitors in the early part of the twentieth century, those who embrace a model of "decline" and imminent disappearance of Jewry are not exclusively or even overly concerned with anti-Semitism, or with the social, economic, or political exclusion of the Jews. Rather, their fears are impelled by the success of Jewry in the postwar period, a success measured in secular, "universal" terms as these have developed in the democratic, capitalist West. Thus, the great challenge to American Jewry, especially in the last half of the twentieth century, has not been that of responding to Gentile antagonism to the Jewish presence. On the contrary, Jews have faced the challenge of "adapting to abundance," in the words of one historian of American Jewry.[82] Many within the Jewish community in the United States view the unparalleled abundance enjoyed by Jews as a mixed blessing. Tolerance and equality lead to higher rates of social and cultural integration, and hence to a vitiated attachment to, and participation in, organized Jewish life. More ominously, the success of integration leads to increasing rates of intermarriage. All of these mean a quantitative loss to "the Jewish People," and point to a qualitative, that is, moral, deficiency.

It may well be that the pessimists will be proven correct, and that the number of Jews in the United States, and in the Diaspora in general, will continue to decline on account of the "mixed blessings" offered by an open society. On the other hand, it may be that the optimists' argument that the quantitative threat is not that serious, and that in any case a smaller, though qualitatively superior Jewish community will surely survive, will prove more accurate. Prophecy, as so many others have remarked, is not usually the privilege of the historian. In the end, as Jonathan Sarna has suggested, it may be that the debate itself is what is of most import.[83] Perhaps the periodic outbreak of intense public concern and worry over the Jewish collective future, and the ensuing debate, itself functions to sustain or reinforce Jewish identity, and hence to help ensure Jewish survival.

*Reference Matter*

# Notes

## Introduction

1. For a discussion of the survey and its reception see Goldberg, 66–67. For a more general discussion of the literature on American Jewish decline see the chapter "The Question of Survival" in Shapiro.

2. "Twelve Men and Women."

3. Quoted in Norden, 40.

4. Georges Friedmann, *The End of the Jewish People?* trans. Eric Mosbacher (New York: Doubleday, 1967).

5. Wasserstein, *Vanishing Diaspora*, vii.

6. "Anyone who studies the history of the Jews will readily discover that there was hardly a generation in the Diaspora period which did not consider itself the final link in Israel's chain." Rawidowicz, 211.

7. There are, it should be pointed out, "optimists" who have argued that the threat to Jewish survival has been overblown. What is significant in this context, again, is that they too possess an unquestioned faith in statistics and social science, and in their ability to move beyond the quantitative and reveal something about the qualitative character of Jewry. They differ from the "pessimists," of course, in the meanings they derive from the data. However, even some former optimists such as Charles Silberman, who in his best-selling book *A Certain People: American Jews and Their Lives* argued that the hand-wringing over intermarriage rates was unwarranted, have turned more pessimistic in the wake of the 1990 Jewish Population Survey. See the discussion in Sarna, 55f.

8. Wistrich, "Do the Jews Have a Future?" 24. A number of articles in *Commentary* in the first half of the 1990s were devoted to exploring implications of the survey. In addition to Wistrich, Norden, "Counting the Jews"; Wertheimer, "Family Values and the Jews"; Sarna, "The Secret of Jewish Continuity."

9. For the purposes of this study I am interested only in those Jewish social scientists who made Jews and Jewish life the principal focus of their research and writings. I do not, therefore, deal extensively with figures such as Emile Durkheim, Georg Simmel, Ludwig Gumplowicz, and others who, while Jewish, did not make the Jews an object of their intellectual work. On the subject of the "Jewish influence" on the development of social scientific disciplines see Käsler; König.

10. This is the first study that examines in detail the relationship between the intellectual, institutional, and ideological aspects, and explores the conceptual framework underlying the various analytical disciplines and categories. Works devoted to particular aspects or themes have appeared over the past few years. The majority of these focus almost exclusively on the issue of race, and the appropriation of racial science by Jewish scholars as a means of apologia and/or internal critique. John Efron's study, *Defenders of the Race*, traces the development of a racial scientific discourse among Jewish scholars, and the political uses to which this was put. In some respects Efron's work and my own complement one another. Yet in fundamental ways the approaches we take and the conclusions we reach are different. First of all, and most important, I stress to a far greater degree the nexus between Jewish social science and Zionism, even as I recognize that non-Zionists were interested and involved in this branch of scholarship. This focus is imperative, given, as I believe my work demonstrates, the fundamental impetus of Zionism to create and develop Jewish social science. Secondly, while Efron's approach is biographical, or prosopographical, I organize my chapters thematically. This facilitates the illumination not only of the leading ideas and issues in social science, but also of those fundamental discursive concepts—for example, progress and degeneration, normalcy and abnormality—through which Jewish social scientific narratives were constructed. Sander Gilman has written a number of important books and articles on the appropriation by Jewish thinkers of racial and medical ideas, and on the complex nature of the internalization of racial images and ideas about Jews by Jewish scientists. See Gilman, *Case of Sigmund Freud*; idem, *The Jew's Body*; idem, *Jewish Self-Hatred*; Stepan and Gilman. On the role of racial thought in pre-State Zionist ideology see Almog, *Zionism and History*, esp. 38–45; Doron, "Rassenbewusstsein und Naturwissenschaftliches"; idem, "Social Concepts Prevalent in German Zionism." Derek Penslar has recently explored the beginnings of a Jewish political economy, and traced Jewish economic thought through the mid-nineteenth century. See Penslar, "Origins." Penslar has offered the most cogent analyses of the interconnections between social-scientific knowledge and social policy generated about and by Jews. See his *Zionism and Technocracy*; idem, "Philanthropy." Alan Levenson has analyzed the function of anthropological and racial ideas in the German Zionist attack upon "assimilation" in Wilhelmine Germany. See Levenson, "German Zionism." On the place of the idea of race in the evolution of American Jewish identity see Goldstein.

11. Accounts of these transformations can be found in the following volumes, among many others: Goldscheider and Zuckerman; Toury, "Der Eintritt der Juden"; Barkai; Rozenblit; Cohen-Albert.

12. A. Cohen, 11.

13. On the history of statistics, and on its relation to the development of the social sciences in the nineteenth and early twentieth centuries, I have found the fol-

lowing works particularly useful: Desrosières, *Politics of Large Numbers*; T. Porter, *Rise of Statistical Thinking*; idem, *Trust in Numbers*; Hacking, *Taming of Chance*. Also still extremely helpful is Koren, *History of Statistics*. A wonderful case study on the use of statistics in addressing questions of national identity and nation-state building is Patriarca, *Numbers and Nationhood*. In addition to the works cited throughout on various aspects of modern social science, see R. Smith; W. Smith, *Politics and the Sciences of Culture*; Oberschall, *Empirical Social Research*; idem, "Two Empirical Roots."

14. There were certainly those who questioned the validity and usefulness of the statistical enterprise. For example, in his 1890 piece "Impressions of a Journey Through the Tomaszow Region," the Yiddish writer I. L. Peretz describes his trip to Tomaszow to collect statistics that will prove that the Jews are not what anti-Semites claim them to be. The piece actually serves to demonstrate Peretz's emerging conviction that statistics reveal nothing meaningful about Jewish life. As he walks around the town he meets with resistance on the part of the people to his fact-gathering. They fear he is a civil servant, and that the information will be used by the Russian state. After being exposed to numerous vignettes of shtetl life, Peretz is alone one evening, and he suddenly asks himself:

What will be the upshot of statistics? Will statistics tell us how much suffering is needed—empty bellies and unused teeth; hunger so intense that the sight of a dry crust of bread will make the eyes bulge in their sockets, as if drawn out by pliers; indeed, actual death by starvation—to produce an unlicensed gin mill, a burglar, a horse thief? While medical science has perfected an instrument for recording the heartbeat, statistical science toys with inane numbers.

The essay is translated in Peretz. On Peretz's trip to the Tomaszow region and the statistical project see Wisse, 19–26. For an example drawn from the circle of the Verein für jüdische Statistik, see the essay by Leo Wengierow, "Die Juden in König-reich Polen," in Nossig, *Jüdische Statistik*. Wengierow begins by lamenting the deplorable level of statistical study of Polish Jewry, and blames this in part on the Jews themselves, who "reject instinctively any attempt at counting," seeing in it authority's interest in higher taxation (294).

15. T. Porter, *Rise of Statistical Thinking*, 6.

16. Ibid., 25.

17. T. Porter, *Trust in Numbers*. The phrase "avalanche of numbers" is derived from Hacking, "Biopower and the Avalanche of Printed Numbers."

18. Hacking, *Taming of Chance*, 1.

19. Ibid., 2.

20. Ibid., 3.

21. The categories are reproduced in Behre, 363.

22. See the census forms contained in *Hamburg in Zahlen*, 20; *Statistik des Deutschen Reichs*, Band I.

23. A replica of the official *Zählkarte* used by the German judiciary before World War I can be found in *Statistik des Deutschen Reichs: Kriminalstatistik für das Jahr 1914*, Band 284, 4–5.

24. On the disappearance of the category of religion from judicial records, see

the *Zahlkarte* in *Statistik des Deutschen Reichs: Kriminalstatistik für das Jahr 1925*, Band 335, 4. For the general population statistics, see *Statistik des Deutschen Reichs: Bevölkerung in den Jahren 1920 und 1921*, Band 307.

25. A comprehensive survey or census of French Jewry, for example, was undertaken in the first decade of the nineteenth century. It was the product of Napoleon's reorganization of the synagogues and communities into consistories. In order to establish the hierarchy of consistories, the requisite number of representatives from each consistory had to be determined. This meant counting the Jews of France. The census was done by the Ministry of Cults, and in 1806 the French Bureau of Statistics presented a report to the Interior Ministry entitled "Sur le nombre des Juifs en France." The survey is discussed in Posener, "Les Juifs sous le Premier Empire: Les Enquêtes Administratives"; idem, "Les Juifs sous le Premier Empire: Les Statistiques générales." Religious statistics in the United States were not gathered officially by the government in the general census. However, the U.S. government did carry out, beginning in 1850, a census of religious bodies, which included a count of Jewish congregations and organizations. It did not, however, count the Jewish population per se. So the demographics with which this study is concerned, and which was of greatest interest to early social scientists, had to be estimated. On the religious census in the United States, and on the attendant problems of estimation of the population, see Engelman.

26. See Fishberg, *Jews*, 3–10; "Jewish Statistics"; Jaffe, "The Use of Death Records"; and the exchange between Jaffe and H. L. Lurie in the same issue. See also Lurie, "Some Problems."

27. Desrosières, 13.

28. The extent of the statistical or social scientific research undertaken about Jews, by Jews and non-Jews, can be seen in the bibliography, which runs to over one hundred pages. It was compiled by the Verein für Jüdische Statistik and published in Nossig, *Jüdische Statistik*.

29. The phrase "collective thought structure" derives from the early-twentieth-century philosopher of science Ludwig Fleck. "Intellectual grammar" can be found in Klingenstein.

30. Zunz. Although, as I note below, Zunz's article was often mentioned, this appears to have been more an attempt to link a newly established body of scholarship to an older, firmly established tradition of work through its most respected representative. Zunz's definition of "statistics" was rooted in the eighteenth-century German definition associated with figures such as Achenwall, and especially Schlözer, a definition that by the early nineteenth century was giving way to what the English called "political arithmetic." Jewish social science, as it came to develop in the late nineteenth century, resembled to a far greater degree this "political arithmetic" than it did Zunz's "Statistik." The disjuncture between Zunz's definition and that of later Jewish social scientists was noted already by Jacobs, "Jüdische Volkskunde," 30–31 (see note 33 below). On German statistics in the eighteenth century, and on the emergence of what later social scientists—including Jewish social scientists—understood by the term, see Desrosières, 16–23; T. Porter, *Rise of Statistical Thinking*, 37–39.

31. The material on Germany (excluding Prussia) was organized and analyzed by

Engelbert. The material on the Austrian Empire was organized by the non-Jewish statistician Gustav Schimmer, and appeared under the title *Statistik des Judenthums*.

32. Neumann, *Fabel*; idem, *Zur Statistik*. On Neumann's immigration studies, and the politics behind them, see Hacking, *Taming of Chance*, 189–99; Regneri. On Neumann in general see Karbe.

33. Jacobs's articles were collected and published in one volume entitled *Studies in Jewish statistics*. For a detailed discussion of Jacobs see Efron, *Defenders of the Race*, chapter 4.

34. Nossig, *Materialien*. In 1894 Nossig published *Sozialhygiene der Juden*. Although not a social scientific work on contemporary Jewry per se, this work nonetheless indicates the way in which social scientific categories and themes had begun to penetrate fin-de-siècle Jewish scholarship. For a detailed analysis of Nossig's work on social hygiene, see Hart, "Moses the Microbiologist."

35. In the 1890s, for example, Hirsch Hildesheimer's newspaper *Die jüdische Presse* published a series of articles refuting anti-Semitic charges about "Jewish criminality," the dangerous overrepresentation of Jews in German secondary schools, and the "unnaturally high" Jewish birth rates. See Hek, "Zur Statistik"; idem, "Schulstatistik der Juden"; idem, "Zur Berufsstatistik." For examples from the Zionist newspaper *Die Welt*, beginning with its first year of publication, see the following: "Die Berufsstatistik der Juden in Deutschland," "Die Enquete über die jüdische Armenpflege," "Jüdische Criminal-Statistik in Oesterreich," "Jüdische Geisteskranke."

36. Detailed summaries of these and other Jewish organizations' efforts at statistical research can be found in Nossig, *Jüdische Statistik*, part II, "The Statistical Work of Jewish Organizations."

37. For the Alliance see, for instance, the work of Legoyt. In the preface to the work the editor of Archives Israélites wrote of the long-standing interest of the Alliance in statistics. Legoyt was the head of the general statistical bureau in the Ministry of Agriculture and Commerce. On Legoyt and his study see Marrus, 16–17. On the *Revue* see, for example, "Chronique et Notes Diverses."

38. While no study of Anglo-Jewish statistics per se exists, a good sense of the significant role played by numbers in British Jewish politics can be gleaned from Eugene Black's *The Social Politics of Anglo-Jewry*.

39. Between 1876 and 1878 the committee sent out the equivalent of census forms to Jewish communities and congregations throughout the country. While admitting the incompleteness of the results, the committee judged the survey successful, having received responses from nearly one thousand places. The committee estimated that in 1880 there were approximately two hundred and fifty thousand Jews in the United States. The survey was published under the title *Statistics of the Jews of the United States* by the Union of American Hebrew Congregations.

40. On the *Jewish Encyclopedia*, including the inclusion of social scientific material, see Schwartz.

41. This was especially true of the article by Zunz, one of the towering figures of nineteenth-century Jewish *Wissenschaft*. For examples see Nossig, "Jüdische Statistik," 13–14; Rost, "Jüdische Statistik"; Blau, "Die bisherigen Leistungen," 152–54; idem, "Sociology and Statistics." On the other hand, we have the brief account by

Arthur Ruppin, published in the ten-year anniversary volume of the bureau. Ruppin mentions only two works, those of Joseph Jacobs and Alfred Nossig, produced before his own book appeared in 1904. These earlier works, according to Ruppin, were not truly scientific. Thus, a genuinely scientific Jewish statistics began, in Ruppin's view, only with the appearance of his own studies. See Ruppin, "Zur Geschichte des Büros," 9–12.

42. See the categories and themes of research presented in Nossig, *Jüdische Statistik*, 19. The categories, drawn directly from general European science, appear already in embryonic form in Nossig, *Materialien*.

43. On the 1897 census, including its numerous shortcomings, see Kabuzan, 153–55. On the censuses in Poland, and the difficulties in using them as sources for social history, see Corrsin.

44. Some of the implications of this tension have been examined by Stepan and Gilman.

45. On this liberal tradition within Central European social science see Massin.

46. See, for instance, Mayr, 356. On Lamarck and his subsequent interpreters see Mayr, 343–60; Jordanova.

47. The literature on this controversy is enormous. For general overviews, see Mayr, 681ff; Proctor, *Racial Hygiene*, 30–38.

48. Jordanova, 111. To a significant degree the debate was infused with, and shaped by, powerful nationalist sentiments and struggles. On the politics of the debate see Proctor, *Racial Hygiene*, chapters 1–2.

49. For example, the prominent German racial scientist Fritz Lenz argued, in Robert Proctor's words, that "the tendency toward 'Lamarckism' is a genetically selected racial characteristic" of the Jew. Proctor, *Racial Hygiene*, 30–55.

50. This is not to say that there were no Jewish scientists who embraced a Mendelian view and applied it to the issues under discussion; they were, however, in the minority. One such scientist, the British Jewish biologist Redcliffe Nathan Salaman, is discussed in chapter 6. He published a number of articles on Jews, race, and heredity from a Mendelian perspective, arguing that "the Jewish facial type . . . is a character which is subject to the Mendelian law of Heredity." Salaman, "Heredity and the Jew," 285.

51. On this see the works cited in note 67 below.

52. Stepan and Gilman, 178–79.

53. Nossig, "Jüdische Statistik," 8.

54. The notion of an internalization of anti-Semitic discourse, resulting in "Jewish self-hatred," is often put forth as a reason for the involvement of Jews in fin-de-siècle medical and social science debates over the nature of Jewry. This, I think, sheds little light on the complex intellectual relationship of Jews to the world of "non-Jewish" society and culture.

55. Stratz.

56. Nossig, "Jüdische Statistik," 8–9.

57. Sorkin.

58. The literature on the history of modern Jewish scholarship focuses in the main on the earliest phase of *Wissenschaft des Judentums*. The concern of this analysis has been to explicate the origins of modern Jewish scholarship within the con-

text of the struggle for emancipation and integration, and the emergence of the Reform movement. Wiener; Schorsch, "Breakthrough into the Past," idem, "Emergence of Historical Consciousness"; idem, "Ideology and History"; Meyer, "Jewish Religious Reform"; idem, "Emergence of Jewish Historiography." A more comprehensive discussion of *Wissenschaft des Judentums* as it developed into the twentieth century in Central Europe can be found in the introductory essay by Kurt Wilhelm to *Wissenschaft des Judentums im deutschen Sprachbericht*. David Myers has recently explored the shifts in the definition and conception of Jewish scholarship in the early twentieth century. His work also provides a sense of the important differences between Central and Western European Jewish *Wissenschaft* and the Eastern European *Hochmat-Israel*. Myers, *Re-Inventing the Jewish Past*. Elsewhere Myers has analyzed the conflicting conceptions of "Science" among German Jewish scholars involved in the creation and development of the Academy of Jewish Scholarship in the first decades of the twentieth century. See Myers, "Fall and Rise." Michael Meyer has analyzed the nexus between changing notions of Jewish scholarship or science and shifts in Jewish collective identity. Meyer, "Jewish Scholarship and Jewish Identity."

59. For comparative analyses see Birnbaum and Katznelson, eds., *Paths of Emancipation*; Jacob Katz, *Toward Modernity*; Endelman, *The Jews of Georgian England*.

60. See, for instance, the discussion in Vital, *Origins of Zionism*, chapter 8ff.

61. See the discussion in Shapira, *Land and Power*, as well as numerous other works.

62. Vital, *Origins of Zionism*, 208.

63. Wassermann, "Zukunft des Judentums," 54.

64. It ought to be noted that despite their opposition to assimilation, and their rhetoric of the need for isolation from the disintegrative effects of Western modernity, Zionists living in Europe or the United States did not feel compelled, as individuals, to necessarily resettle in Palestine. On the variety of ideological and pragmatic approaches to Palestine on the part of early Zionists see Shimoni, esp. chapter 8; Mendelsohn, *On Modern Jewish Politics*. For the particular case of American Zionism see Naomi Cohen, *American Jews and the Zionist Idea* (New York: Ktav, 1975); Ben Halpern, "The Americanization of Zionism, 1880–1930," in Jehuda Reinharz and Anita Shapira, eds., *Essential Papers on Zionism* (New York: New York University Press, 1996).

65. On constructivism see Desrosières, 1–15.

66. For an extended discussion of this point see the introduction to Desrosières.

67. See the discussions in the following works: Weindling, *Health, Race and German Politics*; Stocking, *Race, Culture, and Evolution*; Proctor, "From *Anthropologie* to *Rassenkunde*"; Stepan, *Idea of Race*.

68. On the challenge to racial science from within the scientific community in the 1920s and beyond, see Barkan, *Retreat of Scientific Racism*.

## Chapter 1

1. Nossig, *Jüdische Statistik*, 1.

2. Historians of Zionism have, for the most part, omitted the relationship

between Jewish statistics and Zionism from their narratives. Alfred Böhm, in his two-volume history of the movement *Die Zionistische Bewegung*, noted the connection between the establishment of Jewish statistics and Zionism, and placed Ruppin's social scientific work within the context of the Faction and *Gegenwartsarbeit* (1: 302–3). However, the connection disappears in English-language histories. Walter Laqueur's brief discussion of the Faction in *A History of Zionism* makes no mention of Nossig or the Statistical Bureau. Jehuda Reinharz, in his discussion of the Faction and its role in German Zionism in *Fatherland or Promised Land*, mentions only the Verlag and university project as Faction achievements. Nossig does not appear in the narrative. Jewish social science, as defined here, is absent altogether from Arthur Hertzberg's *The Zionist Idea*, Shlomo Avineri's *Making of Modern Zionism*, and most recently, Shimoni.

3. Nordau, "V. Kongressrede."

4. Ibid., 115–16.

5. Ibid., 113–14.

6. "The best among them in which some sense of Jewish feeling is still alive, is interested solely in the Jewish past, and donates most generously to museums for Jewish antiquities and Jewish art. However, he possesses no interest in the scientific study of the Jewish people in the living present." Nordau, ibid., 115.

7. Indeed, a few years later at the International Statistical Congress meeting in Berlin, Alfred Nossig, the central figure in the initial effort to establish an organized Jewish statistical movement, called publicly for governments to include a category of religion in the next official censuses of their countries. He asked that the International Statistical Institute do what it could to convey to government officials the difficulties posed to Jewish statistics by the lack of such a category, and to convince them to remedy the situation. See the report in *Im deutschen Reich* 10, no. 1 (1904): 35. The Verein für jüdische Statistik officially petitioned, and obtained assurance that the issue of a religious census category would be placed on the agenda of the next international congress. *Im deutschen Reich* insisted that the German and Austrian experience demonstrated that the question could be asked publicly, and that no trouble or problem would ensue from this. For an early formulation of the problem see Nossig, "Jüdische Statistik," 17.

8. Nordau, "V. Kongressrede," *Zionistische Schriften*, 115.

9. See, for instance, "Wir müssen mehr wissen"; B. Friedmann, 1.

10. Any effort to reconstruct the institutional and organizational workings of the *Verein* and the Bureau for Jewish Statistics is severely hampered by the lack of sufficient archival material. In 1931, when the bureau closed, its archives were deposited in the Gesamtarchiv der deutschen Juden in Berlin. The Gestapo eventually confiscated the Gesamtarchiv; it was then seized by Soviet troops. I have been unable to locate the archive of the *Verein* in the material that has recently made its way to the West. On the fate of the bureau's archive see Blau, "Sociology and Statistics," 156.

11. "Aufruf des Komitees zur Errichtung eines Bureaus für Statistik des jüdischen Volkes," printed in Leopold, 145. The call was published in the Zionist newspaper *Die Welt* 6, no. 14 (1902): 8, under the same title.

12. See the discussion of the sections, including the lists of names of personnel, in Nossig, *Jüdische Statistik*, 159–68.

13. On the organizational composition of the *Verein* and of the regional associations during this initial phase see Leopold, 145f.

14. "Satzungen des Vereins für jüdische Statistik," reproduced in ibid., 147.

15. "Instruktionen für die Mitarbeiter an der systematischen Bibliographie der jüdischen Statistik," in Nossig, *Jüdische Statistik*, 27–30.

16. See the discussion of the first plenary meeting of the *Verein* in "Jüdische Statistik," *Die Welt*, 8, no. 6 (1904): 7–8. The financial report, covering the period 1902–03, indicated that the *Verein*'s income (6173.33 Mks.) exceeded its expenses (4855.75), a meager profit attributed mainly to the sale of the organization's 1903 volume. The creation of a permanent statistical bureau demanded far greater funds; hence the establishment of a *Kuratorium*. On the creation of the *Kuratorium* see as well "Zur Organisation der jüdischen Statistik," *Die Welt*, 8, no. 19 (1904): 12–13.

17. In 1904, for example, a Verein für jüdische Statistik started up in Munich, and a Büro für jüdische Statistik in Vienna. On Munich see "Neugründung eines Vereines." On Vienna see "Wiener Versammlungen." For a comprehensive list see "Zur Organisation der jüdischen Statistik."

18. Derek Penslar, in "Philanthropy," and John Efron, in *Defenders of the Race*, have denied the Zionist "origins" of Jewish statistics, stressing the part played by liberal Jewish scientists and organizations in the emergence of a Jewish social science. My argument here is not that liberal or integrationist organizations did not rely on statistics, and in some cases also generate them. As I demonstrate throughout this work, integrationists were instrumental in advancing Jewish social science as an enterprise. However, as an organized, institutionalized undertaking, Jewish statistics began as a Zionist project.

19. Mendelsohn, "From Assimilation to Zionism."

20. Nossig, *Materialien*. Nossig also analyzed the Jewish Question from social scientific and nationalist perspectives in *Versuch zur Lösung der jüdischen Frage* (Lemberg, 1887). For summaries see Gelber, 84–87. For an analysis of these works within the context of early Central European Zionism, see Mendelsohn, "From Assimilation to Zionism."

21. *Volk* is usually translated into English as "people" or "nation," though this fails to capture the full meaning and power of the word in German; *Stamm* is a tribe, but also, in the late nineteenth and early twentieth centuries, a "race." Like many others writing at the time, Nossig used these terms interchangeably, without precisely defining them. Their intended meaning, and the degree to which they carried some biological or racial element, emerged in the course of the descriptive and analytical narrative.

22. Gelber, 85–87.

23. See, for example, the report in *Die Welt* 6, no. 37 (1902): 11, of Nossig's speech on Jewish statistics before the Organization of Jewish Students. "This semester for the first time," *Die Welt* reported, "students sought to take part in the actual workings of modern Jewish institutions. A large number became involved in the Verein für jüdische Statistik founded by Dr. Nossig." See also the report in "Der Gemeindebote." Further evidence for the importance of Zionist university student groups for the emergence of Jewish statistics can be found in the report on the

interest and activities of the Zionist student group Hashmonea, in the section "Berlin," in *Die Welt* 7, no. 15 (1903): 29. See also "Mährisch-Schlesischer Studententag," *Die Welt* 10, no. 39 (1906): 23, in which it was reported that, in the name of the *Kultusgemeinde* of M. Ostrau, the student organization proclaimed the existence and unity of the Jewish nation, and passed the following as one of its official resolutions: "As part of the demand or claim for Jewish autonomy, Jewish statistics will be taken up, and to this end a committee will be put in place in Vienna. Elected to the committee: Egon Zweig, Rudolf Nassau, Felix Winterstein, Hermann Löw and Bernhard Gleitsmann."

24. Nossig, *Jüdische Statistik*, 164. The report also noted that a number of regional Zionist organizations had provided subventions to the *Verein*.

25. Ibid.

26. On the background to this challenge to Herzl's leadership and authority, see Heymann.

27. I have been able to identify all but Kornfeld as Democratic Faction members during the years 1901–02. The board of directors (*Vorstand*) of the *Verein* consisted of Nossig, Buber, Feiwel, Motzkin, Trietsch, Theodor Zlocisti, Alfred Klee, and Kastelianski. Again, all these individuals, save Klee, who at the time was director of the German Zionist Organization, were identifiable as Faction members. The only other significant exception to this was the involvement at the organizational level as early as 1902 of Sigmund Werner, one of Herzl's closest allies. On his involvement in the Committee for Jewish statistics see *Die Welt* 6, no. 47 (1902): 9. Also see the letters from Nossig to Werner related to the *Verein*'s activities, CZA, A162/43.

28. For general discussions of the Faction and its significance within early Zionist debates see Luz, 150f; Reinharz, *Chaim Weizmann*, 65–91; Klausner.

29. On *Gegenwartsarbeit* and its significance for Zionism see Almog, *Zionism and History*, chapter 3.

30. In a letter dated June 9, 1903, for example, Chaim Weizmann wrote to Martin Buber suggesting that Nossig appear, together with Buber and Weizmann, as a speaker at the upcoming Zionist congress on "cultural problems." In addition, Weizmann suggested that Nossig and the German Jewish sociologist Franz Oppenheimer be enlisted for help in setting up "Jewish-social [science] subjects" for the Jewish University. Weizmann, 2: 370.

31. Along with art, poetry, prose, and essays, the *Verlag* dedicated itself to putting out works on social science and the Jews. See the announcements in *Die Welt* 6, no. 12 (1902): 7, which advertised the publication of "wissenschaftliche Monographien zur Anthropologie und Ethnologie des jüdischen Stammes und zur Sociologie der Judenfrage." For an analysis of the Faction and its cultural activities see Berkowitz.

32. Weizmann, 1: 229.

33. *Program and Organization Statutes of the Democratic Faction*, CZA, A126/24/6.

34. Ibid., 5.

35. Ibid., 15.

36. Vital, *Zionism: The Formative Years*, 190. For a response to Vital's interpretation in this regard see Zipperstein, *Elusive Prophet*, 149.

37. Lindenfeld; Patriarca, particularly chapter 1; Hacking, *The Taming of Chance*.

38. Luz, 175–80. This idea of the power of the word "science" is evident as well in earlier Zionist student societies such as The Scientific Society for Russian Jews, Kadimah, and Agudot Iyuniot, societies that stressed their scientific or theoretical character as part of their nationalist agenda. See Klausner, chapter 1; Luz, 179–81; Reinharz, "East European Jews," 68–70.

39. Buber, "Jüdische Wissenschaft," reprinted in *Die Welt*, 5, no. 41 (1901): 1–2.

40. Although his work focuses on the idea of a Jewish renaissance during the Weimar period, Michael Brenner does place the origins of the idea in the pre-Weimar period. See Brenner, 11–35.

41. Nor was this call for a reconceptualization of Jewish Science limited to Zionists. Both Franz Rosenzweig and Hermann Cohen, for instance, made such a call an important part of their efforts at the revitalization of Jewish learning and scholarship in Germany during the first decade of the Weimar Republic. See the discussion in Myers, "Fall and Rise."

42. Thon, "Problem der jüdischen Wissenschaft," 185. For additional examples of this discursive link between Zionism and science, see P. Felix, "Unsere nationale Wissenschaft"; Sigmund Werner, "Unsere socialen Aufgaben"; Lazar Schön, "Geleitwort"; M. Kleinmann.

43. O. Thon, "Problem der jüdischen Wissenschaft," 188. This assault upon the older Science of Judaism was not limited to those affiliated with the Democratic Faction. "Judaism and its science make sense," the Russian Socialist-Zionist leader Nahum Sokolow argued in his 1901 Zionist Congress speech, "and have a right to exist only so long as they are rooted in the nation [*Volkstum*]." *Wissenschaft des Judentums*, tied as it was to the ideals of Reform, was a betrayal in Sokolow's view of the true spirit of Jewry. "One had to dress up the Jewish soul, the Jewish spirit, the entire appearance of the Jew in foreign clothes," he claimed. "We must make this *Wissenschaft* national again, give it originality and freshness." Sokolow, 1. For a discussion of the idea of "Science," and the goal of a scientization of Zionism, see Funkenstein. On the varying definitions of a "Jewish Science" during the nineteenth century, and on the shifts in meaning introduced by Zionist historians during the first decades of the twentieth century see Myers, *Re-Inventing the Jewish Past*.

44. For a discussion of the complex and variegated nature of nineteenth-century Jewish historical writing, see Feiner.

45. Quoted in Luz, 178.

46. Foreword to *Jüdische Statistik*, 4.

47. See, for instance, Weizmann's letter to William Evans Gordon, in Weizmann, 2: 28.

48. On Birnbaum see Doron, *Haguto ha-Tsiyonut*.

49. Natan Birnbaum, "Wissenschaft und Zionismus," in *Zwei Vorträge über Zionismus*, 24. The lecture was first delivered at the opening ceremony of the Jewish National Organization in Vienna, Nov. 27, 1897.

50. Ibid., 14.

51. Birnbaum, "Jüdische Statistik und ihr Wert."

52. Ibid., 335–36.

53. Ibid.

54. *Die Judenprogramme in Russland* (Cologne and Leipzig: Jüdischer Verlag, 1909–10). On this work and its connections with the Zionist program, and on Motzkin's career in general, see Bein, "Arieh Leib Motzkin."

55. Motzkin, "Jüdische Statistik und Zionismus." On liberal integrationist organizations in Germany at the time, Reinharz, *Fatherland or Promised Land*, chapters 1–2.

56. Motzkin, "Jüdische Statistik und Zionismus," 239.

57. Ibid., 239–40.

58. Foreword to *Jüdische Statistik*, 1–2.

59. Nossig, *Jüdische Statistik*; "Zur Organization der jüdische Statistik," *Die Welt* 8, no. 19 (1904): 12–13; *Im deutschen Reich* 10, no. 1 (1904): 35; *Im deutschen Reich* 11, no. 3 (1905)': 167. Individual organizations and communities, including the *Kultusgemeinden* in Berlin, Warsaw, Prague, Posen, Lemberg, Königsberg, and Breslau, also contributed financially to support the publication of *Jüdische Statistik*. See the report in *Im deutschen Reich* 10, no. 1 (1904): 35.

60. On the SAC's decision on funding, see Nossig's report to the committee, "Bericht der statistischen-volkswirtschaftlichen Kommission," CZA, Z2–524; also see *Die Welt* 6, no. 45, (1902): 3.

61. See the discussion in Heymann.

62. See, for instance, Nossig, "Jüdische Statistik," 10–11; Feuchtwang, 218.

63. *ZfDuStdJ* 4, no. 5 (1908): 80.

64. See the notes to the 1906 general meeting of the *Verband* published in the *ZfDuStdJ* 2, no. 6 (1906): 95–96.

65. For a fuller treatment see the discussion of economics below, chapter 7, and the secondary literature cited therein.

66. On the ideological impulses to nineteenth-century *Wissenschaft des Judentums* see the essays collected in Schorsch, *From Text to Context*; Myers, *Re-Inventing the Jewish Past*. On German historiography see Iggers. On the European social sciences see Hughes, as well as the programmatic statements of journals such as the *Archiv für soziale Gesetzgebung und Statistik* (1879), the *Jahrbuch für Sozialwissenschaft und Socialpolitik* (1879), the *Archiv für Sozialwissenschaft und Sozialpolitik* (1904), the *Archiv für Rassen- und Gesellschaftsbiologie* (1904), and the *Zeitschrift für soziale Medizin* (1906).

67. For Austria see Wistrich, *Jews of Vienna*, 131–63, 347–458. For Germany see Schorsch, *Jewish Reactions*; Reinharz, *Fatherland or Promised Land*. The nature of the C.V. and its relationship with German Zionism has generated particular debate among historians of German Jewry. See the exchanges in the section "Jewish Self Defence" in the *Leo Baeck Institute Yearbook* 33 (1988).

68. Foreword to *Jüdische Statistik*, 1.

69. Ibid., 2.

70. Ibid., 2.

71. Stepan and Gilman, 177–78. Ironically, in the Nazi period, Jews were attacked by Nazi scientists and others because of a purported natural inclination to "value-free" and objective science. This, it was claimed, did violence to a nationalist or *völkish* science, which of course the Nazis favored. See the discussion in Proctor, *Racial Hygiene*, 162–66.

72. Hek, "Antisemitische Statistik." See as well the comments of A. Cohen, "Statistik und Judenfrage."

73. Pinkus, "Organization und Separation," 17.

74. Reported in "Jüdische Statistik," *Die Welt* 8, no. 6 (1904): 7.

75. For a contemporary discussion of the relationship between Jewish statistics and the Jewish Question, and the various practical and political uses to which statistics could be put, see A. Cohen, "Statistik und Judenfrage."

76. Nossig, *Jüdische Statistik*, 1.

77. Nossig, "Jüdische Statistik," 9.

78. For an example drawn from earlier Jewish scholarship, see the remarks of Immanuel Wolf in his 1822 essay "On the Concept of a Science of Judaism."

79. Nossig, "Jüdische Statistik," 10.

80. See "Mitteilung," *ZfDuStdJ* 8, no. 6 (1912): 94–95.

81. On this debate, and on the question of politics and science in general during this period see Proctor, *Value-Free Science?* 66f.

82. T. Porter, "Objectivity as Standardization."

83. Jacobs, "On the Racial Characteristics of Modern Jews," in *Studies in Jewish statistics*, iii.

84. Blau, "Jüdische Statistik."

85. Ruppin, *Die Juden der Gegenwart*, 222.

86. Over the course of the nineteenth century the belief that social scientists could discover *laws* of society was increasingly challenged, and the idea of what a descriptive statistics in fact measured and represented came to be modified. Nonetheless, the metaphor of an equivalence of tasks between the natural and social sciences was a powerful one, and played its role in the conceptualization of Jewish statistics. Nossig ("Jüdische Statistik," 9), for example, invoked the two great mid-nineteenth-century figures associated with the idea of a "social physics"—Quételet and Comte—in arguing that Jewish statistics would discover the "laws of national life," and permit "the future of social life . . . to be enunciated." On the debate over the concept of "statistical laws" in German scientific circles see T. Porter, "Lawless Society." For a general discussion of these issues see R. Smith, 17f.

87. Nagel.

88. T. Porter, "Objectivity as Standardization," 31. See as well the similiar observation of Proctor, *Value-Free Science?* 66–70.

89. Quoted in Proctor, ibid, 88.

90. Ruppin, Foreword to *Die Juden der Gegenwart* (1904).

91. T. Porter, "Objectivity as Standardization," 31.

92. T. Porter, *Trust in Numbers*, ix.

93. Proctor, *Value-Free Science?* 92.

94. Nossig, "Jüdische Statistik," 12.

95. Feuchtwang, 218–33. In addition, see the comments of Leo Motzkin ("Jüdische Statistik und Zionismus," 241), who argued that only the Zionist approach to Jewish statistics could be considered truly objective, because only the Zionists represented the universal impulse in Jewry. According to Motzkin, Jewish statistics under the Zionist aegis "is capable of uniting all national elements—the

Jewish *Volk*. Zionists must aspire to take the lead in this, for they represent the most general ideals and they can submit to no particularistic tendencies."

96. Feuchtwang, 218.

97. Ibid., 220.

98. Ibid., 232.

99. This sort of reassurance of nonpartisanship continued to appear in Jewish social scientific writings into the 1920s and beyond. For instance, in a 1924 article published in the *ZfDuStDJ* one finds the following confession: "The Palestine Economic Society [a society dedicated to the scientific research of economic issues related to Jewish settlement in Palestine] rejects on principle the recognition of any party, or a commitment to place itself in the service of any particular tendency. It does so in order not to endanger the objective, purely scientific nature of its research activity." Alony, 87. See as well the reassurances of objectivity in the Jewish statistical enterprise in Guttmann, "Zur Einführung"; Silbergleit, "Das Arbeitsprogramm."

100. Almog, *Zionism and History*, 193f.

101. Motzkin, "Jüdische Statistik und Zionismus," 240.

102. Feuchtwang, 233.

103. Weizmann, letter to Buber, Sept. 1903, in Buber, *The Letters of Martin Buber*, 102–3. In addition, see Buber, letter to the Greater Actions Committee, dated March 1903, regarding the convening of a cultural committee in Berlin. Buber indicated how cultural matters, from the Faction's side, needed to be framed in "non-oppositional terms," in terms of Zionism's interests and Jewry's interests as a whole, idem, 90.

104. On the role of the "imaginary" in nascent nationalist movements, see B. Anderson.

## Chapter 2

1. Ruppin, diaries (manuscript), Central Zionist Archives (hereafter, CZA), A107/950.

2. Ruppin, diary entry, July 21, 1904, CZA, A107/950.

3. On Timendorfer's participation in the early years of Jewish statistics see the report "Jüdische Statistik," *Die Welt* 8, no. 6 (1904): 7–8. On his social welfare activity—he served as president of the Zentralwohlfahrtsstelle der deutschen Juden—see Heuberger, 72.

4. On Thon, see the biographical entries in Weizmann, 4: 345–46; *Encyclopedia Judaica* 15: 1123. Thon, according to Ruppin, knew little to nothing about social science when he joined the bureau. Yet in exchange for lessons in Hebrew, Ruppin agreed to instruct him in the social sciences.

5. J. Thon, "Die jüdischen Gemeinden in Deutschland," "Die jüdische Bevölkerung in Krakau," "Schulbesuch christlicher und jüdischer Kinder in Baden," "Kriminalität der Christen und Juden in Österreich," "Besteuerungs-und Finanzverhältnisse der jüdischen Gemeinden in Deutschland," "Die Berufsgliederung der Juden in Galizien."

6. Penslar, *Zionism and Technocracy*, 91–102. In addition, see Bertisch.

7. On Ruppin's biography see Bein, "Arthur Ruppin"; entry on Ruppin in *Encyclopedia Judaica* 14: 430.

8. The most significant of these was "Die sozialen Verhältnisse der Juden in Preussen und Deutschland," *Jahrbücher für Nationalökonomie und Statistik* (1902).

9. Ruppin, *Die Juden der Gegenwart* (1904). For a sense of the reception of the work, see the following reviews: P. A.; "Die Juden der Gegenwart," in *Israelitisches Familienblatt*; "Die Juden der Gegenwart," in *Literarisches Zentralblatt*.

10. Ruppin, *Darwinismus und Sozialwissenschaft*. On this essay, and on its significance in Ruppin's intellectual development, see Penslar, *Zionism and Technocracy*, 86–88.

11. It should be noted that Ruppin was not fully identified with Jewish nationalism at the time he took control as head of the bureau. Indeed, he had expressed in *Die Juden der Gegenwart* strong reservations about Zionism's viability. This may in part also explain his appointment by the *Verein*. His ideological ambivalence added weight to the enterprise's claim to nonpartisanship. Indeed, Ruppin saw as one of his tasks as director the distancing of Jewish statistics from what he believed to be its "pre-scientific" propagandistic phase, and its development along strict scientific lines. See Ruppin's comments in his diary, CZA, A107/950, 20, 25. In addition, see his judgment about the early works of Nossig and Joseph Jacobs, and his own pioneering role in establishing Jewish statistics as a science, in Ruppin, "Zur Geschichte des Büros."

12. Ruppin was particularly enthusiastic about this project. He had conceived of such a project himself, he wrote, in early 1904. He submitted it to the German publishing house Calvary and Co. only to have it rejected. He consoled himself with the fact that it was too enormous a task to be taken on by a private individual. Diary entry, Dec. 30, 1904, CZA, A107/950.

13. Upon assuming control of the project, Ruppin decided to transform what he called an "old address book" into a scientifically acceptable statistical guide to German Jewry. It was a task that he believed was necessary and long overdue, but that absorbed a great deal of time and with which he quickly grew annoyed.

14. See Ruppin's diary entry, July 1905, CZA, A107/950.

15. On Ruppin's university education see the entries in Ruppin, *Arthur Ruppin: Memoirs, Diaries, Letters*, 47–50; Penslar, *Zionism and Technocracy*, 84–86.

16. Ruppin's diary entry, Dec. 30, 1904, CZA, A107/950.

17. Ibid., 1904–05, 31.

18. Ibid., July 1905.

19. Michaelis.

20. Ibid., 3–4.

21. Ruppin's diary, July 1905, CZA, A107/950.

22. In an attempt to counter the negative reaction to Michaelis's piece, the following issue of the *Zeitschrift* contained a response by Nossig ("Die Auserwähltheit der Juden im Lichte der Biologie"), in which he argued that "chosenness" represented the highest ideals of both enlightened universalism and social Darwinism.

23. As far as I have been able to determine, none of the financial records of the *Verein* or the bureau have survived. It is therefore impossible to determine the actual financial status of the institution.

24.  Ruppin's diary entries, 1905, CZA, A107/950, 3–10. The work in question was published under the title *Die sozialen Verhältnisse der Juden in Russland, auf Grund des amtlich statistischen Materials*. It was the second monograph published in the bureau's official series.

25.  Ruppin's diary entry, Dec. 31, 1905, CZA, A107/950, 10.

26.  In March 1905 Ruppin recorded that he had paid the shekel and joined the Zionist movement officially. He went on to note that together with Feiwel, Trietsch, Buber, Nossig, Idelsohn, Heymann, Elias Auerbach, Israel Auerbach, Thon, and Julius Becker, he became part of the group that challenged, from within the Zionist organization, the official Zionist position regarding a charter. Ruppin's diary entries, CZA, A107/950, December 1904, 30; July 1905, 5–6.

27.  Ibid., 1908, 27–28.

28.  *Die Juden der Gegenwart* was first published in 1904. A revised and expanded version appeared in 1911, and was reissued in 1918 and 1920. The book was translated into English under the title *The Jews of Today*, (trans. Margery Bentwich, New York: Holt, 1913). The two-volume work *Die Soziologie der Juden* appeared in 1930. It appeared in Hebrew under the title *Sozialogia shel ha-Yehudim* (Tel Aviv: A. Y. Stiebel, 1933–34); in English it was translated as *The Jews in the Modern World* (London: Macmillan, 1934) with an introduction by the prominent Anglo-Jewish historian L. B. Namier. A French translation (*Les juifs dans le monde moderne*, trans. M. Chevalley, Paris: Payot) appeared in 1934. In 1940 a slightly altered version, *The Jewish Fate and Future* (London: Macmillan; trans. E. W. Dickes), appeared in English. In it Ruppin took note of the war and of the Nazi threat to the Jews, and he modified his statements about race and biology as a factor in history and contemporary life.

29.  Correspondence in CZA, A107/503, A107/590, A107/950. See as well the correspondence between Ruppin and Jacob Lestschinsky in Lestschinsky's files housed at the Yiddish Scientific Institute (YIVO), RG 339, file 70.

30.  For an analysis of Ruppin and the interconnection between the process of "self-discovery," social science, and Zionism, see Ruveini. Also see the discussion of Ruppin and his social scientific work in Penslar, *Zionism and Technocracy*, chapter 4.

31.  May 9, 1903, reproduced by Ruppin in "Reise nach Galizien" (typed manuscript), CZA, A107/353.

32.  Ruppin's diary entry, Apr. 1903, CZA, A107/905.

33.  Ruppin, "Die Volksvermehrung," 321–23.

34.  Ibid., 322.

35.  Ruppin's diary entry, 1902–03, CZA, A107/950, 15.

36.  Exceptions include the Russian-American social scientist Maurice Fishberg's article, "North African Jews." However, as I have shown in chapter 5, even discussions such as Fishberg's served, ultimately, to highlight some point having to do with Western Jewry.

37.  Ruppin and Thon, *Anteil*.

38.  Blau, "Sociology and Statistics," 149.

39.  Ibid., 149–52.

40.  Ruppin was particularly harsh in his judgment of Nossig and the early scholarly efforts of the *Verein*. However, it is interesting to note that in an unpub-

lished review, written in 1903, of the *Verein*'s *Jüdische Statistik* (CZA, A107/997) Ruppin had quite positive things to say about the volume. The review was written before Ruppin had met and worked with Nossig, an experience that assuredly colored his views.

41. Ruppin, *Die Juden der Gegenwart* (1911), 273.

42. Ruppin's diary entries, Dec. 1910 and Mar. 1911, CZA, A107/950.

43. "Die sozialen Verhältnisse der deutschen Juden," *Die Welt* 6, no. 31 (1902): 6.

44. Zollschan, "The Cultural Value of the Jewish Race," in *Jewish Questions*, 4–5.

45. Zollschan, "Rassenproblem und Judenfrage," 897.

46. Ibid.

47. Böhm, "Zollschans Werk," 678–79.

48. Ibid., 679.

49. Ibid. In 1911 Böhm published an extended review of the newly issued revised version of Ruppin's *Die Juden der Gegenwart*, devoted to illuminating the import of Ruppin's social scientific research for the Zionist project. See Böhm, "Eine neue Grundlegung des Zionismus." In addition, see the review article of Zollschan's 1909 study by the Munich social scientist and Zionist Rudolf Wassermann, "Die Zukunft des Judentums," 54. Wassermann agreed with Zollschan's assessment, proven through statistical and anthropological research, of the imminent disappearance of Western Jewry, and of the impossibility of maintaining the "ghetto-milieu" so as to insure the survival of Eastern European Jewry. "Only Zionism provides a third way, an alternative to the degeneration and dissappearance of European Jewry" ("Auflösung der Rasse oder physische Degeneration, als—den Zionismus").

50. Hugo Hoppe, Review of Alexander Schüler, 184–85. Schüler's work was a popularization of Zollschan's monograph on the "Jewish Race Problem," and was explicitly intended as propaganda for Zionism. According to Hoppe, Ruppin's work, while scientifically exact, was "clearly written and easy to read, and hence had found a wide audience." Zollschan's, in contrast, was far more difficult, and had not found a popular audience. Schüler's work, therefore, "is of first rank as propaganda: it can serve to enlighten the masses on one of the most important theoretical foundations of Zionism" (185).

51. Ruppin invited Felix von Luschan, one of his teachers, and the chair of the anthropology department at the University of Berlin, to contribute the lead article for the premier volume of the *Zeitschrift*. See "Zur physischen Anthropologie der Juden." The eminent British scientist Henry Huxley contributed an article on the anthropology of the Samaritans: "Zur Anthropologie der Samaritaner," *ZfDuStdJ* 2, nos. 8–9 (1906). The statistician Ludwig Knöpfel contributed two articles to the journal: "Stand und Bewegung der jüdischen Bevölkerung im Grossherzogtum Hessen während des 19. Jahrhunderts," *ZfDuStdJ* 2, no. 6 (1906); "Die jüdischen Mischehen im deutschen Reich und die konfessionelle Erziehung der Kinder," *ZfDuStdJ* 2, no. 7 (1906) during the period of Ruppin's directorship. Bruno Blau identifies Knöpfel as a non-Jew. See Blau, "Sociology and Statistics," 156, note 35.

52. On Blau, see the entry in the *Encyclopedia Judaica* 4: 1074–75. Blau's name appears together with Ruppin's on the masthead of the 1908 volume of the *Zeitschrift*; in 1909 Blau appears as the sole editor, and Ruppin as the founder.

53. In addition to his articles related to Jewish subjects, Blau published more general works on the subject of law and criminality. See his *Verantwortlichkeit für fremdes Verschulden nach dem bürgerlichen Gesetzbuch* (Berlin: F. Siemenroth, 1902); *Kriminalstatistische Untersuchung der Kreise Marienwerder und Thorn. Zugleich ein Beitrag zur Methodik kriminalstatistischer Untersuchungen* (Berlin: J. Guttentag, 1903).

54. Blau, "Die jüdische Statistik," 7.

55. Segall's dissertation, a demographic study of Munich Jewry, was supervised by the eminent Munich professor of statistics Georg von Mayr, and completed the year before Segall joined Blau at the bureau. It was later published, under the title *Die Entwicklung der jüdische Bevölkerung in München 1875–1905*, as volume 7 of the *Verein*'s monograph series. On Segall's appointment see the announcement in the "Mitteilungen," *ZfDuStdJ* 5, no. 5 (1909): 79–80. On Segall see the entry in *Jüdisches Lexicon* 5: 340.

56. See the "Mitteilung," *ZfDuStdJ* 7, no. 4 (1911): 64; Blau, "Sociology of the Jews," 153.

57. "Mitteilung," *ZfDuStdJ* 8, no. 6 (1912): 94–95; "Mitteilung," *ZfDuStdJ* 9, no. 12 (1913): 181. Statistical studies sponsored by Jewish organizations were also carried out by individuals with no official connection to the Verein für jüdische Statistik or to the bureau. The Berlin lawyer Bernhard Breslauer, for example, produced two studies, sponsored by the Verband der deutschen Juden, documenting through statistics the continuing discrimination facing Jews in the civil and judicial sectors of the Prussian government. The studies were intended to provide scientific evidence for the *Verband*'s political campaign for greater Jewish representation in official government employment. See Breslauer, *Die Zurücksetzung der Juden im Justizdienst*; idem, *Die Zurücksetzung der Juden an den Universitäten Deutschlands*. On Breslauer and his involvement in liberal Jewish organizations see the biographical entry in *Jüdisches Lexicon* 1: 1163–64.

58. In 1907 the creation of the Vereenigung voor Statistiek en Demographie der Joden in Nederland was announced. Centered in the Hague, and associated with the *Verband* in Berlin, the association was committed to the "social study of Jews in Holland." In 1912 a Verein für jüdische Statistik was started in Frankfurt, and according to a report published one year later quickly attracted 172 members. In 1914 a *Verein* was organized in Lemberg (Lvov). See the report "Verein für Statistik der Juden Galiziens."

59. See "Neugründung eines Vereines," 11.

60. On the activities of the Munich bureau see the annual reports and minutes published as "Mitteilungen" in the *ZfDuStdJ*. On student involvement in the *Verein* see "Beitrag von München," 11.

61. Quoted in Sulzberger.

62. Blau, "Sociology and Statistics," 156. For a list of the bureau's principal publications see the entry for "Synagogue Council of America" in *The Universal Jewish Encyclopedia*.

63. Minutes of meetings of the Verband der deutschen Juden, 1914, CZA, A142/90/10a/b.

64. "Mitteilung," *ZfDuStdJ* 11, nos. 2/3 (1915).

65. For a more general discussion of the responses of German Jewish organizations to the war effort see Matthäus.

66. In his 1881 ethnographic study of Jews, for example, the German anthropologist Richard Andree wrote: "The Jews have since their dispersion never freely searched out military service; they are neither ship captains nor sailors. That they have played as great a role in gymnastics as they have in the stock markets would be a difficult claim to sustain" (80). On military unfitness, Jewish degeneration, and ideas of national integration see Gilman, *The Jew's Body*, chapter 2.

67. Alfred Klee file, CZA, A142/90/10d. On the controversy of the German army's "Counting Jews," and for the Jewish response, see Angress.

68. See, for example, Segall, *Die deutschen Juden als Soldaten*; Theilhaber, *Die Juden im Weltkriege*.

69. Segall, "Die Statistik der Juden 1905–30," 2–3; Blau, "Sociology and Statistics," 155.

70. Between the years 1917–23 the *Zeitschrift* appeared in its full run only in 1919. It appeared again regularly between 1923–27, and then again during the years 1930–31.

71. Gillerman.

72. Ibid; Heuberger. For examples of the sort of social scientific research undertaken by the Zentralwohlfahrtsstelle, and of the participants, see the essays published in *Jüdische Bevölkerungspolitik*.

73. See the announcement in the "Mitteilung," *ZfDuStdJ* 1, no. 1 (new series; 1924): 31.

74. See the report in the "Mitteilung," *ZfDuStdJ* 4, nos. 1–2, (new series; 1927): 30.

75. On the beginnings of YIVO, and the social scientific section of its research, see *Tsvay Jahr Arbeit*; *YIVO Schriften für Ekonomische*; the entry "YIVO" in the *Encyclopedia Judaica*; Dawidowicz, "Max Weinreich." In addition, see Miron.

76. See Lestschinsky's introductory remarks in "Fun der Redaktsia."

77. See the table of contents to *Shriften far Ekonomik un Statistik* 1 (1930).

78. The practical use-value of social scientific knowledge was stressed, for instance, in the discussion of the tasks of the YIVO statistical section. See *Tsvay Jahr Arbeit*, 33–36.

79. On the history of the *Akademie* see Myers, "Fall and Rise."

80. On Täubler's participation in the Verein für jüdische Statistik see the list of names associated with the Berlin working groups in Leopold, 150.

81. Myers, "Fall and Rise," 128.

82. For a contemporary evaluation of the growing importance of social scientific analysis for Jewish historical writing, see Straus.

83. See the editorial comments of Segall, "Mitteilung," and Guttmann, "Zur Einführung," 1–2. And see the programmatic statement of Silbergleit, "Das Arbeitsprogramm." Aside from the publication of the *Zeitschrift*, the *Akademie* also assisted materially in the production of monographs by Jewish social scientists. The major work published during this period was Silbergleit's study of German Jewry, *Die Bevölkerungs- und Berufsverhältnisse der Juden im deutschen Reich*. During this period the *Akademie* also funded the research of Jacob Lestschinsky into the "occupational

structure of Prussian Jewry between 1812 and 1861." The work, however, was never published. On this see Myers, "Fall and Rise," 137–38.

## Chapter 3

1. Ruppin, *Die Soziologie der Juden*, 168.

2. Karl Jeremias, speech on the "physical formation and degeneration of the Jews" at the Fourth Zionist Congress, in *Stenographisches Protokoll der Verhandlungen des IV Zionisten-Kongresses*.

3. I take the phrase "master pathology" from Nye, *Crime*, 140.

4. These categories, of course, continued to be of fundamental interest and importance to Jewish theologians, philosophers, historians, and others. On conversion see the articles collected in Endelman, *Jewish Apostasy*. On intermarriage see Levenson, "Jewish Reactions."

5. Ruppin, *Die Juden der Gegenwart* (1904), 81.

6. Ibid., 71.

7. For an excellent discussion of earlier interpretations of this biblical command, see J. Cohen.

8. Ruppin (*Die Juden der Gegenwart* [1911], 139) among numerous other Zionist social scientists, argued that the ghetto had been one of the fundamental factors in the preservation of the "purity of the Jewish race," and noted approvingly that the British racialist H. S. Chamberlain had put forth a similar idea.

9. The shift that such an approach represented can be more clearly discerned through comparison with the function these themes played in the narratives of Jewish historians. Heinrich Graetz, for instance, concerned himself with the impact intermarriage might have had on the religious beliefs and practices of the Israelites, not on the physical or biological effects of the introduction of "foreign blood." See his discussion in *History of the Jews* 1: 56–57. Nor was this of concern to Graetz when he discussed the historical phenomenon of conversion, for instance his analysis of the Chazars, whose purported conversion to Judaism sometime in the ninth century would figure prominently in the analyses of Jewish and non-Jewish anthropologists and racial scientists. See idem, 3: 139–41. Yet one does find evidence of this widespread scholarly debate over the historical validity of the claim to Jewish racial purity in the work of the Russian Jewish historian Simon Dubnow. At the outset of his work Dubnow stated that his "sociological" approach to Jewish history meant that "the historian fulfills the task of a naturalist, of a biologist, of a psychologist and a sociologist, all in one."(idem, 1: 31). And in his discussion of Ezra's reforms, for instance, Dubnow wrote that the annulment of all mixed marriages and the subsequent banishment of the non-Hebrew wives and children "was a very drastic measure, meaning as it did the dissolution of close family ties and personal attachments; but the sacrifice seemed imperative as a means of fortifying the enfeebled structure of the nation. The segregation of the alien elements from the Judean nation was needed in order to safeguard the purity of its race and religion of its unique national culture." (idem, 1: 349–50).

10. Can a race change its particular characteristics, Ruppin asked in 1911? "There is no doubt that the selective will that privileges certain varieties of plants and ani-

mals can also be found within human races. We have already pointed to Talmud study as such a privilege in racial selective terms. Or blonde hair among German Jews, which we have traced back to the choice of a mate, and to a striving after assimilation." Ruppin referred to the well-known study of German schoolchildren conducted by the renowned German medical professor and anthropologist Rudolf Virchow, which demonstrated a relatively high percentage of blonde-haired German Jewish children. In addition, Ruppin pointed to marital advertisements in newspapers, in which Jews made it clear that they were only interested in partners who appeared "nicht jüdisch," that is, with blonde "Aryan" features. Ruppin, *Die Juden der Gegenwart* (1911), 219. According to Ignaz Zollschan, scientific studies demonstrate that "thoroughbred animals that possess superior characteristics become deteriorated with respect to these very characteristics through intermixture. The same holds good of the human races." Zollschan, "The Significance of the Mixed Marriage," in *Jewish Questions*, 40.

11. For general discussions of the ideas and impact of eugenic thinking during this period within different national contexts, see the essays collected in Adams. Also see Soloway, *Demography and Degeneration*; Schneider, *Quality and Quantity*.

12. On the identification of "outsiders" or "others" within the borders of a community, and on their role in the construction of discourses of health and degeneration, see Pick, 37–39.

13. Nye, *Crime*, 140. Also see Schneider, "Toward the Improvement of the Human Race"; Barrows.

14. Soloway, "Counting the Degenerates"; Searle, "Eugenics and Class."

15. Weindling.

16. See the discussion in Andree, 70f, of the scientific literature, reaching back into the 1840s and 1850s, on the unusually high rates of natural increase among Jews.

17. Levenson, "German Zionism."

18. Zollschan, "The Jewish Race Problem," 404.

19. Ibid., 404–5.

20. "Statistik der Juden in Deutschland," *Die Welt* 8, no. 41 (1904): 12.

21. "Der Verfall," 19. In addition, see the following reports in *Die Welt*: "Judentaufen im XIX Jahrhundert," 3, no. 36 (1899); "Judenehen in Deutschland," 7, no. 18 (1903); "Über die Mischehe in Berlin," 7, no. 30 (1903); "Rückgang der jüdischen Bevölkerung in Dänemark," 10, no. 37 (1906); "Taufen in Wien," 13, no. 37 (1909); "Vierteljahrshefte zur Statistik des deutschen Reichs," 16, no. 48 (1912).

22. "Mixed Marriages," *The Maccabean* 7, no. 5 (May 1905): 216.

23. "Statistisches von ungarischen Juden," *Die Welt* 17, no. 4 (1913): 111.

24. Jeremias, "Uber körperliche Hebung der Juden," 4–5.

25. On the idea of degeneration, disease, and images of national decline see Pick; Chamberlain and Gilman; Nye, *Crime*. On England and the United States, see Kevles. On Latin America see Stepan, *'The Hour of Eugenics.'*

26. J. Thon, "Taufbewegung und Mischehen in Österreich und Deutschland"; idem, *Die Juden in Österreich*; idem, "Taufbewegung der Juden in Österreich." In addition, see the article on Viennese Jewry by the Zionist and racial anthropologist Leo Sofer, "Die soziale Lage." According to Sofer, "the biological conditions of

Viennese Jewry during the first years of the new century are worsening" as a result of declining births and marriages, and increasing rates of divorce and death.

27. J. Thon, "Taufbewegung und Mischehen," 46, 10.

28. Ibid., 12–13.

29. The numbers differed depending upon whether the husband was a Jew or a Christian. If the husband was a Jew, one of every four children was raised Jewish. If the wife was a Jew, one in five. Ibid., 14.

30. Thon does not make this qualifying point in his discussion, remarking only that Jews and Christians must marry "confessionless." Ruppin, in the 1904 edition of *Die Juden der Gegenwart*, also failed to make this distinction. He was taken to task for this in a personal letter from the Austrian-Jewish community leader Maximillian Paul-Schiff, who pointed out that "the State does not care" what the Jews do in this regard. Paul-Schiff to Ruppin, Dec. 6, 1904, CZA, A107/152.

31. J. Thon, "Taufbewegung und Mischehen" 46, 10–12.

32. Ibid., 14.

33. See, for example, Hugo Hoppe's 1914 analysis of Austrian-Jewish population statistics ("Die jüdische Bevölkerung Österreichs," 579–80.) Hoppe began by framing his discussion in terms of Ruppin's as well as Felix Theilhaber's thesis of the crisis of Jewry. The crisis had become, he wrote, an "object of intense interest to Zionists," and so Austrian numbers were deemed significant. Statistics showed that, just as in Germany, since 1891 the Jewish population in Austria had increased at a much slower rate than had the Christian. According to Hoppe, this was due to rapidly declining birth rates, and to increasing rates of conversion and intermarriage (579).

34. Ruppin, "Die sozialen Verhältnisse der Juden in Preussen und Deutschland," 379.

35. Ibid., 377.

36. Ibid., 380.

37. Ruppin, *Die Juden der Gegenwart* (1904), 79.

38. Ibid., 86.

39. Ibid., 87.

40. Ibid., 71–72.

41. "Naturwissenschaftlich wäre es durchaus erklärlich, daß die Mischehen häufiger unfruchtbar sind als die reinen Ehen. Wie verschiedene zoologische Arten sich untereinander nicht kreuzen können, so kann auch schon die Rassen Verschiedenheit in gewissen Masse die Unfruchtbarkeit bedingen." Ruppin, *Die Juden der Gegenwart* (1911), 172.

42. Ibid., 3.

43. Ibid., 4.

44. Ruppin, "Die Verbreitung der Mischehe," 57.

45. Ibid.

46. Zollschan, *Rassenproblem*, 478–79.

47. Ibid., 472.

48. Ibid., 479.

49. Ibid., 487–89.

50. Zollschan, "Rassenproblem und Judenfrage."

51. Ibid., 898.

52. Theilhaber, *Der Untergang der deutschen Juden* (1921), 34.

53. At various points Theilhaber referred to the Jews as "outposts of modernity," "the Americans of the old world," and the "barometer of nations." Ibid., 35, 144.

54. See, for example, Theilhaber's discussion of why Jews gravitate toward the city. He offered five main reasons, combining the social and biological: 1) In the "Jewish *Volkscharacter*" there exists a "striving for sociation" (*Geselligkeit*). "Like a butterfly that flutters around the light, the Jew with his sensitive nervous character seeks out the excitements of the city." 2) For thousands of years the Jew had been predisposed to intellectual pursuits. No other people made study such a central part of life. Intellectual life, Theilhaber suggested, flourished most in the city. 3) The businessman found the most varied opportunities in the big city. 4) The Jew could uproot himself easily because he owned little or no land. Also, the logic of economic development demanded that Jews, like many others, leave agriculture in Europe. 5) The Jew "blends in," or "disappears" in the metropolis. The anti-Semitic spirit of the small village cannot so easily touch him there. See Theilhaber, *Der Untergang der deutschen Juden* (1921), 69–71.

55. His work was praised, as he himself reported, by the leading German social hygienist Alfred Grotjahn because it demonstrated the effects of modern capitalism and capitalist life not merely on the Jews, but potentially upon all the "*besitzenden Klassen*." Theilhaber, ibid., 35. Theilhaber was not alone in this belief in the Jews as indicators of Europe's future. In his work on the Jews of Hesse, for example, Ruppin argued that "die Juden gewissermaßen das Barometer für die übrige Bevölkerung sind und Zustände schon jetzt zeigen, die bei jener erst in der Zukunft zu erwarten sind." This, Ruppin claimed, was the great significance and worth of Jewish statistics for general social science. See the discussion in *Die Juden im Großherzogtum Hessen*, 43f. The argument was taken up by others as well. See, for instance, Knöpfel, 18–19.

56. Theilhaber, *Der Untergang der deutschen Juden* (1921), 10.

57. "The highest good is to bind one's own goals to those of the whole. So sexuality is directed at propagating the whole, understood as a service to the nation." Ibid., 16.

58. Ibid., 19–21.

59. Statistics from the years 1875–1914 showed a substantial decrease, according to the figures he provided, in the number of Jewish births. Even the French, who in the scientific literature were known as the most "child-poor" nation, showed higher numbers than the Prussian Jews: 19–21 percent to 16.5 percent.

60. Theilhaber quoted from a number of prominent non-Jewish social scientists in this connection. For example, the German statistician Georg von Mayr stressed the social, as opposed to the racial, factors involved in Jewish suicide rates. According to Näcke, "the decadence of German Jewry is not a pure (biological) process, born out of the degeneration of the race, but derives from an unhealthy occupational distribution, way of life, types of residence." See *Der Untergang der deutschen Juden*, 151–52.

61. Theilhaber, *Die Schädigung der Rasse*.

62. Ibid., 69–73.

63. Ibid., 75.
64. Ibid., 84, 92.
65. Theilhaber, *Der Untergang der deutschen Juden*, 1921, 96.
66. Ibid., 136. Sombart made these claims in his work *Die Zukunft der Juden*.
67. Jungmann, 3.
68. Conversion did signal a lack of Jewish racial pride, even if it did not biologically effect Jewry. Ruppin, for instance, in a negative review of N. Samter's influential work on Jewish conversion in the nineteenth century published in *ZfDuStdJ* 2, no. 3 (1906): 148, took issue with Samter's thesis that conversion could be countered by instilling in Jews a sense of Judaism's superiority over Christianity as a religion. It is not the religion that needs to be touted, Ruppin wrote. Rather, "far greater results will accrue when Jews are made aware of their value as a *Volksgemeinschaft*, when they are shown what they have contributed and achieved in the realm of human culture, and what they signify as a race." Conversion was only externally, in appearance, a religious act. Fundamentally it was one example of the general sociological rule or law of assimilation. Judaism was a community without the implements or means of power of state to enforce adherence and belonging. Its strength as a *Gemeinschaft* depended on pride in a common past, and sense of worth as a unique people and race. The strongest remedy to conversion was in pride of past (*Ahnenstolz*), pride in what "our forefathers created culturally."
69. Auerbach, "Die jüdische Rassenfrage."
70. Ibid., 333.
71. Ibid., 336.
72. Ibid., 335.
73. Ibid., 334.
74. Ibid.
75. Judt, *Die Juden als Rasse*. The work was published originally in Polish, and then translated into German. The German version was one of the first publications offered by the recently formed Jüdischer Verlag, a Zionist publishing house linked with the cultural wing of the movement.
76. Ibid., 204.
77. Ben-Sasson, 395.
78. Judt, *Die Juden als Rasse*, 205.
79. Sofer, "Über die Entmischung der Rassen."
80. While Darwin's theory of evolution might appear incompatible with polygenist thinking, his position on human races, as George Stocking points out, was "congenial to polygenist thinking." On this, and on the survival of polygenist thought in general after Darwin, see Stocking, "The Persistence of Polygenist Thought," in Stocking, *Race, Culture, and Evolution*, 42–68.
81. Sofer, "Über die Entmischung der Rassen," 12.
82. Zollschan, "The Jewish Race Problem," 405.
83. Zollschan, "Rassenproblem und Judenfrage," 897. The publication of Zollschan's speech in *Die Welt* elicited an angry response from Alfred Waldenberg, a Zionist and racial scientist, who believed he deserved the credit for first alerting Zionists to the dangers posed by intermarriage to the Jewish race. Waldenberg claimed that as early as 1902, in his comparative study of Jewish and non-Jewish

health, he had put forth the thesis that Jewish health was directly related to Jewish racial inbreeding. "The Jewish race has achieved a relatively high immunity from cholera, and a number of acute as well as chronic infectious diseases through inbreeding, and this is an hereditary trait that is weakened or diminished, proportinately, by the introduction of non-Jewish blood." Waldenburg argued that intermarriage produced degeneration and led to "racial suicide," and called for "a superior racial inbreeding" in Palestine. See "Jüdische Rassenhochzucht." His ideas do appear in Zionist works on Jewish anthropology in which the idea of racial purity plays a paramount role. See, for example, Sandler, 26–27.

84. Zollschan, "The Significance of the Mixed Marriage."

85. Ibid., 24.

86. Ruppin's model of assimilation will be discussed in greater detail in the following chapter.

87. Zollschan, "The Significance of the Mixed Marriage," 32.

88. Ibid., 38.

89. Ibid., 42.

90. A. Reibmayr, quoted in Sofer, "Zur Biologie," 89.

91. Sandler, *Anthropologie und Zionismus*, 8. Auerbach also cited Gobineau approvingly in the same context. See the discussion in Levenson, "Jewish Reactions," 191.

92. Sandler, *Anthropologie und Zionismus*, 1.

93. Ibid., 35.

94. Ibid.

95. In an article entitled "Intermarriage and the Jewish-National Consciousness" Sandler identified intermarriage as a direct threat to the Zionist movement itself. Pointing to statistics from Berlin as proof that quantitatively as well as qualitatively intermarriage posed a terrible threat to Jewry, he argued that declining numbers meant diminished strength, and without sufficient numbers of Jews the Zionist dream would remain unfulfilled. See the summary in Levenson, "Jewish Reactions," 189.

96. Sandler, *Anthropologie und Zionismus*, 30.

97. Ibid., 40.

98. Theilhaber, *Der Untergang der deutschen Juden* (1921), 126.

99. Ruppin, *Die Juden der Gegenwart* (1904), 94.

100. Ibid.

## Chapter 4

1. See, for example, the programmatic essay by Nossig, "Jüdisches Statistik." Also see the summary of an early plenary session of the *Verein*, during which Louis Maretzki, a health official and leader of the Berlin Jewish community, emphasized the need for a *Gesundheitsstatistik* of the Jews. See "Jüdische Statistik," *Die Welt* 8, no. 6 (1904): 7–8.

2. See the summary of the report in the *ZfDuStdJ* 1, no. 3 (1904): 16. Nor was the *Verein* alone within Jewish academic circles in addressing itself to these ideas and issues. In Odessa, for example, a Russian-language journal, *The Jewish Medical Voice*,

devoted exclusively to Jews and medicine was started up in 1908. See the announcement and international call for papers in *Die Welt* 11 (1907): 176.

3. See, for example, Ruppin, "Hat der Vater?"; Sichel, "Zur Ätiologie."

4. In addition to the articles drawn from the newspapers and popular journals discussed in this chapter, see Ruppin, "Die jüdische Bevölkerung in Preussen"; A. Friedmann, "Forschungen über Rasse und Degenerationen"; Auerbach, "Rassenmischungen der Juden." For examples from encyclopedias see the articles written by Maurice Fishberg on "Morbidity," "Idiocy," "Insanity," "Nervous Diseases," "Consumption," and "Diabetes" in the *Jewish Encyclopedia*, and the articles "Gesundheitsverhältnisse bei den Juden" and "Sozialhygiene der Juden" by Felix Theilhaber in *Jüdisches Lexicon*. For examples of public lectures on health themes, see the announcement for a lecture at the Café Neptun by the Zionist physician Martin Engländer, entitled "Berichte: Wien."

5. On earlier scientific studies of Jews, by Jews and non-Jews, along medical lines, see Efron, "Images of the Jewish Body"; Mitchell and Kottek; Fuchs and Plaut.

6. On the interrelationship between biology, medicine, and the social sciences at this time see Webster; Weindling, *Health, Race and German Politics*; D. Porter.

7. On the political and socioeconomic contexts of public health in the nineteenth and early twentieth centuries, and on the professionalization of medicine, see Rosen, chapters 6 and 7; Proctor, *Racial Hygiene*; Light, Liebfried, and Tennstedt; Labisch; Kater; Frevert; Huerkamp.

8. On the equation of Jews with disease, and on the emergence of the biological metaphor within the European discourse on the Jews, see Bein, "Der jüdische Parasit"; Weindling, 170. Weindling points out that while, on the one hand, Jews came to be more and more described as bacteria or bacilli, anti-Semites also identified medicine and science as "Jewish," and labeled them threats to the German *Volk* and nation. On the "Jews as disease," see also the short piece entitled "Die Judenfrage und die . . . Cholera" in *Die Welt*, which reported on the links made in Russian public discourse between the Jews and the cholera epidemic.

9. On the image of the Eastern European Jew as dirty and diseased see Aschheim, *Brothers and Strangers*, 60–61 and passim; Wertheimer, *Unwelcome Strangers*, 27–30; Maurer, *Ostjuden in Deutschland 1918–1933*, 109–20.

10. On France see Bein, "Der jüdische Parasit"; for England see Holmes, *Antisemitism in British Society 1876–1939*, chapter 3: "The Health and Morals of the Nation." On the United States see Singerman; Kraut, *Silent Travelers*; idem, "Silent Strangers."

11. Andree, 70.

12. Gilman, *Case of Sigmund Freud*; idem, *The Jew's Body*.

13. For example, in a 1908 article in *Die Welt*, entitled "Eine Judenkrankheit" ("A Jewish disease"), one finds a discussion of the monograph *The Disease of the Jews: Diabetes*, by a Berlin physician, Wilhelm Sternberg. The reality of diabetes as a Jewish disease was taken as a well-established fact by both writer and reviewer. The question to be addressed concerned cause. "It is conclusively demonstrated through the use of statistics that the Jews are represented in disproportionate numbers among diabetics," the reviewer stated, and proceeded to summarize Sternberg's own discussion of the purported link between diabetes and Jewish ritual cooking.

After refuting this hypothesis, Sternberg traced the Jewish propensity to diabetes to biophysical origins: the "well-known neuropathic predisposition" of Jews to the illness, and their propensity to nervous disorders. Dr. X, "Eine Judenkrankheit," *Die Welt* 8, no. 4 (1904): 15. Also see the discussion and scientific literature cited on this question in Fishberg, *Jews*, 297–302.

14. On disease, particularly tuberculosis, as a metaphor in the nineteenth century see Sontag, *Illness as Metaphor*. See also Gilman, *Disease and Representation*.

15. For a full discussion of the various diseases that Jews were believed either to be susceptible to, or to be immune from, and for the scientific literature produced around this issue, see Fishberg, *Jews*, 270–355; Maretzki, "Die Gesundheitsverhältnisse der Juden"; Theilhaber, "Gesundheitsverhältnisse bei den Juden."

16. Quoted in Fishberg, *Jews*, 311.

17. Gilman, *The Jew's Body*. See as well his analysis in *Difference and Pathology*.

18. In 1901, for instance, Ruppin entered an essay contest that asked participants to address the following question: "What can we learn from the principles of heredity that is relevant to domestic political jurisdiction and the administration of states?" He won second prize, and his book-length essay was published in 1902 under the title *Sozialdarwinismus und Sozialwissenschaft*. In a diary entry from December 1901 he recorded his "overriding interest in genetic questions." Dec. 31, 1901, CZA, A107/950, 11. See also Ruveini; Penslar, *Zionism and Technocracy*, 86–88. On Ruppin's life and work in general, see Bein, "Arthur Ruppin."

19. In 1894, for example, Alfred Nossig published a work, *Die Sozialhygiene der Juden und des altorientalischen Völkerkreises*, on the social hygiene of the Jews, in which he set out to establish the equivalency of the biblical and Talmudic laws of purity and modern medical science. In his narrative, which serves as a perfect example of the sort of medicalization of Jewish history mentioned above, traditional Judaism is linked with every idea and practice that produces cleanliness, purity, and health. The image of the Jew as the purveyor of disease is countered with the notion of the Jew as the guardian of medical knowledge, as a central player in the centuries-long story of scientific progress. Judaism is offered as a source of values and rituals that mirror bourgeois notions of normality and respectability in matters of public and private life. For an analysis of this work see Hart, "Moses the Microbiologist."

20. For example, Dr. M. Epstein, in a lecture titled "Illness and Rates of Death among the Jews," and delivered in March 1905 at the Verein für die Statistik der Juden in Munich, argued that the higher rates of mental illness found among Jews can only be explained biologically. This tendency was not a product of "social relations" (i.e., persecutions), but was rather an "inherited neuropathic trait" that had been intensified through inbreeding as well as through the nervousness of the Jew. "Their nervousness is a racial trait. It is a product of the selection process." The talk is summarized in the *Zeitschrift für Demographie und Statistik der Juden* 1, no. 5, (1905): 16.

21. On the politics of Lamarckian versus Mendelian (or Weismannian) inheritance, see the discussion in Proctor, *Racial Hygiene*, 30–38.

22. On the connection between knowledge and practical policy and politics in Jewish statistics, see the foreword to Nossig, *Jüdische Statistik*, 3–4.

23. "Jüdische Geisteskranke," *Die Welt* 2, no. 26 (1898): 11.

24. For example, Dr. Ludwig Werner, one of the leaders of the Jewish gymnastics movement, described the relationship between Zionism, Jewry, and gymnastics in the following way: "Only as an element within Zionism does Jewish nationalism have any justification. Jewish nationalism as an end in itself, without connection to Zionism, is akin to a substance which brings an unconscious, extremely sick man to consciousness, and thereby to full recognition of his situation, without in fact being a genuine means for healing his illness. . . . The medicine required for the Jewish sickness is Zionism! . . . Jewish gymnastics is present-centered and future-oriented work at the same time, in the best sense of the words, for it works for the regeneration of our *Volk*." L. Werner, 5–7. In addition to the examples cited throughout this chapter, see the report on Dr. Alexander Marmorek's trip to Antwerp in which it is written that he understands emphatically the principles of bacteriology, and "is trying to inoculate the many feebled souls with the healing serum of Zionism." *Die Welt* 7, no. 31 (1903): 12; and the article "Entartung" in *Die Welt* in which German Jewry is defined as sick, an "organism showing symptoms of illness (*Krankheitssymptome*).

25. Blau, "Die jüdische Statistik," 7. The ideal of the physician as national leader was enunciated years before by the French sociologist Emile Durkheim: "The duty of the statesman is no longer to push society toward an ideal that seems attractive to him, but his role is that of physician; he prevents the outbreak of illnesses by good hygiene, and he seeks to cure them when they have appeared." Quoted in Nye, "Degeneration," 31.

26. Plaschkes, "Ärzte in der zionistischen Bewegung." In 1912 *Die Welt* argued that the alternative to "tuberculosis, alcoholism, and syphilis" for the Jewish people is their "regeneration in the land of their fathers." "Die Rassenzugehörigkeit der Juden," 1356. For a contemporary evaluation of the need of Jewish physicians to involve themselves in the Zionist effort at "*Rassenhygiene*" and regeneration see Kornfeld.

27. "Die Disposition der Juden." The piece was an excerpt from an article by the same name published originally in the *Politisch-Anthropologische Revue*, one of the leading German scientific journals devoted to issues of race.

28. Ibid.

29. Ibid. Yaakov Shavit has shown the way in which Zionists sought to identify the ancient Hebrews and Phoenicians as racially and ethnically related in order to prove that modern Jewry belonged in Palestine. See his article "Hebrews and Phoenicians."

30. Theilhaber, "Beiträge zur jüdischen Rassenfrage"; idem, "Der Gebärmutterhalskrebs bei den Juden." Decades earlier, the Anglo-Jewish statistician Joseph Jacobs pointed to the anthropological fact that Jewish women menstruated much earlier than non-Jewish women as proof of the racial unity of the Jews. See Jacobs, "On the Racial Characteristics of Modern Jews," xxix.

31. Nossig, *Materialien*.

32. Schimmer.

33. Nossig, *Materialien*, 45.

34. Ibid., 40–41.

35. For a general discussion of the impact of natural scientific thinking, including ideas of race, on German Zionism during this period see Doron, "Rassenbewusstsein und Naturwissenschaftliches Denken."

36. What is significant in this context is Nossig's use of the category to set Jews off from the English in a way that went beyond religious differences, challenging and repudiating the liberal self-perception of Anglo-Jewry.

37. Nossig, *Materialien*, 29–30.

38. On Nossig and Zionism see Ezra Mendelsohn, "From Assimilation to Zionism"; Almog, "Alfred Nossig: A Reappraisal."

39. Mandelstamm, *Stenographisches Protokoll der Verhandlungen des IV Zionisten-Kongresses*. Mandelstamm's speech is reproduced as "Rede Dr. Max Mandelstamms," *Die Welt* 4, no. 35 (1900): 1–7. It was translated into English and published as *How Jews Live* (London: Greenberg, 1900).

Mandelstamm, a physician and optician, had called for the "physical regeneration of the Jews" already in his speech to the Second Zionist Congress in 1898. This talk, together with Nordau's on "*Muskeljudentum*," fueled enthusiasm in Zionist circles for gymnastics, which many believed to be essential to building up not only strong Jewish bodies but a vital Jewish national consciousness. On this, and on the formation of gymnastic societies in early Zionist circles, see George Eisen, "Zionism, Nationalism and the Emergence of the *Jüdische Turnerschaft*." On the idea of the "new Jew" and the *Turnvereine*, see Berkowitz, 99–118.

40. *Encyclopedia Judaica*, 11: 867–69.

41. Mandelstamm, *Stenographisches Protokoll der Verhandlungen des IV Zionisten-Congresses*, 117.

42. Ibid., 126.

43. Ibid., 127–28.

44. Ibid., 125.

45. On the background to this line of argument in general see Gould, chapters 2–3.

46. One example of this sort of argument comes from the work of the Anglo-Jewish statistician Joseph Jacobs, and is discussed in chapter 5. For a full discussion of the discursive link between "Jewish intelligence" and "Jewish superiority" see Gilman, *Smart Jews*.

47. Mandelstamm, *Stenographisches Protokoll*, 128–29.

48. Ibid., 130–31.

49. Avineri, *Making of Modern Zionism*, 101–11; Biale, 177–79; Berkowitz; G. Mosse, "Max Nordau."

50. Nordau, *Degeneration*, 15–18. On Lombroso and his theories of degeneration, see Pick, 111f.

51. Baldwin, 105.

52. Lombroso, in fact, had attempted to account for the high percentage of Jews represented among the insane by referring to the disproportionate number of geniuses among them. See Lombroso, 43–50. The Zionist racial anthropologist Leo Sofer repeated this claim in his summary of scientific opinion on Jewish pathologies. See Sofer, "Zur Biologie," 90. On Nordau's views on degeneration, Zionism, and bourgeois values see Funkenstein, 340–42. On the strong middle-class under-

pinning to Nordau's ideas on degeneration, see George Mosse's introduction to Nordau's *Degeneration*.

53. In a 1911 debate with the French socialist Victor Basch, professor of German literature at the Sorbonne, Nordau argued the following: "Die Elemente, die ein Volk ausmachen, fehlen uns, sagt die Wissenschaft. Wir sind trotzdem ein Volk; die Kriteria, die für ein anderes Volk maßgebend sind, können auf uns nicht angewendet werden, weil wir in anderen, in anormalen Verhältnissen leben. . . . Wir leben ein anormales Leben. Jeder Jude fühlt, bewußt oder unbewußt, den Zwiespalt." See the account in *Die Welt* 15, no. 27 (1911): 634.

54. See the excerpt of the program reproduced under the heading "Jüdisches Turnwesen," in *Die Welt*. In addition, see the article "Die jüdische Turnerschaft" by Ludwig Werner in which the language of illness and medicine was used to illustrate what Werner believed to be the necessary link between gymnastics and Zionism.

55. Concluding his 1901 speech to the Zionist delegates, Nordau called for two immediate and necessary reforms in Jewish life: The Jewish people must wean themselves from early marriages and from traditional schooling. Early marriage, he argued, was "a cancerous sore [*Krebsschaden*] on our *Volksorganismus*," the heder "a barbaric attack on health. It hinders physical development and lays the germs of later illness in the organism." (133). The language Nordau used to describe both early marriage and the heder—the metaphors of cancer and germs that attack the organism of the *Volk*—illustrates well the infusion of medical terminology into early Zionist discourse. Yet it also points to the retention within Nordau's analysis of older Maskilic ideas of causes and symptoms of Jewish degeneration in Eastern Europe. Both early marriage and the heder were favorite targets of Maskilic critics of traditional life. On the heder and on Eastern European Jewish politics see Zipperstein, "Transforming the *Heder*." On Nordau's identification of Western Jewry as degenerate see Baldwin, 112–13; Berkowitz, 107.

56. *Die Welt* 5, no. 18 (1901).

57. Blechmann.

58. Jeremias, "The Physical Inferiority of the Jews," 3–4.

59. Jeremias, *Stenographisches Protokoll der Verhandlungen des IV Zionisten-Congresses*.

60. Gilman, *The Jew's Body*, 40 and *passim*; idem, *Case of Sigmund Freud*, 113–68.

61. On the loss of military strength, and on the discourse of degeneration, see Nye, "Degeneration," 24–28; Soloway, "Counting the Degenerates."

62. Ruppin, *Die Juden der Gegenwart* (1904), 112.

63. Jeremias, *Stenographisches Protokoll*, 120.

64. Ibid., 121.

65. See Jeremias, "Die Hygiene der jüdischen Nerven," 75.

66. Ibid., 73–74.

67. The formal exchange was published as "Offener Brief an den Vorstand des Zentralvereines deutscher Staatsbürger jüdischen Glaubens," *Die Welt* 6, no. 28 (1902): 4–5. See Jeremias, "Offener Brief." Levy, whose letter is reproduced by Jeremias here, was responding to Jeremias's article "Eine öffentliche Irrenanstalt für Juden," in *Allgemeine Zeitung des Judenthums*, May 30, 1902.

68. Ibid.

69. Levy, "Offener Brief," 4.

70. Ibid., 5.

71. In formulating their ideas on the measures necessary for Jewish health and regeneration, many Jewish social scientists—Zionist and non-Zionist—focused on the Jewish family, seeing it as the mediator between the individual and the larger whole. On the significance of the idea and of the image of the family for Jewish social thinkers and social workers, especially during the Weimar period, see Gillerman.

72. In addition, see his article "Die körperliche Minderwertigkeit der Juden," where he emphasized the role of sports in national regeneration efforts.

73. Engländer, *Die auffallend*, 45–46. The work originated as a talk before the Viennese Zionist organization, Zion.

74. Ibid., 15. The review of the book in *Die Welt* stressed Engländer's refutation of Mandelstamm's division of East and West, and saw in the recognition of the illness of Western Jewry further justification for the Zionist movement's activities. "This little book is a true *Volksbuch*," *Die Welt* told its readers, "one that every Jew should read." See *Die Welt* 6, no. 16 (1902): 7.

75. Engländer, *Die auffallend*, 11.

76. Ibid., 12–13.

77. Ibid., 13–14.

78. Ibid., 14–15.

79. Ibid., 16.

80. Ibid., 18.

81. On Krafft-Ebing and his role in the debates on Jewish mental health among Jewish psychiatrists during this period, see Gilman, "Jews and Mental Illness," 153–54.

82. Engländer, *Die auffallend*, 23–24.

83. Theilhaber, *Der Untergang der deutschen Juden*, 69.

84. Ibid., 148–52.

85. Ibid., 157.

86. Engländer, *Die auffallend*, 35.

87. See Ruppin's review of Hoppe's work *Alcohol und Kriminalität* in *ZfDuStdJ* 2, no. 12 (1906).

88. Pick, 42.

89. Cf. Gilman, *Case of Sigmund Freud*, 34–37.

90. The phrase is derived from the work of Spackman.

91. Theilhaber, *Der Untergang der deutschen Juden*, 1921, 158.

92. Hoppe, *Krankheiten und Sterblichkeit*.

93. Ibid., 1.

94. Ibid., 18.

95. See, for example, the discussions in Maretzki, "Die Gesundheitsverhältnisse der Juden," 148–50; Theilhaber, *Der Untergang der deutschen Juden*, 1921, 1–16 and passim; Nossig, *Materialien*, 4, 30–35, 55–56.

96. On the idea of alcoholism as a primary cause of degeneration, see Pick, 87 and passim.

97. Hoppe, "Kriminalität."

98. Ibid., 40. Hoppe took his statistics on Jews in Eastern Europe, as well as on

immigrant Jews in England and the United States, from the works of Ruppin and Jacobs.

99. Ibid., 55–56.

100. Hoppe, *Krankheiten und Sterblichkeit*, 13–17, 42–3; "Kriminalität," 54–56.

101. Hoppe, *Krankheiten und Sterblichkeit*, 60–61. As further proof of his point, Hoppe quoted an assistant physician, H. Fels, who worked in the German Hospital in London. Fels had remarked on the astoundingly high rate of Polish and Russian Jewish mothers, many with as many as eight to fourteen children, who were able to breastfeed their babies. These women, Hoppe wrote, who remain at "an unmodern stage of development," differ markedly from "the hypercivilized Western Europeans. . . . [O]ur modern woman could learn something from the despised and rejected Whitechapel Jews" (51). In addition to Hoppe, and to the other examples provided in this chapter, see the article published in the Jewish newspaper *Ost und West* by a Dr. Augustus Eshner entitled "Krankheits- und Sterblichkeits-Statistik der Juden." Eshner stressed the fact, demonstrated by statistics, that the differences in susceptibility to or immunity from certain diseases among Jews and non-Jews were being effaced by the effects of assimilation. The more Jews give up their isolation and "mix with other races," he argued, "the more they forfeit their characteristic differences, which contemporary statistics on disease and death demonstrate."

102. Hoppe, *Krankheiten und Sterblichkeit*, 26–33.

103. Ibid., 52.

104. Ibid., 55–56.

105. Ibid., 56–57.

106. On Jews and images of mental health and disease see Gilman, "Jews and Mental Illness"; Efron, "The 'Kaftanjude' and the 'Kaffeehausjude.'" On the image of the Jew as mentally ill as a theme in modern French psychiatry see J. Goldstein.

107. This idea that traditional Jewish society and culture represented an expression of the social Darwinian "struggle for existence" through selective breeding did not disappear after World War II. The American sociologist Lewis Feuer, for example, still felt it necessary in 1983 to refute the idea that "Jewish intelligence" was a product of a sociobiological selection process. See Feuer.

108. Leroy-Beaulieu, 151.

109. For additional examples of the application of the social Darwinian notion of "struggle for existence" in the context of Jewish health and disease, see Hoppe, *Krankheiten und Sterblichkeit*, 42; Fishberg, *Jews*, 276f; Maretzki, 139; Ruppin, *Die Soziologie der Juden*, 165.

110. On the romanticization of the *Ostjuden* among Western Zionists see Mendes-Flohr, "Fin-de-Siècle Orientalism."

111. Stern, *The Politics of Cultural Despair*. On the diffusion of this sort of antimodernism within Germany at the time, see, in addition to Stern, Ringer. For a modification of the categorization of this thinking as antimodern, see Herf.

112. For a discussion of this strain of antimodernism, anticapitalism, and degenerationist thinking within early Zionism as a whole see Doron, "Classic Zionism."

113. On the ideal of Bildung in German Jewish life see Sorkin; Mosse, *German Jews Beyond Judaism*.

114. Of course, other factors, both technical and nontechnical, were involved here. Some of these have already been discussed in the introduction and chapter 1, including the issue of religion and the official collection of statistics at the state level. This helped determine that those countries such as Germany and Austria-Hungary, where "confession" was a legally sanctioned category of statistical inquiry, would produce a fuller body of material. For a discussion of this matter and its significance for Jewish statistics, see Knöpfel.

115. See Ruppin, *Die Soziologie der Juden*, 174–84. Both Ruppin and Felix Theilhaber, whose analyses of Jewish vital statistics will be examined in greater detail later, posited the significance of their own work for both Jewish and European social science in large measure on this "predictive element" in Jewish statistics. On this see Ruppin, *Die Soziologie der Juden*, 180–84; Theilhaber, *Der Untergang der deutschen Juden* (1921), 35.

116. Efron, "The 'Kaftanjude' and the 'Kaffeehausjude'"; idem, *Defenders of the Race*, chapter six; Gilman, "Jews and Mental Illness"; Biale, *Eros and the Jews*, 179–80.

117. Hoppe, *Krankheiten und Sterblichkeit*, 59.

118. Ruppin, *Die Juden der Gegenwart*, 101.

119. Ibid., 104.

120. Ibid., 104–5.

121. Ibid., 263–65. On the significance of these categories as markers of national identity within early Zionism as a whole see Almog, *Zionism and History*.

122. Ruppin, *Die Juden der Gegenwart*, 266.

123. Ibid.

124. Ibid., 117–18.

125. Ibid., 292–93.

126. Ibid., 295.

127. Ruppin, *Die sozialen Verhältnisse*.

128. Ibid., 66–68. A decade later W. Kaplun-Kogan, another Zionist social scientist, reached similiar conclusions when he compared the conditions of Polish and German Jewry. His analysis is another example of the sort of interpretive shift of East and West we have been analyzing here. Kaplun concluded that although Eastern European Jewry appeared healthy at present, Western forces of modernization were already at work. The fate of East European Jewry, if it remained vulnerable to the modernizing forces of dissolution, would inevitably be that of contemporary Western Jewry. See Kaplun-Kogan, "Die jüdische Sprach- und Kulturgemeinschaft in Polen."

129. Ruppin, *Die Juden der Gegenwart*, 1. Pages cited refer to the third unrevised edition, issued in 1920.

130. Ibid., 57–71.

131. Ibid., 28.

132. Ibid.

133. Ibid., 29.

134. Ibid., 267.

135. Nye, *Crime*, 134–40, and passim; Pick, 139f; Gates. For an insightful discussion on the collection of suicide statistics in the nineteenth century, and the difficulties in using them to arrive at the "reality" of suicide, O. Anderson, 1–40.

136. On the scholarly debate about suicide during the nineteenth and early

twentieth centuries, and on its significance for sociology as a whole, see Douglas; Giddens, *The Sociology of Suicide*, especially the introduction.

137. Masaryk, *Suicide*, 214. Masaryk noted as well that "religious indifference, skepticism, and unbelief are also prevalent among the Jews, especially among the educated." This was a result of "living with and among irreligious Christians," and taking part in "modern intellectual activities . . . especially in cities" (215). However, he offered no statistics to show how much of an impact this irreligiosity had had on modern Jews.

138. Durkheim, 158.

139. Ibid., 160.

140. Ibid., 167.

141. Ibid., 168.

142. For the official statistics, as well as for summaries of the debates on the question of Jews and suicide, see Hirschberg; Wassermann, "Selbstmord."

143. Ruppin, *Die Juden der Gegenwart* (1904), 108.

144. Ruppin, *Die Soziologie der Juden*, 247–48.

145. Sichel, "Selbstmord."

146. See Theilhaber, *Der Untergang der deutschen Juden* (1921), 136.

147. See, for instance, "Selbstmorde im Jahre 1904," *ZfDuStdJ* 2, no. 12, (1906): 189; "Selbstmorde im Preussen 1907," *ZfDuStdJ* 5, no. 6 (1909): 93.

148. Gilman, *Case of Sigmund Freud*, 169–78. On the place of criminal anthropology and criminology in degeneration theory see Pick, 139f; Nye, *Crime*, chapter 3.

149. For contemporary discussions of the debate see Wassermann, "Kritische"; Paul-Schiff; Fishberg, *Jews*, 407–18.

150. Liszt, unlike many others, rejected the racial explanation, insisting instead that the reasons lie "in the particular occupational status and structure of the Jewish population." Liszt.

151. Wassermann, "Kritische," 75.

152. Ruppin, "Die Kriminalität"; idem, *Die Juden der Gegenwart* (1911), 222f.

153. Ruppin, "Die Kriminalität," 8–9.

154. See, for instance, Doron, "Classic Zionism," 182–94.

155. Nossig, *Materialien*, 30–31.

156. Ruppin, *Die Juden der Gegenwart* (1911), chapter 13.

157. For example: "So it happens that we see in the contemporary Jew a particularly worthwhile human type. He is marked by an unequalled and unprecedented intellectual ability. It is this fact that justifies the existence of the Jews as a *Sondergemeinschaft*" (ibid., 218).

158. Ibid., 222.

159. Ibid.

160. Ibid., 223–24.

161. Ibid., 223.

162. Nossig, *Materialien*, 3–6, 24–26, 55; Weissenberg, "Zur Sozialbiologie," 408.

163. Ruppin, *Die Juden der Gegenwart* (1904), 112.

164. Wassermann, "Die Zukunft des Judentums," 54.

*Chapter 5*

1. Keller, 4.
2. This stood in contrast to the conceptualization of collective identity that relied on the notion of subjectivity. Moritz Lazarus, for instance, who together with Hermann Steinthal pioneered the discipline of *Völkerpsychologie*, defined a nation as a collection of individuals who considered themselves to be part of the nation. Significantly, he drew the distinction and opposition between the natural scientist dealing with other forms of life, and the thinker who analyzes human beings.

The spiritual similarities and differences are independent of the genealogical factor . . . and what a nation does to them is not mainly inherent in certain objective factors such as origin, language, etc. . . . but rather it is inherent in the subjective views of individuals in the nation, who see themselves as belonging to one unified nation. . . . If we were to discuss plants and animals, an expert on wildlife would be the one to classify these according to their different objective markings; . . . but with people, we ask them which nation would they like to belong to. . . . A nation is a pure spiritual entity . . . It is a spiritual product of individuals, who themselves belong to this product. They are not being a nation, rather they are continuously creating a nation. (*Was heisst national? Ein Vortrag von Prof. Dr. M. Lazarus* [Berlin: Dümmler, 1880], quoted in Bacharach, "Jews in Confrontation," 199.)

Nonetheless, Jewish liberals did at times make use of racial-biological language and ideas as well. On this see idem, 200f.
3. Theilhaber reproduced a number of these reviews in the 1921 edition of the work. Theilhaber's critics included fellow Zionists, one of which was the demographer Rudolf Wassermann, with whom Theilhaber worked in Munich. See Wassermann's critique in "Neomalthusianismus und Judenfrage."
4. Segall, "Der Untergang der deutschen Juden," *im deutschen Reich*; idem, "Der Untergang der deutschen Juden," *ZfDuStdJ*. (All subsequent references refer to the longer full-length review from *im deutschen Reich*.)
5. Ibid., 487–88. Segall credited the work of the German statistician Hindelang (*Die neuzeitliche Entwicklung des Fruchtbarkeitsverhältnisse, insbesondere in Bayern*, (Ph.D. diss., Munich, Ludwig-Maxilians University, 1909) with moving demography past this mistaken equation.
6. Segall, "Der Untergang der deutschen Juden," 489; cf. Segall, "Grundzüge."
7. Segall, "Der Untergang der deutschen Juden," 490.
8. Ibid., 490–91. The argument can also be found in Segall, "Stand der jüdischen," 153–54.
9. Segall, "Wirtschaftliche"; idem, *Beruflichen*.
10. Segall, "Berufzählung."
11. Maretzki, "Die Gesundheitsverhältnisse der Juden," 146.
12. Ibid., 148.
13. Ibid., 149.

14. Ibid.

15. Ibid., 150.

16. Efron, "The 'Kaftanjude' and the 'Kaffeehausjude'," 176.

17. Ibid.

18. On Weissenberg's Diaspora nationalism and on its impact on his anthropological thought see the discussion in Efron, *Defenders of the Race*, chapter 5.

19. See, for instance, Weissenberg, "Hygiene"; idem, "Verhalten"; idem, "Zur Sozialbiologie."

20. Weissenberg, "Zur Sozialbiologie," 402.

21. "Mag auch manche Sitte vom Standpunkte der jetzigen Kultur und des modernen Wissens als wesenslos erscheinen, so muß doch in Betracht gezogen werden, daß nicht alle Welt auf der Höhe der modernen Kultur steht." Weissenberg, "Hygiene," 29.

22. Nossig, *Sozialhygiene der Juden*; Hart, "Moses the Microbiologist."

23. See the volumes produced in conjunction with the exhibitions: Eschelbacher and Sindler; Grunwald.

24. In addition to the literature cited in the notes above, see Eisenstadt, *Hygiene und Judentum: Eine Sammelschrift*.

25. Weissenberg, "Zur Sozialbiologie," 410. As proof of the intimate connection between Jews and hemorrhoids Weissenberg noted the linguistic similiarity between the German word *Hämmorhoiden* and the Yiddish phrase "*Mir Jiden*" (we Jews).

26. On the nexus between antifeminism, demographic concerns, and degeneration theory in the European context see Pick, 92–93.

27. Weissenberg, "Zur Sozialbiologie," 406.

28. Ibid., 408.

29. Ibid., 411–12. Also see Weissenberg, "Verhalten," 177.

30. Weissenberg, "Zur Sozialbiologie," 414.

31. Ibid., 417.

32. Ross, 147. In addition see Markel, 5 and passim.

33. Ross, xiii.

34. "Vital Statistics of the Jews in the United States," *Census Bulletin* 19 (Dec. 30, 1890). Billings was assisted by A. S. Solomons, appointed special agent for purposes of the study. Solomons contacted rabbis and communal leaders to obtain lists of congregation families. Of 15,000 surveys sent, Billings records that 10,688 were returned. The surveys were intended to count the Jewish population, and yield information on marriage, births, deaths, sex distribution, occupation, and geographic distribution.

35. "Vital Statistics of the Jews," 5.

36. For an account of these diseases, and the interconnection between epidemics and the politics of immigration, see Markel.

37. Markel, 181.

38. Singerman, 103.

39. On the impact of European racial thinking about the Jews in the United States, and on its role in debates about immigration, see Higham, *Strangers in the Land*, 138–54; Singerman; Chase; Kraut, *Silent Travelers*.

40. Kraut, *Silent Travelers*, 145.

41. The Jews, of course, were not the focus of Boas's anthropological work in general. His studies on headforms and physical anthropology contained research on Italians, Native American Indians, Eskimos, and others, and this research occupied but a small portion of his energies. To be sure, a case can, and has, been made for an intimate connection between Boas's Jewish origins, his immigrant background, and his anthropology. Opponents at the time, and some later historians, have seen in the "cultural turn" advanced by Boas and his disciples an identifiable "Jewish element." However, Boas's intellectual and professional focus was never the Jews. On this see, most recently, Frank.

42. On Boas's Jewish identity see Liss.

43. On the impact of Mendelian genetics on Boas's anthropology see Tanner.

44. In his introductory remarks Boas acknowledged Fishberg's early assistance, and the fact that it was Fishberg's investigations "among the New York Jews [that] indicated the practicability of the present investigation." Boas, *Changes in Bodily Form*, 2. Fishberg was also instrumental in Boas's decision to request funding from the Immigration Commission for the 1908–10 study. See the discussion in Stocking, *Race, Culture, and Evolution*, 174–75.

45. Barkan, *The Retreat of Scientific Racism*, 83.

46. Letter to Professor J. W. Jenks, Mar. 23, 1908. Reproduced in Stocking, ed., *The Shaping of American Anthropology*, 202.

47. Ibid., 203.

48. Stocking, *Race, Culture, and Evolution*, 180.

49. Boas, *Changes in Bodily Form*, 2.

50. Barkan, *The Retreat of Scientific Racism*, 84; Stocking, *Race, Culture, and Evolution*.

51. Boas, "Instability of Human Types," 216.

52. Brill, "Insanity Among Jews"; idem, "Adjustment of the Jew." Brill was born in Austria and immigrated to the United States in 1889, where he held positions in psychiatry at Columbia and New York University. He is best known as the first American translator and interpreter of Freud's writings. "A. A. Brill," entry in *Dictionary of American Medical Biography*, 1: 94.

53. Brill, "Adjustment of the Jew," 223–24.

54. Ibid., 225.

55. Ibid., 229–30.

56. Ibid., 231.

57. Myerson, "The 'Nervousness' of the Jew," 65. Myerson at the time held a number of professional positions, including assistant professor of neurology at Tufts College Medical School, and consulting physician in the Psychopathic Department, Boston State Hospital. The historian of American Jewry Andrew Heinze is currently at work on a study of Jews and the development of American psychology. I have relied here in part on his paper "Judaism Confronts Psychology: Abraham Myerson, Joseph Jastrow and the Psychological Reorientation of American Jewish Thought," delivered at the conference on "Jews and the Biological and Social Sciences," Oxford Centre for Hebrew and Jewish Studies, Oxford, England, August 1998.

58. Ibid., 69–70.

59. Ibid., 71.

60. Ibid., 72.

61. Ibid. Elsewhere, Myerson universalized what in this article he had particularized: the intergenerational tensions, and the beneficial effects of assimilation on the second-generation immigrants is generalized to all populations. See, for example, his article "Mental Hygiene and Family Life," 85–86. In addition, see his discussion of the relation between mental health and disease, and urban life in *The Inheritance of Mental Diseases*, 313ff.

62. Myerson, "The 'Nervousness' of the Jew," 65.

63. Bernheimer, "Philadelphia" (section on health), in *Russian Jew*, 314.

64. Ibid., 316.

65. Wirth, *The Ghetto*. For a recent analysis of the work see Hasia Diner's introduction to the republished edition (New Brunswick, N.J.: 1998). All subsequent page references come from the 1928 edition.

66. Wirth, *The Ghetto*, 65–66.

67. Ibid., p. 66.

68. Wirth acknowledged, following Arthur Ruppin's argument, that there is evidence of intermarriage, but the Jew who intermarried was in fact no longer part of the community. The effect or consequence of this on the racial or physical makeup of Jewry was therefore negligible. In Ruppin's words: "The ghetto from the standpoint of population was a relatively closely inbreeding, self-perpetuating group, to such an extent that it may properly be called a closed community. The combination of various features of ghetto existence tended toward the development and perpetuation of a definite type, which to a marked extent persists to the present day, especially in countries where the circumstances of Jewish communal life have remained relatively unchanged, as, for example, in Eastern Europe and the Orient." Ruppin, *The Jews of Today* (1913). Quoted in Wirth, 68.

69. Wirth cited the following authorities: J. Snowman, "Jewish Eugenics," *Jewish Review* 4; Abraham Myerson, "The 'Nervousness' of the Jew," *Mental Hygiene* 4; and I. S. Wechsler, "Nervousness and the Jew," *Menorah Journal* 10, 121.

70. Wirth, 70.

71. Drachsler. For a discussion of Drachsler's ideas about assimilation within the context of American sociological theories at the time see Gordon, chapter 6.

72. Drachsler, 225.

73. See the entry on Fishberg in the *Encyclopedia Judaica*, 6: 1328–29. It is an indication of how quickly Fishberg established himself in New York that in 1904 he earned an entry in the *American Jewish Yearbook*'s "Biographical Sketches." See *American Jewish Yearbook* 6 (1904): 93.

74. In a footnote at the beginning of his 1905 study on the physical anthropology of Eastern European Jews, Fishberg acknowledged the difficulty he had encountered in the past in obtaining "anthropometric measurements of living people." He then thanked Lee K. Frankel, the manager of the United Hebrew Charities of New York, who "afforded me the opportunity to obtain anthropometric measurements in connection with my work as medical examiner of the charities." Fishberg, *Materials*, 5.

75. For more general discussions of the mass Jewish immigration into America,

see Markel, especially chapter 1; Hertzberg, *The Jews in America*, chapter 10; Howe; Higham, *Send These to Me*.

76. See, for example, *Materials*, 139, 141.

77. Previous discussions of Fishberg have focused exclusively on the North American context of his ideas and activities—the conflict over the immigration of Eastern European Jews into the United States in the first decades of the twentieth century; the debate over the health and disease of Jewry; and the relation between this biophysical status and environmental conditions. The most recent, and the fullest, discussion of Fishberg in the American context is in Kraut, *Silent Travelers*, chapter 6.

78. See especially *Die Rassenmerkmale der Juden*.

79. Fishberg, *Jews*, 473. Fishberg's attack on Zionism in this 1911 work was his most sustained denunciation of the movement to be found in his social scientific writings. He did publish an attack in 1906, in Yiddish, under the title *The Perils of the Jewish Nationalist Movement*.

80. Ibid.

81. Fishberg, *Health Problems of the Jewish Poor*, 6.

82. For a discussion of the ubiquity of the idea of neurasthenia at this time in the American context, see Lutz, especially 1–30. Lutz points out that the great power of a disease such as neurasthenia was its ability to represent or symbolize so many different conditions to so many different people. For example, the American physician George Beard, who is credited with having first formulated nervousness in terms of a quintessentially modern phenomenon, saw it as a sign of civility, of refinement. "Nervousness, according to Beard and many others, was therefore a mark of distinction, of class, of status, of refinement. Neurasthenia struck brainworkers but no other kind of laborer. It attacked those, such as artists and connoisseurs, with the most refined sensitivities. It affected only the more 'advanced' races, especially the Anglo-Saxon" (6).

83. Fishberg, *Health Problems of the Jewish Poor*, 5.

84. Ibid., 15. The medicalization of the heder, as part of a broader critique of traditional "ghetto" Jewish life by Jewish reformers, had already emerged in the late 18th century. See Efron, "Images of the Jewish Body: Three Medical Views from the Jewish Enlightenment," *Bulletin of the History of Medicine* 69, no. 3 (1995). On the heder as a source of pathology in Russian-Jewish discourse, see Steven Rappaport, "Heder and Hygiene: Medicalizing a Social Problem," paper delievered at the annual Association of Jewish Studies Conference, Boston, December 1996.

85. Ibid., 15–16.

86. On the Zionist idea of a "new man" see Berkowitz, *Zionist Culture*, ch. 6.

87. Fishberg, *Materials*.

88. According to the historian of anthropology George Stocking Jr., Fishberg's studies on the mutability of bodily shape, including the form of the head—acknowledged by physical anthropologists as the most "stable" of the various parts of the body routinely measured—were instrumental in shaping Franz Boas's ideas on this subject. Between the 1890s and the 1920s Boas published a number of influential articles on immigrants and the significance of environment over race in determining body shape, strength, and size. See Stocking, *Race, Culture, and Evolution*, 175.

89. Fishberg, *Materials*, 39.

90. Allan Chase identifies Ripley as a professor of economics at MIT and Columbia University. But Ripley is remembered as a "raciologist." See Chase, *The Legacy of Malthus*, 96 and passim.

91. Fishberg, *Materials*, 39–46.

92. For instance, Fishberg's interest in chest measurements stemmed in large part from the significance assigned the chest by military recruiters in Europe—including Russia—and by those who sought to prove the Jews physically incapable of serving in the Army, and by extension of fulfilling their duties to state and society. Fishberg began his discussion by noting the connection in the anthropological literature between "girth of the chest" and the Jews' fitness for military duty. He granted that statistics from Europe indicated that Jews were "deficient in this regard," their chest girth not exceeding the 50 percent of their body height taken as normal or healthy. However, Jews in America who had been measured, he noted, did show such an excess of 50 percent, demonstrating that chest girth was affected by "external influences," and "cannot be considered a stable racial character." Ibid., 50–51.

93. Fishberg, "North African Jews," 55.

94. Ibid., 62.

95. Idem, *Jews*, 272.

96. Ibid., 284.

97. Ibid., 506–13. Fishberg did stress in this work that, while some parts or components of the body, like stature and chest size, were directly influenced by environment, others were the direct result almost exclusively of heredity. The most stable traits, such as pigmentation, or eye and hair color, were the product of genetics, not of socioeconomic conditions. But this, too, in Fishberg's view, demonstrated his point about the historical possibility and fact of Jewish assimilation—in this case through intermarriage and conversion.

98. Alan Kraut has pointed this out in his analysis in *Silent Travelers*, 157ff.

99. Fishberg, *Jews*, 179.

100. "As far as our present knowledge of the origin of racial traits can teach us, we know that the milieu cannot change dark hair into blonde, or the reverse, nor can residence in any country transform a hook nose into a snub nose, or a long head become round by a change of climate. Somatic traits are known to be influenced only by heredity." Fishberg, *Jews*, 179.

101. Ibid., 506–11.

102. Ibid., 191.

103. Ibid., 191–94.

104. Ibid., 196–205.

105. Ibid., 205–9. This was an argument Fishberg would continue to make into the 1920s and 1930s. See, for instance, "Intermarriage Between Jews and Christians."

106. Fishberg, *Jews*, 466.

107. Ibid., 520.

108. Ibid.

109. Ibid., 521.

110. Ibid., 470.

111. Ibid., 469, 473. Fishberg's extended attack upon Zionism is contained in the book's penultimate chapter, entitled "Assimilationism versus Zionism."

112. Ibid., 492.

113. Ibid., 479–80.

## Chapter 6

1. On the emergence and development of modern racial science, and on the different intellectual influences upon it, see Stocking, *Race, Culture, and Evolution*; Proctor, "From *Anthropologie* to *Rassenkunde*"; Stocking, *Volksgeist as Method and Ethic*; Weber; Odom; Stepan, *The Idea of Race*.

2. Ruppin, "Begabungsunterschiede christlicher und jüdischer Kinder," 129–30.

3. Of course, race science was also the product of identifiable political, social, and cultural developments within Europe. These factors have been extensively examined in the standard histories of European racial thinking.

4. On this literature see note 10 in the introduction above.

5. The role of photography in the development of modern criminology and eugenics, and the nexus of statistics, anthropology, and iconography, have been analyzed superbly by Sekula; Green. Sander Gilman has analyzed the role played by iconographic representations of blacks and women in racial texts in "The Hottentot and the Prostitute" in *Difference and Pathology*. Mary Cowling has shown how nineteenth-century scientific disciplines such as physiognomy and phrenology found their way into Victorian painting, and reinforced notions about national and ethnic identities. See Cowling. For an analysis of how the racial and medical notion of "degeneration" affected the theory and practice of art in the nineteenth century, see Bade.

6. By the early twentieth century this notion that cranial capacity or brain weight revealed something vital about an individual's or a group's nature was under serious attack. That it was still taken seriously, though, can be seen from the fact that the third issue of the first volume of the *ZfDuStdJ* included an article devoted to the weight of Jewish brains. See R. Weinberg.

7. The notion of continuity of races over time was central, in the view of racial scientists, to the anthropological enterprise. William Edwards, "the father of French Ethnology," and one of the most important figures in European and American raciology, declared in 1841: "We would not have ethnology if the races could not endure for an unlimited time. Obviously this principle is implied in all ethnological works, but it is important that it be proven." Quoted in Blanckaert, 24.

8. Gobineau, 122.

9. Ibid., 123.

10. Samuel George Morton, *Crania Americana*, 1839. Quoted in Stanton, 30.

11. In an article, published in 1864, the British polygenist Alfred Russel Wallace wrote that "the Jews, scattered over the world in the most diverse climates, retain the same characteristic lineaments everywhere; the Egyptian sculptures and paint-

ings show us that, for at least four thousand or five thousand years, the strongly contrasted features of the Negro and the Semitic races have remained altogether unchanged." See Wallace. The most important French anthropologist of the mid-nineteenth century, Paul Topinard, included the following in his general textbook *Anthropologie*: "The law of the permanence of types rests on the principles of heredity. This can be demonstrated with reference to the identity of five- to six-thousand-year-old Egyptian types, as they are represented on the ancient monuments, as well as the Fellahs who still inhabit the banks of the Nile, and through the identity of the Jewish type both then and now." Topinard, 380.

12. Marrus, 10.

13. By no means were conservative or anti-Semitic German thinkers and writers alone in accepting and using racial ideas to give force to their political and social programs. Scholarship on racial science in Germany documents the wide acceptance of racial thinking among individuals and groups all along the political spectrum, well into the 1920s and 1930s. On the use of racial ideas by leftists and centrists, as well as by conservatives in Germany, see Weindling; Proctor, *Racial Hygiene*, chapter 1; Weiss, 193–236.

14. Andree.

15. See, for example, the dissertation of Bernhard Blechmann, published one year after Andree's book appeared, 1–2; Jacobs, "Are Jews Jews?" 509; Fishberg, *Materials*, 6–7. On Andree and his work within the context of German racial science see Efron, *Defenders of the Race*, 21–22.

16. Andree, 24.

17. Ibid., 24–27.

18. Chamberlain, *Die Grundlagen*, 427–29.

19. Sombart, *The Jews and Modern Capitalism*.

20. On the supposed relationship between intellectual and physical traits in racial and anthropological thinking, see the works on the history of physical anthropology and racial science listed in note 1 above.

21. Sombart, *The Jews and Modern Capitalism*, 271.

22. Luschan, "Zur physischen Anthropologie der Juden." For Luschan's biography, including his rejection of anti-Semitism and its relation to his anthropology, see "Luschan, Felix von," *Encyclopedia Judaica* 11: 583. Also see the entry on Luschan in *Jüdische Lexicon* 3: 1252–53.

23. Luschan, "Anthropologische."

24. In the early 1870s, at the behest of the newly constituted German Anthropological Society, Virchow conducted a survey of close to 7 million children, designed to measure color of eyes, hair, and skin, and shape of skull. The survey demonstrated, as George Mosse has written, that "there was no such thing as a pure German or a pure Jewish race." Pure races, Virchow concluded, did not exist, and science could not establish any clear and simple correlation between particular bodily features (color of hair or shape of nose) and particular races. See the discussions in Mosse, *Toward the Final Solution*, 91–92, and Ackerknecht. See as well Poliakov, chapter 11. On the history of the idea of Aryan and Semite see as well the excellent monograph by Olender.

25. See Luschan's argument in "Anthropologische," 95.

26. Luschan, "Zur physischen Anthropologie der Juden," 2.

27. On what follows, see the following works on the history and theory of photography: Freund; Sontag, *On Photography*; Thomas; English; Trachtenberg; Ivins.

28. See, for example, the essays collected in Trachtenberg.

29. Jacobs, "On the Racial Characteristics of Modern Jews."

30. For a brilliant discussion of this process see the essay by Daston and Galison.

31. Jacobs, *Studies in Jewish statistics*, xvi.

32. Composites, according to the historian of photography Allan Sekula, were the product of

a process of successive registration and exposure of portraits in front of a copy camera holding a single plate. Each successive image was given a fractional exposure based on the inverse of the total number of images in the sample. That is, if a composite were to be made from a dozen originals, each would receive one-twelfth of the required total exposure. Thus, individual distinctive features, features that were unshared and idiosyncratic, faded away into the night of underexposure. What remained was the blurred, nervous configuration of those features that were held in common throughout the sample. (Sekula, 368)

33. Ibid., 368.

34. Jacobs, *Studies in Jewish statistics*, xvi.

35. Galton, 1389. Quoted in Sekula, 386, footnote 80.

36. Jacobs, "On the Racial Characteristics of Modern Jews," xxxiii.

37. Ibid., xxxi–xxxii.

38. Ibid., xvii.

39. Ibid.

40. Ibid., liii–liv.

41. Jacobs, "Are Jews Jews?"

42. Ibid., 506–7.

43. Ibid., 508.

44. Fishberg, *The Jews*.

45. Ibid., 139.

46. Ibid., 198.

47. Ibid., 122–23.

48. Ibid., 170, 172, 173.

49. Ibid., 185. The photographs are reproduced in Hart, "Racial Science," 292.

50. Ruppin, "Gegenwartsarbeit," 64. On the impact of racial ideas on Ruppin's sociology of the Jews, see Ruveini. On Ruppin's life and work in general, see Bein, "Arthur Ruppin."

51. Zollschan, "Rassenproblem und Judenfrage," 898.

52. Cf. Barkan; Efron, *Defenders of the Race*.

53. Hess, 52–53.

54. Ibid., 162–63.

55. Ibid., 52.

56. Shlomo Avineri acknowledges the racial element in Hess's thinking, calling aspects of it "embarrassing" today. Yet the import of this aspect is minimized. Avineri stresses Hess's attack on racial ideology and hatred. The passage in which Hess refers to Jewish racial continuity over centuries is quoted, yet left unanalyzed. Avineri does not discuss Hess's polygenist views. See Avineri, *Moses Hess*, 201–8.

57. Hess, 60.

58. Auerbach, "Die jüdische Rassenfrage." Quoted in Efron, *Defenders of the Race*, 139.

59. Judt, *Die Juden als Rasse*. In the following year Judt published an essay, "Die Juden als physische Rasse," which was an abbreviated version of the book, and included many of the same references to iconography. See "Die Juden als physische Rasse."

60. Judt, "Die Juden als physische Rasse," 414–17.

61. Salaman, "Racial Origins of Jewish Types," 164. For a discussion of Salaman's career, including his ideas on Jews and race, see Endelman, "Decline." I want to thank Professor Endelman for allowing me to read the manuscript of this article.

62. Salaman, "Heredity and the Jew"; idem, "Racial Origins of Jewish Types," "Some Notes on the Jewish Problem," "What Has Become of the Philistines?"

63. Salaman, "What Has Become of the Philistines?" 5. A decade and a half earlier Salaman had argued much the same thing: "All the historic evidence would seem to bear out the contention that from the second century till at least the beginning of the nineteenth, the Jewish people (Ashkenazim) in Europe absorbed into their own midst practically no blood from the races with whom they came in contact." "Heredity and the Jew," 277.

64. Flinders Petrie, "Palace of Apries Memphis," *British Sch. Arch. Egypt* 2, plate XXVIII (1909).

65. Salaman, "Heredity and the Jew," 278. A similar argument, based on genetics and iconography, can be found in "Racial Origins of Jewish Types," 172 and passim, and again in "What Has Become of the Philistines?" 7 and passim.

66. Salaman, "Racial Origins of Jewish Types," 174.

67. "Nor will the likeness between this type (the Philistine) and that we are accustomed to in the heroic statuary of the best Greek period be lost sight of." Ibid., 179.

68. Endelman, "Decline."

69. Ibid., 15.

70. Ibid., 16.

71. Salaman made these points within an explicit discussion of Zionism and Palestine in his book *Palestine Reclaimed*. See Endelman, "Decline," 17–18.

72. Salaman, "Racial Origins of Jewish Types," 180. Salaman's ideas about race, genetics, and Jewish identity can also be found in the more explicit or overt articles he published on Zionism. See, for instance, his analysis of the Jews' "genetic" proclivity for agricultural work, and the import of this for the Zionist project in *The Prospects of Jewish Colonization in Palestine*.

73. Salaman, "What Has Become of the Philistines?" 17.

74. Ruppin, *Die Juden der Gegenwart*, 1911, 263–76.

75. Ibid., 272–73.

76. One can see this already in a book review Ruppin published in 1905: *ZfDuStdJ* 1, no. 5 (1905): 16, of an anthropological study of Polish Jewry. Ruppin praised the work, but faulted the author for not enlarging the selection of photographs.

77. Ruppin, diary entry, April 13, 1923, in *Arthur Ruppin: Memoirs, Diaries, Letters*, 205.

78. Writing about his voyage by ship to Alexandria, Ruppin recorded the following in his diary: "There were about 100 immigrants on board and also a group of Italian Zionists, whom I photographed for my collection of Jewish racial types" (Sept. 6, 1924, Jerusalem). See also his entry for Nov. 23, 1925: "As a precursor of my book on the Jewish race and in the meantime to make use of my photographs of Palestine Jews, I am thinking of publishing *Jüdische Typen in Palästina* [Jewish Types in Palestine] with 200 photographs (anthropological—face and profile) and a very brief text." Ibid., 214, 220.

79. Ruppin, *Die Soziologie der Juden*. Ruppin's desire to include visual images of Jews in his work was spurred by his encounter with the work of the Jena anthropologist and advocate of Aryan supremacy Hans F. K. Günther. In a diary entry from January 1930, Ruppin noted: "A few weeks ago I found in a Tel Aviv bookstore the recently published book by Hans F. K. Günther, *Rassenkunde des jüdischen Volkes*. He includes many ideas and photographs of ancient images that I want to put into my book. With luck, the racial question will occupy a small part of the work." Ruppin, *Tagebücher, Briefe, Erinnerungen*, 422. Ruppin corresponded with Günther during the 1930s, sending him a copy of his own work on the Jews, and in 1933 met with him in Berlin. On Günther's extreme racialism, and on his involvement in the Nazi regime, see Weindling, 311; 462–84.

80. Ruppin, *Die Soziologie der Juden*, 24.

81. Racial scientists took the designations "Sephardic" and "Ashkenazic" as racial categories, and not merely as indicators of geographic or cultural differences. The issue of Sephardic and Ashkenazic racial characteristics was central to the debate over Jewish "racial origins and unity." See the discussion in Efron, "Scientific Racism."

82. In addition to the works discussed in this chapter, see Feist; Günther.

83. Judt, *Die Juden als Rasse*, 1.

84. In particular, the invention of the "halftone" process greatly facilitated the mass reproduction of images in newspapers and books. On this see N. Harris; English, 4.

85. Sekula; Green.

## Chapter 7

1. Segall, "Wirtschaftliche," 49.

2. For early statements regarding the importance of economic statistics for Jewish social science see the following: Jacobs, *Studies in Jewish statistics*, 22 and

passim; "Fragen der körperlichen, geistigen, und wirtschaftlichen"; Nordau, "V. Kongressrede,"125, and foreword to *Jüdische Statistik*, 4. While these early Jewish social scientists may have cast themselves as pioneers in the investigation of Jewish economic life, there was in fact a tradition reaching back into the eighteenth century at least. What changes, of course, is not the object of research, but the methods of investigation and the purposes to which this knowledge was put. On earlier efforts at a scholarly understanding of Jewish economic life see Penslar, "Origins."

3. See the foreword to and the comments of Nossig in *Jüdische Statistik*. For further examples see Pasmanik; Lawin; Segall, "Anteil"; Kaplun-Kogan, "Jüdische Kreditgesellschaften"; I. Koralnik, "Die jüdische Arbeiterschaft in Osteuropa."

4. The relation between social scientific knowledge and social policy and administration has been dealt with by others, most particularly by Derek Penslar. See his *Zionism and Technocracy*; idem, "Philanthropy, the 'Social Question'"; Troen, 20.

5. On the import of economic imagery and themes in modern anti-Semitic discourse see Massing; Bein, "Der jüdische Parasit; Pulzer, *The Rise of Political Anti-Semitism in Germany and Austria*.

6. A number of these studies appeared in Nossig, *Jüdische Statistik*. See the second section, "Statistische Arbeiten jüdischer Organisationen," 168–232. Penslar has recently discussed some of this social scientific literature within the context of an analysis of German Jewish philanthropy and social reform. See his discussion in "Philanthropy, the 'Social Question'."

7. See, for example, Lawin; Fishberg, *Jews*, 362ff.

8. In an 1898 survey of the socioeconomic condition of Galician Jewry, respondents were asked to consider, inter alia, the following questions: "What are the causes of the economic distress of Galician Jewry?" "Have Jewish occupational conditions changed over the past decades, and has this change been favorable or unfavorable?" "Through which means could the general, and together with this specifically Jewish occupational relations be substantially improved?" See Fleischer, 210–11.

9. Alphonse Blum, quoted in Penslar, "Philanthropy, the 'Social Question'," 71. Interest in furthering the economic redistribution of Jewry in the Diaspora could be found as well among Zionists. For instance, Julius Moses, a Mannheim physician and cultural Zionist, called attention in 1903 to the occupational restructuring proceeding among rural Baden Jews. The movement away from traditional Jewish economic activities such as cattle trading and toward "productive labor" such as artisan and crafts work was, in Moses's view, a positive development. He called for stepped-up propaganda within the Jewish community in order to push Jews at a young age into "productive" avenues of the economy. Yet such measures of improvement were, at best, temporary solutions. See Moses.

10. On the discourse of Jewish economic degeneration and its role in the early debates over emancipation see Sorkin, *Transformation*.

11. Fishberg, *Jews*, 368.

12. Ibid., 369.

13. Ibid.

14. Fleischer, 229–31.

15. Segall, "Die Entwicklung der jüdischen Bevölkerung in München 1875–1905." The study was published two years later under the same name in Berlin.

16. Ibid., 29–30.

17. Segall, "Wirtschaftliche"; idem, "Anteil."

18. "Anteil," 50.

19. Ibid., 53.

20. Ibid.

21. Segall, "Wirtschaftliche," 84. Segall made the polemical component to his economic research clear in his 1912 article as well: "There is a constant urge to know how many Jews are high public officials, how many are judges, lawyers, and physicians. One hears repeatedly from the anti-Semitic camp, which accepts the notion that the Jews are the representatives of capitalism, claims that jurisprudence, medicine, and the press have been judaized. On these grounds alone it is necessary to examine more closely occupational categories and activities." "Anteil," 49.

22. "Wirtschaftliche," 51.

23. "While the Jews constituted 4.76% of the Berlin population in general, they made up 24.60% of the gymnasium students in 1906, 18.70% of the Realgymnasium students, 11.40% of those in the Oberrealschulen, 7.10% of the Realschulen, and 30% of the girls' schools." Ibid., 55.

24. Ibid.

25. Ibid., 83. To accentuate what he called the "health" of the German Jewish population, Segall included a brief discussion—seemingly peripheral to a discussion of economic activity—of Jewish military service among university students. Ibid., 56.

26. Ibid., 84.

27. Ibid., 50.

28. Segall responded in particular to an article entitled "Confession and Occupation" by the German Christian socialist and economist Friedrich Naumann. On Naumann and the significance of empirical social science for German religious organizations at the time see Oberschall, *Empirical Social Research in Germany*, 27–36.

29. Segall, "Wirtschaftliche," 78.

30. Ibid.

31. Ibid., 50.

32. Penslar, "Philanthropy, the 'Social Question'," 58–60.

33. Oelsner, "The Place of the Jews"; idem, "Wilhelm Roscher's Theory"; Weinryb; W. Mosse; Mendes-Flohr, "Werner Sombart's: *The Jews and Modern Capitalism*."

34. The analyses of late-nineteenth and early-twentieth-century German political economists were part of a longer tradition of social scientific analysis of Jews and money. The key figure in this regard was, of course, Karl Marx, who produced two essays on the topic. Yet Jewish social scientists did not take up Marx's arguments directly; rather, Sombart, who began his career as a Marxist and who appropriated many of Marx's ideas, was the main focus of their attention. So it is with Sombart's ideas that I deal here. For a discussion of Marx, Jews, and capitalism, and of the history of the commentary on those essays, see Carlebach.

35. Roscher, "Die Stellung der Juden im Mittelalter." Citations here refer to the English translation of this work.

36. Ibid., 22.

37. Sombart's first major statement on the Jews and capitalism appeared in *Der moderne Kapitalismus* (Leipzig: Duncker and Humblot, 1902). In 1911 he devoted an entire work, *Die Juden und das Wirtschaftsleben*, to the subject. On Sombart on Jews and capitalism see Mendes-Flohr, "Werner Sombart's: *The Jews and Modern Capitalism*"; Herf, chapter 6; Carlebach, 214–34; Mitzman. On Sombart's anti-Semitism and his relationship with National Socialism see A. Harris.

38. See Sombart's discussion of "the race problem" in *The Jews and Modern Capitalism*, 263–98.

39. Some historians have expressed surprise and bewilderment over the legitimacy granted Sombart's ideas at the time. On this see the comments of Mendes-Flohr, "Werner Sombart's: *The Jews and Modern Capitalism*."

40. According to Schorsch "[i]n Sombart, the Zionists did not see an anti-Semite, but a Christian scholar who had identified himself openly with Zionism. His endorsement was welcomed as an important vindication." See *Jewish Reactions*, 196–97. For a sense of the public reception of Sombart's ideas see the articles in *Die Welt*: "Bedeutung"; "Befähigung"; "Judaismus und Kapitalismus"; "Oppenheimer über Sombart."

41. Ruppin, *Die Juden der Gegenwart* (1911), 47.

42. Max Weber, while he analyzed ancient Judaism in historical economic and sociological terms, nonetheless rejected the notion that capitalism existed as such before the seventeenth century. Weber's views of Jews and Judaism played a far less significant role in the debate over Jews and capitalism among Jewish social scientists at the time than did those of Roscher, Sombart, and others. I therefore do not take them up here.

43. Pinkus, *Die Moderne Judenfrage*; idem, *Studien zur Wirtschaftsstellung der Juden*. Pinkus's source for this assertion was the work of the eminent biblical scholar Franz Delitzsch, *Jewish Commercial Life in the Time of Jesus* (1875). For a more extended view of Pinkus's attitude toward Sombart see Pinkus, "Werner Sombarts Stellung zur Judenfrage."

44. Pinkus, *Studien zur Wirtschaftsstellung der Juden*, 3–4.

45. Oppenheimer, "Anfänge des jüdischen Kapitalismus," 323. Oppenheimer was both an important European sociologist and a figure who contributed to the theory of Zionist land settlement in the early part of the twentieth century. On his role in the Zionist movement see Penslar, *Zionism and Technocracy*, chapter 3.

46. Ruppin, *Die Juden der Gegenwart* (1911), 216.

47. This link between the economic and criminal pursuits of Jews is examined above in chapter 4. On the idea of "Jewish intelligence" in general at this time, see Gilman, *Smart Jews*.

48. Ruppin, *Die Juden der Gegenwart* (1911), 218.

49. Zollschan, *Rassenproblem*, 353–54.

50. "Bedeutung," 1040–41.

51. Berkowitz.

52. Pinkus, *Studien zur Wirtschaftsstellung der Juden*, 5–10.

53. Jacob Lestschinsky, for instance, detected no notable shift in the occupational distribution of Eastern European Jewry between the years 1897 and 1925. See the summary of Lestschinsky's findings in I. Koralnik, "Die jüdische Arbeiterschaft in Osteuropa."

54. Pasmanik, 27.

55. Ibid., 28.

56. Lestschinsky, "Zur Psychologie der jüdischen Auswanders," 78–79.

57. Theilhaber, *Der Untergang der deutschen Juden*, 1921, 138.

58. Entry, Ruppin's memoirs, Aug. 28, 1898. Quoted in Penslar, *Zionism and Technocracy*, 89.

59. The categories are derived from the work of Ferdinand Tönnies, *Gemeinschaft und Gesellschaft* (Leipzig: Furs, 1887).

60. Ruppin, *Die Juden der Gegenwart* (1911), 6.

61. Ibid., 10.

62. Wassermann, "Juden."

63. Ibid., 269.

64. Similiar arguments were made by Zionist social scientists such as Max Besser and Rafael Becker. See the discussion in Biale, 179–82, and particularly the footnotes, 284–85.

65. Theilhaber, *Der Untergang der deutschen Juden*, 1921, 147.

66. See, for example, Ruppin's discussion of the interdependence of economic independence—through agriculture—and cultural and national regeneration in *Die Juden der Gegenwart* (1911), chapter 15.

67. On this see Berkowitz, especially chapter 6.

68. "Zur Einführung."

69. Zollschan, "Tendencies of Economic Development Among the Jewish People," in *Jewish Questions*, 55.

70. Ruppin, *Die Juden der Gegenwart* (1911), chapter 3.

71. Ruppin, "Die wirtschaftlichen Kämpfe der Juden," 82.

72. See, for example, Horowitz, "The Economic Factor and its Influence"; idem, "Zionism through an Historical Economic Perspective"; idem, "The Economic Problem and its Place in Our National Movement." On these, see Gutwein. In his later writings, however, Horowitz shifted his position, and adopted Roscher's optimistic view about capitalism's power to produce the conditions for Jewish integration into Europe. On Horowitz's economic and Zionist theory see Gutwein.

73. On this see Manor, and the biographical entry on Lestschinsky in the *Encyclopedia Judaica* II: 50–51.

74. Wassermann, "Juden und das deutsche Wirtschaftsleben," 273.

75. Zollschan, "Tendencies of Economic Development Among the Jewish People," in *Jewish Questions*, 64.

76. Ibid., 66.

## Conclusion

1. The phrase "trust in numbers" is taken from T. Porter, *Trust in Numbers*.

2. Stepan and Gilman, 188.

3. The list, in fact, is fairly extensive. The following few examples should suffice to make the point: Auerbach, "Die jüdische Rassenfrage"; Weissenberg, "Beitrag zur Anthropologie der Juden"; Fishberg, *Materials*. Joseph Jacobs read his paper "On the Racial Characteristics of Modern Jews" before the Royal Anthropological Institute in London on Feb. 24, 1885. It was published in the *Journal of the Anthropological Institute*, in Aug. 1885, and again in his *Jewish statistics*. According to Jacobs, he also presented versions of a paper on "The Comparative Distribution of Jewish Ability" to the Aberdeen Meeting of the British Association, and to the Royal Anthropological Institute, in 1886. See "Appendix B" to Jacobs, *Studies in Jewish statistics*, xli. S. Rosenbaum delivered a long paper on the statistics of the Jews of the United Kingdom to the Royal Statistical Society in June 1905; the essay was then published in the *Journal of the Royal Statistical Society*. See S. Rosenbaum. Felix Theilhaber's essay, *Schädigung*, won first prize in the *Gesellschaft für Rassenhygiene*'s 1913 essay contest on the import of environmental factors for racial traits.

4. See, for example, the reviews of the following Jewish social scientific works, all of which appear in the official statistical publication of the German Empire, *Allgemeine Statistisches Archiv*. The following volume numbers, years, and page numbers refer to the specific editions of the journal in which the reviews of the works appear. The Zionist social scientist Davis Trietsch's statistical study *Juden und Deutsche* (1915) 9: 746–47; Felix Theilhaber's *Der Untergang der deutschen Juden*, vol. 13, 1921/22, 334–35; vol. 15 (1919) of the *Zeitschrift für Demographie und Statistik der Juden*, vol. 12 (1920): 364–65; Arthur Ruppin, *Die Soziologie der Juden*, 1931, 21: 475–76; Heinrich Silbergleit, *Die Bevölkerungs- und Berufsverhältnisse der Juden im deutschen Reich*, 1931, 21: 616–17.

5. Rost, "Der Selbstmord bei den Juden."

6. See the notes to chapter 13 in Sombart, *The Jews and Modern Capitalism*.

7. Baur, Fischer, and Lenz. The work, which Robert Proctor identifies as "the most important German textbook on genetics and racial hygiene of the interwar years," went through five editions by 1940. On Baur, Fischer, and Lenz and the significance of their book, see Proctor, *Racial Hygiene*, 46–63; Weindling, 330 and passim.

8. Baur, Fischer, and Lenz, 132, 202.

9. Ibid., footnote 1, 674.

10. Ibid., 693.

11. Although he reproduced many of the negative images about the "Jewish body" found elsewhere, Ripley offered an ambivalent analysis of the condition of modern Jewry. Most important, he argued that in the end the Jews were not a "race" per se, at least not a pure race. Hence, while he used the work of Joseph Jacobs, he rejected Jacobs's argument about the purity of the Jewish race, and argued a line that would very soon be taken up and advocated by Maurice Fishberg.

12. Coon, 432–646.

13. See Pearson, "On the Inheritance of the Mental and Moral Characters"; idem, "On Jewish-Gentile Relationships"; Pearson and Moul; Morant and Samson. On Pearson and Morant and Samson, and on the context of their studies, see Barkan, 151–62.

14. Philippson, "Vorbemerkung," in *Neuste Geschichte des jüdischen Volkes*.

15. Kreppel, ix.

16. I. Cohen, ix–x.

17. See Heuberger; Gillerman.

18. Gillerman, 197.

19. On the *Zentralwohlfahrtstelle* see Lotan; Heuberger.

20. See the list of participants in the conference on population policy sponsored by the *Zentral* in February 1929 in Berlin, in *Jüdische Bevölkerungspolitik* 7; Heuberger, 72.

21. Segall, "Statistik im Dienste."

22. The national conference devoted to Jewish population policy, convened by Jewish social work organizations in Berlin in 1929, highlighted these concerns. See the discussion in Gillerman.

23. Gillerman, 173–74.

24. Troen.

25. The term "re-imagining" is taken from Troen's article, op. cit. Troen argues that this process began in the 1920s and 1930s, with the British mandatory period. As my remarks below indicate, I disagree with this view.

26. See, for example, Mühsam; Sandler, "Die Gesundheitsverhältnisse Palästinas"; "Zur Frage einer medizinischen Hochschule in Palästina"; "Die Tätigkeit der jüdischen Ärztegesellschaft Palästinas"; Mayer. For an analysis of the link between Jewish nationalism and health in the *Yishuv* see Sufian.

27. Penslar, *Zionism and Technocracy*, 3.

28. Ibid., 102.

29. These were collected into a book and published in 1936 under the title *Drei Jahrzehnten in Palästina*, translated as *Three Decades of Palestine: Speeches and Papers on the Upbuilding of the Jewish National Home*.

30. In the late 1910s and 1920s, when these and other essays and speeches were originally conceived and disseminated, this sort of social Darwinist and racialist language was still not identified almost exclusively with right-wing, anti-Semitic groups. By 1936, of course, the invocation of terms such as "racial Jews" (which Nazi theoreticians, including Nazi social scientists, were already using), and the call for a natural selection of immigrants based on racial typologies, was a bit more problematic. Ruppin, one might say, was sixty years old in 1936, and, more or less, "set in his intellectual ways." Nonetheless, as I have argued in a number of places in this book, the ubiquity of this sort of language in Ruppin's, as well as in other Jewish social scientists', writings testifies to the normative—if not the uncontested—nature of these ideas.

31. See the chapter titled "Die Juden-Statistik" in Aly and Roth.

32. On the main institutes of research on Jewry set up during the Third Reich see Weinreich. Much more research needs to be done on these institutes, and on Nazi scholarship on Jews in general. As Alan Steinweis has recently noted, "surprisingly little has been done to augment Weinreich's *Hitler's Professors*, published over fifty years ago." Steinweis, "The Library," 27.

33. These works are discussed in Weinreich, chapters 1–2.

34. I have dealt with these issues at greater length in "The Power of Numbers: Nazi Scholarship, Jewish Scholarship, and Questions of Evidence," paper delivered

at the conference "Intellectual History and Practice," University of California, Berkeley, Oct. 2–3, 1998.

35. Institut zum Studium der Judenfrage, *Die Juden in Deutschland*, 22.

36. Anonymous, 10–11.

37. Steinweis, "Appropriation."

38. Seraphim, 9.

39. For example, in a 1936 speech commemorating the 550th anniversary of the university, University of Heidelberg professor of philosophy Ernst Krieck expressed, albeit ponderously, the belief that: "Each Volk in each period must form its life according to its own law and fate, and to this law of its own, scholarship, with all other spheres of life, is also subject." Ernst Krieck, *Das nationalsozialistische Deutschland und die Wissenschaft* (Hamburg, 1936). Quoted in Weinreich, 21.

40. Hilberg; Aly and Roth.

41. Reproduced in Friedlander and Milton, 128–31.

42. Tartakower, *Ha-Chevrah ha-Yehudit*, 9–10.

43. Barkan, especially part III, "Politics."

44. See Boas, "This Nordic Nonsense"; idem, *Aryans and Non-Aryans*; Fishberg, "Aryan and Semite." And see the discussion by Barkan, 279–340.

45. Barkan, 318–25.

46. Ruppin, *The Jewish Fate and Future*, 11–24.

47. Blau, "Die Entwicklung der jüdischen Bevölkerung."

48. Blau, "The Jew As Sexual Criminal."

49. Dinur, Tartakower, and Lestschinsky.

50. Herskovits.

51. Ibid., 1166–68.

52. For an overview of Jewish social historical writing see Hyman.

53. Baron, "Emphases in Jewish History."

54. Ibid., 30.

55. The article appeared in 1933: Baron, "Ochlosay Yisrael be'yamay ha-Melachim."

56. Baron, "Emphases in Jewish History," 30.

57. Baron, *Contemporary Relevance of History*, 42–43.

58. In footnote 60 Baron did cite a work on the Jewish racial question by David Farbstein, *Die Stellung der Juden zur Rassen- und Fremdenfrage* (Zurich, 1939). Although Baron did not mention this, Farbstein was an original member of the planning committee for the Organization of Jewish statistics.

59. Baron, *Contemporary Relevance of History*, 61.

60. Bloom.

61. Baron, "Modern Capitalism and Jewish Fate."

62. Ibid., 131.

63. Lurie, "On the Use of the Term 'Non-Jewish,'" 79.

64. While Lurie found very little of worth in Jewish statistics as they existed at the time, he did not dismiss the discipline outright. Rather, he called for a more nuanced definition of "non-Jew," which would then allow meaningful comparisons between Jews and other populations to be made. The editors of *Jewish Social Studies* ("A Rejoinder," *Jewish Social Studies* 2 [1940]: 83–84) felt it necessary to respond

to Lurie's article. They agreed that his points were "theoretically unassailable," but insisted that if his argument were taken to its logical conclusion, this "would practically rule out all social statistical information." They did not believe this was a viable alternative, and reminded their readers that "many phases of Jewish social studies are in their scientific infancy. It is easy—too easy—to throw out the infant as not being able to do a full-grown man's work. But it is more useful, although, alas, more difficult, to help the infant to grow to maturity."

65. E. Rosenbaum, "Some Reflections."

66. Ibid., 311.

67. Ibid., 314.

68. Wertheimer, "German Policy and Jewish Politics," 553. For recent examples see Stanislawski; Joselit, especially the appendix, 173–75.

69. Wertheimer, "German Policy and Jewish Politics," 554.

70. Adler-Rudel. But Adler-Rudel also built his study on the statistics derived from prewar Jewish social science research. In addition to the numerous examples found in his best-known book, see his article on East European Jewish workers in Germany, published in the *Leo Baeck Institute Yearbook* 2, 1957. Adler-Rudel began by referring to Klara Eschelbacher's 1920 article on East European Jewish immigration to Berlin, published in the *Zeitschrift für Demographie und Statistik der Juden*.

71. Ismar Schorsch, for instance, relied heavily on Adler-Rudel's numbers for his discussion of East European immigrants in Germany. Schorsch, *Jewish Reactions*, 163 and passim.

72. Jewish historians, it ought to be pointed out, are far from alone in taking this sort of uncritical approach to the census and statistical data from the past. As Richard Steckel has written: "With a few notable exceptions, scholars have given surprisingly little attention to the quality of census data." On this, and for a general discussion of the problems involved for historians in the use of censuses, see Steckel. For other general critical discussions of the uses of statistical data by social scientists see Greenhalgh; Hindess.

73. For examples of the utilization of the 1897 census by early Jewish social scientists see the articles related to Eastern Europe in Nossig, *Jüdische Statistik*.

74. Schorsch, *Jewish Reactions*, 163–65, footnotes on 254–55.

75. In addition to the book on German anti-Semitism, see Schorsch's introductory essay, "Ideology and History."

76. Rozenblit.

77. Ibid., 16, and 214, footnote 16.

78. Honigmann.

79. Ibid., 5.

80. Further on in the study Honigmann also drew directly from these early statistical studies, including the 1903 work *Jüdische Statistik*, and Blau's 1907 study on conversion. Honigmann, 22–23, 29.

81. In *Vanishing Diaspora*, for instance, Bernard Wasserstein wrote that his inspiration derived "from the example of the first generation of Jewish sociologists, demographers, and contemporary historians such as Arthur Ruppin, Jacob Lestchinsky, and Emmanuel Ringelbaum." Wasserstein, *Vanishing Diaspora*, xv. In a review of the book, however, Sander Gilman called Wasserstein "another Theil-

haber," since Wasserstein saw only distress and decay when he looked at contemporary European Jewry. See Gilman, "Review," 1153. Robert Wistrich ("Do the Jews Have a Future?"), on the other hand, produced an argument about Jewish decline and the Diaspora that echoes that of Ruppin, yet makes no mention of these earlier debates.

82. Heinze.

83. Sarna, 56.

# Bibliography

Ackerknecht, Erwin H. *Rudolf Virchow: Doctor, Statesman, Anthropologist*. Madison: University of Wisconsin Press, 1953.

Adams, Mark B. *The Wellborn Science: Eugenics in Germany, France, Brazil and Russia*. Oxford: Oxford University Press, 1990.

Adler-Rudel, Shalom. *Ostjuden in Deutschland 1880–1940*. Tübingen: J. C. B. Mohr, 1959.

A. K. "Der Zionismus im Lichte von Staats- und Gesellschaftslehre." *Die jüdische Presse* 31 (1900).

Almog, Shmuel. "Alfred Nossig: A Reappraisal." *Studies in Zionism* 4, no. 7 (1983): 1–29.

———. "'Judaism as Illness': Antisemitic Stereotype and Self-Image." *History of European Ideas*, 13, no. 6 (1991): 793–804.

———. "The Racial Motif in Renan's Attitude towards Judaism and the Jews." In Shmuel Almog, ed. *Antisemitism Through the Ages*, 255–78. Oxford: Pergamon Press, 1988.

———. *Zionism and History*. Trans. Ina Friedman. New York: St. Martin's Press, 1987.

Alony. "Die ökonomische Gesellschaft in Palästina." *ZfDuStdJ* 1, nos. 3/4 (new series; 1924): 85–90.

Aly, Götz, and Karl Roth. *Die Restlose Erfassung: Volkszählen, Identifizieren, Aussondern im Nationalsozialismus*. Berlin: Rotbuch Verlag, 1984.

Anderson, Benedict. *Imagined Communities*. Rev. ed. London: Verso, 1991.

Anderson, Olive. *Suicide in Victorian and Edwardian England*. Oxford: Clarendon Press, 1987.

Andree, Richard. *Zur Volkskunde der Juden*. Bielefeld: Velhagen & Klasing, 1881.

Angress, Werner T. "The German Army's "Judenzählung" of 1916: Genesis—Consequences—Significance." *Leo Baeck Institute Yearbook* 23 (1978): 117–37.

Anonymous. *Die Wanderung und Verbreitung der Juden in der Welt*. Essen: Küster Verlag, 1938.

"Antiquus." "Jüdische Statistik." *Die jüdische Presse* 34, no. 31 (1903): 338–40.

Aschheim, Steven. *Brothers and Strangers: The East European Jew in German and German-Jewish Consciousness*. Madison: University of Wisconsin Press, 1982.

——. "The East European Jew and German Jewish Identity." *Studies in Contemporary Jewry* 1 (1984): 3–5.

Auerbach, Elias. "Die jüdische Rassenfrage." *Archiv für Rassen- und Gesellschaftsbiologie* 4, no. 3 (1907): 332–61.

——. "Rassenmischungen der Juden." *Jüdische Rundschau* 12, no. 11 (1907): 110–14.

Avineri, Shlomo. *The Making of Modern Zionism: The Intellectual Origins of the Jewish State*. New York: Basic Books, 1981.

——. *Moses Hess, Prophet of Communism and Zionism*. New York: New York University Press, 1985.

Bacharach, Walter Zwi. "Jews in Confrontation with Racist Antisemitism, 1879–1933." *Leo Baeck Institute Yearbook* 25 (1980): 197–219.

——. "Ignaz Zollschan's 'Rassentheorie.'" In Walter Gran, ed., *Jüdische Integration und Identität in Deutschland und Österreich, 1848–1918*, 179–90. Tel Aviv: University of Tel Aviv Press, 1984.

Bade, Patrick. "Art and Degeneration: Visual Icons of Corruption." In J. Edward Chamberlain and Sander Gilman, eds., *Degeneration: The Dark Side of Progress*, 220–40. New York: Columbia University Press, 1985.

Baldwin, Peter. "Liberalism, Nationalism, and Degeneration: The Case of Max Nordau." *Central European History* 13, no. 2 (1980): 99–120.

Barkai, Avraham. *Jüdische Minderheit und Industrialisierung: Demographie, Berufe, und Einkommen der Juden in Westdeutschland 1850–1914*. Tübingen: J. C. B. Mohr, 1988.

Barkan, Elazar. *The Retreat of Scientific Racism*. Cambridge, England: Cambridge University Press, 1992.

Baron, Salo. *Contemporary Relevance of History*. New York: Columbia University Press, 1986.

——. "Ochlosay Yisrael be'yamay ha-Melachim." In Avigdor Aptovitser and Zechariah Schvartz, eds., *Ma'amarim le'zichron Rav Zvi Peretz Chayes*, 76–136. Vienna: Hotsa'at Keren le-Zichron Alexander Kohut, 1933.

——. "Emphases in Jewish History." *Jewish Social Studies* 1, no. 1 (1939): 15–38.

——. "Modern Capitalism and Jewish Fate." *The Menorah Journal* 30, no. 2 (summer 1942): 116–38.

Barrows, Susanna. "After the Commune: Alcoholism, Temperance, and Literature in the Early Third Republic." In John M. Merriman, ed., *Consciousness and Class Experience in Nineteenth Century Europe*, 205–18. New York: Holmes and Meier, 1979.

Baur, Erwin, Eugen Fischer, and Fritz Lenz. *Grundriss der menschlichen Erblichkeitslehre und Rassenhygiene*. Munich: 1921. Trans. as *Human Heredity*, from the 3rd German edition, by Eden Paul and Cedar Paul. New York: Macmillan, 1931.

"Die Bedeutung der Juden für die moderne Wirtschaftsleben." *Die Welt* 13, no. 47 (1909): 1040–41.

"Die Befähigung der Juden zum Kapitalismus." *Die Welt* 13, no. 49 (1909): 1087–88.

Behre, Otto. *Geschichte der Statistik in Brandenburg-Preussen bis zur Grundung des Königlichen Statistischen Bureaus*. Berlin: C. Heymann, 1905.

Bein, Alex. "Arieh Leib Motzkin: A Biographical Sketch." In Alex Bein, ed., *Sefer Motzkin*, 32–116. Jerusalem: Hahanhlah ha-Tsiyonit ve-Hanholat ha-Congress ha-Yehudi ha-Olami, 1938.

———. "Arthur Ruppin: The Man and His Work." *Leo Baeck Institute Yearbook* 17 (1972): 117–41.

———. "Der jüdische Parasit: Bemerkungen zur Semantik der Judenfrage." *Vierteljahreshefte für Zeitgeschichte* 13, no. 2 (1965): 121–49.

"Beitrag von München." *Die Welt* 8, no. 13 (1904): 11.

Ben-Sasson, Haim Hillel. "The Middle Ages." In Haim Hillel Ben-Sasson, ed., *A History of the Jewish People*, 385–723. Cambridge, Mass.: Harvard University Press, 1976.

Berkowitz, Michael. *Zionist Culture and West European Jewry Before the First World War*. Cambridge, England: Cambridge University Press, 1993.

Bernheimer, Charles, ed. *The Russian Jew in the United States*. Philadelphia: J. C. Winston, 1905.

Bertisch, Abraham. "A Study of the Political-Economic Philosophy of Arthur Ruppin and His Role in the Economic Development of the Zionist Settlement in Palestine from 1907–1943." Ph.D. diss. New York University, 1980.

Biale, David. *Eros and the Jews*. New York: Basic Books, 1992.

Billings, John Shaw. "Vital Statistics of the Jews in the United States." *Census Bulletin*, no. 19 (Dec. 30, 1890): 3–23.

———. *Zwei Vorträge über Zionismus*. Berlin: H. Schildberger, 1898.

Birnbaum, Natan. "Jüdische Statistik und ihr Wert." *Ost und West* 2, no. 2 (1902): 334–36.

Birnbaum, Pierre, and Ira Katznelson, eds. *Paths of Emancipation: Jews, States, and Citizenship*. Princeton: Princeton University Press, 1995.

Black, Eugene. *The Social Politics of Anglo-Jewry 1880–1920*. Oxford: Basil Blackwell, 1988.

Blanckaert, Claude. "On the Origins of French Ethnology: William Edwards and the Doctrine of Race." In George Stocking, Jr., ed., *Bones, Bodies, Behavior: Essays on Biological Anthropology*, 18–55. Madison: University of Wisconsin Press, 1988.

Blau, Bruno. "Die bisherigen Leistungen und zukünftigen Aufgaben des Bureaus für Statistik der Juden." In *Statistik der Juden: Eine Sammelschrift*, 152–71. Berlin: Bureau für Statistik der Juden, 1917.

———. "Die Entwicklung der jüdischen Bevölkerung." Manuscript (M.A. 138.585) in the Leo Baeck Institute, New York, 1950.

———. "The Jew As Sexual Criminal." *Jewish Social Studies* 12 (1951): 321–24.

———. "Die jüdische Statistik." *Die Welt* 12, nos. 8 and 9 (1908): 7–8 (no. 8); 5–6 (no. 9).

———. "Sociology and Statistics of the Jews." *Historia Judaica* 11, no. 2 (1949): 145–62.

Blechmann, Bernhard. *Ein Beitrag zur Anthropologie der Juden*. Dorpat: Wilhelm Just, 1882.

Bloom, Harold. *The Anxiety of Influence: A Theory of Poetry*. New York: Oxford University Press, 1973.

Boas, Franz. *Aryans and Non-Aryans*. New York: Information and Service Associates, n.d.

——. *Changes in Bodily Form of Descendants of Immigrants*. New York: Columbia University Press, 1912.

——. "The Instability of Human Types." Reproduced in George Stocking, ed., *The Shaping of American Anthropology 1883–1911. A Franz Boas Reader*. New York: Basic Books, 1974.

——. Letter to Professor J. W. Jenks, March 23, 1908. Reproduced in George Stocking, ed., *The Shaping of American Anthropology 1883–1911. A Franz Boas Reader*, 214–18. New York: Basic Books, 1974.

——. "This Nordic Nonsense." *Forum* (October 1925).

Böhm, Adolf. "Eine neue Grundlegung des Zionismus." *Die Welt* 15, no. 40 (1911): 1053–56.

——. *Die Zionistische Bewegung*. Berlin: Welt-Verlag, 1922.

——. "Zollschans Werk." *Die Welt* 14, no. 28 (1910): 678–79.

Brenner, Michael. *The Renaissance of Jewish Culture in Weimar Germany*. New Haven, Conn.: Yale University Press, 1996.

Breslauer, Bernhard. *Die Abwanderung der Juden aus der Provinz Posen*. Berlin: Verband der deutschen Juden, 1909.

——. *Die Zurücksetzung der Juden im Justizdienst*. Berlin: Verband der deutschen Juden, 1907.

——. *Die Zurücksetzung der Juden an den Universitäten Deutschlands*. Berlin: Berthold Levy, 1911.

Brill, A. A. "The Adjustment of the Jew to the American Environment." *Mental Hygiene* 2, no. 2 (1918): 219–31.

——. "Insanity Among Jews," *Medical Record* 86 (October 1914): 576–78.

Brutzkus, Boris. "Soziologie der Juden." *YIVO Blatter* 4, no. 3 (1932): 271–74.

——. "Die wirtschaftliche und soziale Lage der Juden in Russland vor und nach der Revolution." *Archiv für Sozialwissenschaft und Sozialpolitik* 61, no. 2, (1929): 10–26.

Brutzkus, J. D. "The Anthropology of the Jewish People." In Salo Baron, ed., *The Jewish People, Past and Present*. Vol. 1. New York: Central Yiddish Culture Organization, 1946.

Buber, Martin. "Jüdische Wissenschaft." *Die Welt* 5, nos. 41 and 43, (1901): 1–2 (no. 41); 1–2 (no. 43).

——. *The Letters of Martin Buber*. Nathan Glatzer and Paul Mendes-Flohr, eds. New York: Schocken Books, 1991.

Carlebach, Julius. *Karl Marx and the Radical Critique of Judaism*. London: Routledge, 1978.

Caro, Georg. "Die Juden und das Wirtschaftsleben." *Im Deutschen Reich* 5, no. 17 (1911): 247–52.

Chamberlain, Houston Stewart. *Die Grundlagen des neunzehnten Jahrhunderts*. 13th ed. Vol. 1. Munich: F. Bruckmann, 1919.

Chamberlain, J. Edward, and Sander Gilman, eds. *Degeneration: The Dark Side of Progress*. New York: Columbia University Press, 1985.

Chase, Allan. *The Legacy of Malthus*. New York, 1976.

"Chronique et Notes Diverses." *Revue des Études Juives* 5 (1882): 152–55.

Cohen, Arthur. "Statistik und Judenfrage." *ZfDuStDJ* 1, no. 3 (1905): 11–14.

Cohen, Israel. *Jewish Life in Modern Times*. New York: Dodd, Mead, 1914.

Cohen, Jeremy. *'Be Fertile and Increase, Fill the Earth and Master It': The Ancient and Medieval Career of a Biblical Text*. Ithaca: Cornell University Press, 1989.

Cohen, Naomi. *American Jews and the Zionist Idea*. New York: Ktav, 1975.

Cohen-Albert, Phyllis. *The Modernization of French Jewry*. Hanover, N.H.: Brandeis University Press, 1977.

Coon, Carleton. *The Races of Europe*. New York: Macmillan, 1939.

Corrsin, Stephen D. "Aspects of Population Change and of Acculturation in Jewish Warsaw at the End of the Nineteenth Century: The Censuses of 1882 and 1897." *Polin* 3 (1988): 122–41.

Cowling, Mary. *The Artist as Anthropologist: The Representation of Type and Character in Victorian Art*. Cambridge, England: Cambridge University Press, 1989.

Daston, Lorraine, and Peter Galison. "The Image of Objectivity." *Representations* 40 (1992): 81–128.

Dawidowicz, Lucy. "Max Weinreich: Scholarship of Yiddish." In *The Jewish Presence: Essays on Identity and History*, 163–76. New York: Harcourt Brace Jovanovich, 1960, 1978.

Desrosières, Alain. *The Politics of Large Numbers: A History of Statistical Reasoning*. Cambridge, Mass.: Harvard University Press, 1998.

Dinur, Benzion. "Jacob Lestchinsky, an Obituary" (Hebrew). *Tzion* 31 (1966): 217–21.

Dinur, Benzion, Arieh Tartakower, and Jacob Lestschinsky, eds. *Klal Yisrael: Prakim be-Soziologia shel ha-Am ha-Yehudi*. Jerusalem: Mosad Bialik, 1954.

"Die Disposition der Juden für Geistes- und Nervenkrankheiten." *Die Welt* 10, no. 16 (1906): 18.

Doron, Joachim. "Classic Zionism and Modern Antisemitism: Parallels and Influences (1883–1914)." *Studies in Zionism* 8 (autumn 1983): 169–204.

———. *Haguto ha-Tsiyonut shel Natan Birnbaum*. Jerusalem: Ha-Sifriyah ha-Tzionit al-yad ha-Histadrut ha-Tzionit ha-Olamit, 1988.

———. "The Impact of German Ideologies on Central European Zionism 1885–1914." Ph.D. diss., Tel Aviv University, 1977.

———. "Rassenbewusstsein und Naturwissenschaftliches Denken im deutschen Zionismus während der Wilhelminischen Ära." *Jahrbuch der Institut für deutsche Geschichte Universität Tel-Aviv* 9 (1980): 389–427.

———. "Social Concepts Prevalent in German Zionism, 1883–1914." *Studies in Zionism* 5 (Spring 1982): 1–31.

Douglas, Jack. *The Social Meanings of Suicide*. Princeton, N.J.: Princeton University Press, 1967.

Drachsler, Julius. *Democracy and Assimilation*. New York: Macmillan, 1920.

Dubnow, Simon. *The History of the Jews*. Trans. Moshe Spiegel. South Brunswick, N.J.: T. Yoseloff, 1967–73.

Durkheim, Emile. *Suicide: A Study in Sociology*. Trans. John Spaulding and George Simpson. Glencoe, Ill.: Free Press, 1951.

Efron, John. *Defenders of the Race*. New Haven, Conn.: Yale University Press, 1994.

——. "Images of the Jewish Body: Three Medical Views from the Jewish Enlightenment." *Bulletin of the History of Medicine* 69, no. 3 (1995): 349–66.

——. "The 'Kaftanjude' and the 'Kaffeehausjude'. Two Models of Jewish Identity: A Discussion of Causes and Cures among German-Jewish Psychiatrists." *Leo Baeck Institute Yearbook* 37 (1992): 169–88.

——. "Scientific Racism and the Mystique of Sephardic Racial Superiority." *Leo Baeck Institute Yearbook* 38 (1993): 75–96.

"Ein Verein für jüdische Statistik in Holland." *Die Welt* 11, no. 12 (1907): 16.

Eisen, George. "Zionism, Nationalism and the Emergence of the *Jüdische Turnerschaft*." *Leo Baeck Institute Yearbook* 28 (1983): 247–62.

Eisenstadt, H. L. "Die Renaissance der jüdischen Sozialhygiene." *Archiv für Rassen- und Gesellschaftsbiologie* 5, nos. 5–6 (1908): 707–28.

——, ed. *Hygiene und Judentum: Eine Sammelschrift*. Dresden: Verlag Jac. Sternlicht, 1930.

Endelman, Todd. "The Decline of the Anglo-Jewish Notable." *The European Legacy* (forthcoming).

——. "Die endemischen Krankheiten Palästinas." *Die Welt* 16, no. 8 (1912): 243.

——, ed. *Jewish Apostasy in the Modern World*. New York: Holmes and Meier, 1987.

——. *The Jews of Georgian England*. Ann Arbor: University of Michigan Press, 1999.

Engelbert, Hermann. *Statistik des Judentums im Deutschen Reiche ausschliesslich Preussens und in der Schweiz*. Frankfurt am Main: J. Kauffmann, 1875.

Engelman, Uriah Zvi. "Jewish Statistics in the U.S. Census of Religious Bodies (1850–1936)." *Jewish Social Studies* 9, no. 2 (1947): 27–174.

Engländer, Martin. *Die auffallend häufigen Krankheitserscheinungen der jüdischen Rasse*. Vienna: J. L. Pollack, 1902.

——. "Berichte: Wien." *Die Welt* 7, no. 33 (1903): 12.

English, Donald. *Political Uses of Photography in the Third French Republic 1871–1914*. Michigan: UMI Research Press, 1984.

"Entartung." *Die Welt* 14, no. 6 (1910): 115–17.

Eschelbacher, Max, and Adolf Sindler. *Zur Hygiene der Juden. Zur Errichtung des Pavillons "Hygiene der Juden" auf der Grossen Ausstellung für Gesundheitspflege, soziale Fürsorge und Leibesübungen*. Vienna: Habrith-Verlagsgesellschaft, 1926.

Eshner, Augustus. "Krankheits und Sterblichkeits Statistik der Juden." *Ost und West* 1, no. 6 (1901): 433–38.

Feiner, Shmuel. "Nineteenth-Century Jewish Historiography: The Second Track." *Studies in Contemporary Jewry*. Vol. 10. New York: Oxford University Press, 1994, 17–44.

Feist, Sigmund. *Stammeskunde der Juden: Historisch-Anthropologische Skizze*. Leipzig: Hinrichs, 1925.

Felix, P. "Unsere nationale Wissenschaft," *Die Welt* 2, no. 32 (1898): 2–4.

Feuchtwang, Bertold. "Jüdische Statistik als Kulturarbeit des Zionismus." In Lazar Schön, ed., *Die Stimme der Wahrheit*, 218–33. Würzburg: N. Phillippi, 1905.

Feuer, Lewis. "The Sociobiological Theory of Jewish Intellectual Achievement: A Sociological Critique." In Joseph Maier and Chaim Waxman, eds., *Ethnicity, Identity, and History: Essays in Memory of Werner J. Cahnman*, 93–123. New Brunswick, N.J.: Transaction Books, 1983.

Fishberg, Maurice. "Aryan and Semite, with Particular Reference to the Aryan." In *Aryan and Semite, with Particular Reference to Nazi Racial Dogmas*, 9–19. Cincinnati: Bnai Brith, 1934.

———. Entries for "Morbidity," "Idiocy," "Insanity," "Nervous Diseases," "Consumption," and "Diabetes." In *Jewish Encyclopedia*. New York, 1901.

———. "Health and Sanitation: New York." In Charles Bernheimer, ed., *The Russian Jew in the United States*, 282–303. Philadelphia: John C. Winston, 1905.

———. *Health Problems of the Jewish Poor*. New York: P. Cowen, 1903.

———. "Intermarriage Between Jews and Christians." In *Eugenics in Race and State. Papers of the Second International Congress of Eugenics*. Vol. 2, 125–33. Baltimore: Williams and Wilkens, 1923.

———. *The Jews: A Study of Race and Environment*. New York: Walter Scott Publishing, 1911.

———. *Materials for the Physical Anthropology of the Eastern European Jews*. Memoirs of the American Anthropological and Ethnological Societies. Vol. 1. Lancaster, Pa.: New Era Printing, 1905.

———. "North African Jews." In Berthold Laufer, ed., *Boas Anniversary Volume. Anthropological Papers*, 55–63. New York: G. E. Stechert, 1906.

———. *Die Rassenmerkmale der Juden: eine Einführung in ihre Anthropologie*. Munich: E. Reinhardt, 1913.

———. "The Relative Infrequency of Tuberculosis among Jews." *American Medicine* 2v (1901): 695–99.

Fleck, Ludwig. *Genesis and Development of a Scientific Fact*. Trans. Fred Bradley and Thaddeus J. Trenn. Chicago: University of Chicago Press, 1979.

Fleischer, Siegfried. "Enquete über die Lage der jüdischen Bevölkerungs Galiziens." In Alfred Nossig, ed., *Jüdische Statistik*, 209–31. Berlin: Jüdischer Verlag, 1903.

"Die Fragen der körperlichen, geistigen, und wirtschaftlichen Hebung der Juden." *Die Welt* 4, no. 43 (1900).

Frank, Gelya. "Jews, Multiculturalism, and Boasian Anthropology." *American Anthropologist* 99, no. 4 (1997): 731–45.

Freund, Gisele. *Photography and Society*. Boston: D. R. Godine, 1980.

Frevert, Ute. "Professional Medicine and the Working Classes in Imperial Germany." *Journal of Contemporary History* 20, no. 4 (1985): 637–58.

Friedlander, Henry, and Sybil Milton, eds. *Archives of the Holocaust*. Vol. 20. New York: Garland, 1993.

Friedmann, Alfred. "Neue Forschungen über Rasse und Degenerationen." *Jüdische Rundschau* 8, no. 10 (1903): 80–81.

Friedmann, B. "Zionismus und Weltanschauung." *Die Welt* 6, no. 49 (1902): 1–3.

Friedmann, Georges, *The End of the Jewish People?* Trans. Eric Mosbacher. New York: Doubleday, 1967.

Fuchs, James L., and Mordecai Plaut. "Jewish Medicine and Renaissance Epistemology: Ethical and Scientific Encounters." *Koroth* 9. Special issue published in *Proceedings of the Third International Symposium on Medicine in the Bible and Talmud*, 218–25. Jerusalem, 1988.

Funkenstein, Amos. "Zionism, Science, and History." In *Perceptions of Jewish History*. Berkeley: University of California Press, 1993.

Gates, Barbara T. *Victorian Suicide: Mad Crimes and Sad Histories*. Princeton, N.J.: Princeton University Press, 1988.

Gelber, N. M. *Toldot ha'Tenuah be'Galizia*. Jerusalem: Rubin Mass, 1958.

"Der Gemeindebote." *Beiträge zur Allgemeine Zeitung des Judenthums* 66, no. 22 (May 30, 1902).

"Generalversammlung des Verbandes für Statistik der Juden." *Die Welt* 10, no. 19 (1906): 18.

Giddens, Anthony. Introduction to *Suicide and the Meaning of Civilization*, by Thomas G. Masaryk. Trans. William B. Weist and Robert G. Batson. Chicago: University of Chicago Press, 1970.

———, ed. *The Sociology of Suicide*. London: Cass, 1971.

Giese, Wilhelm. *Die Juden und die deutsche Kriminalstatistik*. Leipzig: F. W. Grünow, 1893.

Gillerman, Sharon. "Between Public and Private: Family, Community and Jewish Identity in Weimar Berlin." Ph.D. diss., University of California, Los Angeles, 1996.

Gilman, Sander. *The Case of Sigmund Freud: Medicine and Identity at the Fin de Siècle*. Baltimore, Md.: Johns Hopkins University Press, 1993.

———. *Difference and Pathology*. Ithaca: Cornell University Press, 1985.

———. *Disease and Representation*. Ithaca: Cornell University Press, 1988.

———. *Jewish Self-Hatred: Antisemitism and the Hidden Language of the Jews*. Baltimore, Md.: Johns Hopkins University Press, 1986.

———. *The Jew's Body*. New York: Routledge, 1991.

———. "Jews and Mental Illness: Medical Metaphors, Antisemitism, and the Jewish Response." *Journal of the History of the Behavioral Sciences* 20, no. 2 (1984): 150–59.

———. Review of Bernard Wasserstein's *Vanishing Diaspora*, *American Historical Review* 102, no. 4 (1997): 1151–53.

———. *Smart Jews: The Construction of the Image of Superior Jewish Intelligence*. Lincoln: The University of Nebraska Press, 1996.

———. *The Visibility of the Jew in the Diaspora: Body Imagery and Its Cultural Context*. Syracuse, N.Y.: Syracuse University Press, 1992.

Glogau, Otto. "Zur jüdischen Volkskunde und Statistik." *Ost und West* 8 (1902): 551–54.

Gobineau, Arthur Comte de. *The Inequality of the Human Races*. Trans. Adrian Collins. New York: H. Fertig, 1967.

Goldberg, J. J. *Jewish Power: Inside the American Jewish Establishment*. Reading, Mass.: Addison-Wesley, 1996.

Goldman, Lawrence. "The Origins of British Social Science: Political Economy, Natural Science and Statistics." *The Historical Journal* 26, no. 3 (1983): 587–616.

Goldscheider, Calvin, and Alan S. Zuckerman. *The Transformation of the Jews*. Chicago: University of Chicago Press, 1984.

Goldstein, Eric L. "'Different Blood Flows in Our Veins': Race and Jewish Self-Definition in Late Nineteenth Century America." *American Jewish History* 85, no. 1 (1997): 29–55.

Goldstein, Israel. "Synagogue Council of America." *The Universal Jewish Encyclopedia* 10 (1943): 131–32.

Goldstein, Jan. "The Wandering Jew and the Problem of Psychiatric Antisemitism in Fin-de-Siècle France." *Journal of Contemporary History* 20, no. 4 (1985): 521–52.

Gordon, Milton. *Assimilation in American Life*. Oxford: Oxford University Press, 1964.

Gould, Stephen J. *The Mismeasure of Man*. Rev. ed. New York: W. W. Norton, 1996.

Graetz, Heinrich. *History of the Jews*. Philadelphia: Jewish Publication Society, 1891–98.

Green, David. "Veins of Resemblance: Photography and Eugenics." *The Oxford Art Journal* 7, no. 2 (1984): 3–16.

Greenhalgh, Susan. "The Social Construction of Population Science: An Intellec tual, Institutional, and Political History of Twentieth-Century Demography." *Comparative Studies in Society and History* 38, no. 1, 1996, 26–66.

Grunwald, Max. *Die Hygiene der Juden, im Anschluss an die internationale Hygiene-Ausstellung Dresden*. Dresden: Historische Abteilung der internationale Hygiene-Ausstellung, 1911.

Günther, Hans F. K. *Die Rassenkunde der jüdischen Volkes*. Munich: Lehmann, 1930.

Gutmann, M. J. "Die Krankheiten der Juden." *ZfDuStDJ* 1–3, no. 1 (new series): 34–44.

Guttmann, Julius. "Die Juden und das Wirtschaftsleben." *Archiv für Sozialwissenschaft und Sozialpolitik* 36, no. 1 (1913): 149–212.

———. "Zur Einführung." *ZfDuStdJ* 4, nos. 1–2 (1927): 1–2.

Gutwein, Daniel. "Economics, Politics and Historiography: Hayyim D. Horowitz and the Interrelationship of Jews and Capitalism." *Jewish Social Studies: History, Culture, and Society* 1, no. 1 (1994): 94–114.

Hacking, Ian. "Biopower and the Avalanche of Printed Numbers." *Humanities in Society* 5, nos. 3–4 (1982): 279–95.

———. "Making Up People." In Thomas C. Heller et al., eds., *Reconstructing Individualism*, 222–36. Stanford, Calif.: Stanford University Press, 1986.

———. *The Taming of Chance*. Cambridge, England: Cambridge University Press, 1990.

Halpern, Ben. "The Americanization of Zionism, 1880–1930." In Jehuda Reinharz and Anita Shapira, eds., *Essential Papers on Zionism*. New York: New York University Press, 1996.

*Hamburg in Zahlen: 100 Jahre Statistisches Amt Hamburg, 1866–1966*. Hamburg: Statistischer Landesamt Hamburg, 1966.

Harris, Abram L. "Sombart and German (National) Socialism." *Journal of Political Economy* 50, no. 6 (1942): 805–35.

Harris, Neil. "Iconography and Intellectual History: The Halftone Effect." In John Higham and Paul K. Conkin, eds., *New Directions in American Intellectual History*, 196–211. Baltimore, Md.: Johns Hopkins University Press, 1979.

Hart, Mitchell. "Moses the Microbiologist: Judaism and Social Hygiene in the Work of Alfred Nossig." *Jewish Social Studies: History, Culture, and Society* 2, no. 1, (1995): 72–97.

———. "Picturing Jews: Racial Science and Iconography." *Studies in Contemporary Jewry* 11 (1995): 159–75.

——. "Racial Science, Social Science, and the Politics of Jewish Assimilation." *Isis* 90, no. 2 (1999): 268–97.

Heinze, Andrew. *Adapting to Abundance: Jewish Immigrants, Mass Consumption, and the Search for American Identity*. New York: Columbia University Press, 1990.

Hek, Willy. "Antisemitische Statistik." *Die jüdische Presse* 29, nos. 39–40 (1898): 441–42.

——. "Die Schulstatistik der Juden in Preussen." *Die jüdische Presse* 29, no. 45 (1898): 495–96.

——. "Zur Berufsstatistik." *Die jüdische Presse* 30, no. 32 (1899): 358–59.

——. "Zur Statistik der Berliner jüdischen Gemeinde." *Die jüdische Presse* 29, no. 13 (1898): 155–56.

Herf, Jeffrey. *Reactionary Modernism: Technology, Culture, and Politics in Weimar and the Third Reich*. Cambridge, England: Cambridge University Press, 1984.

Herskovits, Melville. "Who are the Jews?" In Louis Finkelstein, ed., *The Jews: Their History, Culture, and Religion*. Vol. 2, 1489–1509. New York: Schocken Books, 1949.

Hertzberg, Arthur. *The Jews in America*. New York: Simon and Schuster, 1989.

——. *The Zionist Idea*. New York: Schocken Books, 1959.

Hess, Moses. *Rome and Jerusalem*. Trans. Meyer Waxman. New York: Bloch, 1945.

Heuberger, Rachel. "Die Gründung der 'Zentralwohlfahrtsstelle der deutschen Juden' im Jahre 1917." In Georg Heuberger and Paul Spiegel, eds., *Zedaka: Jüdische Sozialarbeit im Wandel der Zeit: 75 Jahre Zentralwohlfahrtsstelle der Juden in Deutschland, 1917–1992*, 71–78. Frankfurt am Main: Jüdisches Museum, 1992.

Heymann, Michael. "The State of the Zionist Movement on the Eve of the Sixth Congress." In Michael Heymann, ed., *The Minutes of the Zionist Council: The Uganda Controversy*. Volume 1, 14–39. Jerusalem: Israel Universities Press. Reprinted in Jehuda Reinharz and Anita Shapira, eds., *Essential Papers on Zionism*, 210–37. New York: New York University Press, 1996.

Higham, John. *Send These to Me: Jews and Other Immigrants in Urban America*. Rev. Ed. Baltimore, Md.: Johns Hopkins University Press, 1975.

——. *Strangers in the Land*. 2d ed. New Brunswick, N.J.: Rutgers University Press, 1988.

Hilberg, Raul. "The Statistic." In François Furet, ed., *Unanswered Questions: Nazi Germany and the Genocide of the Jews*, 155–71. New York: Schocken Books, 1989.

Hindess, Barry. *The Use of Official Statistics in Sociology*. London: Macmillan Press, 1973.

Hirschberg, Max. "Der Selbstmord bei den Juden mit besonderer Berücksichtigung Bayerns." *ZfDuStdJ* 2, no. 7 (1906): 101–7.

Holmes, Colin. *Antisemitism in British Society 1876–1939*. London: Edward Arnold, 1979.

Honigmann, Peter. "Jewish Conversions: A Measure of Assimilation." *Leo Baeck Institute Yearbook* 34 (1989): 3–39.

Hoppe, Hugo. "Die jüdische Bevölkerung Österreichs." *Die Welt* 18, no. 24 (1914): 579–80.

——. *Krankheiten und Sterblichkeit bei den Juden und Nichtjuden*. Berlin: S. Calvary, 1903.

——. "Die Kriminalität der Juden und der Alkohol." *ZfDuStdJ* 3, no. 3 (1907): 38–42.

——. Review of Alexander Schüler, *Der Rassenadel der Juden*. In *Die Welt* 17, no. 6 (1913): 184–85.

Howe, Irving. *World Of Our Fathers*. New York: Schocken Books, 1976.

Huerkamp, Claudia. "The Making of the Modern Medical Profession, 1800–1914: Prussian Doctors in the Nineteenth Century." In Geoffrey Cocks and Konrad H. Jarausch, eds., *German Professions, 1800–1950*, 66–84. Oxford: Oxford University Press, 1990.

Hughes, H. Stuart. *Consciousness and Society: The Reorientation of European Social Thought, 1890–1930*. New York: Knopf, 1958.

Huth, Alfred. *The Marriage of Near Kin Considered with Respect to the Laws of Nations, the Results of Experience, and the Teachings of Biology*. London: J. & A. Churchill, 1875.

*Hygiene und Judentum: Eine Sammelschrift*. Dresden: Jac. Sternlicht, 1930.

Hyman, Paula, "The Dynamics of Social History." In Jonathan Frankel, ed., *Studies in Contemporary Jewry*, vol. 10 (1994).

Iggers, Georg. *The German Conception of History*. Middletown, Conn.: Wesleyan University Press, 1968.

Institut zum Studium der Judenfrage. *Die Juden in Deutschland*. Munich: F. Eher, 1935.

Ivins, William M., Jr. "New Reports and New Vision: The Nineteenth Century." In Alan Trachtenberg, ed., *Classic Essays on Photography*, 217–36. New Haven, Conn.: Leete's Island Books, 1980.

Jacobs, Joseph. "Are Jews Jews?" *Popular Science Monthly* 55 (1899): 502–11.

——. "The Comparative Distribution of Jewish Ability." *Journal of the Anthropological Institute* 15 (1886): 351–79.

——. *Statistics of Jewish Population in London, etc. 1873–1893*. London: E. W. Rabbinowicz, 1894.

——. *Studies in Jewish statistics: Social, Vital and Anthropometric*. London: D. Nutt, 1891.

Jacobsohn, Bernhard. *Der Deutsch-Israelitische Gemeindebund nach Ablauf des ersten Decenniums seit seiner Begründung von 1869 bis 1879*. Leipzig: W. Schuwardt, 1879.

Jaffe, A. J. "The Use of Death Records to Determine Jewish Population Characteristics." *Jewish Social Studies* 1, no. 2 (1939): 143–63.

Jeremias, Karl. "Die Fragen der körperlichen, geistigen und wirtschaftlichen Hebung der Juden." *Die Welt* 5, nos. 4 and 18 (1901): 8 (no. 4); 3–5 (no. 18).

——. "Die Hygiene der jüdischen Nerven." *Hickls jüdischen Volkskalender* 1 (1902/03): 73–78.

——. "Die körperliche Minderwertigkeit der Juden." *Die Welt* 5, no. 18 (1901).

——. "Offener Brief." *Allgemeine Zeitung des Judentums* 66 (May 30, 1902).

——. "On the Physical Formation and Degeneration of the Jews." *Stenographisches Protokoll der Verhandlungen des IV Zionisten-Kongresses*. Vol. 5, 115–31. Vienna, Eretz Israel: 1901, 3–5.

——. *Stenographisches Protokoll der Verhandlungen des IV Zionisten-Kongresses*. Vol. 4. Vienna: 1901.

————. "Über körperliche Hebung der Juden." *Die Welt* 6, no. 2 (1902): 4–5.

"Jewish Statistics." *The Jewish Review* 1, no. 3 (1910): 199–202.

Jordanova, Ludmilla J. *Lamarck*. Oxford: Oxford University Press, 1984.

Joselit, Jenna Weissman. *Our Gang: Jewish Crime and the New York Jewish Community, 1900–1914*. Bloomington: Indiana University Press, 1983.

"Judaismus und Kapitalismus." *Die Welt* 13, no. 50 (1909): 1113–14.

"Die Juden der Gegenwart." *Israelitisches Familienblatt*, no. 51 (1904).

"Die Juden der Gegenwart." *Literarisches Zentralblatt*, no. 40 (1905).

"Die Juden der Gegenwart." *Mitteilungen aus dem Verein zur Abwehr des Antisemitismus* 14 (Nov.–Dec. 1904).

"Judenehen in Deutschland." *Die Welt* 7, no. 18 (1903): 10.

"Die Judenfrage und die . . . Cholera." *Die Welt* 12, no. 41 (1908): 13.

"Judentaufen im XIX Jahrhundert." *Die Welt* 3, no. 36 (1899): 6.

*Jüdische Bevölkerungspolitik*. Berlin: Schriften der Zentralwohlfahrtsstelle der deutschen Juden, 1929.

"Jüdische Geisteskranke." *Die Welt* 2, no. 26 (1898): 11.

"Jüdische Statistik." *Die Welt* 7, no. 26 (1903): 13.

"Jüdische Statistik." *Die Welt* 8, no. 6 (1904): 7–8.

"Jüdische Statistik." *Im deutschen Reich* 9, no. 7 (1903): 454–55.

"Jüdische Statistik." *Israelitische Monatsschrift* 15, no. 1 (1904): 3–4.

Judt, J. M. "Die Juden als physische Rasse." In Alfred Nossig, ed., *Jüdische Statistik*, 405–23. Berlin: Jüdischer Verlag, 1903.

————. *Die Juden als Rasse*. Berlin: Jüdischer Verlag, 1902.

Jungmann, Max. "Ist das jüdische Volk degeneriert?" *Die Welt* 6, no. 24 (1902): 3–4.

Kabuzan, V. M. "Censuses in Russia and the Soviet Union." *The Modern Encyclopedia of Russian and Soviet History* 6 (1976): 153–57.

Kaplun-Kogan, W. "Jüdische Kreditgesellschaften und Gegenseitigkeit in Russland." *ZfDuStdJ* 9, no. 6 (1913): 89–92.

————. "Die jüdische Sprach- und Kulturgemeinschaft in Polen." *ZfDuStdJ* 11 (1915): 65–74; 12, nos. 1–3, (1916): 4–16.

Karbe, Karl-Heitz. *Salomon Neumann: Wegbereiter sozialmedizinischen Denkens und Handelns*. Leipzig: J. A. Barth, 1983.

Käsler, Dirk. "Jewishness as a Central Formation-Milieu of Early German Society." *History of Sociology* 6, no. 1 (1985): 69–86.

Kater, Michael. "Professionalism and Socialization of Physicians in Wilhelmine and Weimar Germany." *Journal of Contemporary History* 20, no. 4 (1985): 677–701.

Katz, Jacob. "The German-Jewish Utopia of Social Emancipation." In Max Kreutzberger, ed., *Studies of the Leo Baeck Institute*. Vol. 1, 59–80. New York: Frederick Ungar, 1967.

————, ed. *Toward Modernity: The European Jewish Model*. New Brunswick, N.J.: Transaction Books, 1987.

Kautsky, Karl. *Are the Jews a Race?* New York: International Publishers, 1926.

Keller, Evelyn Fox. *Reflections on Gender and Science*. New Haven, Conn.: Yale University Press, 1985.

Kevles, Daniel. *In the Name of Eugenics: Genetics and the Uses of Human Heredity*. New York: Knopf, 1985.

Kisch, Guido. "The Jews' Function in the Mediaeval Evolution of Economic Life." *Historia Judaica*, 6, no. 1 (1944): 1–12.

Klausner, Israel. *Opasitziah le-Herzl*. Jerusalem: Ahi'ever, 1960.

Kleinmann, M. "Der Zionismus im Lichte der Wissenschaft." In Lazar Schön, ed., *Die Stimme der Wahrheit*, 402–6. Würzburg: N. Phillippi, 1905.

Klingenstein, Susanne. *Jews in the American Academy, 1900–1940: The Dynamics of Intellectual Assimilation*. Syracuse, N.Y.: Syracuse University Press, 1998.

Knöpfel, L. "Die Statistik der Juden und die statistischen Amten." In *Statistik der Juden: Eine Sammelschrift*, 13–20. Berlin: Bureau für Statistik der Juden, 1917.

Kolb, G. Fr. *The Condition of Nations Social and Political*. Trans. Emma Brewer. London: G. Bell and Sons, 1880.

König, Rene. "Die Juden und die Soziologie." In Rene König, ed., *Studien zur Soziologie*, 123–36. Frankfurt: Fischer, 1971.

Koralnik, I. "Die beruflichen und sozialen Wandlungen im deutschen Judentum." *Zeitschrift für Jüdische Wohlfahrtspflege und Sozialpolitik* 3, no. 3 (new series; 1930): 80–89.

———. "Demographische Wandlungen im deutschen Judentum." *Schriften für Wirtschaft und Statistik* 1 (1928): 211–28.

———. "Die jüdische Arbeiterschaft in Osteuropa." *ZfDuStdJ* 2, no. 1 (1925): 12–17.

Koren, John, ed. *The History of Statistics: Their Development and Progress in Many Countries*. New York: Macmillan, 1918.

Kornfeld, Siegmund. "Die jüdischen Aerzte und der Zionismus." *Die Welt* 5, no. 16 (1901): 1–3.

Kottek. "Für die freie jüdische Wissenschaft." *Die jüdische Presse* 33, no. 7 (1902): 61–63.

———. "Die jüdische Wissenschaft." *Die jüdische Presse* 33, no. 2 (1902): 13–14.

Kraut, Alan M. "Silent Strangers: Germs, Genes, and Nativism in John Higham's *Strangers in the Land*." *American Jewish History* 76, no. 1 (1986): 142–58.

———. *Silent Travelers: Germs, Genes, and the Immigrant Menace*. New York: Basic Books, 1994.

Kreppel, Jonas. *Juden und Judentum von Heute*. Zurich: Amalthea-Verlag, 1925.

Labisch, Alfons. "Doctors, Workers and the Scientific Cosmology of the Industrial World: The Social Construction of 'Health' and the 'Homo Hygienicus'." *Journal of Contemporary History* 20, no. 4 (1985): 599–615.

Lamberti, Marjorie. "The Centralverein and the Anti-Zionists: Setting the Historical Record Straight." *Leo Baeck Institute Yearbook* 33 (1988): 123–28.

Landau, S. R. *Unter jüdischen Proletariern: Reiseschilderungen aus Ostgalizien und Russland*. Vienna: L. Rosner, 1898.

Landes, David. "The Jewish Merchant: Typology and Stereotypology in Germany." *Leo Baeck Institute Yearbook* 19 (1974): 11–30.

Laqueur, Walter. *A History of Zionism*. London: Weidenfeld & Nicolson, 1972.

Lawin, M. "Beitrag zur Beleuchtung des Elends und der Wohlfahrtspflege der Juden in Russland." *ZfDuStdJ* 2, no. 1 (1906): 10–14.

Lazarus, Moritz. *Was heisst National?* Berlin: Dümmler, 1880.

Legoyt, M. *De Certaines Immunités Biostatistiques de la Race Juive*. Paris: Bureau des Archives Israélites, 1868.

Leopold, Louis. "Arbeiten des Vereins für jüdische Statistik." In Alfred Nossig, ed., *Jüdische Statistik*. Berlin: Jüdischer Verlag, 1903, 145–68.

Leroy-Beaulieu, Anatole. *Israel Among the Nations*. Trans. Frances Hellman. New York: G. P. Putnam's Sons, 1895.

Lestschinsky, Jacob. "Dr. Arthur Ruppin als Statistiker und Soziolog." *Die Zukunft* 48, no. 4 (1943): 232–35.

——. "The Economic and Social Development of the Jewish People." In Salo Baron et al., eds., *Past and Present of the Jewish People*. Vol. 1, 361–90. New York: Central Yiddish Culture Organization, 1946.

——. "Fun der Redaktsia." *Schriften für Wirtschaft und Statistik* 1 (1928): 1–2.

——. "Dos Yiddische Folk in Wandel der letzten hundert Jahren." *Schriften für Wirtschaft und Statistik* 1 (1928).

——. "Zur Psychologie der jüdischen Auswanders." *ZfDuStdJ* 9, no. 5 (1913): 75–80.

Levenson, Alan. "German Zionism and Radical Assimilation Before 1914." *Studies in Zionism* 13, no. 1 (1992): 21–41.

——. "Jewish Reactions to Intermarriage in Nineteenth Century Germany." Ph.D. diss., The Ohio State University, 1990.

——. "Reform Attitudes, in the Past, Toward Intermarriage." *Judaism* 38, no. 3 (1989): 320–32.

Light, Donald, Stephen Liebfried, and Florian Tennstedt. "Social Medicine vs. Professional Dominance: The German Experience." *American Journal of Public Health* 76 (1986): 78–83.

Lindenfeld, David. *The Practical Imagination: The German Sciences of State in the Nineteenth Century*. Chicago: University of Chicago Press, 1997.

Lindenthal, Jacob Jay. "*Abi Gezunt*: Health and the Eastern European Jewish Immigrant." *American Jewish History* 70, no. 4 (1981): 420–41.

Liss, Julia E. "German Culture and German Science in the Bildung of Franz Boas." In George Stocking Jr., ed., *Volksgeist as Method and Ethic: Essays on Boasian Ethnography and the German Anthropological Tradition*, 155–84. Madison: University of Wisconsin Press, 1996.

Liszt, Franz von. *Das Problem der Kriminalität der Juden*. Giessen: Alfred Töpelmann, 1907.

Loewe, Heinrich. *Antisemitismus und Zionismus*. Berlin: H. Schildberger, 1892.

——. *Proselyten: Ein Beitrag zur Geschichte der jüdischen Rasse*. Berlin: Soncio-Gesellschaft, 1926.

Lombroso, Cesare. *Der Antisemitismus und die Juden im Lichte der modernen Wissenschaft*. Trans. H. Kurella. Leipzig: G. H. Wigand, 1894.

Lotan, Giora. "The Zentralwohlfahrtsstelle." *Leo Baeck Institute Yearbook* 4 (1959): 185–207.

Lurie, H. L. "Some Problems in the Collection and Interpretation of Jewish Population Data." *Jewish Social Service Quarterly* 11 (June 1934): 263–68.

——. "On the Use of the Term 'Non-Jewish' in Jewish statistics." *Jewish Social Studies* 2 (1940): 79–84.

Luschan, Felix von. "Die anthropologische Stellung der Juden." *Korrespondenz-Blatt deutscher Gesellschaft für Anthropologie, Ethnologie und Urgeschichte* 23, nos. 9 and 10 (1892): 94–96 (no. 9); 97–100 (no. 10).

———. "The Early Inhabitants of Western Asia." *Royal Anthropological Institute Journal* 41 (1911).

———. *Völker, Rassen, Sprache.* Berlin: Welt-Verlag, 1922.

———. "Zur physischen Anthropologie der Juden." *ZfDuStdJ* 1, no. 1 (1905): 1–4.

Lutz, Tom. *American Nervousness 1903.* Ithaca: Cornell University Press, 1991.

Luz, Ehud. *Parallels Meet: Religion and Nationalism in the Early Zionist Movement 1882–1904.* Trans. Lenn J. Schramm. Philadelphia: Jewish Publication Society, 1988.

Mandelstamm, Max. *How Jews Live.* London: Greenberg, 1900.

———. "Rede Dr. Max Mandelstamms." *Die Welt* 4, no. 35 (1900): 1–7.

Manor, Alexander. *Jacob Lestchinsky: The Man and his Work* (Hebrew). Jerusalem: World Jewish Congress, 1961.

Maretzki, Louis. "Die Gesundheitsverhältnisse der Juden." In *Statistik der Juden: Eine Sammelschrift.* Berlin: Bureau für Statistik der Juden, 1917, 123–51.

Markel, Howard. *Quarantine! East European Jewish Immigrants and the New York City Epidemics of 1892.* Baltimore, Md.: Johns Hopkins University Press, 1997.

Marrus, Michael. *The Politics of Assimilation.* Oxford: Oxford University Press, 1971.

Masaryk, Thomáš G. *Suicide and the Meaning of Civilization.* Trans. William B. Weist and Robert G. Batson. Chicago: University of Chicago Press, 1970.

Massin, Benoit. "From Virchow to Fischer: Physical Anthropology and 'Modern Race Theories' in Wilhelmine Germany." In George Stocking, Jr., ed., *Volksgeist as Method and Ethic: Essays on Boasian Ethnography and the German Anthropological Tradition,* 79–154. Madison: The University of Wisconsin Press, 1996.

Massing, Paul. *Rehearsal for Destruction.* New York: Harper, 1949.

Matthäus, Jürgen. "Deutschtum and Judentum under Fire: The Impact of the First World War on the Strategies of the Centralverein and the Zionistische Vereinigung." *Leo Baeck Institute Yearbook* 33 (1988): 129–47.

Maurer, Trude. "The East European Jew in the Weimar Press: Stereotype and Attempted Rebuttal." *Studies in Contemporary Jewry* 1 (1984) 176–97.

———. *Ostjuden in Deutschland 1918–1933.* Hamburg: H. Christians, 1986.

Mayer, Hermann. "Sanitäre Maßnahmen für die Rückkehr nach Eretz-Israel." In Davis Trietsch, ed., *Volk und Land,* 205–10. Berlin, 1919.

Mayr, Ernst. *The Growth of Biological Thought.* Cambridge, Mass.: Harvard University Press, 1982.

Mendelsohn, Ezra. "From Assimilation to Zionism in Lvov: The Case of Alfred Nossig." *The Slavonic and East European Review* 49, no. 117 (1971): 521–34.

———. *On Modern Jewish Politics.* Oxford: Oxford University Press, 1993.

Mendes-Flohr, Paul. "Fin-de-Siècle Orientalism, the Ostjuden and the Aesthetics of Jewish Self-Affirmation." *Studies in Contemporary Jewry* 1 (1984): 96–139.

———. "Werner Sombart's: *The Jews and Modern Capitalism.*" *Leo Baeck Institute Yearbook* 21 (1976): 87–107.

Meyer, Michael. "The Emergence of Jewish Historiography: Motives and Motifs." *History and Theory* 27 (1988): 160–75.

———. "Jewish Religious Reform and Wissenschaft des Judentums: The Positions of Zunz, Geiger, and Frankel." *Leo Baeck Institute Yearbook* 16 (1971): 19–41.

———. "Jewish Scholarship and Jewish Identity: Their Historical Relationship in Modern Germany." *Studies in Contemporary Jewry* 8 (1992): 181–93.

Michaelis, Curt. "Die jüdische Auserwählungsidee und ihre biologische Bedeutung." *ZdDuStdJ* 1, no. 2 (1905): 1–4.

Miron, Dan. "Between Science and Faith: Sixty Years of the YIVO Institute." *YIVO Annual* 9 (1990): 1–15.

Mitchell, Harvey, and Samuel S. Kottek. "An Eighteenth-Century Medical View of the Diseases of the Jews in Northeastern France: Medical Anthropology and the Politics of Jewish Emancipation." *Bulletin of the History of Medicine* 67 (1993): 248–81.

"Mitteilung." *ZfDuStdJ* 8, no. 8 (1912): 94–96.

"Mitteilung." *ZfDuStdJ* 11, nos. 2–3 (1915).

"Mitteilung." *ZfDuStdJ* 1, no. 1 (new series; 1924): 31.

"Mitteilung." *ZfDuStdJ* 4, nos. 1–2 (new series; 1927): 30.

"Mitteilungen." *ZfDuStdJ* 5, no. 5 (1909): 79–80.

"Mitteilungen des Verbandes für Statistik der Juden." *Die Welt* 8, no. 50 (1904): 13.

Mitzman, Arthur. *Sociology and Estrangement: Three Sociologists of Imperial Germany*. New York: Knopf, 1973.

"Mixed Marriages." *The Maccabean* 7, no. 5 (May, 1905): 216.

Morant, G. M., and Otto Samson. "An Examination of Investigations by Dr. Maurice Fishberg and Professor Franz Boas Dealing with Measurements of Jews in New York." *Biometrika* 28, parts 1 and 2 (June 1936): 1–31.

Moses, Julius. "Statistische Erhebungen über die Berufswahl der jüdischen Jugend in den Landgemeinden Badens." In Alfred Nossig, ed., *Jüdische Statistik*, 202–8. Berlin: Jüdischer Verlag, 1903.

Mosse, George L. *German Jews Beyond Judaism*. Bloomington: Indiana University Press, 1985.

———. *Germans and Jews: The Right, the Left and the Search for a 'Third Force' in pre-Nazi Germany*. New York: H. Fertig, 1970.

———. "The Influence of the Völkish Idea on German Jewry." In Max Kreutzberger, ed., *Studies of the Leo Baeck Institute*. Vol. 1, 81–114. New York: Frederick Ungar, 1967.

———. Introduction to Max Nordau, *Degeneration*, xv–xxxiv. New York: H. Fertig, 1968.

———. "Max Nordau, Liberalism, and the New Jew." *Journal of Contemporary History* 27 (1992): 565–81.

———. *Toward the Final Solution: A History of European Racism*. New York: H. Fertig, 1978.

Mosse, Werner. "Judaism, Jews and Capitalism: Weber, Sombart and Beyond." *Leo Baeck Institute Yearbook* 24 (1979) 3–15.

Motzkin, Leo. "Jüdische Statistik und Zionismus." *Jüdischer Almanach* 1 (1902/03): 233–41.

———, ed. *Die Judenprogramme in Russland*. Cologne: Jüdischer Verlag, 1909–1910.

Mühsam, Hans. "Das hygienische Institut in Palästina." *Die Welt* 14, no. 41 (1910): 1036–38.

Myers, David. "The Fall and Rise of Jewish Historicism: The Evolution of the *Akademie für die Wissenschaft des Judentums* (1919–1930)." *Hebrew Union College Annual* 63 (1992): 107–44.

———. *Re-Inventing the Jewish Past: European Jewish Intellectuals and the Zionist Return to History*. New York: Oxford University Press, 1995.

Myerson, Abraham. *The Inheritance of Mental Diseases*. Baltimore: Williams & Wilkens, 1925.

———. "Mental Hygiene and Family Life." In Earl Williams, ed., *Social Aspects of Mental Hygiene*. New Haven, Conn.: Yale University Press, 1925.

———. "The 'Nervousness' of the Jew." *Mental Hygiene* 4 (1920): 65–72.

Nagel, Thomas. *The View from Nowhere*. Oxford: Oxford University Press, 1986.

"Neugründung eines Vereines für Statistik der Juden." *Die Welt* 8, no. 16 (1904): 11.

Neumann, Salomon. *Die Fabel von der jüdischen Masseneinwanderung*. Berlin: Leonhard Simion, 1880.

———. *Die neueste Lüge über die israelitische Allianz; ein Probestück aus der antisemitischen Moral*. 2d ed. Berlin: Druck und Verlag der Volks-Zeitung, 1883.

———. *Zur Statistik der Juden in Preussen von 1816–1880*. Berlin: Louis Gerschel, 1884.

Nordau, Max. *Degeneration*. New York: D. Appleton, 1895.

———. "V. Kongressrede." In Max Nordau, *Zionistische Schriften*. Cologne: Zionistischen Aktionskommittee, 1909, 1923, 112–39.

Norden, Edward. "Counting the Jews." *Commentary* 92, no. 4 (Oct. 1991): 36–43.

Nossig, Alfred. "Die Auserwähltheit der Juden im Lichte der Biologie." *ZfDuStdJ* 1 no. 3 (1905): 1–5.

———. "Jüdische Statistik, ihre Bedeutung, Geschichte, Aufgabe und Organization." In Alfred Nossig, ed., *Jüdische Statistik*. Berlin: Jüdischer Verlag, 1903.

———. *Materialien zur Statistik des jüdischen Stammes*. Vienna: C. Konegen, 1887.

———. *Die Sozialhygiene der Juden und des altorientalischen Völkerkreises*. Stuttgart: Deutsche Verlags-Anstalt, 1894.

———, ed. *Jüdische Statistik*. Berlin: Jüdischer Verlag, 1903.

Nye, Robert A. "The Bio-Medical Origins of Urban Sociology." *Journal of Contemporary History* 20 (1985): 659–75.

———. *Crime, Madness, and Politics in Modern France: The Medical Concept of National Decline*. Princeton, N.J.: Princeton University Press, 1984.

———. "Degeneration and the Medical Model of Cultural Crisis in the French Belle Epoque." In Seymour Drescher, David Sabean, and Allan Sharlin, eds., *Political Symbolism in Modern Europe: Essays in Honor of George L. Mosse*, 19–41. New Brunswick, N.J.: Transaction Books, 1982.

Oberschall, Anthony. *Empirical Social Research in Germany 1848–1914*. Paris: Mouton, 1965.

———. "The Two Empirical Roots of Social Theory." *Knowledge and Society: Studies in the Sociology of Culture Past and Present* 6 (1986): 67–97.

Odom, Herbert. "Generalizations on Race in Nineteenth Century Physical Anthropology." *Isis* 58 (1967): 5–18.

Oelsner, Toni. "The Place of the Jews in Economic History as Viewed by German Scholars." *Leo Baeck Institute Yearbook* 7 (1962): 183–212.

——. "Wilhelm Roscher's Theory of the Economic and Social Position of the Jews in the Middle Ages." *YIVO Annual of Social Science* 12 (1958–59): 176–95.

Olender, Maurice. *The Languages of Paradise: Race, Religion, and Philology in the Nineteenth Century.* Trans. Arthur Goldhammer. Cambridge, Mass.: Harvard University Press, 1992.

Oppenheimer, Franz. "Die Anfänge des jüdischen Kapitalismus." *Ost und West* 2, nos. 5–7 (1902): 323–32; 391–402; 435–44.

——. "Die Juden und das Wirtschaftsleben." *Die Welt* 15, no. 23 (1911): 535–37.

"Oppenheimer über Sombart." *Die Welt* 16, no. 11 (1912): 331–32.

P. A. "Die Juden der Gegenwart." *Die jüdische Presse* 35, nos. 48–49 (1904): 487–89 (48); 505–7 (49).

Pasmanik, Daniel. "Die ökonomische Lage der Juden in Russland." *Hickls Jüdischer Volkskalender* 4 (1905–06): 23–33.

Patriarca, Silvana. *Numbers and Nationhood: Writing Statistics in Nineteenth-Century Italy.* Cambridge, England: Cambridge University Press, 1996.

Paul-Schiff, Maximillian. "Zur Statistik der Kriminalität der Juden." *ZfDuStdJ* 5, no. 5 (1909): 70–75.

Pearson, Karl. "On the Inheritance of the Mental and Moral Characters." *Journal of the Royal Anthropological Institute* 32 (1903).

——. "On Jewish-Gentile Relationships." *Biometrika* 28, parts 1 and 2 (1936): 32–33.

Pearson, Karl, and Margaret Moul. "The Problem of Alien Immigration into Great Britain. Illustrated by an Examination of Russian and Polish Jewish Children." *Annals of Eugenics* 1 (1925): 5–127.

Penslar, Derek. "The Origins of Jewish Political Economy." *Jewish Social Studies: History, Culture, and Society* 3, no. 3 (1997): 26–60.

——. "Philanthropy, the 'Social Question' and Jewish Identity in Imperial Germany." *Leo Baeck Institute Yearbook* 38 (1993): 51–73.

——. *Zionism and Technocracy: The Engineering of Jewish Settlement in Palestine 1870–1918.* Bloomington: Indiana University Press, 1991.

Peretz, I. L. "Impressions of a Journey Through the Tomaszow Region." In Ruth Wisse, ed., The *I. L. Peretz Reader.* New York: Schocken Books, 1990.

Philippson, Martin. *Neuste Geschichte des jüdischen Volkes.* Leipzig: Gustav Fock, 1910.

Pick, Daniel. *Faces of Degeneration.* Cambridge, England: Cambridge University Press, 1989.

Pinkus, Felix. *Die moderne Judenfrage von den Grundlagen der jüdischen Wirtschafts-geschichte und des Zionismus.* Breslau: Koebner, 1903.

——. "Organization und Separation." *Die Welt* 7, no. 15 (1903): 17–18.

——. *Studien zur Wirtschaftsstellung der Juden.* Berlin: L. Lamm, 1905.

——. "Unsere nationale Wissenschaft." *Die Welt* 2, no. 32 (1898): 2–4.

——. "Werner Sombarts Stellung zur Judenfrage." *Die Welt* 7, no. 20 (1903): 7–8.

Plaschkes, S. J. "Die Ärzte in der zionistischen Bewegung." In Israel Klausner,

Raphael Mahler, and Dov Sadan, eds., *Sefer Yovel l'Natan Michael Gelber*, 271–84. Tel-Aviv: Olamenu, 1963.

Poliakov, Leon. *The Aryan Myth*. Trans. Edmund Howard. New York: Basic Books, 1974.

Porter, Dorothy. "Enemies of the Race: Biologism, Environmentalism, and Public Health in Edwardian England." *Victorian Studies* 34, no. 2 (1991): 159–78.

Porter, Theodore. "Lawless Society: Social Science and the Reinterpretation of Statistics in Germany 1850–1880." In Lorenz Kruger, Gerd Gigerenzer, and Mary S. Morgan, eds., *The Probabilistic Revolution*, 351–75. Cambridge, Mass.: MIT Press, 1987.

———. "Objectivity as Standardization: The Rhetoric of Impersonality in Measurement, Statistics, and Cost-Benefit Analysis." *Annals of Scholarship* 3, nos. 1–2 (1992): 19–59.

———. *The Rise of Statistical Thinking, 1820–1900*. Princeton, N.J.: Princeton University Press, 1986.

———. *Trust in Numbers: The Pursuit of Objectivity in Science and Public Life*. Princeton, N.J.: Princeton University Press, 1995.

Posener, S. "Les Juifs sous le Premier Empire: Les Enquêtes Administratives." *Revue des Etudes Juives* 90 (1931): 1–27.

———. "Les Juifs sous le Premier Empire: Les Statistiques générales." *Revue des Etudes Juives* 93–95 (1932–33): 192–214 (93); 157–66 (95).

Preussischer Landesverband jüdischer Gemeinden. *Jüdische Bevölkerungspolitik*. Berlin: Zentralwohlfahrtsstelle der deutschen Juden, 1929.

Proctor, Robert. "Eugenics Among the Social Sciences: Hereditarian Thought in Germany and the United States." In JoAnne Brown and David K. van Keuren, eds., *The Estate of Social Knowledge*, 175–208. Baltimore, Md.: Johns Hopkins University Press, 1991.

———. "From *Anthropologie* to *Rassenkunde* in the German Anthropological Tradition." In George Stocking Jr., ed., *Bones, Bodies, Behavior: Essays on Biological Anthropology*, 138–79. Madison: University of Wisconsin Press, 1988.

———. *Racial Hygiene: Medicine Under the Nazis*. Cambridge, Mass.: Harvard University Press, 1988.

———. *Value-Free Science? Purity and Power in Modern Knowledge*. Cambridge, Mass.: Harvard University Press, 1991.

Pulzer, Peter. *The Rise of Political Anti-Semitism in Germany and Austria*. Rev. ed. Cambridge, Mass.: Harvard University Press, 1988.

"R." "Jüdisches Turnwesen." *Die Welt* 4, no. 20 (1900): 6.

Rabinowitsch, Sara, and Bertha Pappenheim. *Zur Lage der jüdischen Bevölkerung in Galizien: Reise-Eindrücks und Vorschläge zur Besserung der Verhältnisse*. Frankfurt A/M: Neuer Frankfurter Verlag, 1904.

Ragins, Sanford. *Jewish Responses to Anti-Semitism in Germany 1870–1914*. Cincinnati, Ohio: Hebrew Union College Press, 1980.

"Die Rassenzugehörigkeit der Juden," *Die Welt* 16, no. 44 (1912): 1356.

Rawidowicz, Simon. "Israel: The Ever-dying People." In *Studies in Jewish Thought*, 210–24. Philadelphia: The Jewish Publication Society of America, 1978.

Regneri, Günther. "Salomon Neumann's Statistical Challenge to Treitschke: The

Forgotten Episode that Marked the End of the '*Berliner Antisemitismusstreit*'." *Leo Baeck Institute Yearbook* 43 (1998): 129–53.

Reinharz, Jehuda. "Advocacy and History: The Case of the Centralverein and the Zionists." *Leo Baeck Institute Yearbook* 33 (1988): 113–22.

——. *Chaim Weizmann: The Making of a Zionist Leader*. Oxford: Oxford University Press, 1985.

——. "East European Jews in the *Weltanschauung* of German Zionists, 1882–1915." *Studies in Contemporary Jewry* 1 (1984): 55–95.

——. *Fatherland or Promised Land: The Dilemma of the German Jew, 1893–1914*. Ann Arbor: University of Michigan Press, 1975.

Ringer, Fritz. *The Decline of the German Mandarins*. Cambridge, Mass.: Harvard University Press, 1969.

Ripley, William. *The Races of Europe: A Sociological Study*. London: Kegan Paul, Trench Trubner, 1900.

Rolleston, Humphrey. "Some Diseases of the Jewish Race." *Bulletin of the Johns Hopkins Hospital* 43, no. 3 (1928): 117–39.

Roscher, Wilhelm. "Die Stellung der Juden im Mittelalter, betrachtet vom Standpunkt der allgemeinen Handelspolitik." *Zeitschrift für die gesamte Staatswissenschaft* 31 (1875): 503–26. Translated as "The Position of the Jews in the Middle Ages Considered from the Standpoint of the General Political Economy." Trans. Solomon Grayzel, *Historia Judaica* 6, no. 1 (1944): 13–26.

Rosen, George. *A History of Public Health*. New York: MD Publications, 1958.

Rosenbaum, Eduard. "Some Reflections on the Jewish Participation in German Economic Life." *Leo Baeck Institute Yearbook* 1 (1956): 307–14.

Rosenbaum, S. "A Contribution to the Study of the Vital and Other Statistics of the Jews in the United Kingdom." *Journal of the Royal Statistical Society* 68 (1905).

Ross, Dorothy. *The Origins of American Social Science*. Cambridge: Cambridge University Press, 1991.

Rost, Hans. "Jüdische Statistik." *Soziale Kultur* 27 (1908): 689–96.

——. "Der Selbstmord bei den Juden." In *Bibliographie des Selbstmords mit textlichen Einführungen zu jedem Kapitel*, 32–35. Augsburg: Haas and Grabherr, 1927.

Rozenblit, Marsha. *The Jews of Vienna, 1867–1914: Assimilation and Identity*. Albany: State University of New York Press, 1983.

"Rückgang der jüdischen Bevölkerung in Dänemark." *Die Welt* 10, no. 37 (1906), 19.

Ruppin, Arthur. *Arthur Ruppin: Memoirs, Diaries, Letters*. Trans. Alex Bein. New York: Herzl Press, 1972.

——. "Begabungsunterschiede christlicher und jüdischer Kinder." *ZfDuStdJ* 2, nos. 8–9 (1906): 129–35.

——. *Darwinismus und Sozialwissenschaft*. Jena: G. Fischer, 1903.

——. *Drei Jahrzehnten in Palästina*. Translated as *Three Decades of Palestine*. Jerusalem: Schocken, 1936.

——. "Gegenwartsarbeit." In Lazar Schön, ed., *Die Stimme der Wahrheit*, 61–66. Würzburg: N. Phillippi, 1905.

——. "Hat der Vater oder die Mutter auf die Vitalität des Kindes den grösseren Einfluss?" *Deutschen Medicinischen Wochenschrift* 26 (1901).

——. *The Jewish Fate and Future.* Trans. E. W. Dickes. London: Macmillan, 1940.

——. "The Jewish Population in the World." In Salo Baron et al., eds., *The Jewish People, Past and Present.* Vol. 1, 348–60. New York: The Central Yiddish Culture Organization, 1946.

——. *The Jews in the Modern World.* London: Macmillan, 1934.

——. *The Jews of Today.* Trans. Margery Bentwich. New York: Holt, 1913.

——. *Die Juden der Gegenwart.* Cologne: Jüdischer Verlag, 1904; rev. ed., 1911.

——. *Die Juden im Großherzogtum Hessen.* Berlin: L. Lamm, 1909.

——. "Die jüdische Bevölkerung in Preussen nach der Volkszählung vom 1. Dez. 1900." *Allgemeine Zeitung des Judenthums* 65, no. 46 (1901): 545–46.

——. "Die Kriminalität der Christen und Juden in Deutschland, 1899–1902." *ZfDuStdJ* 1, no. 1 (1905): 6–9.

——. "Die Organisation des jüdischen Proletariats in Russland." *Allgemeine Zeitung des Judenthums* 67, no. 44 (1903): 523–24.

——. "Die sozialen Verhältnisse der Juden in Preussen und Deutschlands." *Conrads Jahrbücher für Nationalökonomie und Statistik* 78 (1902): 374–86; 760–85.

——. *Die sozialen Verhältnisse der Juden in Russland.* Berlin: Jüdischer Verlag, 1906.

——. "Die Verbreitung der Mischehe unter den Juden." *ZdDuStdJ* 5, no. 4 (1930): 53–58.

——. "Die Volksvermehrung." *Die Gegenwart* 31, no. 47 (Nov. 22, 1902): 321–23.

——. "Die wirtschaftlichen Kämpfe der Juden." *ZfDuStdJ* 6, no. 6 (new series; 1931): 81–88.

——. Review of Hugo Hoppe, *Alkohol und Kriminalität* in *ZfDuStdJ* 2, no. 12 (1906): 192.

——. *Soziologie der Juden.* Berlin: Jüdischer Verlag, 1930.

——. "Statistische Untersuchungen über die physiologischen Eigentümlichkeiten der deutschen Juden." *Allgemeine Zeitung des Judenthums* 66, no. 33 (1902): 388–90.

——. *Tagebücher, Briefe, Erinnerungen.* Königstein: Jüdischer Verlag, 1985.

——. "Zahl und Bewegung der jüdischen Bevölkerung in den letzten drei Jahrzehnten." *Allgemeine Zeitung des Judenthums* 67, no. 27 (1903): 320–21.

——. "Zur Geschichte des Büros für Statistik der Juden in Berlin." In *Statistik der Juden: Eine Sammelschrift*, 9–12. Berlin: Bureau für Statistik der Juden, 1917.

Ruppin, Arthur, and Jakob Thon. *Der Anteil der Juden am Unterrichtswesen in Preussen.* Berlin: Verlag des Bureaus für jüdische Statistik, 1905.

Ruveini, Ya'acov. "Sociology and Ideology: Thoughts on the Work of Arthur Ruppin" (Hebrew). *Kivunim* 23 (May, 1984): 25–48.

Salaman, Redcliffe. *Heredity and the Jew.* Cambridge, England: Cambridge University Press, 1911.

——. "Heredity and the Jew." *Journal of Genetics* 1, no. 3 (1911): 273–96.

——. *Palestine Reclaimed. Letters from a Jewish Officer in Palestine.* London: Routledge, 1920.

——. *The Prospects of Jewish Colonization in Palestine.* London: The Contemporary Review Company, 1920.

——. "Racial Origins of Jewish Types." *Transactions of the Jewish Historical Society of England* 9 (1920): 163–91.

———. "Some Notes on the Jewish Problem." In *Eugenics in Race and State. Papers of the Second International Congress of Eugenics*. Vol. 2, 134–53. Baltimore, Md.: Williams and Wilkens, 1923.

———. "What Has Become of the Philistines?: A Biologist's Point of View." *The Palestine Exploration Fund Quarterly* (1925): 1–17.

Sandler, Aron. *Anthropologie und Zionismus: Ein populär wissenschaftlicher Vortrag*. Breslau: Jüdischer Buch- und Kunstverlag, 1904.

———. "Die Gesundheitsverhältnisse Palästinas." *Die Welt* 14, no. 41 (1910): 1038.

Sarna, Jonathan. "The Secret of Jewish Continuity." *Commentary* 98, no. 4 (October 1994): 55–58.

Schimmer, Gustav Adolf. *Statistik des Judenthums in den im Reichsrathe vertretenen Königreichen und Ländern, nach den vom K(aiserlich) K(öniglichen) Ministerium des inneren Angeordneten Erhebungen und nach sonstigen Quellen*. Vienna: Druck der Kaiserlich-Königlichen Hof- und Staatdruckerei, 1873.

Schneider, William. *Quality and Quantity: The Quest for Biological Regeneration in Twentieth Century France*. Cambridge, England: Cambridge University Press, 1990.

———. "Toward the Improvement of the Human Race: The History of Eugenics in France." *Journal of Modern History* 54 (June 1982): 268–91.

Schoeck, Helmut. *Soziologie: Geschichte ihrer Probleme*. Freiburg: K. Alber, 1952.

Schön, Lazar. "Geleitwort." In Lazar Schön, ed., *Die Stimme der Wahrheit*, 5–8. Würzburg: N. Phillippi, 1905.

Schorsch, Ismar. "Breakthrough into the Past: The Verein für Cultur und Wissenschaft der Juden." *Leo Baeck Institute Yearbook* 33 (1988): 3–28.

———. "The Emergence of Historical Consciousness in Modern Judaism." *Leo Baeck Institute Yearbook* 28 (1983): 413–37.

———. *From Text to Context: The Turn to History in Modern Judaism*. Hanover, N.H.: University Press of New England, 1994.

———. "Ideology and History in the Age of Emancipation." In Heinrich Graetz, *The Structure of Jewish History and Other Essays*. New York: Jewish Theological Seminary of America, 1975.

———. *Jewish Reactions to German Anti-Semitism, 1870–1914*. New York: Columbia University Press, 1972.

Schwartz, Shuly Rubin. *The Emergence of Jewish Scholarship in America: The Publication of the Jewish Encyclopedia*. Cincinnati, Ohio: Hebrew Union College Press, 1991.

Searle, G. R. "Eugenics and Class." In Charles Webster, ed., *Biology, Medicine and Society, 1840–1940*, 217–42. Cambridge, England: Cambridge University Press, 1981.

Segall, Jacob. "Der Anteil der Juden in Deutschland an dem Beamtenstande und den freien Berufen." *ZfDuStdJ* 8, no. 4 (1912): 49–60.

———. *Die beruflichen und sozialen Verhältnisse der Juden in Deutschland*. Berlin: M. Schildberger, 1912.

———. "Die Berufzählung in München im Jahre 1907." *ZfDuStdJ* 9, no. 10 (1913): 137–41.

——. *Die deutschen Juden als Soldaten im Kriege 1914–18*. Berlin: Philo-Verlag, 1921.

——. "Die Entwicklung der jüdischen Bevölkerung in München 1875–1905." Ph.D. diss., University of Munich, 1908.

——. *Die Entwicklung der jüdischen Bevölkerung in München 1875–1905*. Berlin: Verlag des Bureaus für Statistik der Juden, 1910.

——. "Grundzüge einer Bevölkerungsstatistik der Juden," *ZfDuStdJ* 12, nos. 4–6 (1916): 43–54.

——. "Mitteilung," *ZfDuStdJ* 4, nos. 1–2 (1927): 1–2.

——. "Stand der jüdischen Bevölkerung in Deutschland auf Grund der Volkszählung von 1 Dezember, 1910." *ZfDuStdJ* 7, no. 11 (1911): 153–57.

——. "Die Statistik der Juden 1905–30." *ZfDuStdJ* 5, no. 1 (1930): 1–3.

——. "Die Statistik im Dienste der jüdischen Gemeinden," *ZfDuStdJ* 6, no. 6 (1910): 81–88.

——. "Der Untergang der deutschen Juden." *Im deutschen Reich* 17, no. 9 (1911): 485–99.

——. "Der Untergang der deutschen Juden." *ZfDuStdJ* 7, no. 11 (1911): 162–65.

——. "Die wirtschaftliche und soziale Lage der Juden in Deutschland." *ZfDuStdJ* 7, nos. 4–8 (1911): 49–58; 76–88; 97–112.

Sekula, Allan. "The Body and the Archive." In Richard Bolton, ed., *The Contest of Meaning: Critical Histories of Photography*, 343–89. Cambridge, Mass.: MIT Press, 1989.

"Selbstmord." *Die Welt* 4, no. 28 (1900): 2–3.

"Selbstmorde im Jahre 1904." *ZfDuStdJ* 2, no. 12 (1906): 189.

"Selbstmorde im Preussen 1907." *ZfDuStdJ* 5, no. 6 (1909): 93.

Seraphim, Peter-Heinz. *Das Judentum im osteuropäischen Raum*. Essen: Essener Verlagsanstalt, 1938.

Shapira, Anita. *Land and Power: The Zionist Resort to Force, 1881–1948*. Stanford: Stanford University Press, 1999.

Shapiro, Edward S. *A Time For Healing: American Jewry Since World War II*. Baltimore, Md.: Johns Hopkins University Press, 1992.

Shavit, Yaakov. "Hebrews and Phoenicians: An Ancient Historical Image and Its Usage." *Studies in Zionism* 5, no. 2 (1984): 157–80.

Sheehan, James. *The Career of Lujo Brentano: A Study of Liberalism and Social Reform in Imperial Germany*. Chicago: University of Chicago Press, 1966.

Shimoni, Gideon. *The Zionist Ideology*. Hanover, N.H.: University Press of New England, 1995.

Sichel, Max. "Der Selbstmord bei den Juden, einst und jetzt." *ZfDuStdJ* 1, nos. 5–6 (1924): 91–107.

——. "Zur Ätiologie der Geistesstörungen bei den Juden." *Monatsschrift für Psychiatrie und Neurologie* 43, no. 4 (1918): 246–64.

Silbergleit, Heinrich. "Das Arbeitsprogramm der Kommission für Statistik und Wirtschaftskunde der Juden." *Korrespondenzblatt des Vereins zur Gründung und Erhaltung einer Akademie für die Wissenschaft des Judentums* 8 (1927): 1–6.

——. *Die Bevölkerungs- und Berufsverhältnisse der Juden im deutschen Reich*. Berlin: Akademie-Verlag, 1930.

Singerman, Robert. "The Jew as Racial Alien: The Genetic Component of American Anti-Semitism." In David Garber, ed., *Anti-Semitism and American History*, 103–28. Urbana: University of Illinois Press, 1986.

Smith, Roger. *The Norton History of the Human Sciences*. New York: W. W. Norton, 1997.

Smith, Woodruff D. "The Emergence of German Urban Sociology 1900–1910." *The Journal of the History of Sociology* 1, no. 2 (1979): 1–16.

———. *Politics and the Sciences of Culture in Germany 1840–1920*. Oxford: Oxford University Press, 1991.

Sofer, Leo. "Die soziale Lage der Wiener Juden." *Die Welt* 10, no. 48 (1906): 16–17.

———. "Über die Entmischung der Rassen." *ZfDuStdJ* 1, no. 10 (1905): 9–12.

———. "Zur Biologie und Pathologie der jüdischen Rasse." *ZfDuStdJ* 2, no. 6 (1906): 85–92.

Sofer, Reba. *Ethics and Society in England: The Revolution in the Social Sciences 1870–1914*. Berkeley: University of California Press, 1978.

Sokolow, Nahum. "Jüdische Literatur und Wissenschaft." *Die Welt* 6, nos. 8 and 9 (1902): 1–5 (no. 8); 4–6 (no. 9).

Soloway, Richard. "Counting the Degenerates: The Statistics of Race Deterioration in Edwardian England." *Journal of Contemporary History* 18 (1982): 137–64.

———. *Demography and Degeneration: Eugenics and the Declining Birthrate in Twentieth-Century Britain*. Chapel Hill: University of North Carolina Press, 1990.

Sombart, Werner. *The Jews and Modern Capitalism*. Trans. M. Epstein. New York: Collier Books, 1962.

———. *Der moderne Kapitalismus*. Leipzig: Duncker and Humblot, 1902.

———. *Die Zukunft der Juden*. Leipzig: Duncker and Humblot, 1912.

———, ed., *Judentaufen*. Munich: G. Muller, 1912.

Sontag, Susan. *Illness as Metaphor*. New York: Farrar, Straus & Giroux, 1978.

———. *On Photography*. New York: Farrar, Straus & Giroux, 1973.

Sorkin, David. *The Transformation of German Jewry, 1780–1840*. Oxford: Oxford University Press, 1987.

"Die sozialen Verhältnisse der Juden in Preussen und in Deutschland." *Mitteilungen aus dem Verein zur Abwehr des Antisemitismus*, 1902.

Spackman, Barbara. *Decadent Genealogies: The Rhetoric of Sickness from Baudelaire to D'Annunzio*. Ithaca: Cornell University Press, 1989.

Stanislawski, Michael. *Tsar Nicholas I and the Jews: The Transformation of Jewish Society in Russia, 1825–1855*. Philadelphia: Jewish Publication Society, 1983.

Stanton, William. *The Leopard's Spots: Scientific Attitudes Towards Race in America 1815–1859*. Chicago: University of Chicago Press, 1960.

*Statistics of the Jews of the United States*. Philadelphia: The Union of American Hebrew Congregations, 1880.

*Statistik des deutschen Reichs*. Band 1. Berlin, 1873.

*Statistik des deutschen Reichs*. Band 284. *Kriminalstatistik für das Jahr 1914*, Berlin, 1920.

*Statistik des deutschen Reichs: Bevöklkerung in den Jahren 1920 und 1921*. Band 307. Berlin, 1924.

*Statistik des deutschen Reichs: Kriminalstatistik für das Jahr 1925*. Band 335. Berlin, 1927.

"Statistik der Juden in Deutschland." *Die Welt* 8, no. 41 (1904): 12.

"Statistisches von ungarischen Juden." *Die Welt* 17, no. 4 (1913): 111.

Steckel, Richard. "The Quality of the Census Data for Historical Inquiry: A Research Agenda." *Social Science History* 15, no. 4 (winter 1991): 579–99.

Steinschneider, Moritz. "Schriften über Medicin in Bibel und Talmud und über jüdische Aerzte." *Wiener klinische Rundschau* 25–26 (1896): 433–35 (25); 452–53 (26).

Steinweis, Alan. "The Appropriation and Exploitation of Jewish social science by Nazi Scholars: The Case of Peter-Heinz Seraphim." Paper delivered at the "Conference on Jews and the Social and Biological Sciences," Oxford, England, August 1998.

——. "The Library of the YIVO Institute for Jewish Research as a Source for Materials on Modern German Antisemitism, National Socialism, and the Holocaust." *German Studies Association Newsletter* 22, no. 2 (winter 1997): 27.

Stepan, Nancy. *'The Hour of Eugenics': Race, Gender, and Nation in Latin America.* Ithaca: Cornell University Press, 1991.

——. *The Idea of Race in Science: Great Britain, 1800–1960.* London: Macmillan, 1982.

Stepan, Nancy, and Sander Gilman. "Appropriating the Idioms of Science: The Rejection of Scientific Racism." In Sandra Harding, ed., *The Racial Economy of Science*, 170–93. Bloomington: Indiana University Press, 1993.

Stern, Fritz. *The Politics of Cultural Despair.* Berkeley: University of California Press, 1974.

Stocking, George, Jr. *Race, Culture, and Evolution: Essays in the History of Anthropology.* New York: Free Press, 1968.

——, ed. *The Shaping of American Anthropology 1883–1911. A Franz Boas Reader.* New York: Basic Books, 1974.

——, ed. *Volksgeist as Method and Ethic: Essays on Boasian Ethnography and the German Anthropological Tradition.* Madison: University of Wisconsin Press, 1996.

Stratz, C. H. *Was sind Juden? Eine ethnographische Studie.* Vienna: F. Tempsky, 1903.

Straus, Raphael. "Zur Forschungsmethode der jüdischen Geschichte." *Zeitschrift für die Geschichte der Juden in Deutschland* 1, no. 1 (1929): 4–12.

Sufian, Sandy. "Healing the Land and Healing the Nation: Malaria and the Zionist Project in Mandate Palestine, 1920–1947." Ph.D. diss., New York University, 1999.

Sulzberger, Mayer. "Joseph Jacobs." *American Jewish Year Book* 17 (1917): 68–75.

Tanner, J. M. "Boas' Contributions to Knowledge of Human Growth and Form." In Walter Goldschmidt, ed., *The Anthropology of Franz Boas: Essays on the Centennial of his Birth*, 76–111. Menasha, Wis.: The American Anthropological Association, Memoir no. 89, 1959.

Tartakower, Arieh. *Ha-Chevrah ha-Yehudit.* Tel Aviv: Masada, 1956.

"Die Tätigkeit der jüdischen Aerztegesellschaft Palästinas." *Die Welt* 16, no. 19 (1914): 457–59.

"Taufen in Wien." *Die Welt* 13, no. 37 (1909): 821.

Theilhaber, Felix. "Beiträge zur jüdischen Rassenfrage." *ZfDuStdJ* 6, no. 11 (1910): 40–44.

———. "Bevölkerungsvorgänge bei den Berliner Juden." *ZfDuStdJ* 3, nos. 4–6 (new series; 1926): 48–57.

———. "Der Gebärmutterhalskrebs bei den Juden." *ZfDuStdJ* 6, no. 11 (1910) 167–68.

———. "Gesundheitsverhältnisse bei den Juden." *Jüdisches Lexikon* 2 (1928): 1120–41.

———. *Die Juden im Weltkriege*. Berlin: Weltverlag, 1916.

———. "Judenthum und Hygiene." *Israelitisches Familienblatt* (May 28, 1930).

———. *Die Schädigung der Rasse durch soziales und wirtschaftliches Aufsteigen beweisen an der Berliner Juden*. Berlin: Louis Lamm, 1914.

———. "Sozialhygiene der Juden." *Jüdisches Lexikon* 5 (1930): 510–13.

———. *Der Untergang der deutschen Juden: Eine sozialwirtschaftliche Studie*. Munich: E. Reinhardt, 1911, 1921.

Thomas, Alan. *The Expanding Eye: Photography in the Nineteenth Century Mind*. London: Croom Helm, 1978.

Thon, Jakob. "Besteuerungs- und Finanzverhältnisse der jüdischen Gemeinden in Deutschland." *ZfDuStdJ* 3, no. 2 (1907): 17–24.

———. "Die Berufsgliederung der Juden in Galizien." *ZfDuStdJ* 3, nos. 8–9 (1907): 113–20.

———. *Die Juden in Österreich*. Berlin: Verlag des Bureaus für jüdische Statistik, 1908.

———. "Die jüdische Bevölkerung in Krakau." *ZfDuStdJ* 1, no. 11 (1905): 5–9.

———. "Die jüdischen Gemeinden in Deutschland." *ZfDuStdJ* 1, no. 9 (1905):1–5.

———. "Kriminalität der Christen und Juden in Österreich." *ZfDuStdJ* 2, no. 1 (1906): 6–10.

———. "Schulbesuch christlicher und jüdischer Kinder in Baden." *ZfDuStdJ* 2, no. 11 (1906): 174–75.

———. "Taufbewegung der Juden in Österreich." *ZfDuStdJ* 4, no. 1 (1908): 6–12.

———. "Taufbewegung und Mischehen in Österreich und Deutschland." *Die Welt* 10, nos. 46–48, 52 (1906): 10–12 (no. 46); 7–9 (no. 47); 6–7 (no. 48); 11–14 (no. 52).

Thon, Osias. "Das Problem der jüdischen Wissenschaft." *Jüdischer Almanach* (1902/03): 183–89.

———. "Demuiot me'Lvov" (Hebrew). *Pirkei Galizia*. Tel Aviv: Am Oved, 1957.

Tobias, Arnold. "Tendenz-Statistik." *Die jüdische Presse* 36, nos. 35–36 (1905): 349–50 (no. 35) 365–66 (no. 36).

Tönnies, Ferdinand. *Community and Society*. Trans. Charles Loomis. New Brunswick, N.J.: Transaction Books, 1988.

Topinard, Paul. *Anthropologie*. Trans. Richard Neuhauss. Leipzig: P. Frohberg, 1888.

Toury, Jacob. *Der Eintritt der Juden ins deutsche Bürgertum, Eine Dokumentation*. Tel Aviv: Diaspora Research Institute, Tel Aviv University, 1972.

———. "Der Eintritt der Juden ins deutsche Bürgertum." In Hans Liebeschutz and Arnold Paucker, eds., *Das Judentum in der deutschen Umwelt, 1800–1850*. Tübingen: Mohr, 1977.

Trachtenberg, Alan ed. *Classic Essays on Photography*. New Haven, Conn.: Leete's Island Books, 1980.

Treitschke, H. von. *A Word About Our Jewry*. Trans. Helen Lederer. Cincinnati, Ohio: Hebrew Union College, 1958.

Troen, Ilan. "Calculating the 'Economic Absorptive Capacity' of Palestine: A Study of the Political Uses of Scientific Research." *Contemporary Jewry* 10, no. 2 (1989): 19–38.

*Tsvay Jahr Arbeit fur dem Yiddishin Visenschaftlichter Institute*. Vilna: YIVO, 1927.

"Twelve Men and Women." *Moment* (Apr. 1995): 66–69.

"Über die Mischehe in Berlin." *Die Welt* 7, no. 30 (1903): 13.

"Verband für Statistik der Juden." *Die Welt* 10, no. 43 (1906): 19.

"Verein für Statistik der Juden." *Die Welt* 13, no. 19 (1909): 415–16.

"Verein für Statistik der Juden." *Die Welt* 14, no. 28 (1910): 690.

"Verein für Statistik der Juden Galiziens." *Die Welt* 18, no. 18 (1914): 440–41.

"Verein für Statistik und Demographie der Juden in Niederland." *Die Welt* 11, no. 21 (1907): 18.

"Der Verein für Statistik der Juden." *Im deutschen Reich* 15, no. 5 (1909) 330–32.

"Der Verfall der jüdischen Bevölkerung in Dänemark." *Die Welt* 10, no. 37 (1906): 19.

"Vierteljahreshefte zur Statistik des deutschen Reichs." *Die Welt* 16, no. 48 (1912): 1491.

Vital, David. *The Origins of Zionism*. Oxford: The Clarendon Press, 1975.

———. *Zionism: The Crucial Phase*. Oxford: The Clarendon Press, 1987.

———. *Zionism: The Formative Years*. Oxford: The Clarendon Press, 1982.

Waldenberg, Alfred. *Das icocephale blonde Rassenelement unter Halligfriesen und jüdische Taubstummen*. Berlin: S. Calvary, 1902.

———. "Jüdische Rassenhochzucht." *Die Welt* 15, no. 37 (1911): 976–78.

Wallace, Alfred Russel. "The Origin of Human Races and the Antiquity of Man Deduced from the Theory of 'Natural Selection'." *Journal of the Anthropological Society* 2 (1864): clxvi–clxvii.

Wassermann, Rudolf. *Beruf, Konfession und Verbrechen: Eine Studie über die Kriminalität der Juden in Vergangenheit und Gegenwart*. Munich: Ernst Reinhardt, 1907.

———. "Ist die Kriminalität der Juden Rassenkriminalität?" *ZfDuStDJ* 7, no. 3 (1911): 36–39.

———. "Die Juden und das deutsche Wirtschaftsleben der Gegenwart." *Preussischer Jahrbücher* 149, no. 2 (1912): 267–75.

———. "Die Kriminalität der Juden in Deutschland in den letzten 25 Jahren (1882–1906)." *Monatsschrift für Kriminal-Psychologie und Strafrechts-Reform* 6 (1909–10): 609–18.

———. "Kritische und ergänzende Bemerkungen zur Literatur über die Kriminalität der Juden." *ZfDuStdJ* 2, no. 5 (1906): 73–77.

———. "Neomalthusianismus und Judenfrage." *ZfDuStdJ* 8, no. 3 (1912): 43–47.

———. "Der Selbstmord bei den Juden in Deutschland." *ZfDuStdJ* 6, nos. 8–9 (1910): 133–34.

———. "Die Zukunft des Judentums." *Die Welt* 14, no. 22 (1910): 54.

Wasserstein, Bernard. "End of the Jewish People?" *The Jewish Quarterly* (Winter 1995): 5–10.

———. *Vanishing Diaspora: The Jews in Europe since 1945*. Cambridge, Mass.: Harvard University Press, 1996.

Weber, Gay. "Science and Society in Nineteenth Century Anthropology." *History of Science* 12 (1974): 260–83.

Webster, Charles, ed. *Biology, Medicine and Society, 1840–1940.* Cambridge, England: Cambridge University Press, 1981.

Weinberg, David. *"Heureux Comme Dieu en France*: Eastern European Jews in Paris 1881–1914." *Studies in Contemporary Jewry* 1 (1984): 26–54.

Weinberg, Richard. "Das Hirngewicht der Juden." *ZfDuStdJ* 1, no. 3 (1905): 5–10.

Weindling, Paul. *Health, Race and German Politics Between National Unification and Nazism, 1870–1945.* Cambridge, England: Cambridge University Press, 1989.

Weinreich, Max. *Hitler's Professors.* New York: YIVO, 1946.

Weinryb, Bernard. "Prolegomena to an Economic History of the Jews in Germany in Modern Times." *Leo Baeck Institute Yearbook* 1 (1956): 279–306.

Weiss, Sheila Faith. "The Race Hygiene Movement in Germany." *Osiris* 3 (2d series; 1987): 193–236.

Weissenberg, Samuel. "Armenier und Juden." *Sonderabdruck aus dem Archiv für Anthropologie Braunschweig* 13, no. 4 (1914): 383–87.

———. "Beitrag zur Anthropologie der Juden: Aaroniden und Leviten." *Zeitschrift für Ethnologie* 39, no. 6 (1907): 961–64.

———. "Hygiene in Brauch und Sitte der Juden." In Max Grunwald, ed., *Die Hygiene der Juden,* 29–43. Dresden: Historische Abteilung der internationalen Hygiene-Ausstellung, 1911.

———. "Das Verhalten der Juden gegen ansteckende Krankheiten." *ZfDuStdJ* 7, nos. 10–12 (1911): 137–46 (no. 10); 158–62 (no. 11); 169–77 (no. 12).

———. "Zur Sozialbiologie und Sozialhygiene der Juden." *Archiv für Rassen- und Gesellschaftsbiologie* 19, no. 4 (1927): 402–18.

Weizmann, Chaim. *The Letters and Papers of Chaim Weizmann.* New Brunswick, N.J.: Transaction Books, 1983.

Wengierow, Leo. "Die Juden in Königreich Polen." In Alfred Nossig, ed., *Jüdische Statistik,* 293–310. Berlin: Jüdischer Verlag, 1903.

Werner, Ludwig. "Die jüdische Turnerschaft." *Die Welt* 8, no. 41 (1904): 5–7.

Werner, Sigmund. "Unsere sozialen Aufgaben." *Die Welt* 4, no. 32 (1900): 1–2.

Wertheimer, Jack. "Family Values and the Jews." *Commentary* 97, no. 1 (Jan. 1994): 30–34.

———. "German Policy and Jewish Politics: the Absorption of East European Jews in Germany (1868–1914). Ph.D. diss., Columbia University, 1978.

———. *Unwelcome Strangers: East European Jews in Imperial Germany.* Oxford: Oxford University Press, 1987.

Wiebe, Karl Friedrich. *Deutschland und die Judenfrage.* Berlin: Institute for the Study of the Jewish Question, 1938.

Wiener, Max. "The Ideology of the Founders of Jewish Scientific Research." *YIVO Annual of Jewish Social Science* 5 (1950): 184–96.

"Wiener Versammlungen." *Die Welt* 8, no. 21 (1904): 4–6.

Wilhelm, Kurt. "Einleitung." In Kurt Wilhelm, ed., *Wissenschaft des Judentums im deutschen Sprachbericht,* 3–58. Berlin: Leo Baeck Institute, 1967.

"Wir müssen mehr wissen." *Jüdischer Volkskalender* 4 (1905–6): 51–52.

Wirth, Louis. *The Ghetto.* Chicago: University of Chicago Press, 1928.

Wisse, Ruth R. *I. L. Peretz and the Making of Modern Jewish Culture*. Seattle: University of Washington Press, 1991.

Wistrich, Robert. "Do the Jews Have a Future?" *Commentary* 98, no. 1 (1994): 23–26.

——. *The Jews of Vienna in the Age of Franz Joseph*. Oxford: Oxford University Press, 1989.

Wolf, Immanuel. "On the Concept of a Science of Judaism." In Michael Meyer, ed., *Ideas of Jewish History*. Detroit, Mich.: Wayne State University Press, 1987.

*YIVO Schriften für Ekonomische und Statistik*. Berlin: YIVO, 1928.

Zimmerman, Moshe. "Jewish Nationalism and Zionism in German-Jewish Students' Organizations." *Leo Baeck Institute Yearbook* 27 (1982): 129–53.

Zipperstein, Steven J. *Elusive Prophet: Ahad Ha'am and the Origins of Zionism*. Berkeley: University of California Press, 1993.

——. "Transforming the *Heder*: Maskilic Politics in Imperial Russia." In Ada Rapoport and Steven J. Zipperstein, eds., *Jewish History: Essays in Honour of Chimen Abramsky*, 87–109. London: P. Halban, 1988.

Zollschan, Ignaz. *Jewish Questions: Three Lectures*. New York: Bloch Publishing Co., 1914.

——. "The Jewish Race Problem." *The Jewish Review* 2 (1912): 391–408.

——. "Rassenproblem und Judenfrage." *Die Welt* 15, no. 34 (1911): 896–900.

——. *Das Rassenproblem unter besonderer Berücksichtigung der theoretischen Grundlagen der jüdischen Rassenfrage*. 5th ed. Vienna: W. Braumüller, 1925. Originally published in 1909.

Zunz, Leopold. "Grundlinien zu einer künftigen Statistik der Juden." *Zeitschrift für die Wissenschaft des Judentums* 1 (1823): 523–32.

"Zur Einführung." *Palästina* 1, no. 1 (1902): 3–5.

"Zur Frage einer medizinischen Hochschule in Palästina." *Die Welt* 16, no. 28 (1912): 842–45.

"Zur jüdischen Rassenfrage." *Die Welt* 16, no. 5 (1912): 141–42.

"Zur Organisation der jüdischen Statistik." *Die Welt* 8, no. 19 (1904): 12–13.

# Index